COMING OF AGE

MOVIE &

VIDEO GUIDE

DON LORT

COMING OF AGE

COMING OF AGE

MOVIE & VIDEO GUIDE

DON LORT

companion PRESS

Cover photo from *Wild Reeds*, courtesy of Strand Releasing.

Copyright © 1997 by Don Lort

COMPANION PRESS
PO Box 2575, Laguna Hills, California 92654

Printed in Canada
First Printing 1997

ISBN: 1-889138-02-9

CONTENTS

ACKNOWLEDGEMENTS

MY THANKS TO STEVE STEWART OF COMPANION PRESS WHO FIRST SUGGESTED I take on this project and who has assisted both by his constant encouragement and in a very practical way by locating all of the photographs included in these pages. Thanks also goes to the many studios who provided photos.

As well, I must thank all those too numerous to mention individually who have expressed support, encouragement and interest in the book. Family, friends and even a few garrulous strangers encountered in bars and buses have all been most helpful.

Finally I must thank the helpful, friendly and knowledgeable staff of Pic-A-Flic Video in Victoria and Videomatica in Vancouver. It is not without reason that newspaper reader polls consistently name these stores the best video retailers in their respective cities.

INTRODUCTION

What is a coming of age film? In simplest terms a coming of age story is one in which a child or a teenager reaches a critical turning point or event that results in a loss of childhood innocence. Not surprisingly, most often this turning point revolves around adolescent sexuality.

As a consequence, the one consistent thread which runs through all of the films in this book is the topic of sexuality. It is, however, sexuality defined in very broad terms. It is not just sex per se, but includes the teenager's emerging sense of him or herself as a sexual being.

Why this emphasis on sexuality? Simply because for most people, especially in our Western society, which lacks recognized rite of passage rituals which initiate the young person into adult society, the discovery of sexuality, in whatever form it takes, is probably the quintessential coming of age experience. It is the one thing about growing up which truly separates the young child from the young adult.

Because of this it is probably the one thing that most parents have the greatest difficulty dealing with in their adolescent offspring. It is unfortunate, as adolescence is a trying and confusing time for both parent and child. It is even more trying and confusing if the adolescent is struggling with the dawning realization that they are gay or lesbian. This is often the case depicted in coming of age films.

One of the problems, however, arising in a discussion of juvenile actors and sexuality is that American society has a strong puritanical streak running through it, a streak which is buttressed by a very vocal religious element which equates nudity with sex and juvenile sex with abuse.

I have even met those who equate swimsuits and underwear with nudity, hence with sex and who would have one believe that sex outside marriage is a sin worse than murder. Let me say right now that I reject this viewpoint, and have for many years been a practicing naturist.

Fortunately the puritanical attitude is not a worldwide phenomenon and is very much a learned response. In some European countries it has been reported that as many as twenty-five percent of all families spend all or part of their summer vacation at nudist or naturist facilities. In some societies the public bath, though these days segregated by sex, is very much a living aspect of the culture.

Cameron Boyd and Jesse Bradford, *King Of The Hill* (1993)

In some of these films sexuality is expressed through simple nudity which, however sensual it may be, occurs in what are patently asexual situations: bathtubs, showers and skinny-dipping scenes, for example. Although I don't subscribe to the view that equates simple nudity with sexuality, because this equation is so strongly held in many sectors of U.S. society, I have reluctantly included this under the concept of sexuality.

Many of the films in this book portray young performers in nude scenes. Is this exploitive? In looking at these films, in most cases I have felt that it was not. In all the films I have included in the book, I have been particularly careful to consider this question as I watch. In none of the films I have included did it seem to me that the performer, as opposed to the character, was uncomfortable with the nude scene. I would not have included a film if it was obvious that an unwilling child or teenager had been coerced into doing a nude scene.

Given a suitable context, and most of such nude scenes for young performers occur in bathtubs, in showers or locker rooms or while skinny-dipping, then a nude scene can have a legitimate place. I don't particularly go looking for nude scenes in films, but I am fully appreciative of the aesthetic qualities of the nude body, regardless of age or gender. I am, therefore, more than willing to welcome on-screen nudity in the right circumstances. I certainly don't consider the mere image of a nude child or teenager to be pornographic, and feel that those who do say more about themselves than the images.

Again, in the U.S. any discussion of sex and sexuality involving minors leads to a discussion of abuse. Therefore it's no surprise that abuse is another major theme in coming of age films: sexual abuse, physical abuse and psychological abuse.

In the films, as so often in real life, these three rarely occur in isolation. Children subjected to one form of abuse are also frequently subjected to others as well. In this respect, however, it must be noted that I, like many of the filmmakers whose work is mentioned in this book, don't automatically assign the term abuse to every instance of sexual relationships between an adult and a young person.

As so many of the films in this book try to make clear, a consenting relationship is possible across the generational boundaries, though I do recognize that the vast majority of such situations are abusive, involving a child with no real option of saying no. I have never been involved in such a relationship, either as a teenager or an adult. I have, however, met several men who look back with a great deal of fondness and nostalgia to just such a sexual relationship which they were a part of, in some cases when they were no more than twelve or thirteen years old.

As the mother of such a young man once told me, the nature of his consent may not have been that of an adult, but at his own level of understanding her thirteen-year-old son was as much a consenting partner as the adult involved. Several of these films, such as *For A Lost Soldier*, *36 Fillette* and *La Petite Amour* examine this kind of consenting relationship. Abusive relationships are also examined in abundance, in such titles as *Sleepers* and *The Boys Of St. Vincent*.

ADOLESCENT FILMS MADE FOR AND BY ADULTS

The other thing that ties all of these films together is that they are treated just as seriously as any adult film—the subject just happens to be children. For the most part, these are adult films made for adults.

So, while we still get the Kevin McAllisters and Dennis the Menaces from the big studios, these are not coming of age movies, these are children's movies made for children. There's a big difference.

Fortunately, many directors outside Hollywood, both foreign directors and independent directors in the United States, have tackled the subject in a serious, thoughtful

James Dean, Natalie Wood, *Rebel Without A Cause* (1955)

and sensitive way. It is a very serious subject and deserves a respectful treatment which does not demean or belittle the teenage protagonist even when the sexuality is treated in a lighthearted or comic manner.

This wider, more realistic, more complete vision of the child is now being seen more often on U.S. screens as well, in films like *Welcome to the Dollhouse, Manny & Lo* and *King Of The Hill.*

To be sure, most of the best of these new images are coming from independent filmmakers. Many are being seen in adaptations of autobiographical books or personal incidents. I don't think that either situation is coincidence, for the best and most realistic stories about young people will inevitably be drawn from the personal history of the writer or filmmaker.

Why is this? Many of these films are of a very personal nature. They grow out of

Jerry O'Connell, River Phoenix, Will Wheaton and Corey Feldman, *Stand By Me* (1986)

incidents in the director's or scriptwriter's own childhood, or have been adapted from autobiographical books. Think of films like *Sunday's Children, King Of The Hill, Au Revoir Les Enfants, Europa Europa,* or *This Boy's Life,* just to mention a very few of the finest.

A quick perusal of the index of directors in the back of this book will read almost like a Who's Who of the profession. I suspect it is the very personal nature of so many coming of age stories which has drawn directors of the calibre of Francois Truffaut, Louis Malles, Agnieszka Holland, Frederico Fellini, George Lucas and Rob Reiner to take on these projects.

Most of these films are not big budget projects. They don't have millions of dollars worth of special effects. They are very much a labour of love for the producers and directors. But they are labours of love which can prove financial success stories because of the lower production costs.

WHY A BOOK ABOUT COMING OF AGE FILMS?

In the most basic terms, because the subject has never been tackled before. Guide books to ever narrower segments of the film market appear on

book shelves almost daily. As the number of films available on videotape keeps increasing, general guides become more and more unwieldy. The best of the general guide books include 20,000 to 25,000 titles. Some CD Rom data bases list in the vicinity of 100,000 titles. One printed British reference book is approaching a quarter of a million film titles.

In this burgeoning field, specialized guide books are becoming ever more common. There are guide books to horror films, guide books to science fiction films, guide books to silent films, guide books to sex in film, even guide books to films which feature full frontal male nudity. What there has not been until now is a guide book to films about children and teenagers.

The only other book which has attempted to look at the subject of youth in film is David M. Considine's 1985 book *The Cinema Of Adolescence,* which now appears to be out of print as well as out of date. More than sixty percent of the films I have included were released after Considine's book was printed. That book also approaches the subject from a different angle, having a more academic outlook and coming at the subject from a thematic point of view. Further, it is limited almost entirely to films produced in the United States.

Gary Grimes and Jennifer O'Neill, *Summer Of '42* (1971)

A stronger impulse for me is my personal interests in children as people. I have been a Big Brother. I have been a stepfather. I have been a teacher. I have also, I hope, been a friend to many children. Watching films about young people, whether sunny films about carefree youngsters gradually learning about life, or gut wrenching films about abuse and exploitation, follows from this prior interest in the real thing.

THE SELECTION OF FILMS

First let me say that this is a very selective group of film titles. I have not included every coming of age film I am aware of. In fact, it hardly represents a substantial proportion of them.

The selection process has involved a number of factors. I started with a list of nearly 1300 titles which might warrant inclusion. From this still growing master list I have selected 200 plus films.

Because the term coming of age is frequently associated with sexuality and sexual experience, there has been a concentration on films which deal with these subjects from gay, lesbian and straight viewpoints.

A vital factor in the consideration process has been the age of the protagonists. I have tried to concentrate on films about school age children and teenagers. Generally the cutoff points have been around eight or nine years old at the lower end and eighteen or nineteen at the upper end. These roughly correspond to the years of public schooling for most North American youngsters and made a convenient yard stick for the selection process.

Another factor considered was availability. I have viewed every film in this book at least once in the past year. With one exception every one was located on a VHS tape. The one exception, *La Revolte Des Enfants*, was seen on a Canadian Broadcasting Corporation French network broadcast. However, this having been said, it does not necessarily follow that all will be found in your local video store.

Some were seen while I was living and teaching in

WHY I WATCH COMING OF AGE FILMS

Adults who watch films about teenagers or children do so for any number of reasons. Some have professional interests: teachers, social workers and so on may find such films of more than passing interest. A friend who works with street youth, for example, asked me for a list of film titles which illustrated the problems of street kids around the world. She felt it might be of help to her in her own endeavours.

Nostalgia also plays an important part for many viewers. We like to think we are reliving the carefree days of our youth while watching the story unfold on screen. If the truth were told, however, for most of us this carefree innocence of youth never was. Nevertheless, we like to think of youth in those terms and some of these films can help us relive a past that never truly existed.

Why do I watch films about youth? The good ones do unquestionably bring about a feeling of nostalgia for a time that never was. My own youth was quite uneventful. I was never abused. I was never seduced by an adult of either gender. Even drugs, alcohol and tobacco rarely entered my life. Perhaps these films are a way to relive the things that never happened to me?

South Korea. Some were obtained as imports from Great Britain through Videomatica of Vancouver, which goes to considerable trouble to obtain titles not otherwise available in North America.

I have also tried to make a varied selection of genres and countries of origin and I've tried to include films from different time periods. The oldest titles in the book date from the early 1930s. The most recent were first screened in 1997.

In origin, they come from more than two dozen countries around the world and almost every continent. (The best I could do for a coming of age film from Africa was *The Kitchen Toto*, in fact a British film, though set in Kenya and filmed by a director who grew up in that country.)

Naturally, for a North American book, the largest number of the films originate from the United States. Don't let chauvinism blind you to the qualities of the other films listed, however. In the past, as I have suggested above, filmmakers from other countries have tended to provide us with far better, more realistic views of the lives of children and teenagers.

In keeping with the desire to provide a variety of films, I have tended to avoid too many instances of remakes and sequels, though some will be found. But how many incarnations of the *Porky's* formula can you sit through and retain your sanity? Generally a remake or sequel has been included only if it has some desirable qualities of its own, is more readily available than the original, or appealed to me for some highly idiosyncratic reason.

I have tended to concentrate on the better films, rather than sit through too much trash. With limited space this only makes sense. There are a few clunkers included, but the percentage is small.

Finally, because I insisted on actually viewing every film in this book, that has also been a factor in determining what was included and what wasn't. Fortunately I have been able to deal with two excellent independent Canadian video stores, Pic-A-Flic in Victoria and Videomatica in Vancouver. My personal collection of tapes and the selections in these two stores account for all but a very small handful of the titles in this book.

Naturally, living in Canada has also affected the selection of tapes available to me. Distribution systems and release dates of video tapes sometimes differ between Canada and the United States. Fortunately both these stores go to the extra effort to import tapes not otherwise available in Canada.

Feel free to disagree with me. After all, how often do any two reviewers react the same way to any given film? I may trash some title you feel is the greatest film ever made. Conversely, I may praise something you feel is garbage.

Don't be afraid to let me know. You won't change my mind, necessarily, but I welcome any and all comments. And if you know of some obscure coming of age title which you suspect isn't on my list, tell me about it. Perhaps it will make it into the next volume.

I welcome your comments. You can e-mail me at wu821@freenet.victoria.bc.ca.

Use and enjoy.

Victoria, B. C., Canada
April, 1997

NOTES TO READER

Review Format

Title: This will be the title as it is given on the cover of the video tape version which I saw. I don't believe there are many included which were released under different titles in Canada and the United States, though this does sometimes happen. Titles are listed in alphabetical order. Titles are listed in alphabetical order. Leading articles are ignored, regardless of language. Thus *Le Petit Amour* follows *Pelle The Conqueror*. Two titles beginning with numbers, *The 400 Blows* and *36 Fillette* are listed as the first titles under F and T respectively.

Star Rating: These are just one man's individual point of view and highly subjective. Every film in this book has something to say, every one has something to offer, even if it is nothing more than a chance to ogle a favourite performer's bare buns. These are just my reactions to the film, my assessment of its worth. Don't agree with me? That's fine. Any star system should be viewed skeptically. I have, following the lead of other books from Companion Press, used a system of five stars which roughly translate as follows:

★ ★ ★ ★ ★ Excellent/Classic

★ ★ ★ ★ Very good

★ ★ ★ Good

★ ★ Fair

★ Poor

Alternative Titles: Frequently this is the title in the original language, or in the country of origin. It may also be variations on the English language title.

Availability: An indication of availability on video tape. I have only indicated a film as available on video tape if I am aware of it having been made regularly available to either the U.S. or Canadian markets. That doesn't mean all of these films will be easy to find. Some are out of print. However, all but a handful are available on tape. I have not tried to indicate Laser Disk availability, though many of these titles are available in that format. As for the new DVD format, at the time of writing it is impossible to say what may or may not be made available.

Date: Normally the year of production or release in the country of origin.

Country Of Origin: Usually the country or countries which raised the finances for the film. This may not necessarily be the country where it was filmed or set. The language or dialogue may also be different.

Color/Black and White

Length: In minutes, usually taken from information on the video cover box.

Language: If not originally in English, an indication of whether it is dubbed into English or subtitled (my own preference).

Director(s)

Screenwriter(s): As essential to the success of the film as the director or the cast.

Source Of Story: When I have been able to determine that a film is based on a story in another medium. Many of the best are, so are some of the worst.

Cast: Some of the cast are listed with the name of the character they play. Cast are listed in alphabetical order not according to the order of importance or their order in the credits. Most of the major characters are listed as well as some minor ones if played by a well known actor or by someone who appears in another film in this book. For some of the films, because of an annoying practice common in some countries of not giving the roles in the credits, all I have been able to do is give the names of the cast members.

Awards: Many of the films in this book have received awards from various film bodies or festivals. The lists of awards are not complete, but I have tried to give some of the more important ones.

Genre: A single sentence giving a brief indication of the nature of the film, such as comedy, drama, documentary, musical or thriller.

Plot: Following my own preference of knowing what the film is about before I watch it, I have concentrated on summarizing the story line of the film rather than spending a lot of space in analysis of the strengths and weakness of the film. Of course, in instances where there are outstanding features, whether good or bad, I have tried to draw your attention to these.

Rateable Features: With all of the films I have given the MPAA rating, or indicated that to the best of my knowledge it has not been rated by that body. For some of the films I have been able to give the Canadian Home Video rating as well. Lack of this latter rating doesn't mean that it hasn't been rated in Canada, only that I haven't been able to determine what the rating is. Also, this Canadian rating system is fairly new, and many older titles are only being marked with the ratings if they are being re-released.

I assume the MPAA system needs no introduction. For those unfamiliar with it, the Canadian Home Video system is similar in appearance, but usually results in less restrictive ratings for films. The relevant parts of the Canadian System are G (equivalent to the MPAA G rating), PG (again equivalent), 14-A (equivalent to the MPAA PG-13 rating, but with a cut off at age 14), 18-A (equivalent to the MPAA R rating, but with a cut off at age 18), R (equivalent to the MPAA NC-17 rating with a cut off at 18).

This section of the review also includes a more or less detailed discussion of the rateable features of the film: sexual situations, nude scenes, violence, coarse language and other particulars which some viewers may find objectionable.

Following the section of the film reviews is an actor, director, genre and sexuality index.

Florence Darel and Ken Higelin, *A La Mode* (1994)

A LA MODE ★★★

(Also known as *In Fashion*)

Credits: VHS/1994/France/Colour/89 minutes
In French with English subtitles.
Director: Remy Duchemin
Screenplay: Richard Morgieve and Remy Duchemin
Based on the novel *Fausto* by Richard Morgieve.
Cast: Maurice Benichou [Lucien], Florence Darel
[Tonie], Francois Hautesserre [Raymond], Ken Higelin
[Fausto], Jean Yanne [Mietek]
Genre: A comedy about a teenage orphan who finds his
true calling when he is apprenticed to a tailor.
Plot: While on a cycling tour of Normandy in 1964, the
parents of Fausto Barbarico (Higelin) are killed when their
tandem bicycle hits a tractor. Now an orphan, the teenager
is sent to the Saint Joseph Orphanage in Paris where he
becomes the butt of several pranks and practical jokes.

Nevertheless, he soon befriends Raymond Lesueur
(Hautesserre), like himself something of an outcast among
the residents of the institution.

As part of the efforts Saint Joseph's makes on behalf
of the boys, the orphanage places them into apprentice-
ships, though this is seemingly done without considering
the teenager's own needs and interests.

Fausto finds himself apprenticed to Mietek Breslauer
(Yanne), a Jewish tailor whose clientele seem mostly to
trade suits for services. Still, his friend Raymond tells
Fausto, it might be a good trade if all the customers were
women, a proposition that Mietek finds preposterous.

Despite the shortcomings of Mietek's business, Fausto
finds he enjoys the trade, though he has dreams of love, of
sex, of outrageous publicity stunts and of haute couture.
He also has dreams of Tonie (Darel), the daughter of a
local mechanic.

To the surprise of everyone, Fausto's outrageous

Francesco Cusimano, *Acla* (1992)

a documentary film about child abuse as his Masters thesis. Knowing of his project, a medical school friend (James) calls Larry to the hospital when badly beaten fourteen-year-old Thomas (Sbarge) is brought into the emergency ward in convulsions with extensive bruises and burns. Immediately, Larry wants to star Thomas in his film but how to contact him? Fortunately, Larry's t-shirt bears the logo "ABUSED? Call ....." and his phone number. Having seen the t-shirt, Thomas makes the first contact. He leaves a message on Larry's answering machine, a message which includes yet another round of abuse when Thomas's parents (Massaro and Schneider) come into the room and the boy takes the chance of leaving the phone off the hook while they beat and berate him.

designs and publicity stunts (Would you believe a jacket made of living grass? Or a suit that resembles a tree trunk?) bring a rapidly increasing trade, nationwide recognition and his name on the shop door. They also bring Tonie into his bed, a situation which leads to her pregnancy and their marriage. As befits a comedy, this film should keep you laughing. Unfortunately, beyond the laughs, there is little substance to the film.

MPAA: Rated R. Fausto and Raymond strip naked while sitting on the orphanage roof. This is a butt shot and although they are obviously nude, little is seen because of lighting and the distance from the camera. Tonie and Fausto make love. During this scene her breasts are seen, as well as a side shot of her buns.

ABUSE ★★★

Credits: VHS/1983/USA/Colour/85 minutes
Writer/Director: Arthur J. Bressan, Jr.
Cast: Mickey Clark [Laura], Kathy Gerber [Kathy Logan], Jack Halton [Professor Rappaport], Steve W. James [Dr. Bennett], Maurice Massaro [Mr. Carroll], Richard Ryder [Larry Porter], Raphael Sbarge [Thomas Carroll], Susan Schneider [Mrs. Carroll]
Genre: A drama which studies the relationship which develops between a documentary filmmaker and one of his subjects.
Plot: Graduate student Larry Porter (Ryder) is producing

After they meet in person, the boy becomes actively involved in the young man's film project, both in front of and behind the camera. They also become involved on a much more personal level, a close friendship developing between the two. Thomas, in addition to struggling with the effects of his parents' abuse, is also in the process of coming to terms with his homosexuality. In fact, when he first saw Larry through a window in the hospital he perceived, almost on an unconscious level, that the man was gay.

It was this, as much as the question of the abuse, which prompted Thomas to contact the man. As the film develops, and as their friendship develops, their relationship soon becomes sexual. Though clearly consensual for both partners, this loving relationship between man and boy is seen by Larry's friends and colleagues as more damaging to Thomas than the horrendous tortures his parents subject him to. With the film complete but the abuse still continuing in the Carroll home, Larry conceives a plan to leave New York with Thomas and head to San Francisco. Although his friends try to talk him out of the plan, Larry is undeterred.

When originally produced, this film, because of the subject matter, found difficulty in getting distribution but it is available today on video tape from Cinevista.

MPAA: Not rated. There are several chilling scenes of horrific physical and psychological abuse throughout the film, including beatings, deliberate burning of the skin and an attempted drowning. Some viewers may be uncomfortable with the positive view the film takes of the sexual relationship between the fourteen-year-old Thomas and the adult Larry.

ACLA ★★★★

(Also known as *Acla's Descent Into Floristella*, or as *La Discesa di Acla A Floristella*)

Credits: VHS/1992/Italy/Colour/86 minutes
In Italian with English subtitles.
Writer/Director: Aurelio Grimaldi
Cast: Luigi Maria Burruano, Francesco Cusimano [Acla], Giuseppe Cusimano [Maurizio], Lucia Sardo, Tony Sperandeo
Awards: This film has been featured at several film festivals in Europe and in Canada, including the Venice Film Festival (1992) and the Vancouver International Film Festival (1993).
Genre: A drama about the hellish brutality endured by a sensitive eleven year old boy sold into indentured labour in the sulfur mines of Sicily in the 1930's.
Plot: One of many children in a desperately poor family, handsome, blond eleven-year-old Acla (Francesco Cusimano) is sold into a form of slavery in the sulphur mines of Floristella. Forced to work long hours virtually nude in the stifling heat carrying heavy baskets of ore to the surface, Acla and the other boys working as loaders are subjected to unceasing physical abuse and sexual advances from the adult miners.

No longer able to tolerate the conditions, especially after a beating meted out when sulphur he is guarding is stolen, Acla runs away. Following his dreams of joining his married sister in Australia, Acla sets out to find the sea, with only the vaguest idea of what the sea is and even less of how to find it.

His disappearance places his family into extreme hardship: they must find Acla, find a replacement for him or return the money. Having spent the money, they set out to find the boy, turning to the police for help. Acla is eventually

found and returned, saving his family from financial disaster and his younger brother Maurizio (Giuseppe Cusimano) from the fate of entering the mines at the age of nine. The cost to Acla is high, however. In the final scenes, black and blue from a beating, Acla returns to the mines, though he never loses his dream of finding the sea.

The two brothers Acla and Maurizio are played by real life brothers Francesco and Giuseppe Cusimano.
MPAA: Not rated. The film features extensive male nudity: the miners habitually wear only a loincloth while working in the mine. Most of the nudity is bare buns, but there are also several scenes of full frontal male nudity, both of boys (including Acla) and of adults. There is also some full frontal female nudity which occurs when one of the unmarried miners visits a prostitute on his Sunday off. There are several scenes of heterosexual activity: Acla watching his parents make love; the unmarried miners visiting the prostitute.

Homosexual activity amongst the miners is common. Frequently this means the boys service the men's desires. As one miner puts it, "It's a miner's fate to screw boys during the week and wives on weekends and holidays." The homosexual activity is widely known and widely talked about.

Acla, although approached many times, resists. Many of the other boys submit in order to earn extra food or a reduction of their contract. The boys are also subjected to vicious physical abuse. Most of them are savagely beaten and when Acla returns to the mine after running away, his entire body is covered with deep blue bruises, scars and open wounds.

THE ADVENTURES OF HUCK FINN
★★★★
Credits: VHS/1993/USA/Colour/108 minutes
Writer/Director: Stephen Sommers
Based on the novel *The Adventures of Huckleberry Finn* by Mark Twain.
Cast: Robbie Coltrane [Duke], Dana Ivey [Widow Douglas],

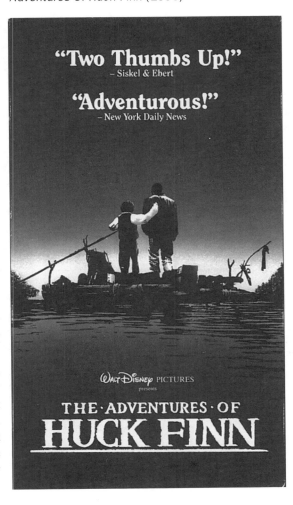

Elijah Wood and Courtney B. Vance, *The Adventures Of Huck Finn* (1993)

"Two Thumbs Up!"
— Siskel & Ebert

"Adventurous!"
— New York Daily News

WALT DISNEY PICTURES
presents

THE·ADVENTURES·OF
HUCK FINN

Ron Perlman [Pap Finn], Jason Robards [King], Courtney B. Vance [Jim], Elijah Wood [Huckleberry Finn]

Genre: The well known Mark Twain adventure tale of a boy and a runaway slave on the Mississippi.

Plot: It hardly seems necessary to summarize this well known and well loved tale. Although I have reservations about some details of the production, Disney's adaptation of the story is definitely one of the better ones yet made, and generally takes fewer liberties with the original text than many other adaptations have. It is not without its faults, however. For example, it lacks much of the biting social satire of Twain's original.

Elijah Wood as Huckleberry Finn gives a generally top notch performance, as is only to be expected from this talented young actor. However, he really was too young to play the role. Twain's Finn was some thirteen or fourteen years old. Wood also seems to have had difficulty maintaining a convincing poor white trash accent. The effect in the film is too studied and too inconsistent to be convincing. Nevertheless, his portrayal of the young boy who gradually comes to see the runaway Jim (Vance) as a real person, with the same fundamental rights as a free man, regardless of the prevailing social milieu, is generally very good, comparing well with the 1938 production with Mickey Rooney. (Rooney was definitely too old to play the part.)

Unfortunately, this film suffers from what I find to be a common Disney fault: an excess of nail-biting, emotion wrenching melodramatic suspense which seems out of place for what surely must be Disney's intended audience. This film has an amazing amount of violence, some of it completely unnecessary and gratuitous. Even as satire, was it really necessary to include the scene of the shooting of two men when Huck and his companions first arrive in Phelps Landing? While the violent deaths of two men and the grinning quip "Welcome to America" may ring true for the contemporary United States, especially for those of us looking in from outside, does it really have a place in what is essentially a family film?

The same question also applies to the shooting of Huck. As for Perlman's savagely vicious Pap Finn, while this is an excellent performance, it seems to me to be too strong for the target audience of most Disney productions. Although some of this violence was imported into the original story, Disney did "clean up" the story. There isn't even a hint in this production that Huck Finn might ever have gone skinny dipping, despite Twain's own words in the original novel. In print, Huck says " ... we was always naked, day and night, whenever the mosquitoes would let us ... I didn't much go on clothes, nohow." But I suppose this is typical of the puritanical streak that runs so deep in American society. The sight of a bare butt might permanently warp a child's psyche, but murder and mayhem are good, clean, wholesome entertainment.

MPAA: Rated PG.

ALL QUIET ON THE WESTERN FRONT ★★★★★

Credits: VHS/1930/USA/B&W/136 minutes
Director: Lewis Milestone
Screenplay, adaptation and dialogue: Maxwell Anderson and George Abbott
Based on the novel by Erich Maria Remarque.
Cast: Ben Alexander [Kemmerick], Lew Ayers [Paul Baumer], William Bakewell [Albert], Russell Gleason [Mueller], Beryl Mercer [Paul's mother], Slim Sommerville [Tjaden], Louis Wolheim [Kat], John Wray [Himmelstoss]
Awards: Academy Awards 1930: Best Director (Milestone); Best Picture; (nomination) Best Cinematography; (nomination) Best Screenplay. National Board Of Review: ten best films list.
Genre: An anti-war epic which follows the experiences of a group of patriotic German high school students who desert their classroom for the greater glory of the trenches during World War I.

Plot: After a rousing speech by their teacher, an entire class of high school boys signs up for active duty in the German Army in 1914. "You are the life of the Fatherland," he tells them. "You are the iron men of Germany. You are the gay heroes who will repulse the enemy." As one they report for duty, but the euphoria quickly evaporates as the boys learn the bitter truths of trench warfare.

In a matter of weeks, the high spirited teenagers have become cynical, battle scarred men. "Nothing but the best for our soldiers at the front," the arm-chair generals in the beer halls declare. But the reality is mud, poor food, terror, emotional breakdown, injury and death. And for what? For abstract notions the young soldiers do not understand. "How do they start a war?" asks a young soldier in one of the many memorable scenes in this film. No one seems able to answer his question.

When one of the group of friends, Paul (Ayers), returns home on leave, his former teacher asks him to inspire a new crop of students to sign up. Instead, in one of the highlights of the film, Paul tells the boys that at the front "we live in the trenches and we fight. We try not to be killed—that's all." He then proceeds to deliver a stinging attack on the war, the military, the system and the society which has deprived him of his youth and most of his classmates of their lives. Returning to the front after his leave he is stunned to find boys as young as sixteen filling out the ranks of his old company.

One of the most effective anti-war films ever produced, *All Quiet on the Western Front* has lost none of its strength in the last sixty five years. I wonder to what extent his work on this film influenced Lew Ayers' decision to be a conscientious objector during World War II? A 1979 television remake of this story is also available.

This film, as originally released, was 140 minutes in length. On video it has been released in both a 103 minute version, and in a 136 minute version which has had most of the original footage restored.

MPAA: Not rated. Canadian Home Video rated PG. There is one brief nude scene of four young soldiers including

Bruno Zanin and Magali Noel, *Amarcord* (1974)

Albert (Bakewell) and Paul bathing in a river. Seen mostly from the waist up, there are brief glimpses of bare buns as they dive beneath the surface. As befits a wartime story, there is some violence, though not as much and not as graphic as might be expected.

AMARCORD ★★★★

Credits: VHS/1974/Italy/Colour/127 minutes
In Italian with English subtitles.
Director: Federico Fellini
Screenplay: Federico Fellini and Tonino Guerra
Cast: Armando Brancia [Aurelio Biondi], Ciccio Ingrassia [Uncle Matto], Pupella Maggio [Miranda Biondi], Magali Noel [Gradisca], Josiane Tanzilli [Foxy], Bruno Zanin [Titta Biondi]

Awards: Academy Awards 1974: Best Foreign Language Film; (nomination) Best Director (Fellini); (nomination) Best Original Screenplay. National Board of Review Awards 1974: five best foreign films. New York Film Critics Awards 1974: Best Director (Fellini); Best Film.

Genre: A comic semi-autobiographical fantasy about growing up in a small coastal town in Mussolini's Italy.

Plot: In a film filled with the larger than life characters so often associated with Fellini, we follow a year in the life of Titta (Zanin), a teenager in 1930's Italy, as he views the antics of his family and fellow townspeople in a series of vignettes. Although seemingly only loosely connected to one another, when taken as a whole these snapshots of town life add up to a remarkable portrait of a particular time and place as seen through the eyes of one teenager. Through Fellini's comic exaggerations, Titta's school, his teachers, his classmates, his family, his neighbours all spring to life before our eyes, leaving us with perhaps a better portrait of the town than a less fantastic portrayal might have.

MPAA: Rated R. There are many sexual situations in the film: the boys fantasize about Gradisca (Noel), a high class courtesan, about Volpina (Tanzilli), the town whore, about the tobacconist with the huge breasts, and about the girls their own age. Titta and the tobacconist play some sexual games, during which her breasts are exposed. Titta's father (Brancia) is seen in a full length rear nude shot getting out of a bath tub. A very young boy is seen running around a farm yard wearing only a t-shirt. Titta's grandfather is constantly boasting about his sexual prowess. In a very funny scene, Titta and several of his friends masturbate together in an old car.

AMERICAN GRAFFITI ★★★★★

Credits: VHS/1973/USA/Colour/112 minutes
Director: George Lucas
Screenplay: George Lucas, Gloria Katz and Willard Huyck
Cast: Candy Clark [Debbie], Richard Dreyfuss [Curt], Harrison Ford [Bob Falfa], Ron Howard [Steve], Paul Le Mat [John], MacKenzie Phillips [Carol], Charles Martin Smith [Terry], Suzanne Somers [blonde in T-Bird], Cindy Williams [Laurie], Wolfman Jack [himself]

Awards: Academy Awards 1973: (nomination) Best Director (Lucas); (nomination) Best Film Editing; (nomination) Best Picture; (nomination) Best Story and Screenplay; (nomination) Best Supporting Actress (Clark). Golden Globe Awards 1974: Best Film - Musical/Comedy. New York Film Critics Awards 1973: Best Screenplay. National Society of Film Critics Awards 1973: Best Screenplay.

Genre: A comedy about four friends having one last fling before going their separate ways after graduating from high school.

Plot: It is the last night of the summer after high school graduation in the year 1962. Four long time friends head out on the town to celebrate, pick up girls or simply cruise the main street. In the hours ahead, though their paths rarely cross during the night, the four friends will each in his own way make some momentous decisions about the future. Go to college, or not? Join the forces? Get a job? Decisions which will affect their entire futures may be made this night. But while the four friends individually contemplate these matters and individually work through the convoluted twists and turns of the night's events, there are more immediate concerns. Girls, music, cars, cruising, necking, parking, racing, proving oneself, drive-ins. The original film of its type, and still the best, the real joys of *American Graffiti* are the great cast, the great music and the wonderful nostalgic feel. Even if we weren't actually there, we can still remember it clearly thanks to George Lucas.

MPAA: Rated PG. Canadian Home Video rated PG. There is a great deal of sexual talk and sexual longing in the film, but little happens on screen. There is one instance of a teenage boy mooning the camera from the back seat of a passing car.

behind the earlier film.

Cast: Jeff Bridges [Jack Kelson], Christian Frizzell [Rollie], Edward Furlong [Nick], Don Harvey [Rainey], Lucinda Jenney [Charlotte], Tracey Kapisky [Molly], Margaret Welsh [Freddie]

Awards: Independent Spirit Awards 1994: Best Actor (Bridges); (nomination) Best Cinematography; (nomination) Best First Feature; (nomination) Best Supporting Actor (Furlong); (nomination) Best Supporting Actress (Jenney).

Genre: A drama about an ex-con and his fourteen-year-old son trying to make it in Seattle.

Plot: When Jack (Bridges) is released on parole from Walla Walla State Penitentiary, the last thing he wants is his fourteen-year-old son Nick (Furlong, in one of his best performances to date). Unfortunately, Nick, who is trying

Rupert Everett and Colin Firth, *Another Country* (1984)

AMERICAN HEART ★★★★

Credits: VHS/1992/USA/Colour/114 minutes
Director: Martin Bell
Screenplay: Peter Silverman

Although it is not specifically stated, this film very obviously owes a great deal to Bell's earlier documentary film *Streetwise*, and reunites several of the principals

to make sense of his own life, desperately needs Jack.

Because of his own immediate needs and his own troubled childhood, however, Jack can't provide for Nick's needs. In fact, he wants Nick to go back to his aunt's farm, where he was living while Jack was behind bars.

When an attempt to ditch Nick at the bus terminal fails, father and son head to Seattle together. Things only seem to get worse. The only work that comes Jack's way is window washing, while Nick is left to his own devices. While Jack tries to kindle a romance with his prison pen-pal Charlotte (Jenney), Nick falls in with a less than desirable element.

Through his relationship with Molly, a teenage prostitute who lives in the same run-down hotel, Nick begins hanging around downtown with drug dealers, pimps, prostitutes and aimless, homeless youth. Circling around in the wings is Jack's old partner Rainey (Harvey), who tries to convince Jack to do one more job with him.

When an argument over shoplifting and drugs causes a further rift between father and son, Nick winds up on the street. Rainey entices the boy and his friend Rollie (Frizzell) into a house breaking, during which Rollie is killed.

In a tearful panic, Nick is re-united with his father and the two make plans to head north to Alaska. However, Jack must first deal with Rainey, a confrontation which will have tragic results.

MPAA: Rated R. The film deals with a number of contentious issues, including teenage prostitution, sexual diversity, street kids, teenage crime and violence. There is some female nudity: Molly's mother is an exotic dancer and is seen topless during a performance. In addition to Molly, several of the other teens are prostitutes, including one cross dressing teenager. Nick himself is picked up by a man when he first runs away from Jack, but jumps from the car when the driver makes a pass at him.

AMONG THE CINDERS ★★★

Credits: VHS/1983/New Zealand/Colour/109 minutes
Director: Rolf Haedrich
Screenplay: Rolf Haedrich and John O'Shea
Based on the novel by Maurice Shadbolt.
Cast: Bridget Armstrong [Helga], Marcus Broughton [Derek], Ricky Duff [Sam], Rebecca Gibney [Sally], Derek Hardwick [grandfather], Amanda Jones [Glenys], Yvonne Lawley [grandmother], Paul O'Shea [Nicholas], Maurice Shadbolt [Frank]
Genre: A drama about an introspective sixteen-year-old boy who must contend with the generation gap, the death of his best friend and his emerging sexuality.
Plot: Nicholas (O'Shea) is a quiet boy with few friends and shy around girls. He retreats even further into himself when his only close friend, a Maori boy named Sam (Duff), is killed in a fall from a cliff while the two boys are on a hunting expedition together.

Nick blames himself for the accident. His own recuperation is not helped when he overhears a conversation between his brother (Broughton) and parents (Shadbolt and Armstrong) speculating on his sex-

ual orientation.

His father and brother note that Nick is a loner. He has no girlfriend and spends long hours reading Oscar Wilde. Thus they speculate that he may be gay, or at the least going through "a homosexual phase."

Shortly after overhearing this conversation, Nicholas heads for his grandparents' home. Grandfather (Hardwick) is a gruff, outspoken old codger prone to drinking but at heart a very loving man, more big kid than old man. When his grandmother (Lawley) dies suddenly, his grandfather abruptly takes Nicholas on a long-discussed hiking trip into the bush. He doesn't even tell the boy his grandmother has died.

During the trip Nicholas encounters Sally (Gibney), a slightly older woman who is suffering from boyfriend problems. Before the day is over, she has coaxed Nicholas out of his shell, out of his clothes and into her bed. A remarkable change for a boy who has been prone to turning tail and running if a girl so much as says hello to him. But then Nicholas feels Sally is "more of a mate" than a "real" girl.

The film relies heavily on voice-overs by young O'Shea to explain the thoughts of the introspective Nicholas, a feature which some may feel detracts from the film.

MPAA: Rated R. Gibney and O'Shea are both seen nude, including some brief, but distant, full-frontal shots when Nicholas and Sally go skinny-dipping together. Gibney has a solo nude scene when Nicholas first encounters her swimming in a pond. The sexual encounter between Nicholas and Sally is more implied than shown.

ANOTHER COUNTRY ★★★★

Credits: VHS/1984/Great Britain/Colour/90 minutes
Director: Marek Kanievska
Screenplay: Julian Mitchell, based on his original play which in turn is based loosely on the lives of Guy Burgess and Donald Maclean.
Cast: Robert Addie [Delahay], Frederick Alexander [Menzies], Philip Dupuy [Martineau], Cary Elwes [James Harcourt], Rupert Everett [Guy Bennett], Colin Firth [Tommy Judd], Michael Jenn [Barclay], Tristan Oliver [Fowler], Adrian Ross-Magenty [Wharton], Ralph Perry-Robinson [Robbins], Rupert Wainwright [Devenish]
Awards: Cannes Film Festival 1984: (nomination) Best Film.
Genre: A drama about love, society, politics and the social order set in an elite British boarding school in the 1930s.
Plot: In the sheltered, circumscribed world of the British Public School, Judd (Firth) and Bennett (Everett) are

outsiders. Both come from the type of wealthy family which can afford champagne and caviar in the midst of the Great Depression. Judd, however, is an avowed Marxist and Bennett is gay.

Despite wide spread sexual activity amongst the students, it is Judd's political eccentricities which are more tolerated by the other students than Bennett's open and hedonistic attitude towards his sexual preferences. Even Judd, one of Bennett's best friends, despite his talk of equality and fraternity, cannot accept the other boy's activities as anything more than a passing schoolboy phase. Casual flirtation at school is one thing: a lifelong orientation is quite another.

After the suicide of Martineau (Dupuy) when he is faced with expulsion after being caught in flagrente delicto with Robbins (Perry-Robinson), Bennett's open courting of the achingly handsome Harcourt (Elwes) is pounced upon by the school prefects.

Notwithstanding the fact that Bennett has "done it" with almost all of them, they are fearful for the school's reputation and their own futures, and cane him as an example. These are, after all, the sons of the elite, the boys who will one day be cabinet ministers and bank presidents. Therefore, they must look to their own interests first.

MPAA: Rated PG. The film deals extensively with questions of sexual orientation and sexual activities amongst the students. It appears that such behaviour is an open secret at the school, acknowledged by both students and staff by turning a blind eye.

Robbins and Martineau are caught in an obvious sexual act early in the film. It is the consequences of getting caught, not the actual act that triggers tragedy.

Bennett and Harcourt share several tender moments together, including one long embrace late at night in a row boat. Bennett talks openly and often about his homosexual longings and desires. And the look of open adoration on the face of junior student Wharton (Ross-Magenty) as he carries out his duties for the seniors is a sure sign that the situation will continue.

There is, however, only one nude scene in the film. An unknown senior student is seen briefly in a full rear shot as he gets out of a bathtub.

Raphael Fejto (2nd from left) and Philippe Morier-Genoud (right), *Au Revoir Les Enfants* (1987)

AU REVOIR LES ENFANTS ★★★★★

(Also known as *Goodbye, Children*)

Credits: VHS/1987/France/ Colour/104 minutes
In French with English subtitles.
Writer/Director: Louis Malle
Based on an incident in Malle's own childhood.
Cast: Francois Berleand [Pere Michel], Stanislas Carre de Malberg [Francois Quentin], Raphael Fejto [Jean Bonnet], Peter Fritz [Muller], Gaspard Manesse [Julien Quentin], Philippe Morier-Genoud [Pere Jean], Francois Negret [Joseph], Francine Racette [Madame Quentin].
Awards: Academy Awards 1987: (nomination) Best Foreign Language Film; (Nomination) Best Screenplay. Cesar Awards (France): Best Cinematography; Best Director (Malle); Best Writing; Best Film; Best Art Direction/Set Decoration; Best Sound. British Academy Awards 1988: Best Director (Malle). National Board of Review Awards 1987: five best foreign films. Los Angeles Film Critics Association Awards 1987: Best Foreign Film. Venice Film Festival 1987: Best Film. European Felix Awards 1988: (nomination) Best Film; (nomination) Best Director. Numerous other awards throughout Europe.
Genre: A semi-autobiographical drama about the impact of the holocaust on one young French boy.
Plot: Occupied France during World War II. The German army is ever present, as are the collaborators and the black marketeers. Twelve-year-old Julien Quentin (Manesse) and his older brother Francois (de Malberg) have returned to their boarding school after the Christmas vacation, a return to cold classrooms and food shortages. Julien discovers that he is to have a new classmate, Jean Bonnet (Fejto). Not just a classmate, Jean also quickly establishes himself as a rival for Julien's position as the academic head of his class.

An uneasy friendship soon develops between the two boys, never really close, always rivals, but never enemies. When Julien notices that Jean does not take part in the religious rituals of the Catholic school, Jean explains this by saying he is a protestant. However, while snooping through Jean's belongings one day, Julien discovers that Jean's name is not Bonnet, but rather Kippelstein.

The secret that the headmaster, Father Jean (Morier-

Gaspard Manesse and Raphael Fejto, *Au Revoir Les Enfants* (1987)

Genoud), is hiding three Jewish boys in the school eventually leaks out to the Germans. The Gestapo come to the school looking for the three boys, and it is an involuntary gesture by Julien which gives Jean's presence away.

The school is closed by the Gestapo. The students are given a mere two hours to pack their belongings and get out. As Julien is packing the last of his things, Jean comes in to the dorms, escorted by a German officer. Jean gives Julien his books, and tells him not to worry about having given him away. The Germans would have got him eventually anyway, he says.

As Jean, the two other Jewish boys and Father Jean are led away by the Gestapo, Julien, in one of the most poignant moments of the film silently raises his hand to wave good-bye to his friend. All that remains is to identify the person who notified the Germans.

One of three holocaust stories in this book (the other two are *Europa, Europa* and *The Two Of Us*). With a heartbreaking story and outstanding performances from both Manesse and Fejto, *Au Revoir Les Enfants* is not to be missed.

MPAA: Rated PG. There is one brief scene in which the boys tease a classmate who appears to be masturbating in class and a shot of Julien in the bathtub, though this is framed so that he is only seen from the chest up.

THE BABY OF MACON ★★★★

Credits: 1993/Great Britain-France-Netherlands-Germany/Colour/118 minutes
Writer/Director: Peter Greenaway
Cast: Nils Dorando [the Baby of Macon], Ralph Fiennes [the bishop's son], Jonathon Lacy [Cosimo Medici], Julia Ormond [the daughter], Philip Stone [the bishop]
Genre: A drama about the exploitation and abuse of children told through the vehicle of a medieval play.
Plot: Peter Greenaway, like so many well known European directors, is something of an acquired taste, many of his films having achieved cult status. In fact, *The Baby of Macon* is already approaching mythic stature despite, or perhaps because of, never having been released in North America, either theatrically or on video. (I was able to view an imported British VHS tape.)

At first glance this film may be stretching the definition of a coming-of-age film. I feel, however, as an allegory for the millions of abused and exploited children in the world today, it warrants inclusion.

The citizens of Macon are presenting a miracle play in their town. Admittedly, this is a Greenaway vision of a miracle play. It holds about as much relationship to the genuine article as a Busby Berkeley musical extravaganza does to a grade school concert. The story of the play is that of a baby born to an old woman in a town where there have been no births for many years. The birth and the boy are quickly hailed as miraculous. The boy's family, especially an older sister (Ormond), attempt to exploit this situation, exchanging the boy's blessings for food and services. This soon brings them into conflict with the local bishop (Stone).

Claiming a monopoly on the miraculous, the church seizes the boy (Dorando), and is soon exploiting him for profit, auctioning off his blessings, his touch, his sweat, his tears and even his urine and his excrement.

Like any Greenaway film, *The Baby of Macon* is visually lush, a quality which even the inevitable image deterioration which accompanies a PAL to NTSC conversion couldn't diminish.
MPAA: Not rated. There are several scenes of violence including instances of murder and heterosexual rape. Ormond, Fiennes and Dorando all appear in full-frontal nude shots, Dorando extensively so.

The true story of the death of innocence and the birth of an artist.

LEONARDO DI CAPRIO
THE BASKETBALL DIARIES
COMING SOON TO A THEATER NEAR YOU.

Leonardo DiCaprio, *The Basketball Diaries* (1994)

THE BASKETBALL DIARIES ★★★

Credits: VHS/1994/USA/Colour/101 minutes
Director: Scott Kalvert
Screenplay: Bryan Goluboff Based on the memoirs of Jim Carroll.
Cast: Lorraine Bracco [Jim's mother], Roy Cooper [Father McNulty], Leonardo DiCaprio [Jim Carroll], Ernie Hudson [Reggie], Michael Imperioli [Bobby], Bruno Kirby [Swifty], Juliette Lewis [Diane Moody], James Madio [Pedro], Patrick McGaw [Neutron], Mark Wahlberg [Mickey]
Genre: A biographical drama chronicling one teenager's descent from star athlete to street junkie.
Plot: Jim (DiCaprio), one of the stars of the St. Vitus High School basketball team, has four absorbing interests: basketball, sex (especially masturbation), drugs and writing his diary, the last frequently being the chronicle of his indulgence in the previous three.

With his three buddies, Neutron (McGaw), Mickey (Wahlberg) and Pedro (Madio), he is ready to take on the world, and if he's stoned at the time, so much the better. His coach, Swifty (Kirby), has Jim pegged for a college basketball scholarship. Despite his love of the game, which he says he plays like a cheetah, the drugs begin to take over Jim's life. He is suspended from school, kicked out of the house by his distraught mother (Bracco) and alienated from his friend Neutron, who rejects the use of drugs.

The death after a long bout of Leukemia of his friend Bobby (Imperioli), a one time team mate at St. Vitus, doesn't help Jim's situation. He soon finds he is rarely out of his drug induced haze. Robbing stores, stealing cars, hustling in public washrooms and pushing drugs himself while living in a ratty cellar. He is trying always, desperately, to find the wherewithal for that next fix. Even being forced to go cold turkey by Reggie, an older black man and one time basketball partner, can't quite keep Jim off the drugs for good. For this he must endure six months in prison, earned for his part in the death of a drug dealer.

Based on the 1960's semi-autobiographical novel by Jim Carroll, the story has been reset in the 1990's, a transformation which has not been totally successful. Certain details of the story, and some of the attitudes of the characters, don't quite ring true for the current decade.

For a better depiction of 1990's lost urban youth, see Larry Clark's *Kids*. Despite this caveat, however, the film is still wrenching. DiCaprio's performance, as one might expect, is powerful and the tale of the relationship between the four friends is timeless.

MPAA: Rated R. Canadian Home Video rated 18-A. *The Basketball Diaries* is full of coarse language and scenes of drug use, though these are not as graphic as some of the scenes in the PG rated *A Hero Ain't Nothin' But A Sandwich,* a reflection, perhaps, of the constantly changing and evolving nature of the MPAA rating system.

There are several sexual scenes in the film, as well as a great deal of sex talk. One of Jim's more frequent pastimes is masturbating, even boasting to Bobby of managing to do it seven times in a single day. He masturbates naked on the roof after dark. He is sexually assaulted in the locker room by his coach. He has sex with a young girl in her apartment. He is fellated by an older man in a public washroom.

DiCaprio, Wahlberg, Madio and McGaw are all seen baring their buns when the four friends moon a passing tour boat from the top of the bluffs. There is one other brief nude scene after dark in the pouring rain on a neighbourhood basketball court. One of the boys who has stripped to his boxer shorts, begins to lose them as he hangs from the hoop.

THE BAY BOY ★★★

Credits: VHS/1984/Canada-France/Colour/107 minutes
Writer/Director: Daniel Petrie
Cast: Mathieu Carriere [Father Chaisson], Peter Donat [Mr. Campbell], Jane McKinnon [Diana Coldwell], Isabelle Mejias [Mary McNeill], Thomas Peacocke [Father McKinnon], Leah Pinsent [Saxon Coldwell], Alan Scarfe [Sgt. Coldwell], Kiefer Sutherland [Donald Campbell], Liv Ullman [Mrs. Campbell], Chris Wiggins [Chief Charlie McInnes], Peter Spence [Joe Campbell]
Awards: Genie Awards (Canada) 1984: Best Motion Picture; Best Supporting Actor (Scarfe); Best Screenplay (Petrie).
Genre: A period drama about a high school boy growing up in a hard hit mining town in the midst of the Great Depression. *The Bay Boy* was one of Kiefer Sutherland's first major roles.
Plot: Like others in the coal mining town of Glace Bay, Nova Scotia, young Donald Campbell's (Sutherland) family is suffering from the economic hard times. While dad (Donat) is trying to establish a soft drink bottling operation, mom (Ullman) is supporting the family by baking and taking in boarders.

Donald, a student at the local parochial school, thinks he may have a priestly vocation, though he can't keep his mind off Diana (McKinnon) and Saxon (Pinsent), the girls next door, daughters of the local police sergeant (Scarfe). Mary McNeill (Mejias), the bright girl with the "reputation," is rarely far from his mind, either.

When Donald sees Sgt. Coldwell murder an elderly Jewish couple, he fears for his own safety, and so only reports hearing gun-shots. The enormity of the act he witnessed, however, preys on his mind, causing nightmares and hallucinations. Finally he feels forced to confront the killer when he sees Sgt. Coldwell viciously beating one of his daughters.

Donald must also deal with school and the church, most especially with Father Chaisson (Carriere), a missionary who has come home to Cape Breton to raise money for his work in the Congo. Father Chaisson, after speaking to the students at the school, arranges an informal contest. By the priest's design, Donald wins. His prize? The chance to visit Father Chaisson's family in one of the neighbouring french-speaking Acadian communities during Christmas vacation.

On the first night of the visit Donald discovers that he must share a bed with the priest who starts to pour out his soul to the boy. In a spiritual torment brought about by his vow of celibacy, Father Chaisson makes a pass at Donald during the night, causing the boy to cut his visit short and return home the next day.

MPAA: Rated R. In addition to his night with Father Chaisson, Donald has another sexual encounter much more to his liking with Mary McNeill. When she invites him to her home to study together while her parents are at

Matthew Broderick, *Biloxi Blues* (1988)

a bingo game, they wind up in bed instead. During the preliminaries to this, Mejias is seen topless. The actual sexual encounters are more suggested than depicted. Considering their high level of sexual drive the teenagers in this film, like the boys in *Summer Of '42*, all display what is, by current standards, an amazing ignorance of basic human anatomy.

THE BEAT ★

Credits: VHS/1986/USA/Colour/102 minutes
Writer/Director: Paul Mones
Cast: Paul Dillon, Marcus Flanagan [Vis], Kara Glover [Kate Kane], Jeffrey Horowitz [Dr. Waxman], David Jacobson [Rex Voorhas Ormine], William McNamara

[Billy Kane], John Savage [Frank Ellsworth]
Genre: A wildly unrealistic drama about competing New York street gangs brought together by a troubled, poetry spouting youth, which tries along the way to deal with questions of mental health, being different, fitting in, racial tensions and drug use.
Plot: Rex (Jacobson) is the new kid at an inner city high school. He also has personality problems. Quickly dubbed a "retard" by his fellow students, he arrives in Frank Ellsworth's (Savage) English class just as the poor, hard-pressed teacher is trying to impart a love of poetry in the members of rival street gangs. Despite poor initial impressions, Rex somehow wins over brother and sister Billy (McNamara) and Kate (Glover), and then most of the other students with his off-beat poetry and the strange imagery of his inner vision.

As is to be expected, the only teacher who understands the boy is Ellsworth: all the other cardboard characters who inhabit the staff lounge at Osmo High would be quite happy to see Rex institutionalized as school psychologist Dr. Waxman (Horowitz) proposes. The doctor's session with Rex leaves the boy severely troubled and leads directly to Rex's suicide. This act, far from being mourned, however, is celebrated as a liberation by his fellow students.

Music or perhaps poetry, it would seem, does indeed have charms to soothe the savage beast. What it may not have is sufficient charms to prevent you from hitting the eject button on your VCR. The Canadian film *Train Of Dreams* and Robin William's *Dead Poet's Society* both present much better and more realistic treatments of the use of poetry as therapy for troubled teenagers.
MPAA: Rated R. There is a great deal of coarse language and sex talk on screen, little of it ringing true: most of it sounds studied and forced. Despite the sex talk, however, there is little action. The only sexual encounter is between Vis (Flanagan) and Kate and that off-screen behind the closed doors of a supply cupboard at the school. Drug use, discussions of drug, and violence abound.

BEAU PERE ★★★

Credits: VHS/1981/France/Colour/ 125 minutes
In French with English subtitles.
Writer/Director: Bertrand Blier, based on his novel.
Cast: Nathalie Baye [Charlotte], Ariel Besse [Marion], Patrick Dewaere [Remi], Nicole Garcia [Martine], Maurice Ronet [Charlie]
Genre: A carefully handled satire about the sexually charged relationship between a precocious fourteen year old girl and her "almost 30" stepfather.

27

Plot: Remi (Dewaere) is a struggling lounge pianist married to Martine [Garcia], a photographer's model. When Martine is killed in a car accident, Remi is left to care for Marion (Besse), her fourteen year old daughter by a previous marriage.

Marion's father Charlie (Ronet) and Remi argue over where Marion should live, Charlie insisting that, as her father, he has both the right and the obligation to look after her. Marion, however, has other ideas. She would much rather live with her beau pere, her stepfather, for she has definite designs on him.

Marion soon runs away from Charlie's home, and returns to Remi, declaring her love and physical attraction for him. Finding Marion waiting in his bed one night, Remi admits his interest, but feels he must refuse, despite every argument Marion can bring to bear on him. Among other things, she says, her grades at school are suffering, a situation that will surely change if only Remi would sleep with her.

Eventually, however, Marion is able to break down Remi's resistance, and the two do make love, though their relationship is fated to end when Remi meets Charlotte [Baye], a fellow pianist, and the mother of a little girl Marion babysits for.

MPAA: Not rated. Most of the sexual encounters between Remi and Marion occur off-screen. There is a limited amount of female nudity which occurs as Marion undresses in a hotel room.

BEETHOVEN'S NEPHEW ★★★

(Also known as *Le Neveu De Beethoven*)

Credits: VHS/1988/France/Colour/103 minutes
Director: Paul Morrissey
Screenplay: Paul Morrissey and Mathieu Carriere Based on a novel by Luigi Magnani.
Cast: Nathalie Baye [Leonore], Jane Birkin [Karl's mother], Mathieu Carriere, Axel Helpap [the school friend], Dietmar Prinz [Karl van Beethoven], Wolfgang Reichman [Ludwig van Beethoven]
Genre: Variously described as a surreal drama, a farce, and a tragi-comedy, this film by Warhol collaborator

Matthew Broderick and Penelope Ann Miller, *Biloxi Blues* (1988)

Morrissey chronicles the obsessive relationship between the composer Beethoven and Karl, his nephew and sole heir.
Plot: On the death of his younger brother, Ludwig van Beethoven (Reichman) managed by somewhat devious means to obtain a court order giving him full custody of his brother's son Karl (Prinz).

Andy Warhol collaborator Morrissey's film begins with this established fact and weaves around it a speculative tale of obsession, jealousy and repressed homosexual desire. A demanding, irascible, ill-tempered bachelor prone to emotional outbursts, Beethoven attempts to control every facet of his nephew's life. In his obsession, he can not allow the boy out of his sight for so much as a minute. Nor can he allow any other influences to affect the boy. Even Karl's mother (Birkin), accused by Beethoven of being a whore, has a thousand obstacles placed in her path every time she attempts to see her son.

When the court orders that Karl be sent to a boarding school, Beethoven moves into an apartment across the street, visiting the school every day. He even sits in on Karl's classes. However, far from inspiring Karl to become a musician as Beethoven intends, his constant attention earns the uncle nothing but loathing and contempt. It even spawns a suicide attempt when Beethoven separates Karl from Leonore (Baye), an attractive young actress and courtesan who invites Karl to come to Paris with her.

So great is Karl's contempt for his uncle that when the composer is stricken with pneumonia, Karl callously and deliberately delays obtaining medical aid for the man, thus earning for himself the reputation as the man who killed Beethoven.

MPAA: Rated R. The film speculates on the nature of the relationship between Beethoven and his nephew, suggesting that the man may have been sexually attracted to his nephew. If so, it is clearly one way. Young Karl has several erotic adventures with women, twice encountering prostitutes while a student at the boarding school and once bedding a maid while he and Beethoven visit a country estate.

In the latter incident, we see Prinz's buns while the two are in bed. Later, after Beethoven has dragged Karl out of the bed, we see the boy, nude from the waist down, running down a hallway. In this latter scene we get a very brief frontal shot of Prinz. The various prostitutes are seen topless and in rear shots.

BILITIS ★

Credits: VHS/1977/France/Colour/95 minutes
Dubbed in English.
Director: David Hamilton
Screenplay: Based on the novel *Les Chansons de Bilitis* by Pierre Louys.
Cast: Mathieu Carriere [Nikias], Patricia D'Arbanville [Bilitis], Bernard Girandeau [Lucas], Gilles Kohler [Pierre], Mona Kristensen [Melissa]
Genre: A soft-core romance about a sexually precocious teenage girl.
Plot: Director David Hamilton is well known as a still photographer specializing in the soft-focus exploration of the bodies of nude teenage girls. Fans of his still photography probably won't be too disappointed by this film: there are a great many young female bodies on view. On the other hand, if you are looking for a first-class story line … .

Bilitis (D'Arbanville) is a high school student spending her summer vacation on the Riviera with Pierre (Kohler) and Melissa (Kristensen). While there, she falls in love with and learns about sex from a young photographer, Lucas (Girandeau). While Pierre is out cheating on Melissa, Melissa is home in bed with Bilitis. Under the guidance of the girl she is also searching for a new man.

MPAA: Rated R. As anyone familiar with Hamilton's still photography would expect, this film has a great many nude scenes and several sexual encounters. These include frequent full-frontal female nudity and a long, loving romantic encounter between Melissa and Bilitis.

BILOXI BLUES ★★★★

(Also known as *Neil Simon's Biloxi Blues*)

Credits: VHS/1988/USA/Colour/105 minutes
Director: Mike Nichols
Screenplay: Neil Simon, based on his play.
Cast: Matthew Broderick [Eugene Morris Jerome], Michael Dolan [Hennessey], Marcus Flanagan [Selridge], Penelope Ann Miller [Daisy], Matt Mulhern [Wykowski], Park Overall [Rowena], Corey Parker [Arnold Epstein], Casey Siemaszko [Carney], Christopher Walken [Sgt. Toomey]
Genre: A semi-autobiographical comedy about a disparate group of boys fresh out of high school thrown together during basic training in the dying days of World War II, as seen through the eyes of Simon's alter ego, Eugene Morris Jerome (Broderick).
Plot: It is 1945, and Eugene Morris Jerome, a rather naive young Jewish boy from New York, finds himself in basic training in Biloxi, Mississippi. An aspiring writer, Jerome finds himself at odds with most of his barracks mates, but especially with Sgt. Toomey (Walken), a sadistic drill sergeant who takes an especial dislike for the young man. In fact, their shared hatred of Toomey is virtually the only common factor linking the young men who have been thrown together by the happenstance of war.

Each of these young men is essentially a misfit, trying in various ways to maintain a minimum of sanity in difficult circumstances. Jerome stays aloof and detached from his fellows, recording his thoughts and observations in a diary.

Epstein (Parker), the only other Jew in the platoon and an intellectual with slightly effeminate mannerisms, becomes the professional victim.

Hennessey (Dolan), the only truly caring and compassionate member of the group, is trying, ultimately unsuccessfully, to hide his homosexuality. Despite their differences, however, in the closing acts of the film, when Jerome is threatened by a drunk, gun wielding Toomey, the platoon pulls together to aid their comrade.

Biloxi Blues is the sequel to *Brighton Beach Memoirs* and was followed by *Broadway Bound*.
MPAA: Rated PG-13. The script includes some coarse language and sex talk, as well as a number of implied sexual situations. The most important of these are the encounters the boys have with the prostitute Rowena (Overall) and an interrupted gay encounter in the barracks washroom involving two young recruits.

BLESS THE BEASTS & CHILDREN ★★★

Credits: VHS/1971/USA/Colour/109 minutes
Director: Stanley Kramer
Screenplay: Mac Benoff
Based on a novel by Glendon Swarthout.
Cast: Miles Chapin [Shecker], Darel Glaser [Goodenow], Bob Kramer [Lally 1], Bill Mumy [Teft], Barry Robins [Cotton], Ken Swafford [Wheaties], Marc Vahanian [Lally 2]
Awards: Academy Awards 1971: (nomination) Best Song "Bless The Beasts And The Children", sung by the Carpenters.
Genre: An at times violent drama about six troubled teenage boys thrown together at summer camp.
Plot: Cotton (Robins), Teft (Mumy), Shecker (Chapin), Goodenow (Glaser), and brothers Lally 1 (Bob Kramer) and Lally 2 (Vahanian) are six teenage misfits. At the Box Canyon Boys Camp no one else will have them. They are thrown together into a single cabin under the leadership of their inept, unsympathetic counselor Wheaties (Swafford). All six are athletically challenged. All six have emotional and psychological problems. All six come from homes where money is abundant but love a scarce commodity. Bed wetting, car theft, sibling rivalry, feelings of abandonment, self destructive behaviour, broken homes, raging fits of temper and drug use are some of the problems which afflict these boys.

The low end of the totem pole at Box Canyon, the six "Bed Wetters" take it upon themselves to liberate a herd of buffalo which has been slated for slaughter in a national preserve. The story follows their trip from the camp to the buffalo pens and their attempts to release the animals.

Intercut with this straightforward road story are a series of flashbacks, some to previous incidents at the camp showing how the boys were thrown together, some to scenes with their parents showing the problems each boy faces. As they travel together, the six boys must deal not only with the practical problems of the trip but also with their own personal and psychological problems. Coming together eventually as a cohesive unit, they accomplish their goal, but not without great cost and tragedy.

Goodenow, because of his gentle nature, is accused by his fellow campers and by his step father of being "a fairy." By the end of the film, he is even using the term to describe himself. Is this supposed to indicate a coming out by a gay youth? I have long suspected that in fact Goodenow is supposed to be a gay teenager at a time when very few directors would have dared to raise this possibility directly, especially not in a sympathetic way. Certainly, the scene by the pond when Goodenow first meets Cotton could be seen as having homoerotic overtones. This is especially true if one considers the number of times Cotton is seen with an arm across Goodenow's shoulders. When the boys spend the night in the open together, these two also seem to be especially close. Goodenow appears to have fallen asleep with his head on Cotton's lap.

MPAA: Rated R. There is a certain amount of violence in the film, as well as coarse language, one scene of marijuana use and a simulated sex scene. Some of the boys are seen masturbating under their blankets at night. There is no actual nudity in the film but there are several scenes of teenage boys dressed only in white briefs. In one particularly revealing shot, Goodenow in a pair of wet, virtually see-through white briefs, walks out of the lake after being talked out of his threat to commit suicide.

BLUE JEANS ★★★★

Credits: VHS/1978/France/Colour/80 minutes
In English and French with English subtitles.
Writer/Director: Hugues Burin des Roziers
Cast: Pierre Bonzans, Gilles Budin, Gabriel Cattand, Gerard Croce, Michel Gibet
Genre: A gentle, bitter-sweet drama about a young French teenager's first forays into the world of love while on an educational holiday in England.
Plot: Thirteen-year-old Julien's exchange trip to the south coast of England finds the boy practicing more than his English. Julien and his friends soon find themselves spending as much time exploring the mysteries of love as the mysteries of the English language.

While young Batissier is soon boasting of his conquests with Maureen, Julien finds himself drawn to Janet. A few days later he is devastated when she apparently disappears, only to reappear with Jean-Pierre, an older French teenager.

To this point Julien's love life has been relatively straightforward, if not overly successful. However, he soon finds himself drawn as much to Jean-Pierre as to Janet. In fact, he becomes the older boy's constant companion, a fact that doesn't go unnoticed by his age mates.

On a bus outing to Margate, Julien is teased and taunted to the point of tears by the other boys calling him queer. When Julien begins to wear a pair of much prized and very distinctive blue jeans which he has begged from Jean-Pierre, the situation is not improved. Turning to a teacher for guidance and consolation when Jean-Pierre's absence has him in tears, Julien says the rumours are a dirty lie. Jean-Pierre is his best pal. That's all.

"That's all?" the teacher replies. "Mais, c'est formidable! It's marvellous to have a real pal, not to be alone. It's nothing to cry about."

"But I don't know where he is," Julien weeps.

Finally finding Jean-Pierre again, but with Janet, Julien throws a fit, jealous of the relationship between the two. Dumbfounded by the intensity of Julien's reaction, Jean-Pierre retaliates by asking if the rumours about Julien's sexuality are true.

On returning to France, Julien, having obtained Jean-Pierre's address from Janet, writes to the older boy inviting him to come to visit, an invitation which Jean-Pierre dismisses. Although the dismissal is of little consequence to Jean-Pierre, Julien is temporarily devastated.

Is Julien going through the earliest stages of coming to terms with being gay? Or is his relationship with Jean-Pierre a form of hero-worship of an older boy who un-questioningly allows the much younger Julien to be his friend? The film doesn't spell out the answer to this question. I have my own ideas, but will leave you to make up your own mind.

MPAA: Not rated. Beyond some sex talk, there is nothing ratable in this film.

THE BLUE LAGOON ★

Credits: VHS/1980/USA/Colour/104 minutes
Director: Randal Kleiser
Screenplay: Douglas Day Stewart
A remake of a 1949 film, based on a novel by Henry DeVere Stacpoole.
Cast: Christopher Atkins [Richard], William Daniels [Arthur Lestrange], Elva Josephson [young Emmeline], Glenn Kohan [young Richard], Leo McKern [Paddy Button], Brooke Shields [Emmeline]
Genre: A romantic adventure tale about two young children growing up alone and learning about love, life and sex on a deserted island in the South Pacific.
Plot: When the ship carrying young cousins Richard (Kohan) and Emmeline (Josephson) to San Francisco with Richard's father (Daniels) burns and explodes in the South Pacific, the two pre-teen children are set adrift in a rowboat with the ship's cook, Paddy Button (McKern).

Eventually coming ashore on a lush, uninhabited tropical island, the two children learn to survive, first under Paddy's instruction and later on their own. As teenagers, Richard (Atkins) and Emmeline (Shields) must cope with the usual teenage problems of puberty and sexual yearnings without the benefit of adults to confide in. Emmeline, of course, eventually becomes pregnant, giving birth to a baby boy, much to the surprise of both teenagers.

Filmed on location in Fiji, some of the photography is beautiful. Unfortunately, few of the performances measure up to the surroundings. Neither Shields nor Atkins makes their character believable. The best performance is unquestionably by Leo McKern as the boozing ship's cook. This film was paid the dubious compliment of a blatant copy two years later in the form of *Paradise* and was followed eleven years later by a sequel, *Return To The Blue Lagoon*. There is an un-doubted fascination with the concept of two innocent teenagers discovering sexuality unencumbered by the trappings of a disapproving adult society. Unfortunately so far none of the attempts to bring this idea to the screen has been better than an unmitigated disaster.

MPAA: Rated R. Canadian Home Video rated 14-A. The film features extensive nudity and partial nudity, both male and female. Both Kohan as the pre-teen Richard and Atkins as the teenage Richard have several full-frontal nude scenes as well as numerous full rear and side shots of both. Atkins spends the vast majority of the film wearing loincloths of varying degrees of brevity. Josephson as the young Emmeline also has several nude scenes, including some full-frontal shots. There are also several shots of the teenage Emmeline nude. These, however, are not Shields but a body double. Shields does appear in assorted loincloths. Almost all of the shots involving full nudity occur while the various characters are swimming. There is one long scene of the teenagers making love for the first time. This is arguably one of the best sequences in the film: the actors all keep their mouths shut and allow the camera to tell the story.

BOYS ★★★

(Also known as *The Girl You Want*)

Credits: VHS/1995/USA/Colour/89 minutes
Writer/Director: Stacy Cochran/Based on the short story *Twenty Minutes* by James Salter.
Cast: Chris Cooper [Mr. John Baker], Lukas Haas [John Baker, Jr.], Jessica Harper [Mrs. John Baker], Charlie Hofheimer [John Cooke], James LeGros [Fenton Roy], John C. Reilly [officer Kellogg Cury], Winona Ryder [Patty Vare], Bill Sage [officer Bill Mortone], Skeet Ulrich [Bud Valentine], Spencer Vrooman [John Murphy], Wiley Wiggins [John Philips], Russell Young [John Van Sleider]
Genre: A romantic drama cum mystery story about a

high school senior involved with an older woman.

Plot: John Baker (Haas) is an unhappy senior at an exclusive New England prep school. Dad (Cooper) has dreams of supermarket moguldom for his son. The boy has dreams of being a writer but feels stifled by the school's attitudes and atmosphere.

Suddenly into the boy's repressed life comes unexpected excitement and romance. Murphy (Vrooman) and Cooke (Hofheimer), two eighth-grade students, ask for his assistance in rescuing a young woman named Patty (Ryder) who they found lying unconscious in a nearby field. With the help of the two younger boys, Baker brings the woman into his room in the dorms.

His budding romantic feelings induce him to conceal her presence. The secret can't last, however, and is soon known throughout the school. It also creates a serious rift between Baker and his best friends and classmates Philips (Wiggins) and Van Sleider (Young).

Patty has secrets of her own which she tries to hide from the boy as well. Although she tries to keep Baker ignorant of her secrets, he eventually discovers them, but not before she and Baker have made love in the grass behind the midway at the county fair.

Both Haas and Ryder do the best they can with the material. However, the overall direction of the film seems at times plodding. Some of the minor characters are not well presented, either. In a strange quirk of the writing, every single student at the school bears some variation of the name John. There are five Johns, one Jon and a Jonathan amongst the named characters in the credit list. No other students are named.

MPAA: Rated PG-13. Canadian Home Video rated PG. Beyond the car accident, there are several minor instances of violence: John Baker, Sr. slaps his son, two boys get into a fist fight in the class room, Philips slams his fist into the wall during an outburst.

There also are occasional, though mostly mild instances of course language and sexual dialogue. Murphy, for example, suggests Baker's interest in Patty is due to the boner in his pants. Baker and Patty kiss on the midway, then later make love in the grass.

THE BOYS OF CELLBLOCK Q
★

Credits: VHS/1992/USA/Colour/90 minutes
Director: Alan Daniels
Screenplay: Ralph Lucas
Based on the stage play by John C. Wall.

Johnny Morina and Henry Czerny, *The Boys Of St. Vincent* (1993)

Cast: Andrew Addams [Timmy], Lewis Alante [Beef], Slade Burrus [Lana], Larry Maraviglia [Padre], Ken Merckx [Boss], David Sochet [Ludes], John Topping [Plunkett], Michael Valdes [Moosemeat]
Genre: A very low-brow, low budget comedy about sexual escapades in a boys' reformatory.
Plot: At the Sunnyvale Juvenile Correction Farm life is

tough. The teenagers (the characters are teens, even if the actors aren't) must put up with Boss (Merckx), the sadistic head of the facility. Padre (Maraviglia) seems more interested in the boy's bodies than their souls. To make matters worse, they have to put up with a new "fish" in their cell. Will new boy Timmy (Addams) fit in? Will his boyfriend on the outside come to his rescue? Will Lana (Burrus) and Padre run away to San Francisco together? Will Beef (Alante) and Ludes (Sochet) find their missing cache? Will the audience care?

This film was adapted from a stage play, and looks it. The whole thing feels very "stagey." Beyond having the entire cast of characters gay, there doesn't appear to be very much original material or even anything interesting occurring on screen.

MPAA: Not rated. There are frequent instances of nudity including full-frontal shots of most of the lead players. As well there is much coarse and sexually suggestive dialogue throughout the film and many suggestive scenes but no actual sex.

THE BOYS OF ST. VINCENT
★★★★★

Credits: VHS/1993/Canada/Colour/184 minutes
(On two tapes, 92 minutes each)
Director: John N. Smith
Screenplay: Des Walsh, John Smith and Sam Grana
A docudrama inspired by actual events in St. John's, Newfoundland.
Cast: Ashley Billard [Brian Lunny age 15], Henry Czerny [Brother Lavin], Kristine Demers [Sheilah], Phillip Dinn [Mike Finn], Brian Dodd [Stephen Lunny age 10], Brian Dooley [Detective Noseworthy], Alain Goulem [Brother Glynn], David Hewlett [Stephen Lunny age 25], Johnny Morina [Kevin Reevey age 10], Lise Roy [Chantel], Sebastian Spence [Kevin Reevey age 25], Greg Thomey [Brother Glacken], Michael Wade [Brother MacLaverty], Timothy Webber [Brian Lunny age 30]
Awards: Independent Spirit Awards (1995): (nomination) Best Foreign Film.
Genre: A docudrama, originally presented as a television mini-series, about the physical, psychological and sexual abuse of young boys and teenagers in a Canadian orphanage.
Plot: Jointly produced by the Canadian Broadcasting Corporation and Canada's National Film Board, *The Boy's Of St. Vincent* is a truly heartbreaking tale. Inspired by, but not a reenactment of, actual events which came to light in the late 1980's, the story is told in two parts.

Part one is the story of the abuse of the children and the high level cover-up by both church and state. Part two covers court trials and Royal Commission enquiries 15 years later when the abuse and the cover up finally become public knowledge.

This story details one of the first instances to be made public of the routine abuse of institutionalized children. Unfortunately, it is not the last: this same basic story has been retold many times over in the years since.

When Kevin Reevey (Morina) first enters the St. Vincent orphanage he is befriended by the institution's superintendent, Brother Lavin (Czerny). What seems at first to be an act of kindness by the man soon becomes a nightmare for the boy. He becomes Lavin's special boy, being routinely sodomized, beaten, caressed and traumatized by the man. He is even told to call Lavin "mom." Nor is Kevin alone. Virtually every Brother on the staff seems to have his special boy.

Bedtime in the dorms is hell as the men come creeping around ostensibly to tuck the boys in, but in fact to fondle and caress them.

When Kevin can no longer take it, he runs away, only to be returned kicking and screaming by the police to a reception which includes an injury-causing belting from Lavin, who suffers from periodic rages. The next day, janitor Mike Finn (Dinn) takes Kevin to the emergency ward at the hospital, and is fired on the spot by Lavin for "interfering in things he knows nothing about." Finn is unable to let it rest, however, and goes to the police with tales of physical and sexual abuse in the orphanage.

Detective Noseworthy (Dooley) begins to investigate, uncovering case after case of abuse. Virtually every boy in the orphanage has been a victim. With the exception of Brother MacLaverty (Wade), virtually every Brother is implicated. Brother Glacken (Thomey) fondles the boys in their beds. Brother Glynn straps Brian Lunny (Billard) so hard he takes the skin off the boy's hands. Even Brian's cocky little brother Stephen (Dodd), despite denials to the police, is visited almost nightly after lights out.

Despite overwhelming evidence, however, the case never proceeds to court. Church, the police chief and the government come to a "gentleman's agreement" not to prosecute and Noseworthy is told to doctor the witness statements from the boys, eliminating all "pornographic" references to sexual matters. After all, the orphanage is about to receive $1,000,000 from the government for renovations and a new hockey arena, and the politicians could be embarrassed if seen to be giving that much money to "a bunch of perverts." The worst offenders are quietly transferred elsewhere, but does the abuse end?

Fifteen years later the scandal eventually comes to light. Glacken, Glynn and Lavin are brought back to

Saint John's to face trial. The victims must also face a trial of sorts. Brian Lunny (Webber), now married with two children of his own, has in his own way learned to forgive. His brother Stephen (Hewlett), whom he has not seen for fifteen years, is only too eager to testify, until it comes out in court that as a teenager he in his turn abused younger boys at the orphanage, and is now living on the streets of Toronto, with a criminal record of drug abuse and male prostitution. Kevin (Spence) wants only to forget, but is unable to. The abuse he suffered in the past affects his daily life in the present, even coming between him and his girlfriend Sheilah (Demers).

MPAA: Not rated. Canadian Home Video rated 18-A. There are several scenes of nude young boys showering while the Brothers watch. Mostly these are rear shots, but there is very brief frontal exposure of one young boy. There are also many stomach churning scenes of the physical abuse of boys, some bordering on torture. Much of this is unflinchingly presented. There are numerous scenes of the sexual abuse of the boys as well: Brothers fondling the boys in their beds at night; Brothers raping boys; Brothers forcing teenagers to perform oral sex; Lavin raping Kevin in the swimming pool. There are also several scenes of the boys describing to the police in detail what the Brothers had been doing to them. The more graphic portions of these scenes and descriptions have usually been deleted when this film has aired on U.S. cable services.

THE BREAKFAST CLUB ★★★★

Credits: VHS/1985/USA/Colour/92 minutes
Writer/Director: John Hughes
Cast: Emilio Estevez [Andrew Clark], Paul Gleason [Richard Vernon], John Kapelos [Carl], Anthony Michael Hall [Bryan Johnson], Judd Nelson [John Bender], Molly Ringwald [Claire Standish], Ally Sheedy [Allison Reynolds]
Genre: A drama about five disparate teenagers forced to spend an entire Saturday together in their high school library while serving detentions.
Plot: It's seven o'clock on a Saturday morning in March, 1984. Five teenagers arrive at the door of their high school to serve a day long detention for various serious misdemeanours. Each is a "type." Each sees the others as a type, and so does the staff. "What do you care?" they ask in their collective essay. "You see us as you want to see us. In the simplest terms and most convenient definitions. You see us as a brain, an athlete, a basket case, a princess and a criminal, correct? That's the way we saw each other at seven o'clock this morning. We were brainwashed."

Over the next eight hours, despite instructions from

Mr. Vernon (Gleason) neither to talk nor to move from their seats, the five manage to overcome their initial hostility towards each other. As the day progresses each learns to accept the others for what they are, as well as to confide their own problems and fears. Beginning to understand the others, each comes eventually to the point where he or she can confront their own problems.

At the end of the day, each of the teenagers has found meaning in new friendships. Each wonders whether their new friendships will stand the test of peer pressure on Monday morning as each re-enters the cliques they left on Friday afternoon.

The Breakfast Club, unlike so many teen angst dramas, gives us solid performances from each member of the cast and depth of understanding of each of the characters. Each of these troubled teens is a whole person. Each has strengths and weaknesses. Each is an essentially likeable but flawed individual. By the film's end we care about each character, and we have been able, as the characters themselves have, to see beyond the stereotypes who walked into the school library at dawn.

MPAA: Rated R. A great deal of coarse language and sex talk.

BUMP IN THE NIGHT ★★

Credits: 1991/USA/Colour/100 minutes
Director: Karen Arthur
Screenplay: Christopher Lofton
Based on a novel by Isabelle Holland.
Cast: Meredith Baxter-Birney [Martha Tierney], Corey Carrier [Jonathon Tierney], Wings Hauser [Patrick Tierney], Christopher Reeve [Muller]
Genre: If Holland's book *Man Without A Face* is about the rarely acknowledged subject of consenting sexual relationships between a man and a boy, this made for television thriller is about the dark side of inter-generational sex, the widely feared problems of child abduction and child pornography.
Plot: On his way to a clandestine before school meeting with his father (Hauser), eight-year-old Jonathon (Carrier) is lured away by convicted child-molester Lawrence Muller (Reeve), posing as a friend of the boy's father. In fact, Muller has paid a child pornography ring $1000 to search out a suitable boy. He is to have Jonathon alone for the day before turning him over to a cameraman.

Taken to an apartment, empty except for a small fortune in photographic and video equipment, Jonathon is able to escape from Muller's clutches, psychologically traumatized but physically unharmed, by climbing through a ceiling hatch in a closet.

MPAA: Not rated. There is no actual sex depicted on-screen, though, of course, sexual abuse of children and child pornography are essential ingredients of this story. Even so, this is more the story of the strained relationship between his divorced parents, alcoholic Martha (Birney) and workaholic Patrick, than of young Jonathon's ordeal.

BURNING SECRET ★★★

Credits: VHS/1988/Great Britain-USA-Germany/Colour/107 minutes
Writer/Director: Andrew Birkin
Based on a story by Stefan Zweig.
Cast: Klaus Maria Brandauer [the baron Alexander], Faye Dunaway [Sonya], David Eberts [Edmond], Ian Richardson [the father]
Awards: Bavarian Film Prize (Germany) 1988: Best Actor (Brandauer).
Genre: A drama concerning love and bitter jealousy involving a beautiful woman, her pre-adolescent son and a handsome baron.
Plot: It is the winter of 1919. Sonya (Dunaway) and her young son Edmond (Eberts) have travelled from Vienna to a spa cum sanatorium in the Austrian Alps in order that the boy may obtain some relief from his asthmatic condition.

Also visiting the spa is the wealthy, urbane baron Alexander (Brandauer). The owner of a flashy car and many heroic stories, the baron easily befriends the boy. They are soon spending every spare moment together. The baron has also started to spend time with Sonya, a relationship which quickly becomes intimate. When Edmond discovers his mother kissing the baron, he is enraged. In a fit of jealousy he returns to Vienna alone. When his mother arrives home shortly after, Edmond is forced to choose: does he tell his father (Richardson) about Sonya's liaison with the baron, or not? Does he betray his father, or two other people he loves passionately?
MPAA: Rated PG. Although there is nothing explicitly stated in the film, it is obvious that the relationship between the baron and the boy involves a great deal of sexual longing for both man and boy. The swimming pool scene, in particular, is fraught with sexual overtones and unspoken desires.

BUSTER & BILLIE ★★★

Credits: VHS/1974/USA/Colour/100 minutes
Writer/Director: Daniel Petrie
Screenplay: Ron Turbeville
Cast: Robert Englund [Whitey], Joan Goodfellow [Billie Joe], Clifton James [Jake], Pamela Sue Martin [Margie Hooks], Jan-Michael Vincent [Buster Lane]
Genre: A dramatic tragedy about a high school senior who finds true love with the class tramp in rural Georgia in 1948.
Plot: Greenwood High School senior Buster Lane (Vincent) is engaged to Margie Hooks (Martin). They are to be married as soon as they graduate. However, in the last few months of the school year, Buster's life is turned upside down when he meets Billie (Goodfellow).

Billie has the well deserved reputation of being the class tramp. Despite this, however, Buster is increasingly drawn to her. As he finds himself falling in love with Billie, he breaks off his relationship with Margie. With the attention Buster is paying to her, Billie's own personality begins to change as well: she is clearly happier. She also becomes unwilling to engage in sex with the other boys in town.

Unable to accept or even comprehend the changes in Billie, when a car load of teenagers finds her alone on a country road, she is chased into the bush. Here she is raped and killed. When he discovers her body, Buster attacks the boys he is certain were responsible, killing two of them in the process. Although arrested and required to stand trial, even the sheriff is sympathetic to his situation, saying he doesn't know how he would have reacted if somebody had raped and killed his girl.
MPAA: Rated R. There are several instances of sexual talk, as well as several sexual situations. The most graphic of these is the brutal rape and murder of Billie Joe by several high school boys. There is also a renowned nude scene involving Vincent and Goodfellow as the two go skinny-dipping together. Vincent is seen in one of the frankest examples of full-frontal male nudity in mainstream American cinema.

CALENDAR GIRL
★★★

Credits: VHS/1993/USA/Colour/86 minutes
Director: John Whitesell
Screenplay: Paul Shapiro
Cast: Stephane Anderson [Marilyn Monroe], Chubby Checker [himself (cameo)], Kurt Fuller [Arturo Gallo], Jerry O'Connell [Scott Foreman], Gabriel Olds [Ned Bleuer], Joe Pantoliano [Uncle Harvey], Jason Priestly [Roy Darpinian], Steve Railsback [Roy's father], Stephen Tobolowsky [Antonio Gallo], Emily Warfield [Becky]
Genre: A teen comedy about three naive boys who go in search of a legend. Their antics, while amusing, would today be considered stalking.
Plot: Scott (O'Connell), Ned (Olds) and Roy (Priestly) are three buddies from a small town in Nevada. Since the age of twelve, when they first encountered a picture of her nude, all three have been in love with Marilyn Monroe.

During the summer of 1962, after graduating from high school they concoct a hare-brained scheme to head to Hollywood to meet the object of their devotion.

Borrowing Roy's father's car they hit the road, aiming to stay with Roy's uncle Harvey (Pantoliano), a would-be film star who is selling bomb shelters until he makes it big. Time is tight, as Roy is facing induction into the army in less than a week. He is also being trailed by the Gallo brothers, (Fuller and Tobolowsky), two hitmen for the Mob trying to recapture the money he appropriated for the trip.

Several misadventures later, after encountering a nude beach, night club bouncers, a cow, dogs and Marilyn's housekeeper, the boys seem to be getting close to achieving their aim. Will they meet the woman they love, or will the Gallo brothers get to Roy first?
MPAA: Rated PG-13. There are several shots of Priestly and Olds nude while they visit the nude beach. These are

Jerry O'Connell, Gabriel Olds and Jason Priestly, *Calendar Girl* (1993)

all rear shots. There are shots of Anderson at the beach as well, including bare buns and bare breasts. There are a large number of unnamed extras in these scenes as well. A pin-up calendar photo of Marilyn Monroe also appears several times.

THE CEMENT GARDEN ★★★★

Credits: VHS/1993/Great Britain-Germany-France/Colour/105 minutes
Writer/Director: Andrew Birkin
Based on the novel by Ian McEwan.
Cast: Ned Birkin [Thomas], Gareth Brown [William],

Alice Coulthard [Susan], Sinead Cusack [mother], Charlotte Gainsbourg [Julie], Jochen Horst [Derek], Andrew Robertson [Jack], Hanns Zischler [father]

Awards: Berlin Film Festival: Best Director (Silver Bear). Dinard Film Festival: Best Film. Birmingham Film Festival: Best Film. Ft. Lauderdale Film Festival: Best Film.

Genre: A drama told primarily from the point of view of a sixteen-year-old boy about four siblings trying none too successfully to hold their family together after the death of their parents.

Plot: This film has recently become available on video tape in North America. The version I saw was a British import which was labeled as a "director's authorized version." Watching it, I was not aware of any differences between this and the theatrical version I had seen previously.

Jack (Robertson), Julie (Gainsbourg), Susan (Coulthard) and Thomas (Ned Birkin) have been living with their parents in an isolated house in a derelict area of London. After their father (Zischler) dies, their mother (Cusack) becomes sick. She soon dies as well, leaving the four children alone.

Caring for the two younger children falls on the shoulders of eighteen-year-old Julie and sixteen-year-old Jack. In order to prevent eight-year-old Thomas and twelve-year-old Susan being taken into care, the children decide to keep their mother's death a secret, encasing her body in cement in an old metal cabinet in the basement. Unfortunately, their lives soon begin to fall apart.

The dishes remain unwashed. Jack goes for weeks without a bath or change of clothes. The children argue about all the chores which need to get done. Thomas, being victimized by bullies at school, announces he wants to become a girl.

To make matters worse, the body in the basement is beginning to smell. Julie's boyfriend Derek (Horst) is beginning to get suspicious, and he's upset that he isn't trusted with the secret.

Although Jack's hygiene problems seem to be cured by a nude run in the rain during a late night thunderstorm, and Thomas's cross-dressing is accepted by his siblings and his best friend William

(Brown), Derek's suspicions grow stronger until finally he takes a sledge hammer to the cement filled cabinet.

Running throughout the film are Jack's increasingly erotic feelings towards his older sister, culminating in a scene of brother-sister incest. This proves to be the final straw for Derek.

Although this last will probably be disturbing to some, the two have obviously been building towards this point almost from the first minutes of the film, and the act seems less shocking than one might expect. It is carefully handled and presented as a fully consensual act for both teenagers. Something which is a natural outgrowth of things which have gone before.

Ned Birkin is the director's son. Charlotte Gainsbourg is his niece.

Charlotte Gainsbourg, *The Cement Garden* (1993)

MPAA: Not rated. There are several instances of juvenile nudity in this film. Julie appears bare breasted during the incest scene. Thomas is seen nude in a rear scene in his bed. Jack appears nude several times. He is seen running naked in the back yard during a thunderstorm. While dark, this sequence includes both full-frontal and bare-buns shots.

Later, he is seen nude indoors in an extended sequence leading up to the incest scene with Julie. Effectively speaking, for almost the last ten minutes of the film, Jack is nude.

In addition to the brother-sister incest involving Jack and Julie, Jack also masturbates several times. Thomas, with his siblings' encouragement, frequently indulges in cross-dressing.

THE CHILDREN OF NOISY VILLAGE ★★★★

(Also known as *Alla VI Barn I Bullerbyn*, as *The Six Bullerby Children*, or as *The Children of Bullerby Village*)

Credits: VHS/1986/Sweden/Colour/87 minutes
Dubbed in English.
Director: Lasse Hallstrom
Screenplay: Astrid Lindgren, based on her novel.
Cast: Linda Bergstrom [Lisa], Ellen Demerus [Britta], Crispin Dickson Wendenius [Lasse], Henrik Larson [Bosse], Harald Lonnbro [Olle], Anna Sahlin [Anna]
Genre: A slice of life film with little in the way of plot line about six young children from three families growing up together in a small Swedish village in the 1920s. It is unfortunate that it appears only to be available in a dubbed version, but given its nature as a family film, this is probably inevitable.
Plot: It would be hard to miss with Lasse Hallstrom (*My Life As A Dog* and *What's Eating Gilbert Grape*) directing a film based on a book by Astrid Lindgren (the Pippi Longstocking series of children's books) and this beautifully evocative and nostalgic film is no disappointment.

There is no discernable continuous story line here, just a series of incidents and vignettes taken from one long, glorious, barefoot summer in the lives of six young children, the oldest perhaps ten or eleven, the youngest about eight. The story is told from the point of view of Lisa (Bergstrom) and we watch as she, her brothers Lasse (Wendenius) and Bosse (Larson), their neighbours Britta (Demerus) and Anna (Sahlin), and the boy down the road, Olle (Lonnbro) spend a carefree summer together. The six inseparable friends play together, do chores together, tease each other and have adventures, both real and imagined, together.

Befriending a neglected dog, helping with the hay-ing, boarding a pirate ship, shopping for mother, sleeping out in the hayloft, setting traps for crayfish, hunting for pearls buried on a deserted island, thinning seedlings in the fields, or skinny-dipping in the lake, whatever these children do becomes fun.

Those responsible for this film obviously have a very acute sense of what children and childhood are like. Unlike so many American directors, Hallstrom portrays very real children. So carefully has he captured the feeling that a cameraman simply followed these kids around for the summer recording what he saw, that at least one person I know has wondered if there was even a detailed script.

A sequel featuring the same cast was released in 1987. To the best of my knowledge, this has not yet been made available in North America.
MPAA: Not rated. Very much a family film, but one not just for the kids. There is one scene of the children swimming together in a lake. Being rural Sweden, all six children swim nude. Wendenius and Bergstrom are seen in full-length rear shots on the shore while Lasse undresses. The other four children are in the water for the entire shot, and though presumably also nude, this is only implied.

CHINA, MY SORROW ★★★★

(Also known as *Niu Peng*, and as *Chine, Ma Douleur*)

Credits: VHS/1989/France/Colour/86 minutes
In Mandarin and Shanghaiese with English subtitles.
Director: Dai Sijie
Screenplay: Dai Sijie and Shan Yuan Zhu
Cast: Chang Cheung Siang, Guo Liang-Yi [Four-Eyes], Sam Chi-Vy [Baimao], Tieu Quan Nghieu [the monk], Troung Loi, Vong Han Lai
Awards: A Cannes Film Festival selection, and winner of the Prix Jean Vigo.
Genre: A comedy about a young teen learning vital lessons about life, survival, and relationships in a re-education centre during the Cultural Revolution in China.
Plot: Yes, this is a French film. Though shot by a Chinese director, with Chinese dialogue and an entirely Asian cast, this film was produced in France with French financing. This arrangement was reportedly to avoid censorship problems in China.

The period of the Cultural Revolution was not a good time for romance, as thirteen-year-old Tian Ben (Guo), known to one and all as Four Eyes, discovers to his detriment.

He is arrested for playing a love song to his thirteen-year-old neighbour. As a purveyor of obscene records, Four Eyes is sent to a Niu Peng, a re-education centre, far away in the hills to serve his time with other enemies of the people.

The youngest inmate in an open detention centre, where there are no walls, no barbed wire and no Red Guards, Four Eyes befriends a teenage pick-pocket named Baimao (Sam) and an aging Buddhist monk (Tieu). His new found friends help him retain his sense of self and family in an atmosphere dedicated to the elimination of individuality. Even within the confines of the centre, where most of the inmates are adults, the two irrepressible boys find time and inspiration for fun and practical jokes.

MPAA: Not rated. Other than Four Eyes' romantic feelings towards his young neighbour at the beginning of the film, the only sexual situation occurs at the camp. Sex is very much on the minds of the two teenage inmates, but they have no outlet. Consequently, on one occasion they decide to embarrass the camp chief. By putting a piece of wet paper on his foot while he sleeps they hope to make him horny, and induce him to "pop off in his shorts."

CHRONICLE OF A BOY ALONE ★★★★

(Also known as *Chronicle Of A Lone Boy*, and as *Cronica De Un Nino Solo*)

Credits: VHS/1964/Argentina/B&W/86 minutes
In Spanish with English subtitles.
Director: Leonardo Favio
Screenplay: Zuhair Jorge Jury and Leonardo Favio
Cast: Oscar Espindola, Leonardo Favio, Beto Gianolo, Tino Pascali, Diego Puente [Polin]
Genre: A drama about a poor Argentine boy who escapes from a juvenile detention centre.
Plot: Polin (Puente), a boy who seems no more than eleven or twelve years old, has been sent to a strict juvenile detention centre. His entire life must be lived in unison with his fellow inmates: his every action regulated by the warden's whistle.

A resourceful boy, Polin soon finds a way to escape from custody, making his way back home to the shantytown where he lives. He is soon back to thieving, picking pockets and running from the authorities. His institutional haircut, however, marks him for derision by his peers. It also marks him for the police.

When he is stopped with his friend Fabian's horse, the policeman, noting the shaved head, takes him into custody again. As the film ends, we see the young boy in the secure grip of the cop being led off to the precinct office, his brief period of freedom again at an end.

Despite a very leisurely pace, this is a surprisingly rewarding film. It has been greatly enhanced by the remarkably powerful, stark and moody black and white photography.

MPAA: Not rated. There is a great deal of implied violence and psychological abuse directed towards the young inmates at the centre. While he is enjoying his freedom from the centre, Polin goes skinny-dipping with a friend in a river on the edge of town. Three boys, including Polin, are seen in extended nude scenes, including a considerable number of casual, unaffected full-frontal shots.

CLASS ★★

Credits: VHS/1983/USA/Colour/98 minutes
Director: Lewis John Carlino
Screenplay: Jim Kouf and David Greenwalt
Cast: Jacqueline Bisset [Ellen Burroughs], John Cusak [Roscoe], Rob Lowe [Skip Burroughs], Stuart Margolin [Balaban], Andrew McCarthy [Jonathon Ogner], Cliff Robertson [Mr. Burroughs], Casey Siemaszko [Doug]
Genre: A teenage sex comedy about an awkward youth who finds true love in the arms of an older woman.
Plot: Jonathon (McCarthy) is a new scholarship student at Vernon Academy, an exclusive boys prep school. More than a little awkward—in fact, he's a walking disaster area—Jonathon has difficulties adjusting to his classmates, especially his roommate Skip (Lowe), and quickly becomes the butt of several practical jokes.

After yet another fiasco, Jonathon is banned from the Halloween dance. To compensate, Skip gives him some money, and tells him to go to Chicago and not to return until he gets laid.

Several disasters later, Jonathon meets Ellen (Bisset), an older woman who takes pity on him. She also seduces him.

Returning to school two days later, Jonathon suddenly finds himself the "big man on campus". Weekends in Chicago with Ellen become a regular thing, until she accidently learns he is not the North Western grad student he claims to be.

Ellen abruptly disappears from Jonathon's life until Skip invites Jonathon home for the Christmas vacation. Jonathon then discovers that Ellen is Skip's mother, precipitating several more crises. These finally come to a head when Skip learns of the relationship between his best friend and his mother.

This might have been a far better film if more emphasis had been placed on the relationships between Ellen, Skip and Jonathon. The film has been padded with too many high school hijinx. For a better treatment of a similar theme, see the French film *Le Petit Amour*.

MPAA: Rated R. There are several love scenes involving McCarthy and Bisset as the relationship between Jonathon and Ellen grows, though there is little nudity. Virtually the only skin we see is a couple of bare breasts when a school girl has her blouse ripped open. However, we are treated to shots of Lowe and McCarthy in bra and panties.

CLAYFARMERS ★★★

Credits: VHS/1988/USA/Colour/60 minutes
Director: A. P. Gonzalez
Screenplay: Michael Moore
Cast: Aaron Denny [Randy], Todd Fraser [Dan], Liam McGrath [Gary], Nicholas Rempel [Mike], Asbury Ward [Jim]
Genre: A short drama about homophobia and child abuse both real and alleged, set in a small farming community.
Plot: Twelve-year-old Gary (McGrath) and his slightly older step brother Randy (Denny) live in a rural California community. Gary's father Jim (Ward), an alcoholic, regularly physically abuses the boys and his wife. Abuse which only gets worse when he has been drinking.

As a measure of relief from his pain, Gary regularly escapes to the company of Dan (Fraser) and Mike (Rempel), two hired hands on a neighbouring farm. The two young men have an ambiguous relationship to each other. They may be gay. Certainly there seems to be a real love between them, though it goes unspoken. They are also outsiders in the close knit little community and only marginally accepted.

After a particularly savage attack by his stepfather, Randy commits suicide. Gary, clearly upset at being blamed for the "accident" goes for comfort from Dan and Mike. When Jim finally tracks his son down, Gary and the two young men are skinny-dipping together in a small pond.

Seeing Dan hugging his nude son, Jim drags Gary away and belts him. He is soon spreading stories around the town that Dan and Mike are gay, and have been molesting Gary.

The film poses questions about and takes issue with the prevalent puritanical attitudes in contemporary American society. The attitude that gay men are child molesters. That nudity equates with sex. That sexual diversity is worse than murder. That the outsider is the

Brad Renfro and Joseph Mazzello, *The Cure* (1995)

pariah, the easy scapegoat. That beatings and physical abuse of children is good parenting, but tenderness, hugs and physical comforting equate with sexual abuse.

Dan is seen by the community as harming Gary by hugging him when he needs comforting. Jim, who has driven his stepson to suicide can be upheld as a good parent.

MPAA: Not rated. Dan, Mike and Gary go skinny-dipping together. Most of this is butt shots only, but there is some very brief frontal exposure of the adults. McGrath is only seen in rear or unrevealing side shots. Although clearly in love with each other, neither Mike nor Dan seems willing or able to voice, let alone act upon their feelings. Though accused of molesting Gary, Dan's embrace at the pool is clearly therapeutic for the boy, not abusive or exploitive and grows out of Dan's own history as an abused child.

COLEGAS ★★★

(Also known as *Pals*)

Credits: VHS/1980/Spain/Colour/117 minutes
In Spanish with English subtitles.
Director: Eloy de la Iglesia
Screenplay: Gonzalo Goicoechea and Eloy de la Iglesia
Cast: Jose Manuel Cervino [Esteban], Jose Luis Fernandez Equia [Pirri], Antonio Gonzales Flores [Antonio], Rosario Gonzales Flores [Rosario], Jose Luis Manzano [Jose], Enrique San Francisco [Rogelio]
Genre: A sometimes comic drama about two friends from a poor neighbourhood in Madrid trying to raise the money for an abortion which highlights the world wide problem of unemployment among young people.
Plot: Jose (Manzano) and Antonio (Antonio Flores), teenage buddies in a poor neighbourhood in Madrid, are looking for work. Well, maybe they are. At the best of times it is only a very half-hearted search. Then a problem crops up. Antonio's sister Rosario (Rosario Flores) announces she's pregnant, and Jose is the father.

Together the three teens try to come up with a strategy to deal with this new crisis. Antonio says the choices are simple, either Rosario has the baby or she doesn't.

"How can we have a baby?" Rosario asks.

"Well, that's it. An abortion," her brother replies.

But an abortion costs money, so the three try to devise schemes to raise the cash. Nobody will lend it, so Jose and Antonio turn to Jose's fifteen-year-old brother Pirri (Equia) and his street gang connections, but they won't work with anybody over the age of fifteen. They try holding up a tobacconist, but are scared off without the cash. They try hustling in a local gay steam bath, but get nowhere with that. They finally turn to Rogelio (San Francisco), a local crime boss. He has a job for them: smuggling hashish from Morocco, secreted in condoms inserted into their rectums.

Rogelio also has another scheme for the three to consider. Instead of an abortion, he suggests selling the baby to a wealthy foreign couple who will adopt the child, earning for the teenagers ten times what an abortion would cost.

In the end, however, Rosario decides, quite literally at the last minute, not to have the abortion and, in an altercation with Rogelio, which leads to the shooting of Antonio, she also decides not to sell the baby.

MPAA: Not rated. There are several scenes of nude teenage boys, including full-frontal shots of Manzano and Equia. There are also shots of bare breasted girls and several scenes of sexual activity, including teenage couples making love and shots of two teenage boys, the younger brothers of Jose, masturbating in bed.

Joseph Mazzello and Brad Renfro, *The Cure* (1995)

CRISS-CROSS ★★★

(Also known as *Alone Together*)

Credits: VHS/1992/USA/Colour/101 minutes
Director: Chris Menges
Screenplay: Scott Sommer, based on his novella.
Cast: David Arnott [Chris Cross], Steve Buscemi [Louis], Paul Calderon [Blacky], Keith Carradine [John Cross], James Gammon [Emmett], Goldie Hawn [Tracy Cross], Arliss Howard [Joe], Christy Martin [Termina], J. C. Quinn [Jetty], Damian Vantriglia [Buggs]
Genre: A sometimes slow moving but not unrewarding drama about the internal turmoil in a boy's life brought

about by his parents' divorce.

Plot: Newcomer David Arnott plays twelve-year-old Chris Cross, a boy who seems to live in little more than a pair of old cut-offs. Chris and his mother Tracy (Hawn) have been living in a hotel room in Key West since his parents were divorced. Dad (Carradine) is a former Vietnam bomber pilot who has been living in a monastery under a vow of silence since the break-up of his marriage. A break-up caused in no small part by his inability to deal with his war time experiences—he accidently bombed a children's hospital and has been overwhelmed by the enormity of that action.

Tracy is trying to hold down two jobs in order to support herself and her son. Chris, in the meantime, is delivering papers and doing odd jobs around the hotel in an attempt to help out.

When Chris accidently hears that his mom has a new "act" at the bar where she is a cocktail waitress, he sneaks in and discovers that she is working as a stripper. Already upset about his mother's relationship with Joe (Howard), a man who says he is in Key West on holidays, this new revelation proves too much for Chris. He hitchhikes north to Miami to find his father. Unable to reconcile his parents, or himself to their divorce, Chris reluctantly returns home with his mom.

When he accidently stumbles across a cocaine operation, Chris attempts to cut himself in on the action, hoping to earn some big money and get his mother out of the bar. Although he ultimately achieves the latter goal and is able to break up the relationship between his mother and Joe, it doesn't come about in quite the way he planned: he is apprehended in the middle of a drug deal and the court places him on probation for a year.

David Arnott puts in a very creditable performance in what is, to the best of my knowledge, his only major film appearance. His portrayal of a confused kid trying to get his parents back together again has the right note of reality about it, and the scenes where he confronts his father are among the more memorable in the film.

MPAA: Rated R. Canadian Home Video rated 14-A. There is a certain amount of kid-type sex talk in the film: Chris wants to live with his girlfriend Termina (Martin) so they can have orgasms together—though he isn't quite sure what that means.

He comes close to finding out though. Chris and Termina, alone in her bedroom one day, start a little round of you-show-me-and-I'll-show-you, a game which is interrupted by the unexpected return of Termina's father.

In the scene where the two rush to get dressed again, we get a full-length rear shot of Chris nude. There is also some adult female nudity in the bar scenes, including some shots of Tracy in G-string and pasties.

CROSS MY HEART ★★★★

(Also known as *La Fracture Du Myocarde*)

Credits: VHS/1991/France/Colour/105 minutes
In French with English subtitles.
Writer/Director: Jacques Fansten
Cast: Lucie Blosier [Claire], Sylvain Copans [Martin], Benoit Gautier [Julien], Olivier Montiege [Antoine], Nicholas Parodi [Jerome], Cecilia Rouaud [Marianne]
Genre: A gentle drama which manages to be sweet without being cloying about a boy trying to make it on his own after his single mother dies.
Plot: Twelve-year-old Martin (Copans) is obviously upset about something and his friends are concerned. When he disappears from school after being sent to the principal for not paying attention, they head out in search. They find him at home and soon discover the truth. His mother has died suddenly and Martin is terrified of the prospect of being sent to an orphanage.

In a move typical of the spontaneous, well meaning generosity but lack of foresight of children, Martin's classmates swear themselves to secrecy, vowing to help him. They stand up for him in class, they help him with his homework, they cook, clean and provide food for him. They even help to bury his mother in an old clock case at the edge of the woods. All to no avail, because eventually the truth must come out, and Martin is taken into care. Even then, their efforts don't cease. They try to enlist the aid of a favorite teacher, asking him to adopt Martin. Sadly, he tells them, he can't. The law won't allow a gay man to adopt a child, a situation which does not sit well with Martin's classmates, who exclaim loudly over the unfairness of this.
MPAA: Not rated. Strictly PG level material.

THE CURE ★★★★

Credits: VHS/1995/USA/Colour/95 minutes
Director: Peter Horton
Screenplay: Robert Kuhn
Cast: Bruce Davison [Doctor Stevens], Joseph Mazzello [Dexter], Brad Renfro [Erik], Diana Scarwid [Gail], Annabella Sciorra [Linda]
Genre: A heartwarming and heart wrenching drama about the tragedy of children with AIDS.
Plot: Eleven-year-old Dexter (Mazzello, in a performance which tugs all the right strings without becoming maudlin) has AIDS, a result of a transfusion of tainted blood.

Loner Erik (Renfro) lives next door. Both boys are outsiders with few friends. Erik's mother's irrational fear of Dexter's illness causes her to forbid her son from seeing his neighbour. Despite this, over the course of the summer the two boys become best friends.

As Dexter's illness becomes worse, the two boys, inspired by a supermarket tabloid report, head off together for New Orleans to find a miracle cure. Their odyssey is forced to an early end when Dexter's illness becomes worse. The two boys return home and Erik soon must deal with his best friend's inevitable final hospitalization and death.

MPAA: Rated PG-13. Canadian Home Video rated PG. There is nothing overtly, or even covertly, sexual about this film; however, as in real life, many of the townspeople obviously associate AIDS with being gay. As a result, both boys are taunted about their sexual orientation. Dexter because he has AIDS, Erik for associating with him.

DAZED AND CONFUSED
★★★★

Credits: VHS/1993/USA/Colour/103 minutes
Writer/Director: Richard Linklater
Cast: Joey Lauren Adams [Simone], Ben Affleck [Obanion], Michelle Burke [Jodi], Rory Cochrane [Slater], Adam Goldberg [Mike], Cole Hauser [Benny], Christina Hinojosa [Sabrina], Sasha Jenson [Don], Milla Jovovich [Michelle], Deena Martin [Shavone], Matthew McConaughey [Wooderson] Parker Posey [Darla], Esteban Powell [Carl], Anthony Rapp [Tony], Marissa Ribissi [Cynthia], Wiley Wiggins [Mitch]
Genre: A comedy about a group of Texas high school students celebrating the last day of classes in May, 1976.
Plot: What *American Graffiti* did for the 1960s, so *Dazed and Confused* does for the mid 1970s.

A large group of small town high school students celebrates the end of classes in a galavanting night long party which begins with the sounding of the last bell and ends at dawn at the outskirts of town and passes through school yards and football fields, drive-ins and pool halls along the way.

Like so many other films of this genre, there is little in the way of a linear plot. Nevertheless, director Linklater and his superb ensemble cast have done a masterful job of evoking a time, a place and the awkwardness of youth searching for their role in life.

My only serious complaint with the film is that sometimes there is too much soul searching. The beer bust at the Moon Tower in particular tends to drag at times. But then such affairs frequently do in life as well. In total, *Dazed and Confused* has captured the period with a portrait that is more real than the reality of the times, and set the whole to a great '70s sound track.

Dazed And Confused (1993)

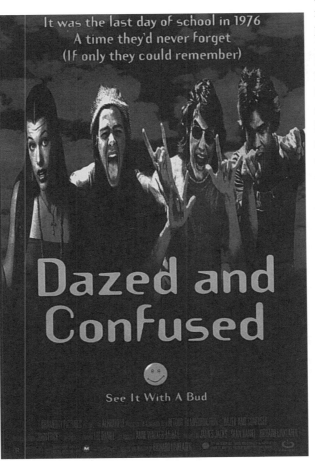

MPAA: Rated R. Canadian Home Video Rated 14-A. The rating was earned for course language, frequent drug and alcohol use, some violence and sex talk.

DEAD POETS SOCIETY ★★★★

Credits: VHS/1989/USA/Colour/128 minutes
Director: Peter Weir
Screenplay: Tom Schulman
Cast: Josh Charles [Knox Overstreet], Gale Hanson [Charlie Dalton], Ethan Hawke [Todd Anderson], Dylan Kussman [Richard Cameron], Robert Sean Leonard [Neil Perry], Norman Lloyd [Mr. Nolan], Alexandra Powers [Chris Noel], Allelon Ruggiero [Steve Meekes], Kurtwood Smith [Mr. Perry], James Waterson [Gerrard Pitts], Robin Williams [John Keating]
Awards: Academy Awards 1989: (nomination) Best Picture; (nomination) Best Actor (Williams); (nomination) Best Director (Weir); (nomination) Best Original Screenplay. British Academy Awards 1989: Best Film. Cesar Awards (France) 1991: Best Foreign Film.
Genre: A boarding school drama about the relationships between students, their parents, and a special teacher, and the conflicts between parental aspirations and filial dreams.
Plot: At Welton Academy in the early 1950s seventy-five percent of all graduates go on to the Ivy League. Academic and discipline standards are strict. Most of the students expect to follow in the footsteps of their fathers, or the path their parents have laid out for them.

Into this setting John Keating (Williams) arrives. At first viewed skeptically by the students, he soon comes to be seen as an exciting breath of

Ethan Hawke and Robin Williams, *Dead Poets Society* (1989)

fresh air. Although himself a graduate of Welton, he employs some highly unorthodox teaching methods and encourages his students to think for themselves. The boys actually begin to welcome the study of poetry!

However, Keating is soon under fire from administration and parents for his methods. He becomes the scapegoat when tragedy strikes.

Neil Perry (Leonard) has had his future planned for him by his father (Smith). He is to go to Harvard and enter the medical profession, no questions asked. Neil would rather go on stage. When he goes against his father's instructions and takes a part in a community production of "A Midsummer Nights Dream," his father withdraws him from Welton despite the boy's obvious success as an actor.

Unable to deal with the family pressures and unwilling to give up his dream of an acting career, Neil commits suicide in his father's study. The parents and the headmaster (Lloyd) conduct an enquiry which is nothing more than a witch hunt. They place the blame squarely on the shoulders of Keating, resulting in the teacher's dismissal. The students, coerced into complicity and unable to change this decision, nonetheless still manage to make their feelings known.

Whatever your feelings about Robin Williams as an actor, you may be surprised by his performance in this film. Although given top billing, in many ways his role is subservient to those of the outstanding ensemble cast of younger actors. And while he can't quite completely abandon his customary clowning, this is one of the most restrained and serious performances of William's career.

MPAA: Rated PG. Other than a few romantic entanglements, sexuality is not overt. However, Williams bases his poetry class on the writings of gay poet Walt Whitman. He has the students call him "captain, my captain" from a Whitman poem.

THE DELTA ★★★★

Credits: 1996/USA/Colour/85 minutes
Writer/Director: Ira Sachs
Cast: Thang Chan [Minh Nguyen "John"], Colonious Davis [Ricky Little], Shane Gray [Lincoln Bloom], Rachel Zan Huss [Monica]
Awards: Official selection at Toronto International Film Festival 1996, Sundance 1997 (dramatic competition), San Francisco International Film Festival 1997, Los Angeles

Outfest 1997, San Francisco Gay & Lesbian Film Festival 1997.

Genre: A drama about a brief gay love affair which crosses boundaries of class and race.

Plot: In a Memphis far removed from the city tourists normally see, in a Memphis of bars, peep shows, drugs, alcohol, anonymous sex and pool halls, two youths meet while cruising in the park after dark.

Lincoln (Gray) is a white teenager from a wealthy middle-class family. Minh (Chan) is an unemployed mixed-race immigrant, the son of an Afro-American father and a Vietnamese mother. Both are experiencing internal turmoil occasioned by the conflicts and struggles in their lives.

Lincoln has a steady girlfriend Monica (Huss), but looks for gay sex in dark places. Minh is gay, of mixed race ancestry and ultimately feels abandoned by the father he has never known. When a second meeting occurs between the two, the persuasive Minh induces Lincoln to take his father's boat down the river. For little more than twenty-four hours the two have a brief, but ultimately doomed love affair before parting, Lincoln to return to Monica and his family, Minh to his gay roommate, the pool halls and violently tragic sexual encounters.

This dark and moody film is one which grew on me, both as I watched it and afterwards as I contemplated its volatile and hypnotic mix of class conflict, sexuality and racial identity as they intersect in the violent and unforgiving atmosphere of the contemporary United States.

MPAA: Not rated. There is some coarse language and sexual dialogue and some instances of serious violence, especially at the ending of the film. There are a number of scenes of sexual activity, including Lincoln and Minh together on several occasions: in a car in the park, on the boat and embracing in the water. There is also some nudity. Both male leads have brief bare buns shots, and Monica is seen topless briefly.

DEVIL IN THE FLESH ★★

(Also known as *Il Diavolo In Corpo*)

Credits: VHS/1987/Italy, France/Colour/110 minutes
In Italian with English subtitles.
Writer/Director: Marcho Bellocchio
A remake of the 1946 French film *Le Diable Au Corps*, which was in turn based on the novel by Raymond Radiguet.

Shane Gray, *The Delta* (1996)

Cast: Riccardo de Torrebruna, Maruschka Detmers [Giulia], Anita Laurenzi, Frederico Pitzalis [Andrea]

Genre: This Italian romantic drama is another variation on the older woman, younger man theme.

Plot: Giulia (Detmers) is the beautiful but unstable young woman. Andrea (Pitzalis) is the handsome young high school student. He is also the son of Giulia's psychiatrist. Giulia's fiance Giacomo is on trial, accused of being a terrorist. During the trial, Giulia meets and carries on an affair with Andrea. Although discovered by Giacomo's mother and warned off by Andrea's father, the two continue to meet and make love.

MPAA: Not rated. Also available in an R Rated version. The film includes several nude scenes and scenes of sexual activity primarily involving Giulia and Andrea. The film is well known for an explicit oral sex scene involving the two principles, a scene which is cut from the R rated version of the film.

THE DEVIL'S PLAYGROUND ★★★★

Credits: VHS/1976/Australia/Colour/107 minutes

Writer/Director: Fred Schepisi

Cast: Simon Burke [Tom Allen], Alan Cinis [Waite], Peter Cox [Brother James], Michael David [Turner], John Diedrich [Fitz], Arthur Dignam [Brother Francine], Gerry Duggan [Father Hanrahan], John Frawley [Brother Celian], Thomas Keneally [Father Marshall], Charles McCallum [Brother Sebastian], Nick Tate [Brother Victor]

Awards: Australian Film Institute Awards 1976: Best Film; Best Director (Schepisi); Best Screenplay; Best Cinematography; Best Actor (Tate); Best Actor (Burke).

Genre: A drama about sexual tensions and frustrations played out within the walls of a Catholic seminary for teenage boys preparing to enter the priesthood where the rules are so strict that showering in the nude is forbidden, even behind closed doors.

Plot: Tom Allen (Burke) is a thirteen-year-old boy with an infectious smile and the crookedest set of teeth I have ever seen on film. A student at the seminary, he doesn't seem to fit in; he is habitually late for mass and for class, he is the butt of everybody's practical jokes and teasing, he is untidy, and he wets the bed. Nicknamed "Piss The Bed," the image of Tom rinsing out his wet sheets in the morning is a recurring motif.

Like most of the boys and the teaching brothers, Tom has trouble dealing with his sexual urges. Some, like young Turner (David), turn to mysticism, flagellation, and religious fanaticism to mask their sexual frustrations. For others, like the spiritually tortured Brother Francine (Dignam), the outlet is fantasy and voyeurism at the local public swimming pool on their day off. But for all, the sexual tension runs high, until even the Reader's Digest becomes a source for erotic stimulation, and the dictionary a dirty book.

A wrestling match on the lawn, or casual physical contact between two boys in the corridor becomes fraught with sexual overtones. For Tom, the outlet is masturbation, a habit as well known as his bed wetting. He admits in the confessional to indulging two or three times a day. Tom is constantly teased about it by others, especially by Fritz

Simon Burke (right), *The Devil's Playground* (1976)

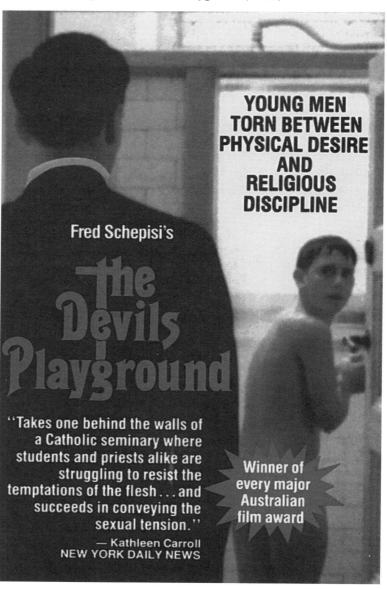

Fred Schepisi's

The Devil's Playground

YOUNG MEN TORN BETWEEN PHYSICAL DESIRE AND RELIGIOUS DISCIPLINE

"Takes one behind the walls of a Catholic seminary where students and priests alike are struggling to resist the temptations of the flesh...and succeeds in conveying the sexual tension."
— Kathleen Carroll
NEW YORK DAILY NEWS

Winner of every major Australian film award

(Diedrich), an older boy and one of Tom's few real friends at the seminary.

Eventually events conspire against Tom's vocation: he meets an attractive young girl, with whom he shares a first kiss; the elderly Sebastian (McCallum), the only truly sympathetic Brother, dies; Fitz is expelled from the seminary and Tom forbidden to contact him. After an agonizing, accusatory night in prayer, Tom runs away from the seminary. Picked up hitch-hiking, he is surprised and relieved to discover that his flight is understood and supported by at least two of the teaching brothers.

MPAA: Not rated. The film is concerned almost entirely with the sexuality and sexual frustrations of the boys and the teaching brothers, though for the most part it is mostly talk. Tom is seen once shoving a hand in his pocket after coming across a magazine ad for a brassiere. His wrestling matches with Waite (Cinis) are obviously sexually driven, at least on Waite's part. It is one such wrestling match which leads to the most sexually explicit scene in the film. The two boys drop their pants and engage in mutual manipulation which a horrified Waite, though the instigator, cuts short before completion.

There is also a considerable amount of nudity in the film. Burke appears in a full-length rear shot when he is

Simon Burke and Charles McCallum, *The Devil's Playground* (1976)

caught, contrary to regulations, showering without his swimsuit. Dignam appears nude in two scenes, both including full-frontal shots: once in the locker room of the local public swimming pool and once swimming under water in a fantasy scene. The locker room scene also includes several unknown adult extras, also in full-frontal shots. The underwater fantasy involves several full-frontal shots of nude women.

ERNESTO ★★★★

Credits: VHS/1983/Italy/Colour/95 minutes
In Italian with English subtitles.
Writer/Director: Salvatore Samperi
Based on the novel by Emberto Saba.
Cast: Martin Halm [Ernesto], Virna Lisi [Mother], Michele Placido [Stablehand], Lara Wendel [Emillio/Rachel]
Genre: A drama about a gay teenager with "a socialist tongue and a capitalist stomach" exploring the confusing world of love and sex in the Italian city of Trieste just prior to World War I.
Plot: Though blessed with head turning good looks, sixteen-year-old Ernesto (Halm) is a fundamentally unlikable teenager with an amazing knack for attracting would be lovers.

He is a spoiled, selfish, amoral dandy who is too lazy to work despite professing socialist principles. A sharp sarcastic tongue ever ready to give voice to insolent disrespect does not help this manipulative youth who is really interested in one person and one person only: himself. Nevertheless he seems to have a certain charisma which attracts people to him. People Ernesto feels no qualms about dumping the minute their presence no longer fills his needs.

Ernesto's own sexual orientation does not appear to be in question. He is a more than willing partner when a stevedore (Placido) at the firm where he is an apprentice clerk proposes a sexual relationship. The relationship continues for some time, but the callous Ernesto simply walks away from it when it no longer serves his purpose.

More ambivalent is his relationship with the fifteen year old twins Emillio and Rachel (both played by Lara Wendel in a dual role). Ernesto is first attracted by the androgynously beautiful Emillio, or Illo as he is called, when the two catch sight of each other at a violin concert. Thus begins a love affair between the two boys. Ernesto can nevertheless casually shunt Illo to one side when their two families, thinking Ernesto is attracted to Rachel, begin to discuss marriage. Needless to say, this new situation engenders a screaming jealous rage in Illo.

MPAA: Not rated. There is a fair amount of sex talk in this film. Ernesto has several sexual experiences including a visit to a female prostitute and a number of encounters, including both oral and anal sex, with the stevedore. During one of these there is a buns only nude shot of Halm as the man embraces the boy. There is also a kissing scene involving Ernesto and Illo. Illo and Rachel engage in some cross dressing, switching clothes on occasion. One gets the feeling that the motivation for this is not just the stated one of confusing their family.

Marco Hofschneider, *Europa, Europa* (1991)

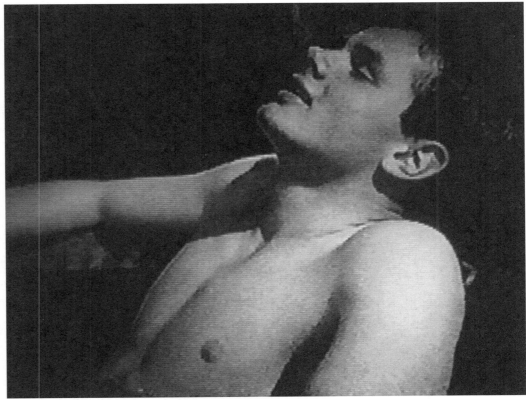

EUROPA, EUROPA ★★★★★

Credits: VHS/1991/Germany, France/Colour/110 minutes
In German and Russian with English subtitles.
Writer/Director: Agnieszka Holland
Based on the memoirs of Solomon Perel.
Cast: Klaus Abramowsky [the father], Julie Delpy [Leni], Delphine Forest [Inna], Michele Gleizer [the mother], Marco Hofschneider [Solomon Perel], Rene Hofschneider [Isaak], Andrzej Mastalerz [Zanek], Nathalie Schmidt [Basia], Ashley Wanninger [Gerd], Andre Wilms [Robert], Hanns Zischler [the captain]
Awards: Academy Awards 1991: (nomination) Best Adapted Screenplay. Golden Glove Awards 1992: Best Foreign Film. National Board Of Review Awards 1991: Best Foreign Film. New York Film Critics Awards 1991: Best Foreign Film. It has been reported that because of the subject matter, Germany refused to nominate the film for an Oscar in the Best Foreign Film category.
Genre: The incredible and harrowing biography of a Jewish teenager in World War II Germany.
Plot: As a teenager, Solomon Perel (Marco Hofschneider) lives a charmed life. In 1938, as the persecution of Jews in Germany begins to heat up in earnest, his family leaves their home in Peine (near Hannover), moving to Lodz in Poland. This proves only a temporary haven, for the

German army is soon to follow. As the Wehrmacht drives eastward, his parents send young Solly and his brother Isaak (Rene Hofschneider) eastwards towards the Soviet Union. Solly escapes to Russian held territory, but is separated from Isaak at the border. Several years in a Russian orphanage at Grodno (now in the Belarus Republic) follow, during which Solly becomes a dedicated, committed young communist.

This new life is shattered when once again the Germans push east. The teenager is able to conceal his Jewish identity, adopting the name Joseph Peters. As Joseph (or Jupp) he becomes the darling of the German troops, acting as a Russian interpreter. He even receives an offer of adoption from a German Army captain (Zischler). Only one German soldier discovers Jupp's secret, but Robert (Wilms) has deadly secrets of his own: he is gay. The two outcasts agree to protect each other.

Jupp's efforts to conceal his Jewish identity and the fact that he is circumcised become ever more desperate: rather than strip for a medical exam, he submits to an emergency extraction of a perfectly good tooth; despite his urges, he stops short of sexual intercourse with Leni (Delpy); his relief at seeing another boy showering in his underwear is almost palpable; as is his terror when called to the front of the class to be a model for the teacher's "How to recognize a Jew" lecture.

In an excruciating sequence, he even tries to reverse his circumcision. Somehow, by some miracle, by lies, by quick thinking, by adaptability, Solly survives the war, only to risk being shot as a traitor by the Russians. His saviour? His brother Isaak who recognizes him at the very last minute.

An absurd tale? A wild flight of fancy by some overly imaginative script-writer? No. A true story of one teenager's will to survive. As his brother tells Solly in the closing minutes, "Don't tell anybody your story. They won't believe you."
MPAA: Rated R. Canadian Home Video rated 14-A. Marco Hofschneider has several nude scenes, including some full-frontal shots. Solly has sex with the Nazi Party official who is escorting him from the eastern front to Berlin. Although Robert, the gay German soldier, is ob-

Marco Hofschneider, *Europa, Europa* (1991)

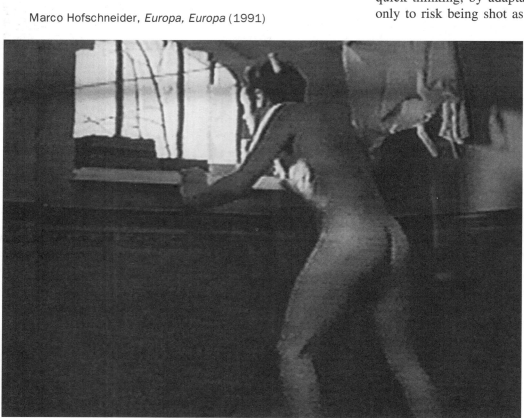

Mark Lee, *The Everlasting Secret Family* (1988)

viously charmed by Jupp, there is no suggestion that their relationship becomes sexual. In fact, as Robert lies dying in the trenches, Jupp kisses the man. Robert comments on the fact that in the end he received a kiss from the boy.

THE EVERLASTING SECRET FAMILY ★★

Credits: VHS/1988/Australia/Colour/93 minutes
Director: Michael Thornhill
Screenplay: Frank Moorhouse
Cast: Beth Child [the Pottery Woman], Arthur Dignam [the Senator], Paul Goddard [the Son], Mark Lee [the Youth], John Meillon [the Judge], Dennis Miller [Eric, the Chauffeur], Heather Mitchell [the Wife]
Genre: A drama about secret societies and homosexual intrigue at the highest levels of Australian society.
Plot: This film must represent the radical religious right's

worst nightmares. A secret society of wealthy and influential homosexuals recruiting beautiful schoolboys from the halls of the most exclusive boarding schools in the country with the open connivance of the teachers in order to use the teenagers as high class callboys to provide pleasure for themselves and their powerful friends in industry and government.

In a strangely anonymous world where only the chauffeur (Miller) has a name, the Youth (Lee) is chosen from the halls of St. Michael's School to become the companion of the Senator (Dignam), a high ranking member of the Secret Family. As the Youth becomes closer to the man, he also becomes more and more concerned with retaining his youthfulness, seemingly his one hold on the senator.

When for the sake of political appearances the Senator marries, the Youth is slowly put to one side, becoming no more than a baby-sitter and companion to his former lover's son. In revenge, the Youth vows to seduce the Senator's son (Goddard) and recruit him into the Family, little realizing that this was the intention from the start.

An at times confusing film, *The Everlasting Secret Family* frequently takes unexpected and unexplained twists and turns, and many points about the story are left hanging in the air, ultimately never to be resolved.

MPAA: Not rated. Gay themes run throughout this film, although there is little in the way of explicit on-screen sex. Mark Lee is seen nude in several rear shots while he and the senator are together in a hotel room after the Youth is first introduced to the Family. There are also some scenes of the Youth tying the Judge (Meillon) up at the beginning of leather and bondage sessions. There is also one scene of the Youth with the Pottery Woman (Child) in which her breasts are shown.

THE 400 BLOWS
★★★★★

(Also known as *Les Quatre Cents Coups*)

Credits: VHS/1959/France/B&W/97 minutes
In French with English subtitles.
Director: Francois Truffaut
Screenplay: Marcel Moussey and Francois Truffaut
Cast: Patrick Auffay [Rene Bigey], Jean-Claude Brialy, Guy Decomble [the teacher], Jacques Demy, Georges Flamant [M. Bigey], Jean-Pierre Leaud [Antoine Doinel], Claire Mauruer [Mme. Doinel], Jeanne Moreau, Albert Remy [M. Doinel], Francois Truffaut
Awards: Acadamy Awards: (nomination) Best Story and Screenplay. Cannes Film Festival 1959: Best Director (Truffaut). New York Film Critics 1959: Best Foreign Film.
Genre: This is a drama about a young teenager at odds with his family and the world at large whose exploits eventually land him in reform school.
Plot: Antoine (Leaud, in an outstanding performance in his film debut) is a young teen. A teller of tall tales, he seems always to be in trouble with his parents, his school and the authorities.

Antoine's antics, however, are more mischievous and ill-considered than truly criminal. Unhappy at home in a tiny Paris apartment, his relationship with his mother and stepfather is difficult. His grades at school are poor. To complicate matters, while playing hooky one day he catches sight of his mother in an amorous embrace with another man.

Returning to school three days later, he tells the school he was absent because his mother has died. Caught in the lie later in the day, he is beaten by his stepfather and runs away from home.

Still later, while suspended from school for plagiarism, he steals a typewriter from his stepfather's office. Unable to pawn the machine, he is apprehended trying to return it.

Arrested and forced to spend a lonely night in jail, Antoine is placed into a strict reform school where, the

Albert Remy and Jean-Pierre Leaud, *The 400 Blows* (1959)

smallest of all the inmates, he is cut off from all contact with his old friends. Finally, unable to take it any longer, Antoine escapes from the school during a soccer game and in one of cinema's best known sequences, runs until he reaches the ocean.

The 400 Blows is the first of five films Truffaut

Marco Mestriner and Lorenzo Lena, *The Flavor Of Corn* (1991)

directed over a period of twenty years detailing the loves and adventures of Antoine Doinel, all starring Leaud.

MPAA: Not rated. Leaud has one brief full-length rear nude scene. After having a bath, Antoine jumps from bath towel to bed in his parents' apartment. There is also a certain amount of sex talk while Antoine is being interviewed by a psychiatrist at the reform school. The doctor wants to know about the boy's sexual past. Antoine, fidgeting and nervous, finally confesses to a total lack of sexual experience but no lack of desire.

THE FLAVOR OF CORN ★★★

(Also known as *Il Sapore Del Grano*)

Credits: VHS/1991/Italy/Colour/93 minutes
In Italian with English subtitles.
Writer/Director: Gianni Da Campo
Cast: Lorenzo Lena [Lorenzo], Marco Mestriner [Duilio], Alba Mottura, Mattia Pinoli, Egidio Termine
Genre: A drama about a young teacher who finds himself developing a close relationship with one of his twelve-year-old students.
Plot: Lorenzo (Lena), a university student, has taken a temporary teaching position in a small Italian town. What

seems at first to be a straightforward assignment is soon complicated by a number of emotional entanglements.

Lorenzo is first attracted to Cecilia, a young woman who is theoretically engaged to a married man. When the increasing complications of this relationship lead to a break up between Lorenzo and Cecilia, the young man finds that an even more complicated situation is rising in his emotional life.

Duilio (Mestriner), a twelve-year-old boy in his literature class, has developed a passionate attachment to the young man. Several invitations to the family home for dinner and encouragement in the relationship by Duilio's grandparents lead to increasing closeness between man and boy.

The attachment leads to several exchanges of gifts and some close, physical tenderness including holding hands and kisses. Although Duilio's stepmother is suspicious of the relationship, there is no suggestion of a sexual liaison between the two. Nevertheless, the love each feels for the other is evident. It is also evident that the man's attention is benefitting the boy, who blossoms academically and emotionally under Lorenzo's attention.

One of Duillo's gifts to Lorenzo is a small manuscript of poems the boy has written. Eventually even the father, who fears losing the boy, and the stepmother, who suspects sexual activity, come to the realization that the relationship is not a threat. The two truly love each other and Lorenzo would not do anything to harm the boy. Unfortunately, however, the school year must come to an end, and with it Lorenzo's temporary teaching post.

MPAA: Not rated. Lorenzo makes love with a young woman in the compartment of a railway coach. Duilio kisses Lorenzo on the lips. Gabriel, one of Lorenzo's students, is seen masturbating in the back of the classroom, hoping to attract the attention of one of the girls.

FLIGHT OF THE INNOCENT
★★★★

(Also known as *La Corsa Dell' Innocente*)

Credits: VHS/1992/Italy, France/Colour/105 minutes
In Italian with English subtitles.
Director: Carlo Carlei
Screenplay: Carlo Carlei, Gualtiero Rosella
Cast: Sal Borgese, Manuel Colao [Vito], Francesca Neri, Frederico Pacifici, Jacques Perrin
Genre: A visually-stunning thriller about a young boy on the run through Italy after he witnesses the killing of his entire family.
Plot: The Putorti family are poor Calabrian farmers. Because without money you are nothing, they have

supplemented their meager income with a little kidnapping for profit—their victim being Simone Rienzi, the young son of a wealthy Siena family. When the Putorti family is massacred by a rival gang, only ten-year-old Vito (Colao) escapes: even the young kidnap victim is killed in the crossfire.

Terrified, Vito runs. Because he is able to identify one of the killers, they pursue. The chase takes them first to Rome, where Vito shelters with his cousin Orlando. When the killers catch up to him again, they shoot Orlando then trail Vito who by this time has been apprehended by the police and placed in a children's home for his protection.

The stay in the home and the security it provides, are both short lived. Soon Vito is on the run again. Now carrying the ransom money, he heads north to Siena, intending to return it to Simone's family. Entering the Rienzi home unannounced, he is found by Simone's mother who deludes herself into believing Vito is Simone returned to her.

The killers have also tracked down Simone's family. Through some faked evidence they have persuaded them the boy is still alive and will be returned after the payment of an additional ransom demand. Vito, putting his own life on the line, convinces Simone's father of the truth, then engineers a shoot out between the killers and the police before a seemingly fairy tale ending.

MPAA: Rated R. The film has a great many violent scenes as the various gangs battle it out.

Thandie Newton and Noah Taylor, *Flirting* (1989)

FLIRTING ★★★★

Credits: VHS/1989/Australia/ Colour/100 minutes

Writer/Director: John Duigan

Cast: Nicole Kidman [Nicola Radcliffe], Thandie Newton [Thandiwe Adjewo], Felix Nobis [Jock Blair], Kiri Paramore ["Slag" Green], Josh Picker ["Backa" Burke], Bartholomew Rose ["Gilby" Fryer], Noah Taylor [Danny Embling]

Genre: A wry, insightful comedy about two teenagers, both misfits, one black, one white, who are too cool to use the word love.

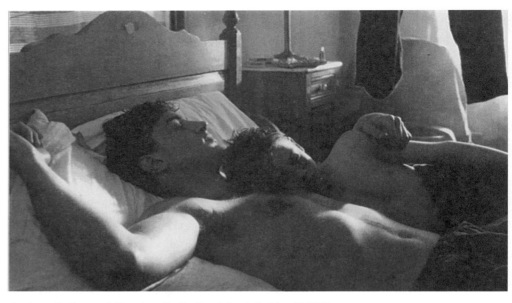

Andrew Kelley and Maarten Smit, *For A Lost Soldier* (1993)

Plot: The sequel to *The Year My Voice Broke*, this is the second of John Duigan's tales about growing up in the Australian Outback in the 1960s.

It's 1965, and Danny Embling (Taylor) has been sent away to St. Alban's boarding school. A slight, quiet, academic boy with a sardonic outlook on life, Danny is an outsider, the butt of jokes and teasing from many of the other boys. His only real friend at school is Gilby (Rose), a rather pompous, affected, self-important, would-be intellectual.

Then Danny's life changes. He meets a girl from the sister school across the lake. Thandiwe is from Uganda. Her father is a writer, a lecturer and a political activist. Despite the best efforts of both schools to limit contacts between boys and girls, Danny and Thandiwe manage to meet clandestinely and fall in love, though they never use the word.

When political events in Uganda cause Thandiwe to return to Africa, the two teenagers, having picked up some unlikely allies amongst their fellow students, meet in a local motel room to say good-bye, an episode which results in Danny's expulsion from St. Alban's.

MPAA: Rated R. Canadian Home Video rated 14-A. There are a number of scenes of sexual activity. Long past lights out one night, Danny and Thandiwe meet secretly in a boat house, engaging in a little mutual touching, though remaining fully clothed.

Later, just before Thandiwe leaves Australia, she and Danny spend the night together in a motel room. During this scene, Newton appears briefly topless. In common with most boarding school films, there is also a great deal of sexual angst and desire evident. Both the boys and the girls suffer equally from repressed desires and talk about it frequently.

There are two scenes involving male nudity. At the beginning of the film, several boys drop their pajamas to compare stripes after being caned. The group includes Green (Paramore) and Burke (Picker). As part of this sequence, Danny also gets his pants pulled down and his bare butt photographed.

Later, about eight or ten teenage boys are seen in a shower sequence. During the horseplay, there are several brief instances of full-frontal exposure.

THE FOOL KILLER ★★★★

(Also known as *Violent Journey*)

Credits: VHS/1965/USA/B&W/100 minutes

Director: Servando Gonzalez

Screenplay: Morton Fine and David Friedkin Based on the novel by Helen Eustis.

Cast: Edward Albert [George Mellish], Dana Elcar, Henry Hull, Salome Jens, Charlotte Jones, Arnold Moss, Anthony Perkins [Milo], Sindee Ann Richards.

Genre: A suspense drama with many striking visual moments about a twelve-year-old boy on the run from an abusive foster home who teams up with a mysterious young man in the years immediately following the American Civil War.

Plot: After George Mellish (Albert, in his screen debut), an orphan, is whipped by his Scripture quoting foster parents, he runs away from home. Hopping freight trains and slogging it out on foot, he heads west.

Along the road he encounters Dirty Jim, an old widower living alone in a filthy, rundown cabin. Jim proceeds to fill

George's head with stories of The Fool Killer, an eight-foot giant with a sharp chopper who preys on fools.

Some days after leaving Jim's home George meets Milo, a mysterious Civil War veteran who is suffering from amnesia. They team up, George soon coming to love Milo as a brother. All is not well, however, and Milo soon begins to display some very erratic behaviour. When they attend a camp meeting at George's urging, Milo becomes visibly disturbed at George's frenzied reaction to the hell fire preaching. The next morning, Milo has disappeared and the preacher is found hacked to death.

Alone again, George wanders into a nearby town where he is taken in by a kindly couple who run the general store. Although paddled severely for stealing candy, George learns to love Sam and his wife. His tranquility is shattered, however, when Milo appears, expecting George to hit the road again. He is tempted, but George now has loving, understanding parents, a good home, good clothes on his back and good food in his belly. His refusal prompts a violent, and frightening response from Milo.

The suspense in this film is greatly enhanced by striking, often stark, photography. Using the black and white stock to great advantage, cinematographer Alex Philips, Jr. frequently fills the screen with dark, brooding shadowy images.

MPAA: Not rated. Although there is an undercurrent of violence and death throughout the film, very little is actually shown on-screen. The most violent act portrayed is the whipping that sparks George's initial flight, and even this is framed in such a way that we don't actually see the blows connect. Albert is seen nude in a full-length rear shot when George runs into a river to join Milo for a swim.

FOR A LOST SOLDIER
★ ★ ★ ★ ★

(Also known as *Voor Een Verloren Soldaat*)

Credits: VHS/1993/Netherlands/Colour/92 minutes
In English, Dutch and Frisian with English subtitles.
Writer/Director: Roeland Kerbosch
Based on the autobiographical novel by Rudi van Dantzig.
Cast: Andrew Kelley [Walt], Jeroen Krabbe [Jeroen as an adult], Derk-Jan Kroon [Jan], Freark Smink [Heit], Maarten Smit [Jeroen, age 12]
Genre: A sensitive drama which deals in a positive way with a young boy's exploration of his own sexual orientation and with the controversial subject of a consenting sexual relationship between a twelve-year-old boy and a young soldier.
Plot: In the winter of 1944, food is scarce throughout the Netherlands, especially in Amsterdam. To ease the burden on his family, twelve-year-old Jeroen (Smit) along with many other children, is sent to a small fishing village in the province of Friesland for the duration of the war.

At first lonely in this new environment, despite having his friend Jan (Kroon) staying in the same village, Jeroen must adjust to Heit (Smink), a fisherman, and his family.

Language differences (the villagers speak Frisian, not Dutch—some theatrical prints of this film have Dutch subtitles as well as English for the Frisian dialog), a new school, wooden shoes, outdoor plumbing and weekly baths in a portable tub in the kitchen are all obstacles. He must also deal with his feelings towards Jan and towards his older foster brother, Heit's son.

When Canadian soldiers arrive in the village, Jeroen finds a new friend and soul mate in Walt (Kelley), one of the liberators. Their relationship quickly turns to love and a consenting sexual encounter between man and boy ensues. Unfortunately, Jeroen's joy is shattered when the Canadians suddenly pull out, and Walt must leave town without even saying good-bye to the boy. Jeroen is left with little more than warm memories and a single photograph which doesn't even include Walt.

The sexual aspect of the relationship between Jeroen and Walt may be shocking to some, but it is

Maarten Smit and Andrew Kelley, *For A Lost Soldier* (1993)

carefully handled and the boy is clearly a consenting partner. It is also obvious from earlier scenes in the film that Jeroen is already experiencing gay sexual feelings long before he and Walt make love.

In one scene his eyes linger on Jan's nude body, and in another he reaches out towards Heit's son, not quite touching the older boy, though obviously wanting to.

MPAA: Not rated. Smit appears nude once, bathing in a tub in the kitchen. Kroon also appears nude lying in the sun after Jan dives into a wrecked aircraft. There is brief full-frontal exposure when he roles over. Kelley appears partially nude in a shower scene.

FOREIGN STUDENT ★★★

Credits: VHS/1994/USA/Colour/96 minutes
Director: Eva Sereny
Screenplay: Menno Meyjes
Based on the novel by Philippe Labro.
Cast: Hinton Battle [Sonny Boy Williamson], Charles Dutton [Howlin' Wolf], Robin Givens [April], Edward Herrmann [Zach Gilmour], Marco Hofschneider [Phillippe Le Clerc], Rick Johnson [Cal], Charlotte Ross [Sue Ann]
Genre: A sometimes slow-moving romantic drama about interracial love at a small Virginia college in the mid 1950s.
Plot: Marco Hofschneider stars as Phillippe Le Clerc, an eighteen-year-old French student who has won a scholarship to attend one semester at Virginia's Asheland-Stuart University in the fall of 1955. Arriving in the town he comes face to face with two alien and totally bewildering concepts: American football and racial segregation.

Alessandro Di Sanzo, *Forever Mary* (1988)

The situation is bad enough when he finds obstacles in his path as he attempts to attend a blues concert in a black hall. It is severely aggravated by the appearance of April (Givens), a beautiful young black school teacher. His attraction to April quickly becomes romantic, and even sexual, placing both himself and April at risk before his ultimate return to France.

MPAA: Rated R. Givens and Hofschneider are seen nude while Phillippe and April are making love in a storage shed, though the nudity is very brief and incomplete. Hofschneider's buns are seen briefly and Given's breasts are partially exposed.

FOREVER MARY ★★★

(Also known as *Mery Per Sempre*)

Credits: VHS/1988/Italy/Colour/100 minutes
In Italian with English subtitles.
Director: Marco Risi
Screenplay: Sandro Petraglia and Stefano Rulli
Based on the book by Aurelio Grimaldi, who later directed the film Acla.
Cast: Claudio Amendola [Pietro], Francesco Benigno [Natale], Alessandro Di Sanzo [Mary], Alfredo Li Bassi, Roberto Mariano, Michele Placido [Marco Terzi], Maurizio Prollo, Tony Sperandeo, Salvatore Termini
Genre: A drama about the relationship between an Italian teacher and his students, inmates at a reform school.

The Rosaspina reform school in Palermo, Sicily, is home to a rough collection of teenage boys incarcerated for such various offenses as breaking and entering, manslaughter, theft and assault.

A disparate group, the inmates include Natale (Benigno), serving nine years for manslaughter, Pietro (Amendola), a repeat offender in for stealing a stereo, fourteen-year-old Claudio, who broke into a clothing store, and Mario (Di Sanzo), a crossdressing teenage prostitute who prefers to be called Mary, who assaulted and nearly killed a customer who shortchanged him.

Into this unstable milieu comes Marco (Placido), a teacher between jobs who has taken the assignment as a temporary post until he is able to take up a permanent position in a regular high school.

Teaching these boys is not easy.

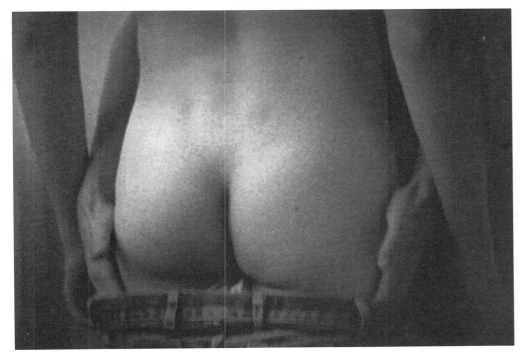

Claus Bender Mortensen, *Friends Forever* (1986)

FREEDOM IS PARADISE

★★★★

(Also known as *SER*, or as *Svoboda Eta Rai*)

Credits: VHS/1989/USSR/ Colour/75 minutes
In Russian with English subtitles.
Writer/Director: Sergei Bodrov
Cast: Alexander Bureyev [father], Svetlana Gaitan [Klava], Volodya Kozyrev [Sasha], Vitautus Tomkus [camp commandant]
Awards: Montreal International Film Festival: Grand Prize
Genre: A drama about a thirteen-year-old reform school runaway who is searching for his imprisoned father.

Mary declares his love for Marco. Claudio is raped by Carmello and ostracized and beaten by the other boys when he reports the incident. The guards are vicious and uncaring. The headmaster clashes with Marco almost from the moment the teacher walks in the front gate.

The boys can't respect Marco because he doesn't employ physical punishment and because he is seen as simply another liberal do-gooder. In the end, Marco is inevitably faced with a difficult decision. He is offered a post at a regular school at a much higher salary. Should he take the new position, or stay with the boys who have come, in their own grudging ways, to accept him?

One could profitably compare this film with the Canadian film *Train of Dreams* which also covers much of the same ground, the sympathetic teacher in a reform school who gradually earns the respect of his involuntary students.

MPAA: Not rated. Frequent coarse language and violence. There are several scenes with sexual overtones: Mary with a john, Mary kissing Marco, Tony masturbating in class while daydreaming about his young wife and a hilarious class discussion about the synonyms and euphemisms for penis. As well, there are several scenes of seduction and attempted rape, both heterosexual and homosexual involving various inmates.

Plot: Sasha Grigoryev (Kozyrev) is an inmate at a reform school for boys fourteen and under. At least he is supposed to be. In fact, he is constantly on the run, escaping whenever he can. He is also trying to get whatever news he can of his father, his only living relative.

At every turn Sasha is told to forget him. The prostitute Klava (Gaitan), Shasha's only friend on the outside, tells him to forget his father. The authorities tell him to forget the man. Only by accident does the boy discover that his father is an inmate at a labour camp in Archangel.

With this information and renewed energy, Sasha once again escapes from incarceration and heads north to find his father.

After arriving at the gates of the labour camp. Shasha is allowed just one night for the difficult and uncomfortable reunion during which the father (Burayev) tells his life story to his son. The story begins with the man's own birth in a prison hospital. The next morning, father and son are again separated, each returning to his own form of incarceration.

MPAA: Not rated. The film includes full-frontal nude scenes of Klava walking around in her apartment. There are also several nude scenes of Sasha. These include full-frontal shots of him and several other pre-adolescent boys in a shower as well as a humiliating episode in the reform school where the boys are required to drop their pants for an inspection.

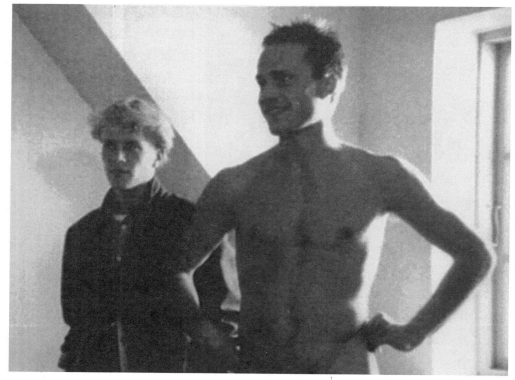

Thomas Sigsgaard and Morten Stig Christensen, *Friends Forever* (1986)

There is also one scene with decidedly erotic over-tones which occurs when Klava takes Sasha into her bed, cuddling and kissing the boy.

FRESH ★★★★★

Credits: VHS/1994/USA/ Colour/114 minutes
Writer/Director: Boaz Yakin
Cast: Natima Bradley [Rosie], Ron Brice [Corky], Giancarlo Esposito [Esteban], Cheryl Freeman [Aunt Francis], Samuel L. Jackson [Sam], Jean Lamarre [Jake], Luis Lantigua [Chuckie], Sean Nelson [Fresh], N'Bushe Wright [Nichole]
Awards: Independent Spirit Awards 1995: Debut Performance (Nelson); (nomination) Best Supporting Actor (Esposito). Sundance Film Festival 1994: Special Jury Prize, Filmmakers Trophy.
Genre: A drama about drug dealing, murder and revenge amongst pre-teens in the heart of Harlem.
Plot: Twelve-year-old Fresh (Nelson, in an outstanding first appearance) is one of twelve siblings and cousins living with his Aunt Francis (Freeman) in a tiny inner-city apartment. While he dreams of becoming a millionaire, Fresh runs drugs for two different pushers: smack for Esteban (Esposito) and crack for Corky (Brice) and his vicious lieutenant Jake (Lamarre).

When not running drugs, Fresh is in the park learning

chess from his father (Jackson), who also tries to impart lessons in life and philosophy to his young son.

Already upset about the situation his sister Nichole (Wright) is in (she's sexually involved with the married Esteban and probably working as a prostitute), when Fresh sees Jake casually gun down a young boy on the basketball courts, simultaneously killing Fresh's girlfriend Rosie (Bradley), he begins to plot revenge.

Using strategy lessons learned on the chess board, Fresh coldly, methodically sets up a labyrinthian series of moves and counter moves which one by one take out Jake, Nichole's pimp and Esteban. Check and mate.

While one can't help cheering the intelligence, resourcefulness and cunning of Fresh, one can't help decrying the insanity of a society as casually violent as the one reflected in this film. Rosie, Fresh's buddy Chuckie (Lantigua) and the young basketball ace are the children gunned down in the film, but the bullets which take their lives have just as surely killed the childhood of the boy still living.

MPAA: Rated R. Canadian Home Video rated 18-A. The dialogue is liberally sprinkled with coarse language. There are several scenes of murder, including the gunning down of children and the beating to death with a chain of a drug dealer.

Nelson and Esposito both have nude scenes. Nelson is seen curled up on a bed in the fetal position, in a state of shock after witnessing the casual murder of his girl friend. Esposito is seen nude in a romantic scene. There is also some sex talk, most noteworthy when a desperate, pregnant drug addict offers to provide sexual favours to Fresh in exchange for a free fix.

FRIENDS ★★

Credits: VHS/1971/Great Britain/Colour/101 minutes
In English, and French with English subtitles.
Director: Lewis Gilbert
Screenplay: Jack Russell and Vernon Harris
Based on an original story by Lewis Gilbert.
Cast: Anicee Alvina [Michelle Latour], Sean Bury [Paul Harrison], Joan Hickson [lady in book shop], Ronald

Lewis [Mr. Harrison], Sady Rebbot [Pierre], Pascale Roberts [Annie], Toby Robbins [Mrs. Gardner]

Genre: A drama about a teenage couple who set up housekeeping in the south of France.

Plot: There is probably a wonderful story hidden somewhere in this tale of teenage friends who become lovers after they run away together. Unfortunately, Gilbert and his cast haven't found it and the film editor seemingly can't decide whether this is a love story or a travelogue extolling the natural beauties of the Camargue.

Fifteen-year-old Paul (Bury) is the poor little rich English boy who, bored with life in Paris with his single father (Lewis), steals cars for kicks. Fourteen-year-old Michelle (Alvina) is the orphaned French girl who has reluctantly come to live with her uncaring cousin (Roberts).

They meet in the zoo, and after Paul drives his father's car into a lake, they run away to the cottage in the Camargue which Michelle's artist father owned. "Just for a few days" stretches into a year and friends become lovers, kids become parents.

These two teenagers display all the youthful zest of a middle aged couple. It's too bad, because the story could have had a great deal to say about teenage pregnancies and the realities of kids trying to be adults before their time.

Friends was followed in 1974 by *Paul And Michelle*.

MPAA: Rated R. Alvina has several topless scenes: when her cousin's boyfriend (Rebbot) tries to make a pass at her; getting into a bathtub at the cottage; making love on the beach with Paul; in bed with Paul.

Bury appears in a couple of full length butt shots: undressing before the fireplace before getting into a bathtub; getting into bed with Alvina. Paul and Alvina are seen making love several times.

FRIENDS FOREVER
★★★★

(Also known as *Venner For Altid*)

Credits: VHS/1986/Denmark/ Colour/95 minutes
In Danish with English subtitles.

Director: Stefan Christian Henszelmann

Screenplay: Stefan Christian Henszelmann and Alexander Korschen

Cast: Morten Stig Christensen [Mads], Thomas Elholm [Henrik], Lill Lindfors [the singer], Claus Bender Mortensen [Kristian], Henrik Ohlers [the landlord], Thomas Sigsgaard [Patrick], Christine Skou [Sophie]

Genre: A drama about a Danish high school student confronting his own and his society's attitudes towards homosexuality after he learns that his best friend is gay.

Plot: Kristian (Mortensen), the new boy at school, is pulled two ways in making new friends. He is drawn at first to Henrik (Elholm), an intellectually stimulating and somewhat eccentric classmate who studies astronomy, practices Tai-Chi and works as a photographer's model. But Henrik's odd ways and somewhat androgynous appearance have him labeled as a "faggot."

Fearing he will be tarred with the same brush for associating with Henrik, Kristian soon distances himself from his erstwhile friend. When chance takes Henrik away, Kristian enters into the entourage surrounding Patrick (Sigsgaard).

Patrick is a popular, charismatic boy. He is athletic. He is good looking. He is a ringleader in classroom pranks and hijinx. He also is living in a rented room, away from his parents. Kristian and Patrick quickly become close friends. Patrick introduces Kristian to an older woman (Lindfors), the singer at the night club where Patrick works. He also helps Kristian get a part time job. In turn, Kristian helps Patrick academically.

The friendship seems on firm footing until Kristian discovers Patrick in a loving embrace kissing Mads (Christensen). Kristian must now confront his own feelings about homosexuality, a confrontation which is not

Elodie Bouchez and Pascal Cervo, *Full Speed* (1996)

Stephane Rideau and Meziane Bardadi, *Full Speed* (1996)

easy for the boy. It is made even more difficult when Patrick comes out at school and a classroom discussion of homosexuality brings reprisals from the school administration.

Friends Forever is important for asking us to examine, to challenge, and to eschew stereotyping. In a media which still all too often presents gay characters as wimpy, effeminate queens, it is refreshing to see a production where the stereotypes are challenged as effectively as they are in the characterizations of the straight Henrik and the gay Patrick.

MPAA: Not rated. There are several scenes of nudity and sex. A teenage girl has her sweater ripped off in a classroom prank, leaving her topless. An adult man is seen in an extended nude sequence, including full-frontal shots, as he wanders around the apartment where Patrick rents a room. Kristian's bare buns are seen as the singer slowly removes the boy's jeans before they make love in her hotel room. Patrick and Mads are both seen nude while engaged in sex when Kristian bursts in on them in Patrick's bedroom. Shortly after this, Mads is seen in a full-frontal nude shot.

FULL SPEED ★★★★

(Also known as *A Toute Vitesse*)

Credits: 1996/France/Colour/85 minutes
In French with English subtitles.
Writer/Director: Gael Morel
Cast: Romain Auger [Rick], Meziane Bardadi [Samir], Elodie Bouchez [Julie], Stephane Rideau [Jimmy], Pascal Cervo [Quentin]
Genre: A drama about four friends on the verge of adulthood coming to terms with changes in their lives. This film re-unites some of the cast and crew of the earlier French film *Wild Reeds* and covers some of the same thematic ground but it is not a sequel.
Plot: Julie (Bouchez), Quentin (Cervo) and Jimmy (Rideau) are three nineteen-year-olds who, despite having little in common, have been close friends for years. Julie is now a college student. Quentin, although having foregone a higher education, has just won a literary award for his first novel. Jimmy is a tough, unemployed working class rapper.

Into the world of this trio, a fourth teenager, Samir

(Bardadi), appears when Quentin catches sight of him at a party. Samir is Algerian and gay. He is, two years after the event, still overwhelmed by the shooting death of his then sixteen-year-old boy friend Rick (Auger).

Can Quentin take the place of Rick? Without a doubt Samir finds himself attracted to the young author, and it would seem at first that Quentin may have some feelings for the young Arab. However, when Samir's attentions are about to go beyond a kiss, Quentin storms out in disgust.

In the meantime, Julie, who has always been Quentin's girlfriend, has left him for Jimmy. In large measure this is a result of Quentin's decision to move to Paris to pursue his writing career. Tragically, however, Julie and Jimmy are not destined for happiness. Jimmy dies following a gay-bashing, but even his death can't bring the remaining three friends back together in the way they were before.

MPAA: Not rated. There are two scenes of shootings as well as several scenes of fist fights and other forms of physical violence, much of it racially motivated.

The film revolves in large measure around Samir's homosexuality and the reaction of the other characters to this. There is a some sexual talk in the dialogue as various characters relate some of their early sexual experiences.

Samir is seen kissing Quentin on a number of occasions. He is also seen masturbating after Quentin has refused his advances. Julie and Jimmy are seen in an extended lovemaking sequence which includes bare buns shots of both actors, as well as brief shots of her breasts.

The Genesis Children (1971)

THE GENESIS CHILDREN ★★

Credits: VHS/1971/USA/Colour/84 minutes
Director: Anthony Aikman
Screenplay: Anthony Aikman and Billy Byars
Cast: Max Adams, Butch Burr, Vincent Child, Bubba Collins, Peter Glawson, Jack Good, Mike Good, Greg Hill, Jeremy Hoellack [the narrator], David Johnson
Genre: An adventure tale about eight boys on an isolated Italian beach.
Plot: "Wanted. Boys to act in a play to be performed before God at Pavicelli. Come unprepared for your parts. No rich rewards. Time of the performance is sunset today."

Answering this ad, eight American boys in Rome, the youngest maybe twelve, the oldest about fifteen, are thrown together on an isolated beach for what seems to be intended as a journey of survival and self-discovery.

Watched over by a mysterious man who is now priest, now choirmaster, now diplomat, now military policeman, the boys lose little time before stripping naked and cavorting on the beach.

Despite frequent references to *Lord of the Flies*, and attempts at profundity and mystical navel-gazing in the narration, the primary purpose of this film from Lyric Studios is to get the eight boys nude as often as possible in what the producers seem to hope is an artistic manner. (Many of the boys also appeared in other nudist films from the same source.)

Unfortunately the film is too arty to satisfy the voyeur, and too poorly made to satisfy the film connoisseur.

This film could have done for the young male figure what David Hamilton's films have done for the young female figure. Unfortunately the artistic levels of *The*

Genesis Children do not come up to that limited standard.

MPAA: Not rated. From the opening minutes to almost the last frame, the film is filled with images of nude adolescent and pre-adolescent boys, including numerous full-frontal shots of all eight principals. There is, however, no suggestion of sexuality beyond one ambiguous exchange between two of the boys.

Is this film pornographic? No. Parts of it attempt to be sensual, but it is not erotic. The film is saved by the fact that most of the nudity seems quite natural and the boys don't seem the least self-conscious in front of the cameras.

LE GRAND CHEMIN ★★★★

(Also known as *The Grand Highway*)

Credits: VHS/1987/France/Colour/107 minutes
In French with English subtitles.

Writer/Director: Jean-Loup Hubert

Cast: Anemone [Marcelle], Raoul Billery [the priest], Richard Bohringer [Pelo], Vanessa Guedj [Martine], Antoine Hubert [Louis], Marie Matheron [Solange], Christine Pascal [Claire], Daniel Rialet [Simon], Pascale Roberts [Yvonne]

Genre: A comedy with an edge about a young boy who unknowingly reconciles a feuding couple when he is forced to spend two weeks with them.

Plot: Claire (Pascal), a woman deserted by her husband, is due to give birth to her second child. She takes her eight-year-old son Louis (Hubert) to stay with an old friend, Marcelle (Anemone) who lives in a small village in the Loire valley. Marcelle and her husband Pelo (Bohringer) have been fighting bitterly since the death in infancy of their only son, who would have been the same age as Louis.

Neither Marcelle nor Pelo has been able to deal with their loss, and Louis's presence reopens old wounds as the adults use Louis as a battle ground. Louis, oblivious to the reasons for the fighting, is having adjustment problems of his own. The village of Rouans is definitely not Paris!

The boy is helped along the way by Martine (Guedj), the ten-year-old daughter of Marcelle's neighbour. Together, the two children get into any amount of mischief: spying on the villagers from the cemetery hedge, getting sick on stolen green apples, climbing to the roof of the church, peeing through the gargoyles onto the heads of nuns. Louis survives various crises and eventually his presence, especially his bonding with Pelo, brings about a reconciliation between Marcelle and her husband.

This film was remade in the USA in 1991 as *Paradise*, with Elijah Wood, Melanie Griffith, and Don Johnson. Antoine Hubert is the son of the film's director.

MPAA: Not rated. Louis and Martine discuss sexual matters several times as well as playing childish sex games.

Solange (Matheron) and Simon (Rialet) make love in the grass while Louis and Martine watch from the hay loft. The two children go to the barn to play you show me. Spying on the lovers proves to be more fun. Rialet is seen nude in a rear shot during this scene. Matheron is seen topless in a couple of shots.

Hubert is seen nude twice. While Marcelle gives Louis a stand up bath in the kitchen the boy is facing the camera but keeps his hands cupped in front of him. When Martine dumps a handful of cirvelles down the front of his swim trunks, Louis retreats to the garden to clean up, pulling his clothes off in order to get rid of them. This is a rear shot only.

HEAVEN HELP US ★★★★

Credits: VHS/1985/USA/Colour/102 minutes
Director: Michael Dinner
Screenplay: Charles Purpura
Cast: Malcolm Danare, [Caesar], Patrick Dempsey [Corbet], Kevin Dillon [Rooney], Stephen Geoffreys [Williams], John Heard [Brother Timothy], Mary Stuart Masterson [Danni], Andrew McCarthy [Michael Dunn], Jay Patterson [Father Constance], Kate Reid [Grandma], Wallace Shawn [Father Abrazzi], Donald Sutherland [Brother Thadeus]
Genre: A comedy about life in a strict Catholic boys school in Brooklyn in the year 1965.
Plot: Michael Dunn (McCarthy) is a new student at St Basil's. The school in Brooklyn is run by Brother Thadeus (Sutherland), a strict task master who oversees a staff of teaching brothers, some of whom border on the sadistic.

Despite some initial setbacks, Dunn soon falls in with a group of misfits. Rooney (Dillon) is a failing student who calls everybody faggot, perhaps to cover his doubts about his own sexuality. Caesar (Danare) is the overweight would-be intellectual. Williams (Geoffreys) is a handsome, carefree boy whose sole recreational activity seems to be masturbating. Dunn also makes the acquaintance of Danni (Masterson), a girl who is trying singlehandedly to run her disabled father's coffee shop and care for him as well.

The pranks played by Dunn and his friends eventually land them on the receiving end of a brutal beating by Father Constance (Patterson). When Dunn responds with his fists, decking the teacher before the entire school, he is greeted by a standing ovation. Brother Thadeus suspends Dunn and his friends for two weeks, and then fires Constance on the spot.
MPAA: Rated R. The film is filled with talk about sex:

Patrick Dempsey, Malcolm Danare, Andrew McCarthy, Kevin Dillon and Stephen Geoffreys, *Heaven Help Us* (1985)

these boys seem to talk or think about little else. Williams is constantly teased about his masturbating. He confesses to have indulged 168 times in the space of a single month, proudly pointing out that equals 5.6 times per day.

The priests who run the school are obsessed with sex. In one of the funniest scenes of the film, Father Abrazzi (Shawn) kicks off a school dance with a rousing denunciation of lust. Although there is no on-screen sex, there is one lengthy nude scene. Swim classes at St. Basil's are conducted in the buff and a long line of boys is seen standing along the edge of the pool. For the most part, when the boys face the camera, they have their hands covering their genitals and most of the rear shots are partially blocked, showing only the upper half of the boys' buns. However, in the very first shot in the pool, one boy at the very right-hand edge of the screen is standing with his arms folded across his chest and Danare half turns towards the camera as he walks to the edge of the pool. All of the boys are seen in full-length rear shots as they enter the pool, though it is difficult to pick out any of the principals, other than Danare.

A HERO AIN'T NOTHIN' BUT A SANDWICH ★★★

Credits: VHS/1978/USA/Colour/107 minutes
Director: Ralph Nelson
Screenplay: Alice Childress, based on her novel.
Cast: Erin Blunt [Carwell], Kenneth "Joey" Green [Jimmy Lee], David Groh [Cohen], Kevin Hooks [Tiger], Helen Martin [grandma], Larry B. Scott [Benjie], Glynn Turman [Nigeria], Cicely Tyson [Sweets], Paul Winfield [Butler]

Genre: A highly didactic drama about the rehabilitation of a teenage drug addict.
Plot: Benjie (Scott) is a thirteen-year-old Afro-American boy living with his mother (Tyson), stepfather (Winfield) and grandmother (Martin) in Los Angeles. Upset by his father's disappearance and not comfortable with his stepfather, Benjie turns to drugs in an attempt to smother his inner pain.

In a progression whose rapidity stretches credulity, Benjie proceeds from his first joint through skin popping heroin to mainlining. In what seems to be less than a week, a bright, creative young teen has become a hopeless drug addict stealing from his family and running drugs for his supplier (Hooks) to get his next fix.

Even the death of his twelve-year-old pusher Carwell (Blunt), the distancing of his erstwhile friend Jimmy Lee (Green) and several weeks in a rehabilitation centre can't ease his pain or lessen his need. Only his eventual reconciliation with his stepfather seems to solve his problems.

The film suffers from being overly preachy, from being too simplistic in its view of the teenage drug problem and from too obvious a feel-good ending. Scott is highly commendable in his portrayal of the young druggie. Unfortunately, some of the adult performances don't quite measure up.
MPAA: Rated PG. If this film were released today, it is highly unlikely it would garner such a liberal rating. It contains a great deal of coarse language, graphic scenes of drug use and a lengthy nude scene by Scott. This includes some very brief full-frontal exposure while Benjie's mother tries to "wash the devil" out of him by giving the protesting boy an indigo blue bath.

HEY BABU RIBA ★★★

Credits: VHS/1986/Yugoslavia/Colour/109 minutes
In Serbo-Croatian with English Subtitles.
Writer/Director: Jovan Acin
Cast: Nebojsa Bakocevic, Relja Basic, Dragan Bjelogrlic, Goran Radakovic, Marko Todorovic, Gala Videnovic, Milos Zutic
Genre: A drama about teenagers in Yugoslavia in the early days of the Tito regime told as they look back

Kevin Dillon (left) and Malcolm Danare (right), *Heaven Help Us* (1985)

Hey Babu Riba (1986

from the vantage point of middle age to one decisive summer.

Plot: Four old friends from Belgrade meet at the funeral of a woman they had all been in love with as teenagers. In a series of flashbacks to the summer of 1953, they relive some of the antics of their high school years.

Pop, Glen, Kicha and Sacha had been inseparable as The Foursome, and Esther had been the fifth member of the group. Together, they row, play jazz and yearn for things western. Separately, they fall in love and lose their virginity, the boys to an older woman, Esther to an older man.

After her mother dies and Esther becomes pregnant by a local Communist party official, the boys spirit the girl out of the country to Italy where her father is living in exile. It's the last time any of the boys see Esther.

MPAA: Rated R. There is some on-screen nudity, principally female breasts. As well there are a number of sex scenes, mostly involving a teenager and an adult of the opposite sex.

For the boys, the reward for this activity is not just their sexual initiation. The woman also supplies them with scarce, hard to come by western-made clothing as payment for their services.

HIDDEN PLEASURES ★★★

(Also known as *Los Placeres Ocultos*)

Credits: VHS/1977/Spain/Colour/97 minutes
In Spanish with English subtitles.
Director: Eloy de la Iglesia
Screenplay: Rafael Sanchez Campoy and Eloy de la Iglesia
Cast: Simon Andreu, German Cobos, Antonio Corencia, Tony Fuentes, Charo Lopez, Angel Pardo, Beatriz Rossat
Genre: A drama about the frequently stormy relationship which develops between a wealthy middle-aged gay man, a poor straight teenager and the boy's girlfriend.
Plot: Eduardo, a middle-aged Madrid banking executive is the object of a certain amount of envy from family and friends. He's good-looking. He has a good job and lots of money. He comes from a good family. It is, they say, a

Kasper Andersen and Allan Winther, *The Hideaway* (1991)

wonder that no woman has snatched him up.

But Eduardo has other interests, especially in the teenage boys from poor neighbourhoods who hustle their bodies in the streets and parks of the city, and whose services he is more than willing to pay for. His eye is caught by Miguel, yet another poor kid trying to help support his family while he goes to school.

Miguel is uncompromisingly straight: he has a girlfriend, Carmen, as well as an adult lover, Rosa. Nonetheless, Eduardo begins a campaign of seduction and corruption in an effort to win the boy over. He finds a better job for Miguel. He takes the boy to dinner in expensive restaurants. He plies Miguel with wine. He provides prostitutes for the boy. He hires the boy to work extra hours typing a manuscript. He helps Miguel buy a much desired motorcycle.

Although the other boys in the barrio begin to hassle Miguel about his relationship with Eduardo, Miguel tells the man he views him as a father, as a replacement for the man who abandoned the family many years earlier. In time, Eduardo learns to accept that this relationship will always be non-sexual.

With this new understanding, Eduardo, Miguel and Carmen become a trio, keeping constant company.

MPAA: Not rated. Despite being a story with strong gay themes, almost all of the nudity in this film consists of bare breasts. There are also a number of sexual situations. Again, despite obvious implications of past and present gay sex and teenage boys hustling on the streets of Madrid, almost all of the on-screen sex is straight.

THE HIDEAWAY
★★★★

(Also known as *Mov Og Funder*, or as *Mov And Funder*)

Credits: VHS/1991/Denmark/ Colour/70 minutes

In Danish with English subtitles.

Director: Niels Grabol

Screenplay: Niels Grabol and Per Daumiller

Cast: Kasper Andersen [Mov], Kristine Horn [Rikke], Ditte Knudsen [the mother], Allan Winther [Funder]

Genre: A drama about the relationship between a lonely twelve-year-old boy and an injured fugitive.

Plot: Twelve-year-old Mov (Andersen), also known as Martin, is feeling very much alone. Mom (Knudsen) has a new boyfriend and little time for her son. Dad is supposed to spend time with Mov, but must go to Stockholm instead. Even Rikke, (Horn), the girl downstairs, seems to have little time for Mov these days. The boy is feeling an acute sense of abandonment. Then into his life comes Funder (Winther).

Funder is twenty-two years old and an ex-con. He is

Allan Winther and Kasper Andersen, *The Hideaway* (1991)

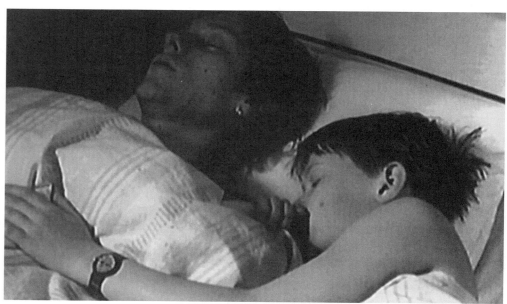

also badly wounded and on the run after having been involved in an altercation at the bar across the street. Mov agrees to help the young man, hiding him in his private corner of the basement of the apartment building.

Responding to Funder's need for food and care, Mov soon finds himself growing emotionally attached to the young man: Funder's need for assistance fills a void in the boy's emotional life. In several touching and gently humorous scenes, Mov even begins to emulate his new hero's appearance and mannerisms. Mov slicks back his hair with his mother's facial cream. He joins Funder in shaving, a thoroughly unnecessary activity on the boy's part. And when he finally catches sight of the young man's actions, he follows Funder's lead in hiding behind crossed hands when his mother walks in on them while they are showering together.

When the police finally catch up with Funder, Mov proves willing to risk himself to help the man escape, and for his part, Funder is willing to sacrifice his own freedom to save the boy from physical danger. A friend in need truly is a friend indeed.

MPAA: Not rated. Mov and Funder are both seen in full-frontal nude shots during and after a shared shower. There are also some minor instances of female nudity as well as some scenes of violence early in the film.

HOPE AND GLORY ★★★★

Credits: VHS/1987/Great Britain/Colour/117 minutes
Writer/Director: John Boorman.
Cast: Ian Bannen [Grandfather George], Jean-Marc Barr [Bruce], Sammi Davis [Dawn], Sebastian Rice Edwards [Bill], David Hayman [Clive], Sarah Miles [Grace], Geraldine Muir [Susie], Derrick O'Conner [Mac]
Awards: British Academy Awards: Best Film; Best Supporting Actress. Los Angeles Film Critics Association Awards: Best Director (Boorman); Best Film; Best Screenplay. The National Society of Film Critics: Best Film; Best Screenplay. Golden Globe Awards; Best Film-Musical/Comedy. The National Society of Film Critics: Best Director (Boorman); Best Screenplay (Boorman); Best Cinematography. Academy Awards: (nomination) Best Cinematography; (nomination) Best Director

(Boorman); (nomination) Best Original Screenplay; (nomination) Best Picture. National Board of Film Review: Ten Best Films of the Year.

Genre: A comedy about the effects of World War II on the lives of ordinary people as seen through the eyes of a young boy in working-class London.

Plot: Life around him is becoming increasingly fragmented by the War, though seemingly it has little effect on young Billy (Edwards). His sixteen year old sister Dawn (Davis) becomes pregnant by a young Canadian soldier

Sebastian Rice Edwards with director John Boorman, *Hope And Glory* (1987)

(Barr). The houses on his street and their residents become casualties of German bombing raids. His father (Hayman) signs up and mom (Miles) looks increasingly to Uncle Mac (O'Conner) for comfort. When their own home burns down, Billy and his family move to the country to live with grandfather (Bannen), an eccentric old man who lives in a house by the Thames.

Through it all, the war seems little more than a new and generally distant source of games and play for Billy and his friends. Hopalong Cassidy at the local cinema seems more real to them than news reels of events on the continent. Their play does, however, become increasingly violent and destructive as the war comes closer and closer to home. Smashing things up and playing with unexploded ammunition become the order of the day, and when their school is hit in a raid, the boys give forth with a rousing cheer, "Thank you, Adolf."

MPAA: Rated PG-13. There are some instances of coarse language, as well as some sexual incidents. Pauline, after her house has been destroyed and her mother killed in an air raid, allows all the young boys in Roger's gang to peer down the front of her panties. On a couple of occasions Bill watches as his sister Dawn and her boyfriend make love, once in the ruins of a bombed-out house and once in her bedroom, seen through the keyhole of her door.

I LIVE WITH ME DAD ★★★

Credits: VHS/1985/Australia/Colour/86 minutes
Director: Paul Moloney
Screenplay: Peter Pinney
Based on a short story by Derry Moran.
Cast: Rebecca Gibney [the Social Worker], Peter Hehir [Sid], Haydon Samuels [Chris]
Genre: A drama about a homeless man and his seven-year-old son living on the streets of Melbourne.
Plot: Sid (Hehir) is unable to hold down a job. An alcoholic, he is haunted by memories of his daughter who died in a house fire. He lives on the streets with his son Chris (Samuels), twin brother of the dead girl.

The local social worker (Gibney) threatens to take Chris from him and place the boy in care if Sid can't find work and a place to live. In order to support himself and keep Chris with him, Sid jumps at every opportunity to earn a few dollars.

When a bar buddy offers him twenty dollars to use Chris as a model for calendar photos, Sid readily agrees, realizing only just in time that the so-called friend is a boy-lover, and the photographer is producing kiddie-porn. This is but one of many adventures and misadventures on the road to the inevitable happy ending.
MPAA: Not rated. There is no sex portrayed on screen. The sex suggested by the episode involving the child pornographer is handled entirely off-screen: Sid comes into the studio while Chris is still being prepared for the shot. The boy is shirtless, but no sexual activity has yet taken place. It is suggested that a previous model, seen leaving the studio, has been molested. The young boy tells his waiting mother he never wants to go back there again.

IF ... ★★★★★

Credits: VHS/1969/Great Britain/ Colour and B&W/111 minutes
Director: Lindsay Anderson
Screenplay: David Sherwin
From the original script *Crusaders* by David Sherwin and John Howlett. This film also owes a great deal to the 1930 French film, *Zero de Conduite.*
Cast: Sean Bury [Jute], Geoffrey Chater [Chaplain], Arthur Lowe [Mr. Kemp], Mary MacLoed [Mrs. Kemp], Malcolm McDowell [Travis], Christine Noonan [the girl], Robert Swann [Rowntree], Hugh Thomas [Denson], Richard Warwick [Wallace], Mona Washbourne [Matron], Rupert Webster [Bobby Philips], David Wood [Knightly]
Genre: A violent black comedy which is a much acclaimed perennial favourite about teenage alienation and rebellion in a boarding school in England.
Plot: Travis (McDowell, in his first film), Wallace (Warwick) and Knightly (Wood) are seniors at College House. They are also rebels against the strict customs of the school. Against the world of Scums and Whips, of savage rituals and minute regulations. Their world is also a world of yearnings and dreams and frustrated desires, of sexual longings and philosophical musings, of salacious matrons and groping masters. A world where Whips cane their fellow students and senior students lust after the junior boys.

Travis, Wallace and Knightly declare "death to the oppressor" after one particularly savage caning. A series of further incidents and punishments involving the three rebels leads to the final, climactic carnage, leaving us with the question if ... .

David Sust and Marisa Paredes,
In A Glass Cage (1986)

Parts of this film were shot in colour and parts in black and white. Although much speculation has been raised about the artistic significance of this, Anderson himself has stated that it was strictly an economic decision. Money became short towards the end of the shooting schedule and he was forced to switch to black and white stock. As the film was not shot sequentially, the black and white segments are distributed throughout the film.

MPAA: Rated R. There is a great deal of sex talk in this film, both straight and gay: the rebels lust after centre-folds, the Whips, especially Rowntree (Swann), lust after Bobby Philips (Webster). Travis and the girl (Noonan) have a wild sexual fantasy in a road-side cafe. Wallace and Philips are lovers: Philips gazes longingly at Wallace working out in the gym, and later joins him in bed.

There is also a fair amount of nudity. Mrs. Kemp (MacLoed) is seen walking through the boys dorms while the students are absent on a military exercise. The girl and Travis make love in the cafe. Wallace, Travis, and Knightly are forced to take a cold shower as a disciplinary measure. A large number of extras are seen in the showers.

This shower scene was actually shot twice. In the version of the film released in the United States, the extras in the showers either have their backs to the camera, or towels around their waists. In the version of the film released in many other parts of the world, some of the boys are seen in full-frontal shots. I have seen a badly faded 35 mm print of this latter version in repertory theatres in Canada, but the VHS tape available from Paramount was mastered from the US version of the film.

IN A GLASS CAGE ★★★

(Also known as *Tras El Cristal*)

Credits: VHS/1986/Spain/Colour/110 minutes
In Spanish with English subtitles.
Writer/Director: Agustin Villaronga
Cast: Gisela Echevarria [Rena], Gunter Meisner [Klaus], Marisa Paredes [Griselda], David Sust [Angelo]
Genre: A dark, disturbing psycho-sexual thriller which examines the long term effects of systematic torture and abuse on a young boy.
Plot: As a young boy during World War II, Angelo (Sust) was subjected to physical and sexual abuse and torture at the hands of Klaus (Meisner). Klaus, a Josef Mengele-type figure, had spent the war years conducting experiments on young boys in the concentration camps. During these experiments he kept detailed accounts of his actions and the sexual arousal these acts produced. Now, years later, Angelo is out for revenge, but it is a revenge darkly coloured by his own descent into madness brought about by his treatment at the hands of Klaus.

Angelo tracks Klaus to the villa where he is now living in exile with his wife Griselda, (Paredes) and young daughter Rena, (Echevarria). Finding Klaus confined to an iron lung, Angelo insinuates himself into the household, hiring on as a nurse. He begins to isolate Klaus, killing Griselda, dismissing the maid and co-opting Rena.

Angelo's revenge then begins in earnest, but it is a revenge made more chilling by his own evident psychological and sexual involvement in what he is doing. And what vicious revenge it is. No simple bullet through the brain for Klaus. Angelo begins to act out the man's wartime diaries, taking Klaus's role as his own. He induces several young boys from the town to come into the house where he proceeds first to torture and then to murder them before the eyes of the captive Klaus.

MPAA: Not rated. This film has many disturbing scenes of torture, murder and the sexual abuse of children. The film opens with scenes of a nude boy, bound and hung from the ceiling by his hands, then being hit with a heavy board, then kissed and caressed by his torturer. The dialogue includes long passages of Angelo reading from Klaus's wartime diaries, describing the erotic stimulation he received when he killed young boys in the concentration camps.

THE INCREDIBLY TRUE ADVENTURE OF TWO GIRLS IN LOVE ★★★★

Credits: VHS/1995/USA/Colour/94 minutes
Writer/Director: Maria Maggenti
Cast: Sabrina Artel [Vicky], Stephanie Berry [Evelyn Roy], Dale Dickey [Fugina], John Elson [A.J.], Laurel Holloman [Randy Dean], Maggie Moore [Wendy], Nicole Parker [Evie Roy], Toby Poser [Lena], Nelson Rodriquez [Frank], Kate Stafford [Rebecca Dean]
Genre: A contemporary romantic drama which is undoubtedly the best American example yet of a very rare breed indeed, a lesbian coming of age story.
Plot: Randy Dean (Holloman), called by some a "diesel dyke," is a seventeen-year-old high school student living in "your typical lesbo household," which includes herself, her lesbian aunt (Stafford), and her aunt's lover.

She also works part-time in the family business, a service station. She has for some time been carrying on a relationship with Wendy (Moore), an older, married woman. Her life begins to change dramatically, however, the day a beautiful Afro-American girl drives in to have her car attended to.

Thus begins a beautiful love affair between Evie (Parker) and Randy. An affair which survives the inevitable harassment both girls face at school. Which

"It makes the big studios' romantic comedies look artificial and old hat. First love, straight or gay, has rarely been so expertly enacted." **David Ansen**, Newsweek

"Fresh & endearing, as much a coming-of-age story as a romantic comedy." **Jay Carr**, Boston Globe

Laurel Holloman and Nicole Parker, *The Incredibly True Adventure Of Two Girls In Love* (1995)

survives Wendy's jealousy, and her husbands violent outbursts. Which survives the recriminations from A.J. (Elson), Evie's old boy friend. Which survives Evie being abandoned by her erstwhile friends. Which survives even the shrieking outrage of Evie's mother (Berry) when she walks into a house awash in dirty dishes, empty bottles and leftover food to find Evie and Randy in bed together.

When the two girls escape to a motel room in order to find some breathing room, the entire cast assembles on their doorstep screaming mutual recriminations before the inevitable reconciliation.

MPAA: Rated R. Canadian Home Video Rated 14-A. The film is concerned entirely with lesbian themes. Randy

and Wendy share a passionate embrace and kiss early in the film. Holloman and Parker are both seen nude during a long, romantic lovemaking scene in Evie's bed. This involves bare breasts and bare buns but not full-frontal nudity.

THE INHERITORS ★★★

(Also known as *Die Erben*)

Credits: VHS/1985/Austria/Colour/89 minutes
In German with English subtitles.
Director: Walter Bannert
Screenplay: Walter Bannert and Erich Richter
Cast: Klaus Novak, Roger Schauer, Johanna Tomek, Nikolas Vogel [Thomas]
Awards: This film was featured at the 1984 Cannes Film Festival. Montreal World Film Festival: Jury Award for Best Cinematography.
Genre: A drama about sex, violence, politics and neo-Nazis among contemporary German teenagers.
Plot: As home life continues to deteriorate for Thomas (Vogel), a handsome, fresh-faced German schoolboy, he finds himself drawing closer and closer to the violent youth group attached to a Neo-Nazi political party.

Despite, or because of, opposition from his shrewish, insensitive mother, his seemingly uncaring father and his more liberal classmates, Thomas becomes deeply involved with the movement.

Eventually, after the suicide of his sensitive, musical and possibly gay brother, Thomas leaves home and leaves school. He becomes involved full-time in the youth group's violence, taking part in a summer of para-military training. Eventually, the violence reaches the stage where Thomas takes part in a murder committed for purely personal rather than political reasons.

MPAA: Not rated. Between bouts of violence, the teenagers in this film also find time to engage in a variety of sexual escapades: they seem to have a particular love for straight oral sex.

Much of the sex is choreographed to the music of Gustav Mahler. In the course of this sexual activity, several of the young actors, including Vogel, appear on screen nude. This is mostly rear shots, but includes some very brief full-frontal male scenes.

THE INKWELL ★★★★

Credits: VHS/1994/USA/Colour/112 minutes
Director: Matty Rich
Screenplay: Tom Ricostronza and Paris Qualles
Cast: Vanesa Bell Calloway [Frances Phillips], Morris Chestnut [Harold Lee], Suzanne Douglas [Brenda Tate], Adrienne-Joi Johnson [Heather Lee], Duane Martin [Jr. Phillips], Joe Morton [Kenny Tate], Jada Pinkett [Lauren Kelly], Phyllis Yvonne Stickney [Dr. Wade], Larenz Tate [Drew Tate], Glynn Turman [Spencer Phillips]
Genre: A romantic comedy about an Afro-American teenager who finds himself and love during a summer vacation spent on Martha's Vineyard. This film bears more than a passing similarity to *Summer Of '42*.
Plot: It's 1976. Sixteen-year-old Drew (Tate), a New York City kid who's father (Morton) is an ex-Black Panther, is none too thrilled about the prospect of spending any part of his summer vacation on Martha's Vineyard, a place he dismisses as nothing more than "a big pile of dirt and some salty water."

To make matters worse, they are going to spend the two weeks with wealthy, conservative relatives. His uncle (Turman) is a black Republican who constantly bates Drew's father. Drew also needs to work through some personal problems. His only friend is a rag doll named Iago. His personal transportation is a beat up tandem bicycle. He is still troubled about an accidental house fire he started. His parents are feuding. And he's a virgin.

Upon arrival on the island, cousin Junior (Martin) takes Drew in hand. Junior, however, is a loudmouthed jerk who pictures himself as the epitome of all that's cool. He also liberally dispenses advice on how Drew should cure the problem of his virginity. Drew, however, finds his own way to deal with the problem.

He first attracts the attention of Lauren (Pinkett), the most sought after girl in town. When she stands him up, he finds consolation in the arms and the bed of Heather (Johnson), a young woman whose husband has been cheating all over town.

MPAA: Rated R. This film includes a lot of sex talk, as well as a number of implied sexual situations. Nothing explicit is played out on-screen, however. The director has managed to avoid any on-screen nudity, even in a scene where Drew and Junior visit a nude beach with several friends.

JACK THE BEAR ★★★

Credits: VHS/1993/USA/Colour/98 minutes
Writer/Director: Marshall Herskovitz
Screenplay: Steven Zaillian. Novel by Dan McCall.
Cast: Danny DeVito [John Leary], Miko Hughes [Dylan], Andrea Marcovicci [Elizabeth Leary], Gary Sinise [Norman Strick], Robert J. Steinmiller, Jr. [Jack], Reese Witherspoon [Karen]
Genre: Drama about a single father trying to raise his two sons alone after the death of his wife.
Plot: John Leary (DeVito), is a man who won't grow up. Raising his sons Jack (Steinmiller) and Dylan (Hughes), coping is difficult for Leary, and twelve-year-old Jack is frequently left to care for his younger brother.

Jack, though in most ways more mature than his father, has problems of his own. Trying to understand the death of your mother is hard enough. Having your father little more than a big kid with a drinking problem only makes matters worse. And you still have all the normal twelve-year-old concerns like school, homework and how to survive that first date with Karen (Witherspoon).

Still, the Learys are a family and must hold together if they are to survive. This is tested by a series of incidents. First Dylan disappears, abducted by Norman (Sinise), a sinister Neo-Nazi racist living next door. Then, with dad once again out of work and drinking, Jack and Dylan are taken to live with grandparents. Finally, after Jack returns home, father and son must fend off an attack by Norman.

Inevitably, of course, the family is reunited, dad matures and Jack is able to just be a kid again, dealing with more typically twelve-year-old concerns.

MPAA: Rated PG-13. Rated for coarse language and violence. Jack and Karen share a kiss, and Dylan is seen a couple of times in his underwear, but there is no sex or nudity. After Dylan is found following his abduction, it is stated quite clearly that he was not molested.

JOSH AND S.A.M. ★★★★

Credits: VHS/1993/USA/Colour/97 minutes
Director: Billy Weber
Screenplay: Frank Deese
Cast: Joan Allen [Caroline], Sean Baca [Curtis Coleman], Maury Chaykin, Noah Fleiss [Sam], Ronald Guttman [Jean-Pierre], Jake Gyllenhaal [Leon Coleman], Udo Kier, Christ Penn [Derek Baxter], Martha Plimpton ["the Liberty Maid"], Jacob Tierney [Josh], Stephen Tobolowsky [Thom Whitney]
Genre: Although predictable in places, this comic road-movie adventure-tale for and about kids is a much better film than a short synopsis might lead you to believe.
Plot: Twelve-year-old Josh (Tierney) is a computer whiz-kid with an over-active imagination. His seven-year-old brother Sam (Fleiss) is a gullable misfit who is having problems at school. Both boys are having difficulty adjusting to their parents' divorce and pending re-marriages.

The boys are also at odds with each other. To complicate matters, mom (Allen) is in California and dad (Tobolowsky) is in Orlando. When the two boys fly to Florida to spend the last two weeks of their summer vacation with dad, their two stepbrothers Curtis (Baca) and Leon (Gyllenhaal) lead Josh to believe that dad thinks his son is gay because he isn't interested in sports.

Meanwhile, Josh has let Sam believe the younger boy is not a real boy at all, but a S.A.M., a Strategically Altered Mutant, destined to become a child warrior sent off to fight a war in Africa. A series of coincidences conspire to apparently confirm Josh's tall tale.

Already upset by his father's reported feelings towards him, when Josh believes he has killed Derek Baxter (Penn), a man they meet during a delay in Dallas on their return home to California, the two boys take off.

Sam believes they are headed up the Underground Roadway to Canada and freedom for himself. A long series of comic adventures ensues, during which they meet The Liberty Maid (Plimpton), the girl who is to drive them to the border and Sam's emancipation from his fate as a killer S.A.M. They do reach the city of Calgary, but their stay is short before their eventual reconciliation with their father and each other.

MPAA: Rated PG-13. This rating was earned for some minor coarse language and violence. Although Josh and The Liberty Maid share the same bed in a motel room, there is no indication that this scene is supposed to suggest a sexual relationship developing between them.

JUST ONE OF THE GUYS ★★

Credits: VHS/1985/USA/Colour/100 minutes
Director: Lisa Gottlieb
Screenplay: Dennis Feldman and Jeff Franklin
Cast: Stuart Charno [Reptile], Sherilyn Fenn [Sandy], Toni Hudson [Denise], Joyce Hyser [Terry], Billy Jacoby

[Buddy], Leigh McCloskey [Kevin], Clayton Rohner [Rick], William Zabka [Greg]

Genre: A teen comedy about gender roles.

Plot: When Terry (Hyser), a high school senior doesn't win a student journalism contest, she blames it on the teacher's gender bias. To prove her point, she changes schools. Borrowing clothes from her fifteen-year-old brother Buddy (Jacoby), she masquerades as a boy and re-enters the contest under her new persona.

The producers of the film get a great deal of fairly puerile comedic mileage from the problems caused by Terry's cross-dressing masquerade: how to deal with school washrooms, how to deal with gym class, jock straps, locker rooms, group showers and so on. Better handled are the romantic entanglements.

At her new school, Terry finds herself romantically drawn to a shy, handsome loner named Rick (Rohner) who begins to suspect that Terry is gay. At the same time Terry discovers that Sandy (Fenn), among several other girls at her new school, is coming on to her. Meanwhile, her boyfriend Kevin (McCloskey), an antediluvian chauvinist jerk who doesn't know about her cross dressing venture is on the verge of dropping her because she has cut her hair and is pursuing career goals. She must also contend with the school bully Greg (Zabka), a stereotypical muscle-bound jock.

As I have already suggested, this film suffers from too many stereotypes. Too many stereotypes lead to too many predictable situations. This is unfortunate, because the idea behind the film is a good one and the social realities that lead to Terry's cross-dressing charade are serious ones and deserve better than they are given here.

MPAA: Rated PG-13. There is some incidental male nudity and partial nudity in locker room scenes: boys wearing jock straps and boys in a very steamy shower. There is one topless scene when Terry opens her shirt to prove to Rick that she really is a girl. There is a lot of sexual talk and innuendo, particularly from Buddy, who does eventually find himself in bed with Sandy.

KES ★★★★

Credits: VHS/1970/Great Britain/Colour/113 minutes
Director: Kenneth Loach
Screenplay: Barry Hines, Kenneth Loach, Tony Garnett
Based on the novel *Kestrel For A Knave* by Barry Hines.
Cast: Bob Bowes [Mr. Gryce], David Bradley [Billy],
Fredde Fletcher [Jud], Brian Glover [Mr. Sugden], Lynne
Perrie [Mrs. Casper], Colin Welland [Mr. Farthing]
Genre: A drama about a young teenager with no
prospects who finds temporary relief from his dreary, unin-
spiring school, family and community through the train-
ing of a young kestrel (hawk).
Plot: Thirteen-year-old Billy Casper (Bradley) is a boy with few options in life. Already he has a police record for "nick-ing" goods from local shops. Even without his record he would be marked as a boy going nowhere. He has the reputation of the housing estate to live down. He must endure almost daily abuse, both physi-cal and psychological, from his brother Jud (Fletcher), from his teachers and from the news agents he delivers papers for.

Leo Fitzpatrick (upper right), Justin Pierce (lower left)
and Chloe Sevigny (lower right), *Kids* (1996)

Mum (Perrie) is little help. She has little money and though she obviously cares about her younger son, she seems at times to be totally at sea when it comes to parenting.

Approaching school-leaving age, Billy's options are severely limited. Despite his passionate proclamation that "I'll not go down t'pit," the town of Barnsley's only industry, coal mining, seems certain to be his fate.

The only bright spot in Billy's life is Kes, the young kestrel he finds on a local farm. With the aid of a book he nicks from a local shop, Billy carefully, patiently, lovingly trains the young hawk. His skills with the bird, and his evident love for her are the inspiration for Billy's longest and most coherent speech in the whole film. They also bring him an unexpected bonus: unrestrained respect from

a teacher. For one brief moment the boy is able to climb out of his dreary surroundings. But not for long, for tragedy is about to strike.

This is the first feature film from acclaimed British director Kenneth Loach. As in so many of his later films chronicling the lives of working class Britons, most of the actors in Kes are residents of the area where the filming occurred. A consequence of this is the use of the local dialect. Unlike some of Loach's later films, Kes has not been subtitled for North American audiences. As a result, the south Yorkshire dialect may require some careful attention, especially at first. Kes benefits greatly from the superb photography of Chris Menges who later di-rected *Criss-Cross* and *Second Best*.

MPAA: Not rated. Frequent coarse language. There is frequent violence directed against Billy and the other boys in his neighbourhood. Bradley is seen nude several times in the school locker rooms and showers. For the most part these are bare butt shots, but there is brief frontal exposure in one scene when he climbs over the shower wall to escape from a cold shower being administered by a sadistic gym teacher.

KIDS ★★★★

Credits: VHS/1996/USA/ Colour/91 minutes
Director: Larry Clark
Screenplay: Harmony Korine
Cast: Leo Fitzpatrick [Telly], Justin Pierce [Casper],
Chloe Sevigny [Jenny]
Awards: Independent Spirit Awards 1996: Debut
Performance (Pierce).
Genre: A gritty, hard-biting, rough-edged drama with the look and feel of a documentary, about teenage sex, sexuality and AIDS.

Cameron Boyd and Jesse Bradford, *King Of The Hill* (1993)

Plot: Kids is a first-time directing effort from Clark, who is better known for his still photography about life at the edge. If you are familiar with Clark's photography, this film may surprise you. Although the subject matter may be familiar, the imagery is, I feel, much more subdued and much less explicit than one would have expected from Clark.

Clark's cameras track Telly (Fitzpatrick) and Casper (Pierce), a couple of bored, directionless New York City teens, for a single day. From the opening scene where Telly talks a reluctant fourteen-year-old girl into losing her virginity, to the closing one, where Casper rapes a drugged out Jenny (Sevigny), a day in the life of these boys revolves around sex. Talking about it, doing it or just thinking about it. The only things to vary the routine are drugs and casual, random violence.

Interwoven with the boys' sexual bragging is the girls' point of view, especially that of Jenny who has just been diagnosed HIV+. The infection has undoubtedly been picked up from Telly, her only previous sexual partner. Telly, ignorant of his own infection, sees no reason to change his behaviour.

MPAA: Not rated. Canadian Home Video rated 18-A.

Originally given an NC-17 rating by the MPAA, this film was released unrated instead. Despite all of the sexual goings on, there is very little nudity in this film. Even a late night skinny-dipping party somehow doesn't quite make it to screen. Almost the only bare skin we see is Fitzpatrick's buns as Telly has sex with the reluctant fourteen-year-old.

KING OF THE HILL ★★★★★

Credits: VHS/1993/USA/Colour/103 minutes
Writer/Director: Steven Soderbergh
Based on the memoirs of A. E. Hochner
Cast: Karen Allen [Miss Mathet], Amber Benson [Ella McShane], Cameron Boyd [Sullivan], Jesse Bradford [Aaron Kurlander], Adrien Brody [Lester], Joseph Chrest [Ben], Lisa Eichhorn [Mrs. Kurlander], Spalding Gray [Mr. Mungo], Jeroen Krabbe [Mr. Kurlander], Elizabeth McGovern [Lydia]
Genre: A drama about poverty, children who must fend for themselves and the importance of family ties set in St. Louis in the midst of the Great Depression.
Plot: Aaron (Bradford, in an exceptional performance) is

a gifted twelve-year-old attending school in a wealthy neighbourhood despite living in a seedy, run-down hotel with his parents (Eichhorn and Krabbe) and younger brother Sullivan (Boyd).

Dad is struggling to survive as a salesman. Mom is ill and must be sent to a sanitarium. Sullivan is sent to live with relatives. Aaron resorts to telling ever more fantastic tales about his family to hide the truth of his poverty from his well-fixed, well-fed classmates. Notwithstanding Aaron's tales, they still look down on him as a charity case.

When dad gets a new job on the road, Aaron is left to cope on his own, virtually abandoned. When all dad's schemes for providing for Aaron during his absence fall through, the boy must survive by his own wits. This process becomes more difficult when his own money-making ideas come to naught and the hotel prepares to evict the Kurlanders for non-payment of rent.

His running battle with hotel security in the form of Ben (Chrest) accelerates and his allies gradually disappear. Ella (Benson), the epileptic girl next door moves out. Lester (Brody), the older youth down the hall is arrested. the old man across the hall reaches the end of his financial tether and commits suicide.

Aaron has no money and no food and can't leave the room even to pee for fear Ben will padlock the door. He is reduced at one point to serving himself a meal of cut outs from magazine illustrations. Perseverance and dogged determination pay off in the end, however, when dad gets a new, steady, government job and the family can move into a good apartment. Aaron even manages to sneak his most prized possessions out of the hotel right beneath the nose of the ever vigilant Ben.

While Aaron is left to fend for himself, he must also deal with the first stirrings of sexual awareness. The girls at school are eyeing him. Ella, the epileptic girl next door, introduces him to the pleasures of the dance. She even rewards him with his first kiss. And what exactly is the old man across the hall doing with beautiful young Lydia (McGovern)

MPAA: Rated PG-13. This rating is a result of occasional mild cursing and the suicide scene.

Jesse Bradford, *King Of The Hill* (1993)

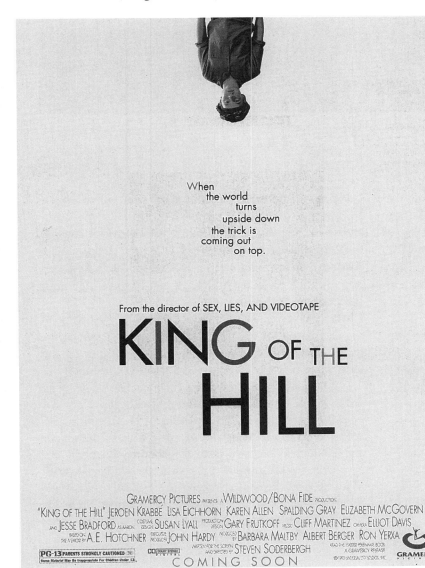

When the world turns upside down the trick is coming out on top.

From the director of SEX, LIES, AND VIDEOTAPE

KING OF THE HILL

GRAMERCY PICTURES PRESENTS A WILDWOOD/BONA FIDE PRODUCTION "KING OF THE HILL" JEROEN KRABBÉ LISA EICHHORN KAREN ALLEN SPALDING GRAY ELIZABETH McGOVERN AND JESSE BRADFORD AS AARON COSTUME DESIGN SUSAN LYALL PRODUCTION DESIGN GARY FRUTKOFF MUSIC CLIFF MARTINEZ CAMERA ELLIOT DAVIS BASED ON THE MEMOIR BY A.E. HOTCHNER EXECUTIVE PRODUCER JOHN HARDY PRODUCED BY BARBARA MALTBY ALBERT BERGER RON YERXA WRITTEN FOR THE SCREEN AND DIRECTED BY STEVEN SODERBERGH READ THE HARPER PERENNIAL BOOK A GRAMERCY RELEASE

PG-13 PARENTS STRONGLY CAUTIONED Some Material May Be Inappropriate For Children Under 13. DOLBY STEREO DIGITAL

COMING SOON

GRAMERCY PICTURES

KIPPERBANG ★★★★

(Also known as *P'tang, Yang, Kipperbang*)

Credits: VHS/1982/Great Britain/Colour/85 minutes

Director: Michael Apted

Screenplay: Jack Rosenthal

Cast: John Albasiny [Alan Duckworth], Mark Brailsford [Abbo], Garry Cooper [Tommy], Abigail Cruttenden [Ann], Maurice Dee [Jeffrey Whitaker], Chris Karallis [Shaz], Frances Ruffelle [Eunice], Alison Steadman [Estelle Land], Robert Urquhart [Headmaster]

Genre: A nostalgic comedy about young English teenagers shortly after World War II.

Plot: Fourteen-year-old Alan Duckworth (Albasiny), known to his friends as Quack Quack, has three obsessions: world peace, the England - Australia Test Match, and sex. Well, maybe not sex so much as a desire to kiss Ann (Cruttenden), the most beautiful girl in school.

Lying in bed in the morning, daydreaming in class, walking home from school, just before he goes to sleep at night, the desire to kiss Ann is ever present. And the prayers are

Edwin Mahinda and Ronald Pirie, *The Kitchen Toto* (1987)

constant. Please, God, if not tomorrow, at least before the end of term. Unfortunately, Ann has her eyes on Jeffrey Whitaker (Dee), and Alan is the class nerd: the girls forget to even put his name forward when they vote on the dishiest boy in class.

Alan finally gets his big chance when he is chosen to star in the school play. His part calls for him to kiss Ann. Can he actually do it … ?

Originally made for British television, Kipperbang was released theatrically in North America in 1984.

MPAA: Rated PG. Alan and his friends seem always to have sex on their minds. They talk about it constantly. For most of the boys, it's all just talk: the most action they ever get is lining up in class for a chance to rub up against the breasts of one of the girls.

THE KITCHEN TOTO ★★★★

Credits: VHS/1987/Great Britain/Colour/96 minutes
Writer/Director: Harry Hook
Cast: Phyllis Logan [Janet Graham], Edwin Mahinda [Mwangi], Bob Peck [John Graham, the police chief], Ronald Pirie [Edward]
Awards: The Evening Standard British Film Awards 1987: Best Newcomer (Hook).
Genre: An involving drama of choices, racial tensions and loyalties set against the backdrop of the struggle for independence in Kenya in the 1950s.
Plot: Twelve-year-old Mwangi (Mahinda), after witnessing the murder of his father, a Christian preacher, at the hands of Kikuyu freedom fighters, goes to work for the local white police chief (Peck) as the new kitchen toto.

While working for the police chief and his disapproving wife (Logan), the serving boy eventually befriends his employer's young son, Edward (Pirie). The two boys become companions, though never close friends: the master and servant relationship is never forgotten by either boy.

Forced by the freedom fighters to take the Thenge Oath of loyalty and obedience, Mwangi is eventually must make a choice. Does he kill the police officer, as demanded by his tribesmen? Or does he side with the family which has given him employment and shelter?

Writer/director Harry Hook grew up in Kenya during the 1950s, the time frame for this film.

MPAA: Rated PG-13. Edwin Mahinda appears nude, including full-frontal exposure, in an early scene. When Mwangi is first given employment, the police chief's insensitive wife submits the boy to a bath while he stands naked on the lawn in front of the house, watched by a boorish, sniggering Edward.

Timothy Bottoms and Eileen Brennan, *The Last Picture Show* (1971)

LAKKI, THE BOY WHO GREW WINGS ★★★★

(Also known as *Lakki - Gutten Som Kunne Fly*, and as *Lakki - The Boy Who Could Fly*)

Credits: VHS/1992/Norway/Colour/104 minutes
In Norwegian with English subtitles.
Writer/Director: Svend Wam
Based on a novel by Per Knutsen.
Cast: Anders Borchgrevink [Lakki], Nina Gunke, Gabriel Paaske, Bjorn Skagestad
Awards: Giffoni Film Festival 1992: Best Picture.
Genre: A drama about a deeply troubled teenager trying to deal with a multitude of personal and family problems.

Plot: Lakki (Borchgrevink) is a young teenager with many problems and few real friends. His parents are divorced. His mother has had a succession of lovers. Her latest is Lakki's gym teacher, a man who has physically assaulted Lakki in the locker room at school.

His father has a pregnant live-in girlfriend who doesn't get along with the boy. In fact, she forbids his presence in her home. Neither parent has time to spend with their son.

Lakki hasn't yet come to terms with his parent's divorce, blaming himself in part for their separation. He has frequent flashbacks to his childhood and the happier days when they were a family. He may also be struggling with his own sexual identity. Certainly he has an almost phobic reaction to being touched.

In the course of the film his only sexual experience is with an older man, a scripture quoting fanatic who puts the make on Lakki before brutalizing the boy. Lakki retaliates by beating the man senseless with a bicycle chain. As if this were not enough, strange scars on his back appear to be growing into a pair of fully feathered wings. Or are they? Is this actually happening or is it just an hallucination? An escape from the darkness which seems to surround him?

MPAA: Not rated. The film includes a great deal of physical violence, some of it directed at Lakki, some of it perpetrated by him. There is also a lot of male nudity, including full-frontal shots of a very young Lakki getting out of a bathtub and an adult running down a hall.

The teenage Lakki, Borchgrevink, has numerous nude and partially nude scenes, all of them rear shots or obscured frontal shots. In addition to discussions of sexual matters, the young Lakki watches his parents make love. The teenage Lakki is seen being sexually assaulted by an older man. He appears to masturbate in one scene while thinking of his childhood. There are also scenes of drug use.

LAMB ★★★

Credits: VHS/1985/Ireland/Colour/110 minutes
Director: Colin Gregg
Screenplay: Bernard MacLaverty, based on his novel.
Cast: Ian Bannen [Brother Benedict], Ian McElhinney [Maguire], Liam Neeson [Michael Lamb (Brother Sebastian)], Hugh O'Connor [Owen Kane], Dudley Sutton [Haddock], Frances Tomelty [Mrs. Kane]
Genre: Drama about a Catholic priest and member of an Irish teaching order, on the run with an abused ten-year-old student.
Plot: Owen Kane (O'Connor), is an abused ten-year-old boy brought to St. Kiaran's school, a residential treatment centre for boys, by his mother (Tomelty) when she feels unable to deal with his problems.

At the centre he is befriended by Brother Sebastian, also known as Michael Lamb (Neeson). The only truly sympathetic brother on the staff, Lamb is not without problems of his own. His father is dying and he is tormented by spiritual doubts.

Brother Benedict (Bannen), the head of the facility, beats Owen for graffiti he knows the boy probably didn't write. He justifies his actions by saying that somebody had to be punished, so it might just as well be Owen. Shortly after this occurs, Lamb and the boy run away together. Using an advance of the money coming to Lamb from his

father's will, the two head to England posing as father and son. At first it seems more like a holiday, and Owen soon comes to love the man who is the closest thing to a father he has ever had.

Inevitably, however, problems set in. Michael can't get work. His money is running out. Furthermore, the Irish authorities are looking for them, charging Lamb with kidnapping the boy and misappropriation of school funds. As well, the medication Owen needs to control his epilepsy is running out. Even though they leave hotels behind and move into a London squat with several gay men, money is almost at an end with no safe way to obtain more. The decision is made to return to Ireland where Lamb sets in motion a tragic plan ironically founded on his love for the boy which is to end forever the abuse that has been Owen's lot in life.

Although this film probably stretches the definition of a coming of age story, the relationship which develops between man and boy while they are together in London warrants its inclusion in this book, despite the ending of the story.

MPAA: Not rated. Lamb is clearly worried at one point about the possibility that Haddock (Sutton), one of the gay residents of the London squat, may have designs on Owen, especially when the Irishman comes home to find the two of them alone together, the boy smoking a joint. However, nothing sexual actually occurs in the film. The violence directed towards the boy is all implied or spoken of rather than shown.

LANDSCAPE IN THE MIST ★★★★

(Also known as *Topio Stin Omichli*)

Credits: VHS/1988/Greece, France, Italy/Colour/126 minutes
In Greek with English subtitles.
Director: Theo Angelopoulos
Screenplay: Thanassis Valtinos, Tonino Guerra and Theo Angelopoulos
Cast: Alika Georgouli, Eva Kotamanidou, Tania Palaiologou, Stratos Tzortzoglou (Orestes), Michalis Zeke
Genre: A haunting, mystical, at times surreal drama about two young children on the run through Greece in search of their father.
Plot: Thirteen-year-old Voula and her seven-year-old brother Alexander, having heard many times from their mother (who wanted the children to have something to dream about) that their father is living in Germany, take off one wet winter night in search for the man.

On foot, hitchhiking and jumping trains they gradually work their way north towards the Germany of their dreams. As they journey northwards they pass through a succession of events and landscapes in turn harsh and real, mythical, mystical and surreal.

As the two children search for their father, they encounter a succession of men who might be father figures for them, even if only temporarily. Each of these chance encounters, however, leaves something to be desired. Their

motorcycle, but he is about to begin his military service. Besides, he is gay. In the end, they are left only with the never met, almost mythic father in far off Germany.

MPAA: Not rated. There is one scene, which plays out off camera, during which Voula is raped by a truck driver who has picked up the children by the side of the highway. It gradually becomes evident during a scene in a night club that in all likelihood Orestes is gay, though the whole question is very skillfully downplayed. He is gay, and the discovery seems to upset Voula, but he is also the one man they meet who is genuinely out to help them.

THE LAST PICTURE SHOW
★★★★★

Credits: VHS/1971/USA/Black and White/118 minutes
Director: Peter Bogdanovich
Screenplay: Larry McMurtry and Peter Bogdanovich
Based on the novel by Larry McMurtry.
Cast: Sam Bottoms [Billy], Timothy Bottoms [Sonny Crawford], Eileen Brennan [Genevieve], Jeff Bridges [Duane Jackson], Gary Brockette [Bobby Sheen], Ellen Burstyn [Lois Farrow], Barc Doyle [Joe Bob Blanton], Clu Gulager [Abilene], Kimberly Hyde [Annie-Annie Martin], Ben Johnson [Sam the Lion], Cloris Leachman [Ruth Popper], Cybill Shepherd [Jacy Farrow], Randy Quaid [Lester Marlow], Sharon Taggart [Charlene Duggs]
Awards: Academy Awards 1971: Best Supporting Actor (Johnson); Best Supporting Actress (Leachman); (nomination) Best Supporting Actor (Bridges); (nomination) Best Supporting Actress (Burstyn); (nomination) Best Picture; (nomination) Best Director; (nomination) Best Adapted Screenplay; (nomination) Best Cinematography. Golden Globe Awards 1972: Best Supporting Actor (Johnson). New York Film Critics Awards 1971: Best Screenplay; Best Supporting Actor (Johnson): Best Supporting Actress

Timothy Bottoms and Jeff Bridges, *The Last Picture Show* (1971)

uncle washes his hands of them, saying he doesn't want to get involved. A truck driver picks them up, then rapes Voula. A restaurant owner feeds Alexander, but only after the boy has cleaned every table in the place. The youngest member of an acting troupe, Orestes (Tzortzoglou), gives them shelter and a lift in the troupe's bus and on his

(Burstyn). National Board Of Review Awards 1971: Ten best films of the year; Best Supporting Actor (Johnson); Best Supporting Actress (Leachman). National Society Of Film Critics Awards 1971: Best Supporting Actress (Burstyn).

Genre: A slice-of-life drama about growing up in a small north Texas town in the early 1950s.

Plot: In a bleak, dusty, wind-swept town near Wichita Falls, Sonny (Timothy Bottoms) and Duane (Bridges) and their friends come face to face with the realities of their fading community. It is a community where teenagers pair off, not for love but because there is nobody else. It is a community where everybody knows everybody else and knows exactly what everybody else is doing at any minute of any day.

When Duane and Jacy (Shepherd) book into a motel room together, their friends are waiting outside to hear the details. When Sonny and Ruth Popper (Leachman), the emotionally unstable wife of Sonny's football coach, have an affair, the whole town knows. When the boys pool their funds to hire a prostitute to initiate Billy (Sam Bottoms), a mute teenager with an obsession for sweeping, it doesn't take long for the entire community to know. When the preacher's son Joe Bob Blanton (Doyle) abducts a little girl, half the town has assembled before he reaches the town jail.

Bogdanovich has managed in this film, which is visually enhanced by stark black and white photography, to capture in exquisite detail the bleakness of a dying town and the end of innocence for the main characters. "This really is the epitome of what a coming of age story is all about. Characters one cares about facing up to the harsh truths of the adult world in a story which gives the audience some greater insight into the world of youth as they come face to face with the realities of work, adult life, love, friendship, sexuality and death."

MPAA: Rated R. The film includes a number of scenes of sexual activity: Sonny and Charlene making out in the front seat of a pickup truck; Duane and Jacy in the pickup; Billy and a prostitute in the back seat of a car; Duane and Jacy in a motel room; Sonny and Ruth Popper in her bedroom.

There are also a number of nude scenes, the most significant being a skinny-dipping sequence in an indoor pool. In this scene both Brockette and Hyde appear in full-frontal nude shots. Several others performers, mostly unnamed, also appear in side and rear shots in this sequence. Shepherd is seen topless in this scene as Jacy undresses on the diving board as part of her initiation. Sharon Taggart also has a topless scene and Sam Bottoms has a brief bare butt scene as he gets dressed after his session with the prostitute.

THE LAST PROSTITUTE ★★★

Credits: VHS/1991/USA/Colour/93 minutes
Director: Lou Antonio
Screenplay: Carmen Culver
Based on the play by William Borden.
Cast: Sonia Braga [Loah], David Kaufman [Bert], Dennis Letts [Mr. Hancock], Dru Mouser [Carol Ann], Cotter Smith [Joe], Woody Watson [Raleigh], Wil Wheaton [Danny]

Chris Furrh (right), *Lord Of The Flies* (1990)

Genre: A made for cable drama about a teenage boy who, over the course of a summer, learns about the human and personal side of a former prostitute, seeing beyond her past to the individual inside.

Plot: It's summer time. Kennedy is president. Danny (Wheaton) and Bert (Kaufman) are heading off to summer camp. Well, that's what they tell their parents. In fact, they are about to hit the road in search of a legend.

The legend is Loah (Braga) and according to Danny's late uncle Charlie she's the best in the world. The best prostitute, that is. Being randy teenagers, Danny and Bert are eager to lose their virginity. How better to do so than with the best in the world?

When they track down Loah in a small Texas town, however, they find she has retired to a respectable life of breeding horses. Arriving on her doorstep broke, having lost all their money along the road, the two boys reluctantly accept employment on Loah's farm for the duration of the breeding season. While living on her farm and watching Loah's interactions with her neighbours, Danny gradually comes to see her as a real person. Bert, on the other hand, never gains any insight into her character; never sees her as anything other than a hooker who ought to put out for him. When she won't, he takes it upon himself to destroy her by revealing her past to the man she loves.

MPAA: Rated PG-13. As might be expected in a PG-13 rated film originally made for cable TV, other than a lot of talk, the sex is merely hinted at, and Wil Wheaton's shower scene only suggests that he might be nude.

THE LEATHER BOYS ★★★

Credits: VHS/1963/Great Britain/B&W/103 minutes
Director: Sidney J. Furie
Screenplay: Gillian Freeman
Based on the novel by Eliot George.
Cast: Johnny Briggs [the boyfriend], Colin Campbell [Reggie], Gladys Henson [Gran], Dudley Sutton [Pete], Rita Tushingham [Dot]
Genre: Drama about a teenaged couple whose marriage is on a shaky footing trying to come to terms with their lives.
Plot: Something of a cult classic, the themes which put this film on the fringe when first produced now seem far less shocking.

Dot (Tushingham), a fifteen-year-old English school girl, is floating on cloud nine. She's engaged and about to marry her teenage boyfriend Reggie (Campbell), a motorcycle mechanic. Reggie is as eager for the wedding as Dot, despite the obvious problems the couple will face with finances and accommodation.

What neither teenager expects is to encounter sexual problems. However, after the church wedding and a honeymoon at Butlin's Holiday Camp, sexual difficulties set in almost immediately. Reggie may be as eager as ever, but now that it's legal, the excitement seems to have gone for Dot. She complains, in fact, that sex is all Reggie ever seems to want and seems set on becoming a frumpy middle-aged housewife before her eighteenth birthday.

Six months after the wedding they are fighting like cats and dogs and are soon separated.

Reggie moves into a spare bedroom at the home of his grandmother (Henson). Here he shares space and a bed with his best buddy Pete (Sutton). Several attempts at reconciliation, including a faked pregnancy by Dot, fail to get the couple back together again.

Meanwhile Pete has persuaded Reggie to join him in looking for work at sea, an idea which the latter agrees to after finding another guy in Dot's bed. However, even going to sea turns out to be a letdown for Reggie. Instead of heading off to New York or Australia, the only ship hiring is a coastal freighter headed no further than Cardiff and the thought of working on board ship with Pete quickly loses its appeal for Reggie when he comes to the sudden realization that Dot's accusation that he and Pete "look like a couple of queers" is indubitably correct.

MPAA: Not rated. Although the film revolves around questions of sexual behaviour, sexual orientation and sexual frustrations, there is no on-screen sex. Even Pete's homosexuality, while obvious by the end of the film, is neither shown nor spoken of but left to be implied by the scenes in the gay bar.

LEMON POPSICLE ★★★

Credits: 1978/Israel/Colour/100 minutes
Dubbed in English.
Director: Boaz Davidson
Screenplay: Boaz Davidson and Eli Tabor
Cast: Anat Atzmon [Nili/Nicki], Yiftach Katzur [Benz/Benjie], Zachi Noy [Yudelah/Hughie], Jonathan Segal [Momo/Bobby], Ophella Shtrel [Stella]
Genre: A teenage comedy about three boys desperate to lose their virginity which also manages to deal with the serious questions of personal relationships, teenage pregnancy and abortion.
Plot: I have seen this film on video tape, but not in North America. The tape I saw had been dubbed in English (with Korean subtitles!) and Americanized as well: the names of the principal characters had been changed, the kids spend their summer at camp rather than a kibbutz and they attend Roosevelt High School.

The story follows three Tel Aviv high school boys during the summer of 1960 as they desperately try to find ways to "lose it" before school lets out for the summer.

Bobby (Segal) is the good-looking boy who is essentially shallow and unfeeling. Hughie (Noy) is the fat kid who thinks he's a lady killer. Benjie (Katzur) is the shy, romantic boy who falls deeply in love. Together they search for ways to lose their virginity, either with Stella

(Shtrel), the sex-starved wife of an absent sailor or with a cheap prostitute who gives all three boys a severe case of crabs. As well, all three boys fall madly in love with Nicki (Atzmon). She, however, has her eye on Bobby. The minute she gets pregnant, however, he drops her, leaving Benjie to pick up the pieces when the rest of the boys go off to the kibbutz for the summer. Seriously in love with Nicki, Benjie arranges an abortion and helps her to get her life in order again, only to be devastated when she returns to Bobby's arms the moment he returns home.

The three principal characters in this film bear more than a passing resemblance to the three principals in the earlier American film *Summer of '42*. This film was the first of seven films in the *Lemon Popsicle* series made in Israel by Davidson. This is the only one I have come across and so far I have not found it in North America.

The same director essentially remade this film for the American market in 1982 as *The Last American Virgin*. Despite the bad dubbing, I think *Lemon Popsicle* is by far the better film.

MPAA: Not rated: Several sexual encounters occur during the film, involving one or the other of the three boys with either Stella, the prostitute or Nicki. The film also tries to deal with questions of teenage pregnancy, illegal abortions and sexually transmitted diseases. Benjie is seen in a bare buns shot when he is with the prostitute. As well several extras bare their buns in a school locker room when a group of boys line up to measure up their assets.

LEOLO ★★★★

Credits: VHS/1992/Canada, France/Colour/115 minutes In French with English subtitles. Also available dubbed, and in a hybrid version with dubbed narration but with the dialogue in French with English subtitles.

Writer/Director: Jean-Claude Lauzon

Cast: Roland Blouin [the father], Pierre Bourgault [the Word Tamer], Eric Cadorette [Buddy Godin], Maxime Collin [Leo], Giuditta Del Vecchio [Bianca], Julien Guiomar [the grandfather], Yves Montmarquette [Fernand], Alex Nadeau [Fernand, age 16], Ginette Reno [the mother], Genevieve Samson [Rita]

Awards: Cannes Film Festival 1992: (nomination) Best Film. Genie Awards (Canada) 1992: Best Costume Design; Best Film Editing; Best Original Screenplay.

Genre: A haunting black comedy about a gifted twelve-year old boy growing up in a very pedestrian and highly dysfunctional blue collar family.

Plot: In a working class neighbourhood in Montreal in the 1950s, Leo Lozeau (Collin) inhabits a world where dividing lines are blurred, where dichotomies converge. It becomes increasingly difficult for the boy and the viewer to differentiate between health and sickness, between fantasy and reality, between fact and fiction, between love and hate, between sanity and madness, between strength and weakness, between past, present and future.

Because his father (Blouin) is crazy and Leo is not, the boy dreams of an alternate sire: an Italian peasant and a contaminated tomato.

He is not Leo Lozeau, the boy declares, but rather Leolo Lozone. But sanity is hard to define in Leo's world. His father is obsessed with laxatives and shit. His brother Fernand (Nadeau, later Montmarquette) is obsessed with building up his body so he will no longer fear the local Anglo tough. His grandfather (Guiomar) is obsessed with Bianca (Del Vecchio), the same teenage girl Leo is obsessed with. His sister Rita (Samson) presides over a netherworld of insects and reptiles in the cellar of their apartment building and for a fee consumes Leo's share of the weekly laxatives.

In and out of Leo's world wanders the Word Tamer (Bourgault), gathering old photographs and letters from trash bins. In his searches, he finds discarded pages of Leo's journal where the boy has recorded his passage through life, his dreams, his fantasies, and his family's gradual slide into madness.

MPAA: Rated R. Canadian Home Video rated 14-A. There are several instances of nudity: Bianca appears topless while assisting the grandfather in his bath; the grandfather is seen nude when Leo attempts to murder him; Leo appears nude in the closing moments of the film, lying in a tub surrounded by ice cubes in the psychiatric hospital.

There are several scenes of sexual activity. Leo and another boy are seen fondling and being fondled by a teenage girl. Twelve-year-old Buddy Godin (Cadorette), a boy who "will fuck anything that moves," is seen in the infamous cat sequence while the narrator tells us the boy regularly prostitutes himself with his hockey coach.

Leo masturbates several times. (You may never look at liver in quite the same way ever again.) Befitting the father's obsession with defecation, there are also frequent scenes of people sitting on the toilet.

LESSONS AT THE END OF SPRING ★★★★

Credits: VHS/1989/USSR/Colour/75 minutes In Russian with English subtitles.

Writer/Director: Oleg Kavan

Cast: Alexandr Feklistov [the teacher], Yuri Mazhuga [Lvovskiy], Yuri Nazarov [Vasiliek], Danya Tolkachev [Vadim the boy]

Genre: A drama set in the USSR during the Khrushchev era about a young teenager wrongly incarcerated as a

Lord Of The Flies (1990)

political prisoner whose youthful optimism and indomitable spirit serve to keep him sane while the adults around him slowly sink into madness and despair.

Plot: On his way to attend the cinema on a spring afternoon, eighth-grader Vadim Nikolayevich (Tolkachev) is picked up by the police. Accused of having taken part in a political demonstration, he is thrown into a prison where he is the youngest inmate.

Vadim is placed in a cell with three adults, Lvovskiy (Mazhuga), Vasiliek (Nazarov) and the teacher (Feklistov). Like Vadim, the three men are all political detainees who consider themselves more fortunate than, and above the level of the mere criminals in the same prison. Each one is viewed with disdain by the others and suspected of being an informant.

Throughout his ordeal, Vadim never gives up hope that he will be released. He never seriously wavers in his protestations of innocence, regardless of the psychological pressure placed on him by the prison authorities to sign a false confession.

When he is finally released, he returns home full of recriminations. His mother never answered his letters. She

did not work hard enough to have him released. She, on her part, claims to have had no idea where he was. Thinking he was a runaway, she had instituted a missing persons search. When the truth becomes clear, Vadim vows never to forget his treatment or the lies he was told by the prison authorities.

MPAA: Not rated. Being a boy in an adult prison, during his incarceration Vadim is subjected to frequent sexually suggestive comments and leers from the adults. While showering, one heavily tattooed man stands and openly stares at the boy's nude body.

The prison barber and bath attendant openly makes a pass at the boy's genitals while Vadim is standing being brushed off and disinfected after a haircut. As a result, the boy later sidles away from the man and tells him to keep his hands off. His cell mates also tell Vadim that he should feel lucky he is a political prisoner, for if he had been jailed with the criminals, they would have "turned him into a girl double fast." Tolkachev has an extended nude scene while in the showers, including lengthy and frank full-frontal exposure.

LILIES ★★★★

Credits: VHS/1996/Canada/Colour/96 minutes
Director: John Greyson
Screenplay: Michel Marc Bouchard.
English version by Linda Gaboriau.
Based on the play *Les Feluettes ou la Repetition d'un Drame Romantique* by Michel Marc Bouchard.
Cast: Jason Cadieux [young Simon], Brent Carver [Countess de Tilly], Alexander Chapman [Lydie-Anne], Ian D. Clark [chaplain/Father Saint Michel], Matthew Ferguson [young Bilodeau], Danny Gilmore [Vallier], Aubert Pallascio [older Simon], Marcel Sabourin [the bishop]
Awards: Genie Awards (Canada) 1996: Best Motion Picture; three other awards. Montreal International Film Festival 1996: Best Canadian Film (audience choice award). Locarno Film Festival 1996.
Genre: A drama about friendship, jealousy, love and revenge, truth, lies and deception.
Plot: In 1952, an aging bishop (Sabourin) arrives at the gates of a prison to hear the confession of a dying inmate. The inmate Simon (Pallascio) is a lifer whose relationship with the bishop goes back to their boyhood when they were classmates in Roberval.

Simon's confession, however, is no ordinary confession. He is out for revenge and it is the bishop's confession he wishes to hear. With the help of several other inmates, aided and abetted by the prison chaplain (Clark), Simon has conceived a play to be performed before the captive bishop. Within the confines of the prison chapel, we are taken back forty years, to the year 1912 and the small town of Roberval.

In their youth, Simon (Cadieux), Bilodeau (Ferguson) and Vallier (Gilmore) had been school friends. They were more than just friends, however. As the prisoner's play unfolds we see that Simon and Vallier are lovers. Bilodeau, afraid to admit his own feelings for Simon, is both attracted and repelled by the handsome youth. He is also driven to the point of irrationality by his jealousy of Vallier's hold over Simon. But Simon is changing. He has been beaten by his father for his relationship with Vallier. Further, he is attracted by, and even engaged to, the exotic and romantic Parisienne Lydie-Anne (Chapman), who has arrived in town. Still, the truth of the matter is that the one person he has ever truly loved is Vallier.

Seizing a fortuitous opportunity, the jealous Bilodeau sets fire to a school building, trapping Simon and Vallier. Although Simon is rescued, Vallier perishes in the fire. It is testimony from Bilodeau which pins the blame for the fire and the death on Simon, thus beginning Simon's lifetime behind bars. And it is revenge for Bilodeau's boyhood actions and the desire by Simon to hear Bishop Bilodeau admit his culpability which are the motive behind the prison play.

Because of the conceit that this is a play performed by inmates within the walls of a prison, all the female roles in the 1912 scenes are played by men. This film has been released on video tape in Canada (by Alliance Releasing Home Video). Director Greyson is well known for his often audacious look at gay themes in his films, which include *Urinal* and *Zero Patience*.
MPAA: Not rated. Canadian Home Video rated 14-A. Gay themes predominate in this film. The young Simon and Vallier exchange kisses several times. Simon and Bilodeau also exchange kisses. Simon and Vallier make love in a bathtub. As Vallier, Danny Gilmore has several nude scenes, including full-frontal shots. As the young Simon, Cadieux also appears nude several times, but in rear shots only.

LITTLE GIANTS ★★★

Credits: VHS/1994/USA/Colour/106 minutes
Director: Duwayne Dunham
Screenplay: Tommy Swerdlow, Michael Goldberg, James Ferguson and Robert Shallcross
Cast: John Madden [himself], Rick Moranis [Danny], Ed O'Neill [Kevin], Devon Sawa [Junior], Susanna Thompson [Patty], Mary Ellen Trainor [Karen O'Shea], Shawna Waldron [Becky "Icebox" O'Shea], Brian Haley [Mike Hammersmith], Sam Horrigan [Spike],
Genre: A comedy about a group of inept misfit kids who want to play football. This is a story which has been told several times before, in the *Bad News Bears* series and the *Mighty Ducks* series. This time around the sport is football.
Plot: When The Icebox (Waldron) is passed by when the cut is made for the Urbania, Ohio football team for no reason other than her gender, she is more than a little upset. It is particularly galling because she is clearly the best football player in town and the coach (O'Neill) is her uncle.

Wasting no time, she and the others who have not made the official team form one of their own, with her father (Moranis) as coach. The rivalry between the two teams is intensified by the lifelong rivalry between the coaching brothers. Although the outcome of the game and the story is utterly predictable, it is fun while it lasts.

The young actors generally acquit themselves well and you can't help cheering for the misfits, especially The Icebox, as she rides rough shod over the competition while trying to make sense of her budding romantic interest in teammate Junior (Sawa). This unexpected romantic turn in her life causes much internal conflict for Becky as she tries to attract Junior's attention.

Will he respond better to her as a pre-teen cheerleading vamp like her cousin? Or does she have a better chance as the best damn twelve-year-old footballer in town?

MPAA: Rrated PG. There are a few shots of young boys in their underwear and a number of the requisite jokes about jock straps. There is a growing romance between The Icebox and Junior, but it goes no further than being mutually grossed-out while watching a couple of teenagers kissing.

THE LITTLE GIRL WHO LIVES DOWN THE LANE ★★★

Credits: VHS/1976/Canada, France/Colour/90 minutes
Director: Nicholas Gessner
Screenplay: Laird Koenig, based on his novel.
Cast: Jodie Foster [Rynn Jacobs], Scott Jacoby [Mario], Martin Sheen [Frank Hallet], Mort Shuman [officer Miglioriti], Alexis Smith [Mrs. Hallet]
Genre: A romantic thriller about a thirteen-year-old girl with many secrets living in a small New England town.
Plot: New to town, Rynn Jacobs (Foster) starts to attract attention from the local townspeople when they begin to realize that her poet father has not been seen for some time. First Mrs. Hallet (Smith), the abrasive real estate agent who leased the house to them, finds excuses to barge into the house looking for him. Always Rynn's father is busy working and can't be disturbed, or is out of town meeting with a publisher.

Then Frank Hallet (Sheen), the woman's son, starts to show up. Frank's presence is even more upsetting to Rynn because he is a known child molester. Even the police get in the act, though officer Miglioriti is pacified when he believes he meets Mr. Jacobs. Only Mario (Jacoby), Miglioriti's nephew and as much a loner as Rynn, is able to make friends with the girl, learning her secrets and eventually becoming her accomplice and her lover.

MPAA: Rated PG. Although this is a story about death and murder, there is almost no on-screen violence. There is no on-screen nudity or sex, although at one point Rynn scrubs Mario's back while he is sitting in the bathtub, later getting into bed with him. The attempts by Frank Hallet to seduce Rynn are also handled discretely, despite the increasingly violent and abusive nature of his behaviour.

A LITTLE ROMANCE ★★★★

Credits: VHS/1979/USA/Colour/110 minutes
Director: George Roy Hill
Screenplay: Allan Burns
Based on the novel *E=MC2 Mon Amour* by Patrick Cauvin.

Cast: Thelonious Bernard [Daniel], Broderick Crawford [himself], Graham Fletcher-Cook [Londet], Arthur Hill [Richard King], Sally Kellerman [Kay King], Diane Lane [Lauren], Laurence Olivier [Julius], Ashby Semple [Natalie]
Awards: Academy Awards 1979: Best Original Score; (nomination) Best Adapted Screenplay.
Genre: A romantic comedy about two young teenagers travelling across Europe to fulfil a fantasy.
Plot: Lauren (Lane in her screen debut), a twelve-year-old American girl, is thoroughly bored living in Paris with her mother (Kellerman) and stepfather (Hill). A gifted child who reads existential philosophy for pleasure, her only real friend is Natalie (Semple), a good-hearted but homely girl who is gullible, gushy and nowhere near Lauren's intellectual equal.

While spending a day on a movie set with her mother, Lauren meets Daniel (Bernard), a movie-mad thirteen-year-old French boy who has wandered away from a school field trip to watch the film crew. Her intellectual equal, Daniel is nonetheless from a different world.

The only child of a less than scrupulously honest taxi driver, father and son live alone in a small apartment. The chance encounter blossoms quickly into romance and just as quickly the lives of the two youngsters take another rapid turn. An accident in a park introduces them to Julius (Olivier), a scoundrel, a pickpocket and a con man. He is also something of a romantic, telling the young couple of a legend which says that if two lovers kiss in a gondola under The Bridge of Sighs in Venice at sunset when the bells of the Campanile toll they will love each other forever.

With Lauren's permanent return to the United States imminent, she persuades Daniel that they must go to Venice to fulfil the legend. Taking Julius with them to ease the border crossing into Italy, the two young lovers run away to Venice. Needless to say, they are pursued by parents and police and a series of adventures and misadventures places the successful completion of their quest in jeopardy.

This is a better than average example of the young lovers on the run genre of romantic tale.

MPAA: Rated PG. There are a few minor instances of mild cursing and coarse language. Nudity is confined to shots of classical statuary in a museum and overt sexuality exists only in the form of conversations.

Lauren teases Natalie by intimating that she has "done it" with Daniel. Lauren's parents jump to the conclusion that the relationship between the two kids is sexual and panic about the possibility that Julius might molest their daughter.

THE LITTLEST VIKING ★★★

Credits: VHS/1989/Norway/Colour/85 minutes
Dubbed in English.
Director: Knut W. Jorfald, Lars Rasmussen and Paul Trevor Bale
Screenplay: Knut W. Jorfald and Lars Rasmussen Based on the book *Sigurd Drakedreperen* by Torill Thorstad Hauger.
Cast: Anders Bidsvoll [Tord], Christian Breivik [Reim], Per Jansen [Orm Viking], Rulle Smit [mother], Terje Stromdahl [Jarl Haakon], Kristian Tonby [Sigurd Dragonslayer]
Genre: A children's adventure tale about a twelve-year-old boy in Viking-era Norway.
Plot: Young Sigurd (Tonby) is a Viking prince, the younger son of Jarl Haakon (Stromdahl). Sigurd doesn't like all the weapons practice he must put in every day with his teacher Orm Viking (Jansen). He doesn't like Orm and the feeling is mutual. Furthermore, Orm wants to become Jarl himself. That would necessitate killing off Sigurd's father, his older brother and Sigurd.

To make matters even more difficult for Sigurd, he is a gentle, sensitive boy who doesn't like the idea of killing or even hurting others. He runs and hides, for instance, when he is faced with the demand that he flog a young slave boy he himself caught stealing. When his brother is killed during a raid by the Ilugi from the neighbouring village and shortly after this his father is killed during a reprisal raid, Sigurd is faced with a dilemma.

He is now Jarl and must avenge the deaths of his kin. To complicate matters even more, the Jarl of the neighbouring Ilugi village, Tord Ilugison (Bidsvoll), is a boy little older than Sigurd himself and by happenstance a newly made friend.
MPAA: Rated PG. Canadian Home Video rated G. Some scenes of violence and death. Breivik and Tonby have a brief nude scene. This is a long-distance rear shot and occurs when the two boys remove their clothes to dry off after Reim rescues Sigurd from a raging river he has fallen into. The two nude boys sit on the river bank in the sun.

THE LONG DAY CLOSES
★★★★★

Credits: VHS/1992/Great Britain/Colour/83 minutes
Writer/Director: Terrence Davies
Cast: Leigh McCormack [Bud], Ayse Owens [Helen], Anthony Watson [Kevin], Marjorie Yates [Mom]
Genre: The second of Terrence Davies' autobiographical reminiscences of growing up gay and Catholic in a less than pristine working class district in Liverpool.
Plot: Bud (McCormack) is twelve-years-old and leaving

Corey Haim, *The Lost Boys* (1987)

primary school behind. It is the early 1950s, and the setting is working class Liverpool. We are to be treated to an examination of this time and place through the eyes of one child on the verge of adolescence.

The Long Day Closes is not so much a movie, however, in the traditional narrative sense as a succession of exquisitely framed photographs from a family album. But not just any photo album. None of Aunt Hildegaard's out of focus snapshots here. Rather we have some eighty minutes of somber, moving, poignant and intensely beautiful vignettes from a young boy's life, filled with the things that fill a boy's day: home, a new school, neighbours, music, church. But above all, there is family, mom, and the pictures.

This film is an intense visual and aural experience: a treat for eyes and ears. The cinematography under the direction of Michael Coulter and the sound track filled with film clips and pop songs of the '50s and earlier really deserve a theatrical setting. Any film loses impact when seen on the television screen: this one more than most.

MPAA: Rated PG. Although director Terrence Davies is gay, there is very little that is overtly gay about the film, or young Bud's character. To be sure, the other boys at his new school taunt him from time to time with calls of "Who's a fruit, then?" However, the closest we get to a real suggestion of Bud's sexual orientation is an early scene of the boy at an upstairs window, staring entranced at a group of young bricklayers working shirtless in the sun.

LORD OF THE FLIES ★★★★★

Credits: VHS/1963/Great Britain/B&W/91 minutes
Writer/Director: Peter Brook
Based on the novel by William Golding.
Cast: James Aubrey [Ralph], Tom Chapin [Jack], Hugh Edwards [Piggy], Elwin [Roger], Tom Gaman [Simon], Nicholas Hammond
Genre: A dramatic re-telling of the classic tale of the descent into savagery of English school boys stranded on a tropical island after an airplane crash.
Plot: After their aircraft is downed in the tropics, a group of English school boys, the oldest little more than twelve

Matthew Barry, *Luna* (1979)

or thirteen, is forced to fend for themselves on an otherwise uninhabited island.

From grey flannel shorts and crisp white shirts, the boys, despite the best of efforts and intentions, quickly become little savages. School uniforms soon become rags. The rags become loincloths or get shed completely, war paint and masks become the norm.

Sacrificial offerings are made to the much feared and semi-mythical "Beast" as the conflict between "good" and "evil" overwhelms and divides the boys. In a political allegory which may never lose its relevance, fear of the unknown drives the boys, individually and collectively, to choose the savage and authoritarian ways of Jack over the more civilized and democratic ways of Ralph.

While Ralph agonizes over why things went wrong, Jack willingly, though perhaps not consciously, leads the slide into savagery. Meanwhile Piggy, as the voice of reason and pragmatism, and Simon, as the embodiment of mysticism, look on from the outside. Eventually, after the murders of Simon and Piggy, Ralph is left alone, hunted across an island set ablaze by the little savages.

This is decidedly the better of the two filmed versions of Golding's classic. Brook's version of the story is extremely close to the original novel and the performances by all of the young actors are superb, despite the fact that none had previously appeared on-screen and very few were ever to do so again.

MPAA: Not rated. Unlike the 1990 U.S. version of this film, where none of the boys ever appears in anything less than ragged underwear, by the end of Brook's film most of the youngest boys are quite content to have completely shed their clothing. Many of the others wear various abbreviated and makeshift loincloths. At different times in the film there are a number of casual nude scenes, including some full-frontal shots.

LORD OF THE FLIES ★★

Credits: VHS/1990/USA/Colour/90 minutes
Director: Harry Hook
Screenplay: Sara Schiff
Based on the novel by Sir William Golding.
Cast: Badgett Dale [Simon], Chris Furrh [Jack], Balthazar Getty [Ralph], Danuel Pipoly [Piggy], Andrew Taft, Edward Taft
Genre: An Americanized and updated remake of the 1963 film based on Golding's book, this is again a drama about the descent into savagery of a group of schoolboys stranded by an aircraft disaster.
Plot: Although not a particularly bad film in it's own right, this version of Golding's novel is, in comparison, decidedly inferior to the 1963 film. Although the young

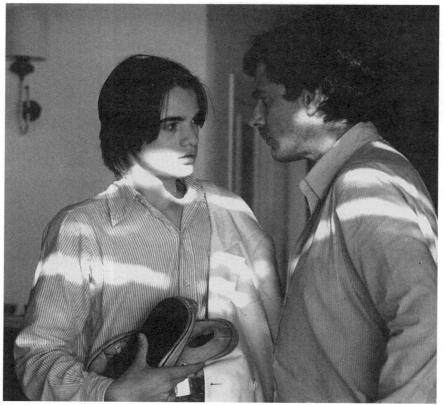

Matthew Barry and Thomas Milian, *Luna* (1979)

actors, particularly the leads, put in creditable performances, they are poleaxed by a terrible script.

Although all of the major elements of Golding's novel
are present in Hook's adaptation, some aspects of the story
have been tampered with in such a way as to materially
affect the entire story line. Foul-mouthed kids from an
American military prep-school, some of whom have been in
trouble with the law, don't seem such unlikely candidates
for the descent into savagery. Nor do they seem to fall as far
as the angelic Kyrie singing choir boys from the 1963 film.

Chris Furrh's Jack forms a gang, not a tribe. There is
more dirt, but less war paint and no masks for the
American boys. And not one of the American boys sheds
that last vestige of conventional civilization, his clothing.

Sure, by the end of the film, all the boys are running
around in their underwear, most of which is filthy, and
some of which is in shreds. But not one of these boys goes
nude. Not even when they are swimming.

MPAA: Rated R. This rating was earned primarily for the
almost non-stop profanities spouting from the mouths of
these kids. There is a very small amount of sex talk as Jack
and Ralph early in the film discuss their own lack of any
sexual experience. Nudity appears in a very brief flash of
Chris Furrh's buns as Jack is wrestling with Ralph (Getty)
just before Piggy (Pipoly) is killed.

THE LOST BOYS ★★★

Credits: VHS/1987/USA/Colour/97 minutes
Director: Joel Schumacher
Screenplay: Janice Fischer, James
Jeremias and Jeffrey Boam
Cast: Corey Feldman [Edgar Frog], Jami
Gertz [Star], Corey Haim [Sam], Edward
Herrmann [Max], Barnard Hughes
[Grandpa], Jamieson Newlander [Allan
Frog], Jason Patric [Michael], Kiefer
Sutherland [David], Dianne Wiest [Lucy]
Genre: A campy, comic farce about two
teenage brothers who encounter a gang of
young vampires in a California seaside town.
Plot: With their newly divorced mom Lucy
(Wiest), Sam (Haim) and Michael (Patric)
move from Phoenix to Santa Carla,
California to live with their eccentric
grandfather (Hughes). What seems at first to
be a sleepy seaside town where nothing ever
happens soon turns into a nightmare.

Attracted by the beautiful Star (Gertz),
Michael becomes involved with a hard-party-
ing crowd of bleach-blonde motorcycle riders
led by David (Sutherland). Sam, meanwhile,
has met the Frog brothers at a local comic shop.

Dedicated to "Truth, Justice and the American Way,"
Alan (Newlander) and Edgar (Feldman) inform him there
are vampires loose in the town. With information gleaned
from comic books, Sam soon comes to believe that
Michael's new friends are in fact of the Undead and about
to take Michael into their fold. Worse, he comes to suspect
that his mother's new employer Max (Herrmann) is the
chief vampire. With the help of the fearless Frog brothers,
Sam sets out to rid the town of this menace.

MPAA: Rated R. Canadian Home Video rated 14-A. Lots
of blood and gore, though most of the violence seems to
consist of people screaming. Michael and Star make love
once, though there is no nudity involved. Sam is seen in
the bathtub, but there are so many bubbles, even Haim's
navel is concealed.

LUCAS ★★★★

Credits: VHS/1986/USA/Colour/100 minutes
Writer/Director: David Seltzer
Cast: Kerri Green [Maggie], Corey Haim [Lucas],
Thomas E. Hodges [Bruno], Ciro Poppiti [Ben], Winona
Ryder [Rina], Charlie Sheen [Cappie], Courtney Thorne-
Smith [Alise]
Genre: A better-than-average teenage romance about an
intellectual who falls for the beautiful new girl at school.

Plot: Lucas (Haim) is the school wimp, the butt of everybody's jokes, the kid with the oversize glasses, the uncombed hair and the outstanding intellect who, at fourteen, has been accelerated into high school. A lover of insects and classical music, Lucas is also a clown with a proclaimed aversion to superficiality (although, in a neighbourhood of million dollar mansions, he feels it necessary to hide his own very humble origins).

During summer vacation he meets Maggie (Green), the new girl in town, and is immediately smitten. Though she is two years older than Lucas, they become good friends. When school starts up again in September, however, Lucas is dismayed to find that Maggie is falling for Cappie (Sheen), the handsome captain of the football team and one of the few people at school willing to stand up for Lucas.

When she joins the cheerleading team, Lucas, in desperation to regain her attention, tries out for football. Although both coach and principal tell him he can't play, Lucas insists on suiting up for the big game. When he is severely injured during the game, he becomes the surprise school hero, even winning over the bullying football jock Bruno (Hodges).

MPAA: Rated PG-13. There is some brief incidental male nudity involving rear shots of uncredited extras in a shower scene, as well as some sex talk as Lucas delivers a lecture on male anatomy to Bruno. Having been teased about the size of his penis, Lucas responds by implying that the football star may be gay. "I don't get semi-erect around other males, the way some of you fellows do … . You can tell the fags in a warm shower by who's got the longest dong."

LUNA ★★★

Credits: 1979/Italy/Colour/142 minutes
Director: Bernardo Bertolucci
Screenplay: Giuseppe Bertolucci, Clare Peploe and Bernardo Bertolucci
Cast: Matthew Barry [Joe], Roberto Benigni [the upholsterer], Franco Citti [Mario], Jill Clayburgh [Caterina], Tomas Milian [Giuseppe]
Genre: A drama about the relationship between a lonely teenage drug addict and his jet-setting international opera-star mother.
Plot: When his father dies shortly before his mother (Clayburgh) is due to leave on a European singing tour, fifteen-year-old Joe (Barry) is suddenly forced to accompany her instead of being left alone in New York. It soon becomes evident that Joe is a very lonely boy.

Although she is able to give him all the creature comforts, his mother Catarina seems often to be unaware of his existence. She needs her secretary to remind her after a performance that the next day is Joe's sixteenth birthday. Joe's already precarious emotional state isn't helped by overhearing this conversation.

At the hastily planned party the next day, Catarina sees Joe and a local girl, Arianna, together. Thinking they are necking, she is devastated to observe Joe shooting heroin. The crisis this discovery engenders threatens her relationship with her son and even her career. Eventually it even leads to incest and mum supplying her son with drugs.

Matthew Barry and Jill Clayburgh, *Luna* (1979)

Joe, meanwhile, is trying to support his habit by stealing cash from his mother. There is also one ambiguous scene which suggests he may be prostituting himself to pay for the drugs. As if this were not enough for the boy, his mother chooses this time to inform him that Douglas, the man who died in New York, was not his real father. In one last attempt to help her son, she puts him on the trail of Giuseppe (Milian), his biological father.

Unfortunately, the subject of incest is not as well handled in this film as it is in Louis Malle's *Murmur of the Heart*. The circumstances leading to the incestuous encounter are too heavy going, too laden down with psychological baggage to be satisfactory. The circumstances of the sexual encounter don't quite ring true. The film is also hampered by Matthew Barry's performance. His Joe is too stolid, too uninspired, too unengaging to really do justice to the role.

Look for brief appearances by renowned physical comedian Roberto Benigni (of *Johnny Stecchino* fame) as a curtain hanger and by Franco Citti (a regular in the films of Pasolini) as the man who tries to pick up Joe in the bar.

MPAA: Not rated. There is a considerable amount of coarse language and, befitting Joe's addiction, several scenes of drug use. Joe and Arianna make love once in a dark movie theatre. Joe and his mother share several long, passionate kisses after one of which Catarina urges her son not to fight it any longer. There is also the previously mentioned scene in which Catarina masturbates her son while he is suffering from withdrawal symptoms.

Joe and Catarina both have nude scenes. Joe is seen curled up on his bed under the influence of the drugs. This shot includes some brief, dark, partial-frontal exposure. Catarina is seen nude as she undresses and showers. You don't actually see her face in the nude shots, so it may be a body double. There is also an extended sequence in the first minutes of the film of a nude toddler, the infant Joe.

MACHO DANCER ★★★

Credits: VHS/1988/Philippines/Colour/136 minutes
In Tagalog with English subtitles.
Writer/Director: Lino Brocka
Screenplay: Ricardo Lee and Amado Lacuesta
Cast: Charlie Catalla [Mama Charlie], Daniel Fernando [Noel], Jacklyn Jose [Bambi], William Lorenzo [Dennis], Allan Paole [Pol], Princess Punzalan [Pinning], Bobby Sano [Greg]
Genre: A drama about a poor country youth who comes face to face with the harsh realities of city life in the seamy underside of Manilla.
Plot: Pol (Paole) is a poor country kid trying to help support his hardworking single mother. Unskilled and unschooled, he earns his money as a call boy. When his regular American lover Larry announces he is leaving the Philippines, Pol's friend Greg (Sano) suggests the youth try his luck in Manilla.

Within hours of arriving in the city, Pol has entered into a seamy world of sleazy gay bars, violence, police corruption, drug dealing, juvenile prostitution, live sex stage shows and sexual tourism. Pol finds work as a dancer on the stage of Mama Charlie's which at least has the advantage of being slightly less offensive than some of the other gay bars.

Sharing a room with Noel (Fernando), one of Mama Charlie's other boys, Pol is also soon enmeshed in his roommate's search for his seventeen-year-old sister Pinning (Punzalan).

Macho Dancer (1988)

Jason London, *The Man In The Moon* (1991)

MPAA: Not rated. There are many scenes of nude and nearly nude youths and young men engaged in erotic stage shows in the gay bars of Manilla. These range from relatively tame dance routines where the performers wear backless loincloths through highly erotic shower cum striptease routines to such outright sleaze as a row of nude youths sitting on stage masturbating. There are also a number of scenes of straight sex.

MADAME ROSA ★★★★

(Also known as *La Vie Devant Soi*)

Credits: VHS/1977/France/Colour/105 minutes
In French with English subtitles.
Writer/Director: Moshe Mizrahi
Based on the novel by Emile Ajar.
Cast: Stella Annicette [Madame Lola], Michal Bat-Adam [Nadine], Samy Ben Youb [Momo], Elio Bencoil [Moishe], Claude Dauphin [Dr. Katz], Gabriel Jabbour [Mr. Hamil], Simone Signoret [Madame Rosa], Mohamed Zinet [Kadir]
Awards: Academy Awards 1977: Best Foreign Film.
Genre: A story about an aging ex-prostitute who shelters and raises the children of other prostitutes and her special

relationship with one young teenager in her care.

Plot: Madame Rosa (Signoret), an aging ex-prostitute has for some years been caring for a mixed assortment of children, the sons and daughters of active Paris prostitutes. As she grows older, however, she finds herself less and less able to carry the load. Her health is deteriorating. Her past as an inmate of Auschwitz is coming back to haunt her. Gradually she finds herself relying more and more on the help of Momo (Ben Youb), a handsome fourteen-year-old Arab boy who is the last of her foster children.

Momo, however, is becoming obsessed with finding his roots. Who was his father? Who was his mother? Why don't they contact him? Why are his the only parents who don't provide financial support? When his father (Zinet) does appear, the truth is no comfort to Momo.

MPAA: Not rated. There is a certain amount of sex talk in the film, and it is obvious that Momo is a very knowing young man. It being the only occupation he knows much about, he is also at risk of falling into the sex trade himself.

In one scene, when money runs short, he tries to take to the streets. He winds up being paid by another prostitute to stay off the street. Having found out what he was up to, Madame Rosa extracts a promise that he will never, ever take to hustling.

One of the other residents of the apartment building is the transsexual Madame Lola (Annicette), the proverbial hooker with the heart of gold. According to Momo, she used to be a boxer but got some injections and now she peddles her ass in the Bois de Boulogne.

THE MAN IN THE MOON ★★★

Credits: VHS/1991/USA/Colour/99 minutes
Director: Robert Mulligan
Screenplay: Jenny Wingfield
Cast: Tess Harper [Abigail Trent], Ernie Lively [Will Sanders], Jason London [Court Foster], Bentley Mitchum [Billy Sanders], Gail Strickland [Marie Foster], Emily Warfield [Maureen Trent], Sam Waterston [Matthew Trent], Reese Witherspoon [Dani Trent]
Genre: An at times melodramatic tale of first love, loss

and the bonds between sisters set in rural Louisiana in the late 1950s.

Plot: Dani (Witherspoon) and Maureen (Warfield) are sisters growing up in the rural south. Maureen, the elder, is set to enter college. Dani is a young teenager just beginning to understand the romance of love, though she's more at home in the local swimming hole than in a Sunday dress. In fact, while she's skinny-dipping in that swimming hole one day, an unknown but handsome sixteen-year-old boy dives in.

Despite this rather unorthodox introduction to Court Foster (London), and despite a rather shaky start to their relationship, Dani is soon head over heels in love with her new neighbour. Unfortunately, although willing to be friends with Dani, Court is far more enamored of her older sister.

Having just broken up with her long-time boyfriend Billy (Mitchum) after Billy's father (Lively) put the make on her at a dance, Maureen is equally attracted to Court. The jealous love triangle which ensues pits sister against sister, a standoff which won't end until Court's untimely death in a farming accident. His death brings the two sisters back together in their mutual need to mourn their loss.

The relationship between Court, Maureen and Dani is what gives this film it's strength and makes it worth watching. Multifaceted and complex, each of these three characters is well drawn and well portrayed. The story line could have used some reworking.

MPAA: Rated PG-13. Canadian Home Video rated PG. Dani and Court are both seen nude, but I wonder if Dani's scenes weren't done by a body double. The shots very carefully and pointedly hide her face when she is nude. All her nude scenes are rear shots. Court is seen nude jumping into the pond. This includes some full-frontal shots, but they are short, far away and slightly off focus. Court and Maureen are seen making love behind a clump of bushes.

THE MAN WITHOUT A FACE ★★★

Credits: VHS/1993/USA/Colour/115 minutes
Director: Mel Gibson
Screenplay: Malcolm MacRury
Based on the novel by Isabelle Holland.
Cast: Mel Gibson [Justin McLeod], Gaby Hoffmann [Megan], Geoffrey Lewis [Chief Stark], Fay Masterson [Gloria], Richard Masur [Carl], Nick Stahl [Chuck Norstadt], Margaret Whitton [Catherine]

Genre: A drama about the friendship which develops one summer between a twelve-year-old boy and a disfigured, reclusive man in a small town on the coast of Maine.

Plot: Chuck (Stahl) is a boy who's self image is virtually nil. Feeling stifled as the only male in an otherwise all female household, the twelve-year-old also considers himself "the family retard." He wants to escape from his mother (Whitton), his half-sisters Gloria (Masterson) and Megan (Hoffmann) and a never ending parade of stepfathers. His goal? To enter Holyfield, the military academy his father had attended as a boy. Unfortunately, he has already failed the entrance exam. During his summer vacation he conceives a plan: he will get a tutor to help him study, and retake the exam in August. He persuades Justin McLeod (Gibson), a badly scarred, rarely seen neighbour who lives alone in an old house, to take on the task.

During the summer, a genuine friendship develops between the two as Chuck learns both academics and self-confidence. At the end of the summer, however, Chuck's improving self image suffers a major set back. After a family crisis, Chuck runs to McLeod for comfort. The next

Emily Warfield and Jason London, *The Man In The Moon* (1991)

morning the police chief (Lewis) finds Chuck running around McLeod's home in his underwear. Combined with an incident in McLeod's past, police and townspeople accuse the man of molesting the boy. Rather than put the boy through the anguish of testifying about their relationship, McLeod agrees to a stipulation that he never see Charles again.

The screenplay has taken major liberties with Isabelle Holland's original novel. It has been transformed from the story of a fourteen-year-old boy beginning to come to grips with his homosexuality to that of a twelve-year-old boy whose new found happiness and self confidence is shattered when a trusted friend and teacher is wrongly accused of molesting him. An important story, but not the one Holland told.

MPAA: Rated PG-13. The film deals in its later stages with the sexual abuse of children and false accusations of sexual abuse. There are some minor instances of coarse language. Although it is suggested that Chuck is beginning to experience sexual desires, in the film, unlike the book, they are all strictly heterosexual. Gloria and one of her boyfriends are caught in bed together, though little is actually seen on screen.

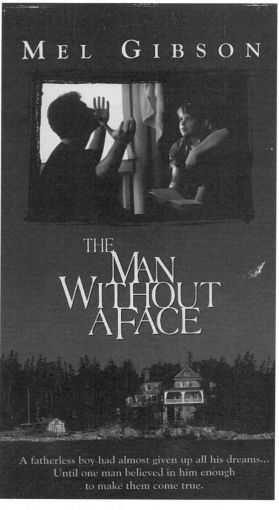

Mel Gibson and Nick Stahl, *The Man Without A Face* (1993)

MANNY & LO ★★★★★

Credits: VHS/1996/USA/Colour/89 minutes
Writer/Director: Lisa Krueger
Cast: Cameron Boyd [Chuck], Glenn Fitzgerald [Joey], Paul Guilfoyle [country house owner], Scarlett Johansson [Amanda (Manny)], Aleksa Palladino [Laurel (Lo)], Mary Kay Place [Elaine]
Genre: A drama which explores the strange symbiotic relationship which develops between a middle-aged kidnap victim and her juvenile captors.
Plot: Teenager Laurel (Palladino), who is known as Lo, is on the run from a succession of foster homes. Along the way she has picked up her younger sister Amanda (Johansson), also called Manny.

Driving an old stolen car, the two girls survive by syphoning gas, stealing groceries and sleeping in display homes in new subdivisions. Although it becomes increasingly evident that Lo is pregnant, she puts her weight gains down to their junk food diet. When even Lo can no longer deny her condition, she stops at a clinic to get an abortion. However, because of the advanced stage of her pregnancy, her request is denied. Some days later they find an apparently empty house hidden deep in the woods. Here Lo decides to hole up until the birth of her baby.

Desperate for medical help, Lo makes a momentous decision. The two girls kidnap Elaine (Place), an employee of a nearby maternity shop. At first Elaine refuses to cooperate and is kept shackled in a locked room. When she eventually discovers Lo's pregnancy, however, her attitude begins to change. Though the relationship experiences a series of ups and downs and even severe crises, in the end Elaine is there when Lo gives birth. And despite the fact that Elaine has earlier turned down the suggestion that she adopt the baby, it is clear by the end of the film that she, the two girls and the baby are becoming the family that Manny has desperately been seeking from the very first frame.

MPAA: Rated R. Canadian Home Video rated 14-A. The dialogue includes a great deal of coarse language. Lo and Joey (Fitzgerald) make love in the cab of a "monster truck" early in the film. Manny is seen once in a bathtub, but is thoroughly concealed by soap suds throughout the scene.

MAYA ★★

Credits: VHS/1965/USA/Colour/91 minutes
Director: John Berry
Screenplay: John Fante. Based on the book *The White Elephant* by Jalal Din and Lois Roth.
Cast: Jairaj [Gammu Ghat], I. S. Johar [One Eye], Sajid Kahn [Raji], Jay North [Terry Bowen], Sonia Sahni [Sheela], Clint Walker [Mr. Bowen]
Genre: A children's adventure tale set in India.

Plot: After his mother dies, Terry (North) arrives in India to live with his father (Walker). His father is a big-game hunter and guide who has lost his nerve and his fortune after being attacked by a tiger. He is also less than thrilled at the prospect of caring for his teenage son.

When dad tries to send him back to his grandparents in the United States, Terry jumps off the train and runs away into the jungle where he meets Raji (Kahn), whose father has just died. The two boys head off across India together to deliver a sacred baby white elephant to a distant temple, a task imposed on Raji by his dying father.

With blonde boy and white elephant suitably disguised with brown mud, the boys and the beasts fend off the attacks of assorted bad guys. Naturally they find the true meaning of friendship, and Terry finds a reconciliation with his father just before the hit-you-over-the-head-with-the-message-just-in-case-you-didn't-get-it ending.

Maya suffers from a poor story line and is seriously marred by a less than stellar performance from North and occasional lapses into racist humour. This film is remarkable only for the shots of North standing nude by the river bank.

This film spawned a short-lived TV series.

MPAA: Not rated. North appears nude in a full-length rear shot as Terry dries off after having fallen into a river.

North was thirteen at the time this film was shot and his nude scene was one of the first by a big name actor as Hollywood abandoned the old production code in the 1960s. It is difficult, if not impossible, to imagine many child actors of comparable stature consenting to this scene today.

MEATBALLS ★★

Credits: VHS/1979/Canada/Colour/94 minutes
Director: Ivan Reitman
Screenplay: Len Blum, Dan Goldberg, Janis Allen and Harold Ramis
Cast: Harvey Atkin [Morty], Russ Banham [Crockett], Jack Blum [Spaz], Kristine Debell [A. L.], Kate Lynch [Roxanne], Chris Makepeace [Rudy], Bill Murray [Tripper], Sarah Torgov [Candace]
Awards: Canadian Genie Awards 1980: Best Actress (Lynch).
Genre: A comedy focusing on the counselors at a children's summer camp.
Plot: Camp Northstar, under the leadership of Morty (Atkin), is the poor neighbour of Camp Mohawk down the road. Many of the campers are from lower income families and most are physically and socially inept. The teenage Counselors-In-Training are worse. In fact, most of them are distasteful stereotypes thrown together for no reason other than to make fun of them.

The senior staff members Tripper (Murray) and Roxanne (Lynch) attempt with little success to keep a lid on the hijinx while dealing with the problems of the children, the ongoing rivalry with Camp Mohawk and their own complex relationship which swings from sniping battles to romantic liaisons.

Against this backdrop of pranks and mischief is played out a sweet and gentle story of the relationship between Tripper and twelve-year-old camper Rudy (Makepeace). The boy is a lonely, unhappy kid dumped into camp by his all too busy father. Feeling unwanted at home, and out of place at camp, Rudy tries to run away, but is talked out of it by Tripper.

The personal attention and friendship of Tripper is repaid by devoted hero worship from the boy. By finding an activity Rudy enjoys and excels in and encouraging him to become even better, the man pulls the shy and athletically inept youngster from his shell. Under Tripper's tutelage Rudy grows and gains the self-confidence and self-respect he has been lacking to the point where he becomes the camp hero.

MPAA: Rated PG. Although sexual desires and sex talk run rampant throughout this film, on-screen sexuality is limited to talk, angst ridden yearnings, snide comments and lots of nubile bodies in bikinis.

Although an affair between Tripper and Roxanne is implied, the details are left to the imagination.

MISCHIEF ★★★

Credits: VHS/1984/USA/Colour/97 minutes
Director: Mel Damski
Screenplay: Noel Black
Cast: Maggie Blye [Claire Miller], D. W. Brown [Kenny], Jami Gertz [Rosalie], Graham Jarvis [Mr. Miller], Doug McKeon [Jonathon], Chris Nash [Gene], Terry O'Quinn [Claude Harbrough], Kelly Preston [Marilyn], Catherine Mary Stewart [Bunny]
Genre: A teenage sex comedy about growing up in the 1950s, with more than just a few passing references, both thematic and specific, to *Rebel Without A Cause*.
Plot: The time: 1956. The place: small town Ohio. Jonathon (McKeon) is a high school senior with one burning desire: to lose his virginity, preferably with Marilyn (Preston), a blonde bombshell.

Small town life changes dramatically with the arrival of Gene (Nash), the sophisticated, charismatic, motorcycle-riding new kid from Chicago. Gene undertakes to educate Jonathon in the ways of the world. He simultaneously gains the attention of every attractive girl in town. Most especially, however, he captivates and is captivated by Bunny (Stewart). This mutual attraction sets up the primary conflict in the story, between Gene and Bunny's steady boyfriend Kenny (Brown), son of the wealthiest family in town.

Gene, meanwhile, is concealing family secrets. His widower father regularly beats the boy. Eventually, after yet another clash, Gene finds himself homeless. Jonathon finally achieves his desires, but learns some unwelcome truths about Marilyn in the process. Bunny finds herself forced with a difficult decision. Does she go with the exciting but penniless Gene or stay with the wealthy, respectable but boring Kenny?

MPAA: Rated R. The dialogue includes a great deal of sex talk. In fact, much of the film is concerned with sexual matters, especially Jonathon's attempts to lose his virginity and Gene's efforts to assist him reach this goal.

McKeon and Preston are both seen nude when Marilyn and Jonathon make love for the first time. Preston has a brief full-frontal scene, McKeon is seen only in rear shots.

MON ONCLE ANTOINE ★★★★

Credits: VHS/1971/Canada/Colour/104 minutes
In French with English subtitles.
Also available in a dubbed version.

Director: Claude Jutra

Screenplay: Clement Perron and Claude Jutra

Cast: Lynn Champagne [Carmen], Jean Duceppe [Antoine], Jacques Gagnon [Benoit], Claude Jutra [Fernand], Helene Loiselle [Madame Poulin], Olivette Thibault [Celine], Lionel Villeneuve [Jos Poulin]

Awards: Canadian Academy Awards: Best Feature Film; Best Director (Jutra); Best Screenplay.

Genre: A wistful, nostalgic drama about a fifteen-year-old boy growing up in a depressed asbestos mining community in 1950's Quebec.

Plot: Considered by many to be one of the best Canadian films ever made, most of the action in *Mon Oncle Antoine* takes place in a twenty-four-hour period beginning in the early morning on Christmas Eve.

After serving at early morning mass, fifteen-year-old Benoit (Gagnon) returns to his uncle's general store to help prepare for Christmas. A shy, handsome boy with a winsome smile, over the next twenty-four hours Benoit will witness all the activities of his small town from the vantage point of the store, truly the spiritual and social heart of their community.

Quietly, and without comment, Benoit will observe the infidelity of his aunt (Thibault) with the store clerk (Jutra), the alcoholism and confessions of his uncle (Duceppe), the stirrings of his own sexual desires, especially for Carmen (Champagne), the young girl working at the store and the social realities of the town's dependence on the mine and it's Anglo boss.

Especially, however, Benoit must come face to face with death when he accompanies his inebriated uncle, who also acts as undertaker and funeral director in the town, to an outlying farm to collect the body of a fifteen-year-old boy who has died suddenly after a brief illness.

MPAA: Not rated. There are some instances of bare breasts as a female customer tries on a girdle in the back of the store while Benoit and another boy watch.

Jutra is seen briefly in a side nude shot as Fernand pulls on his pants getting out of Celine's bed.

Benoit has a few sexual fantasies and on one occasion makes a few tentative, groping overtures towards Carmen.

MOON CHILD ★★★★

(Also known as *El Nino de la Luna*)

Credits: VHS/1995/Spain/ Colour/120 minutes
In Spanish with English subtitles.

Writer/Director: Agustin Villaronga

Cast: Hedi Ben Amar [Mid-E-Mid], Lucia Bose [the director], Lisa Gerrard [Georgina], Maribel Martin [Victoria], Enrique Saldana [David], David Sust [Edgar]

Awards: Official entry at Cannes Film Festival, The Chicago International Film Festival, The World Film Festival.

Genre: A drama about a twelve-year-old Spanish orphan who runs away to north Africa because he believes himself to be the child god which the prophecies of a remote tribe predict.

Plot: According to the mythology of a remote sub-Saharan people, a great fire in the sky will be the portent which announces the arrival of a pale and radiant child god.

David (Saldana), a twelve-year-old Spanish orphan, comes to believe that he is this Moon Child. However, before he can take up the burdens of this prophetic destiny, he must endure some very human travails. Blessed (or cursed) with telekinetic powers, he is placed in the care of a centre for the study of the paranormal.

Never at ease in the centre and obsessed with images of the moon, he soon uncovers sinister plans in conjunction with an attempt by the centre to breed a Moon Child. Convinced that he himself is the Moon Child, David takes Georgina (Gerrard) and Edgar (Sust), the couple chosen by the centre for the breeding program, and flees.

Pursued by agents of the centre, Edgar is soon killed but David and the pregnant Georgina escape across the Mediterranean. They head for the home of Edgar's father in a remote army outpost in the Sahara. Recruiting the aid of Mid-E-Mid (Ben Amar), a young slave boy, David makes his way south. At first he is pursued by Victoria (Martin), a member of the centre staff. She has come to retrieve David and Georgina and salvage the Moon Child project. Once she catches up with David, however, she comes to believe in the truth of his contention that he is the Moon Child and in the end assists the boy's entry into the village he believes is waiting for him.

MPAA: Not rated. Georgina and Edgar have a fairly explicit sexual scene which David witnesses.

Gerrard is seen in full-frontal nude shots, and Sust in full-length rear shots while the couple mates as part of the centre's breeding program.

Later, in the desert, after Georgina's delivery, she and young David appear in a scene which has overtones of sexuality and eroticism, both of them apparently nude.

Saldana is also seen in a very dark full-length rear nude shot in the opening minutes of the film.

Lea Massari and Benoit Ferreux, *Murmur Of The Heart* (1971)

MURMUR OF THE HEART
★★★★★

(Also known as *Le Souffle Au Coeur*)

Credits: VHS/1971/France/ Colour/118 minutes
In French with English subtitles.

Writer/Director: Louis Malle

Cast: Jacqueline Chauveau [Helene], Benoit Ferreux [Laurent], Fabien Ferreux [Thomas], Daniel Gelin [the father], Corinne Kersten [Daphne], Michael Lonsdale [the priest], Lea Massari [the mother], Marc Wincourt [Marc]

Awards: Italian Golden Grail 1971 - 72: Best Actress (Massari).

Genre: Definitely one of the great coming-of-age films, this comedy of manners concerns a fourteen-year-old boy whose discovery of sex eventually leads to an incestuous incident with his mother.

Plot: Laurent (Benoit Ferreux), the son of a wealthy gynecologist (Gelin) and his beautiful young wife (Massari) is growing up in Dijon. The year is 1954. The French are still engaged in Indo-China.

Laurent, however, has more important things on his mind. SEX! He masturbates, sometimes alone, sometimes with his brothers. He compares penis sizes with his brothers. He has an affectionate, but innocent, affair with a younger boy which begins at school and continues into a scout camp where the two boys share space in the tent.

He receives unwelcome attention from his confessor at school. He is treated to a session in a high class brothel. He spends the night with a young girl while at a hotel with his mother. Indeed, sex seems to intrude into every aspect of his life at home, at school, at church, even at scout camp.

When he comes down with scarlet fever while at camp, he is bed ridden for days afterwards and develops a heart murmur. The doctor prescribes a stay at a mineral water spa. While staying at the hotel with his mother, he makes several new friends and sexual discoveries. More importantly, however, his relationship with his mother takes several new and unexpected turns.

Even though the subject matter of this film may be distasteful to some, the mother and son incest is very carefully handled. It flows so naturally out of the circumstances of the film that few should be offended by it. Malle treats the subject in a much better way than Bertolucci did in the film *Luna*, for example. However one may feel about the matter in the abstract, in the

Lea Massari and Benoit Ferreux, *Murmur Of The Heart* (1971)

specific environment of this film it is obviously not a case of coercion, but a mutually agreeable, indeed mutually needed, albeit thoroughly spontaneous event. It is obvious that this is not a case of abuse, but of shared needs and desires.

MPAA: Rated R. The film includes a number of nude scenes. The prostitute who initiates Laurent is seen bare breasted. Massari is seen nude in a rear shot, with some brief shots of her bare breasts while Laurent watches his mother in the bathtub in their hotel room.

Benoit Ferreux is seen nude in two scenes. At the spa, Laurent must undress before receiving a shower of mineral waters. This includes a brief full-frontal shot as well as butt shots. Later, there is a full-length rear shot when Laurent jumps out of the bathtub as his mother pours cold water over his head to rinse out the shampoo.

MY AMERICAN COUSIN ★★★★
Credits: VHS/1985/Canada/Colour/94 minutes
Writer/Director: Sandy Wilson
Cast: Richard Donat [Major Wilcox], Camille Henderson [Shirley Darling], Margaret Langrick [Sandy Wilcox], Jane Mortifee [Kitty Wilcox], T. J. Scott [Lenny McPhee], John Wildman [Butch Walker]
Awards: Toronto Festival of Festivals 1985: International Critics Prize. Genie Awards (Canada) 1986: Best Film; Best Director (Wilson); Best Actor (Wildman); Best Actress (Langrick).
Genre: Drama about a twelve-year-old girl's first love.
Plot: Summer, 1959, in Canada's Okanagan Valley. Amid the cherry orchards and the beaches of Penticton, twelve-year-old Sandy Wilcox (Langrick) has a serious problem. "Dear Diary," she writes. "NOTHING EVER HAPPENS!" Then out of the blue, there's a knock on the front door. Her

teenage cousin Butch (Wildman) arrives for a vacation.

To a kid from a small town where the one and only radio station at most plays rock and role for a couple of hours on Saturday afternoon and *Rebel Without A Cause* has yet to play the local theatre, cousin Butch from California is a suave and exotic distraction. He arrives driving a big red Cadillac convertible and has the charisma and animal magnetism of a young James Dean.

Sandy is swept off her feet by his good looks and his reckless ways. Although her father, Major Wilcox (Donat) puts Butch to work picking cherries, Butch seems more interested in making the acquaintance of as many of the local girls as possible.

Too soon, however, reality sets in. Butch's gauche and patronizing parents arrive on the scene. Mamma wants her car back, and dad has the news that it's safe for Butch to come home. His girl isn't pregnant. She was only a few days late. As Butch and his parents drive away, her mother (Mortifee) tells a very doubtful Sandy, "As you grow older, you'll find boys are like buses. If you miss one, another will be along any moment."

My American Cousin was followed in 1989 by a sequel of sorts, *American Boyfriends*, also starring Langrick and Wildman.

MPAA: Rated PG. Beyond a great deal of angst and a fatherly attempt at a birds and bees speech, there is nothing explicitly sexual in the film, and only a few minor instances of violence.

MY BODYGUARD ★★★

Credits: VHS/1980/USA/Colour/97 minutes
Director: Tony Bill
Screenplay: Alan Ormsby
Cast: Adam Baldwin [Ricky Linderman], Matt Dillon [Melvin Moody], Ruth Gordon [granny Peache], Kathryn Grody [Ms. Jump], John Houseman [Mr. Dobbs], Chris Makepeace [Clifford Peache], Martin Mull [Larry Peache], Craig Richard Nelson [Mr. Griffith], George Wendt [the engineer]
Genre: A comedy about a teenager who stands up to the school tough and simultaneously makes friends with a much feared older and taller boy.
Plot: It's the first day of school. Fifteen-year-old Clifford Peache (Makepeace) is a new student at a big school in central Chicago. At school, Cliff quickly finds himself at odds with local tough Melvin Moody (Dillon) whose activities include intimidation of most of the younger students, taking their lunch money as protection payments.

He also encounters Ricky Linderman (Baldwin), an older boy whose reputation proceeds him. According to rumors, "He killed a kid." "He raped a teacher." "He …"

A slight, normally unassertive boy, Cliff decides to take a stand against Moody. He won't pay the protection money. When he offers Linderman a job as his personal bodyguard, he is initially turned down. Persisting in his entreaties, Cliff finally befriends Linderman, eventually learning the truth about the fatal accident which gave birth to the boy's reputation.

Moody, meanwhile, has hired his own "bodyguard," escalating the war between himself and Clifford. In the final fist fight in the park which is sparked by the destruction of the motorcycle Linderman has been rebuilding, Clifford finds himself taking on Moody, one on one.

Dillon's homophobic obsession makes him a closet case suspect. He refers to Makepeace as a fruit and a faggot on more than one occasion.
MPAA: Rated PG. Cliff and his father use a telescope to spy on women in adjoining buildings and granny spends her time picking up men in a bar. There are, however, several scenes of fist fights and intimidation.

MY FATHER'S GLORY ★★★★★

(Also known as *La Gloire De Mon Pere*)

Credits: VHS/1991/France/ Colour/ 110 minutes
In French with English subtitles.
Director: Yves Robert
Screenplay: Jerome Tonnerre, Louis Nucera, Yves Robert. Based on the writings of Marcel Pagnol.
Cast: Philippe Caubere [Joseph], Julien Ciamaca [Marcel], Paul Crauchet [Edmond des Papillons], Victorien Delamare [Paul], Therese Liotard [Tante Rose], Joris Molinas [Lili des Bellons], Didier Pain [Oncle Jules], Nathalie Roussel [Augustine]
Genre: A beautiful, lyrically evocative drama about a young boy's relationship with his family and his environment set in the hills surrounding Marseille at the beginning of the twentieth century. Based on the autobiographical writings of renowned French writer and film director Marcel Pagnol.
Plot: Julien Ciamaca, in a standout performance, is Marcel. The handsome, brilliant son of a primary schoolteacher, Marcel observes life with a wry interest as his family grows. The birth of a brother and a sister, the marriage of his aunt, the birth of a cousin, the sniping relationship between his radical humanist father (Caubere) and traditional religious uncle (Pain); everything around him is viewed with a keen eye, and a touch of whimsy.

The summer Marcel is eleven, father and uncle rent a cottage in the country. Here the boy first experiences a love which is to last him his entire life; a love for the hot, dry hills of Provence. Well water, spring water, chasing cicadas in the scrub, open air showers in the summer sun, new friends and dining al fresco all combine to make this summer the happiest time of his life. So much so that as summer comes to an end Marcel concocts a plan to run away and live as a hermit in a cave where he and his new friend Lili (Molinas) found shelter from a sudden rain storm.

However, not all is sunshine in these hills for Marcel must deal with the duplicity of adults when he discovers that despite assurances, his father and uncle don't plan to take him on a promised hunting trip. And when his father proves not to be omnipotent, not to be above mere human frailties, Marcel must once again deal with the reality of the world around him. "I had caught my superman in the act of being human. I loved him even more for it."

My Father's Glory was followed by *My Mother's Castle*.

MPAA: Rated G. Canadian Home Video rated PG. Despite this rating, there are two nude sequences including full-frontal exposure of both Ciamaca and Delamare and full-length rear shots of both these boys as well as of Molinas.

In the first, Marcel and Paul are seen showering and playing outdoors under a hose. After their shower, they are seen running through the house and up the stairs.

In the second nude scene, after getting caught in a cloudburst Marcel and Lili strip and dry off in front of the fireplace before running upstairs.

MY FIRST SUIT
★★★★

Credits: VHS/1985/New Zealand/Colour/29 minutes
Director: Stewart Main
Screenplay: Peter Wells
Cast: Conrad Crawte [Stevie], Heather Lindsay [mum], Heather Pitt [Aunt Irene], Martin Sanderson [dad]
Genre: A short, nostalgic comedy set in the late 1960s about a gay teenager's first tentative steps towards understanding his own sexuality.
Plot: Stevie (Crawte) is a skinny, gawky, bespectacled teenager. Six months ago his parents separated and he is presently living with his Auntie Irene (Pitt). It is now a week to go until the school dance. Both mum (Lindsay) and dad (Sanderson) insist on buying their son his first suit in order that he may be properly attired for the big event.

Needless to say, he winds up with two, both bought from the same shop. Despite all this parental concern and attention, Stevie has a little difficulty concentrating on the task of obtaining the titular garment. There are simply too many handsome, muscular, half-naked men around in real life, in magazines, on television and in store displays. With all this beefcake to ogle, how can a young puppy like Stevie concentrate on something as mundane as buying a suit?

On the night in question, after dutifully visiting each parent, Stevie chucks the dance, takes the bus into town and goes to the pictures. There, in the warm black, under the shimmering projector light, he meets a tall dark

Chris Makepeace (left), *My Bodyguard* (1980)

stranger, and his real romantic life begins.

Although short, and definitely lighthearted, this little comedy is important for being a positive, sensitive, sympathetic picture of a gay teenager who, though still learning, is nevertheless completely comfortable with his emerging sexuality. You know Stevie won't become a suicide statistic.

My New Suit has been released on VHS packaged jointly with the American short *Clayfarmers*.
MPAA: Not rated. There are one or two shots, in the form of black and white stills, of bare butts. There are also several shots of Crawte wearing a pair of white briefs.

MY LIFE AS A DOG ★★★★★

(Also known as *Mitt Liv Som Hund*)

Credits: VHS/1985/Sweden/Colour/101 minutes
In Swedish with English subtitles.
Also available dubbed in English.
Director: Lasse Hallstrom
Screenplay: Annette Mandoki
Based on a novel by Reidar Jonsson.
Cast: Ing-Marie Carlsson [Berit], Anton Glanzelius [Ingmar], Melinda Kinnamen [Saga], Anki Liden [the mother], Kicki Rundgren [Aunt Ulla], Manfred Serner [Erik], Tomas von Bromssen [Uncle Gunnar]
Awards: Academy Awards 1987: (nomination) Best Adapted Screenplay; (nomination) Best Director (Hallstrom). Golden Globe Awards 1987: Best Foreign Film. Independent Spirit Awards 1987: Best Foreign Film. New York Film Critics: Best Foreign Film. National Board of Review: five best films of the year. Swedish Film Institute: Best Film; Best Actor (Glanzelius). Swedish Film Critics' Association: Best Film. The Union of Danish Film Critics: Best European Film. Danish Film Academy: Best Foreign Film.
Genre: A gentle comedy about an unhappy, confused young boy who is sent to the country to live with relatives when his terminally-ill mother is hospitalized. Along the way he meets a remarkable cast of colourful characters, from a soccer playing tomboy to a sex-obsessed senior citizen.
Plot: Truly one of the classic films about children, *My Life As A Dog* follows several months in the life of Ingmar (Glanzelius), an irrepressible imp with a mischievous grin and a knack for attracting trouble. Ingmar and his older brother Erik [Serner] are sent away to relatives for the summer when their mother's illness becomes critical. Erik goes to their grandmother, Ingmar to Uncle Gunnar [von Bromssen] in a small village in rural Smaland.

The village is home to a memorable population of eccentrics. There is Saga [Kinnamen], a twelve-year-old girl who is the star player on the boys' soccer team and boxes with them as well. There is Manne, a boy with green hair who's grandfather, an inveterate and usually unsuccessful tinkerer, owns the barn where the children play. There is old Mr. Arvidson who lives downstairs and likes to hear Ingmar read lingerie ads from the mail-order catalogue. There is old Mr. Fransson, who's sole occupations are repairing his roof and swimming in ice covered streams. There is Berit [Carlsson], a well developed young blonde woman who agrees to be the model for a local sculptor's vision of The Earth Mother. And there is Uncle Gunnar, who works in the local glass factory and is building a gazebo for himself. On somebody else's land!

Amongst these people, Ingmar must slowly come to terms with his changing life. His mother's illness proves fatal. His beloved mutt, Sickan, has been put down, though nobody has the heart to tell him. And he is experiencing conflicting feelings about Saga, one minute pounding her furiously in the boxing ring, the next cuddling asleep with her in her parents' home.
MPAA: Not rated. There is a certain amount of sex talk in this film. Erik tries to give a group of younger children a sex lecture which leads to a very painful scene in which Ingmar gets stuck in a bottle.

Ingmar and a young neighbour indulge in a little childish sex play before the boy leaves for the country. There is also some female nudity.

Berit is seen nude while posing for the sculptor. This includes some brief full-frontal shots as she tries to roll out of the way when Ingmar falls through the skylight.

Saga appears topless once or twice as she complains to Ingmar about her growing breasts, though she is only twelve-years-old and appears to be just entering puberty. After one such session she tries unsuccessfully to get Ingmar to show her if he has grown, too.

MY MOTHER'S CASTLE ★★★★

(Also known as *Le Chateau de Ma Mere*)

Credits: VHS/1991/France/Colour/98 minutes
In French with English subtitles.
Director: Yves Robert
Screenplay: Jerome Tonnerre and Yves Robert
Based on the writings of Marcel Pagnol.
Cast: Philippe Caubere [Joseph], Julien Ciamaca [Marcel], Paul Crauchet [Edmond des Papillons], Victorien Delamare [Paul], Therese Liotard [Tante Rose], Joris Molinas [Lili des Bellons], Didier Pain [Oncle Jules], Jean Rochefort, Nathalie Roussel [Augustine], Julie Timmerman [Isabelle], Philippe Uchan [Bouzigue], Georges Wilson
Genre: A comedy about a young boy's first love and his continually deepening understanding of his parents.
Plot: In this sequel to *My Father's Glory*, we again follow the life of Marcel (Ciamaca) and his family and the boy's continuing love for the hills of Provence. This time round, Marcel pleads with his father Joseph (Caubere) to return to the hills. They can, Marcel says, commute to Marseille every day if they borrow his uncle's bicycle. Although unwilling to attempt this, Joseph has, unknown to Marcel, arranged for the family to spend Christmas and Easter in the villa in the hills. It is not long before the trips to the villa occur every weekend.

Marcel is in for another surprise. On a trip into the hills to pick thyme for his mother he finds a beautiful young girl, Isabelle (Timmerman), sitting on the rock and seemingly lost. He is instantly smitten and Isabelle, a pretentious, domineering girl with an overactive imagination, soon has Marcel eating from her hand. She subjects the boy to increasingly humiliating games which culminating in feeding him a live grasshopper. No amount of teasing from his brother Paul (Delamare) or his friend Lili (Molinas) can deter him, however. His eyes are not to be opened until he catches Isabelle out in a lie.

MPAA: Rated PG. Canadian Home Video rated PG. Marcel's relationship with Isabelle is strictly puppy love. Nothing more serious than a gallant kissing of her hand passes between them.

Young Delamare is seen in an outdoor showering scene reminiscent of the one in *My Father's Glory* but this time the shot is filmed through the window and his nudity is no more than implied.

MY NAME IS IVAN ★★★★★

(Also known as *Ivan's Childhood*, as *The Childhood Of Ivan*, as *The Youngest Spy* or as *Ivanovo Detstvo*)

Credits: VHS/1962/USSR/B&W/84 minutes
In Russian with English subtitles.
Director: Andrei Tarkovski
Screenplay: Vladimir Bogomolov and Michail Papava
Based on the story Ivan by Vladimir Bogomolov.
Cast: Kolya Burlyayev [Ivan], S. Krylov [Katasonich], V. Maliavina (Masha), Y. Zharikov [Galtsev], Valentin Zubkov [Holin]
Awards: Venice Film Festival 1962: Best Film.
Genre: A wrenching anti-war drama about the devastating effects of World War II on one twelve-year-old boy in Russia.
Plot: A testament to the power of black and white cinematography, *My Name Is Ivan* is filled with outstanding visuals and would be worth watching for that reason alone. The visuals, moreover, are married to a first class story line brought to life by great performances.

Ivan (Burlyayev) is a twelve-year-old war orphan, the only surviving member of his family following the German invasion of Russia. Although early in the war he had been evacuated to a children's home far from the fighting, he ran away, heading for the fighting in the west, bent on revenge for his family's deaths.

His contribution to the war effort? Spying behind enemy lines. When he is threatened with being sent to a military school, he insists on getting his way. A determined boy with an occasionally vicious temper, Ivan is trying hard to be a man beyond his years. This is difficult, however, when he is subject to bouts of a child's tears and recurring dreams and nightmares about his family.

Eventually he persuades the Russian military that he can be more use as a partisan than a military student and cajoles his old friends Holin (Zubkov), Senior Lieutenant Galtsev (Zharikov) and Katasonich (Krylov) to take him across the river to the German side where he heads steadfastly off into the gloom alone, the last time that any of the men will see him.

MPAA: Not rated. For a wartime tale set at the front lines, there is surprisingly little violence. A few bodies are seen, but no killings actually occur on-screen. The only hint of sexual behaviour occurs when Holin attempts to seduce Masha (Maliavina), a lonely, distraught nurse, though he gets no further than forcing an unwelcome kiss on her.

Early in the film, Burlyayev is seen in a long full-length rear nude shot as Ivan steps into a tin bath in the barracks, continuing to stand while he bathes.

MY OWN PRIVATE IDAHO ★★★★

Credits: VHS/1991/USA/Colour/105 minutes
Writer/Director: Gus Van Sant.
Cast: Chiara Caselli [Carmella], Flea [Budd], Rodney Harvey [Gary], Udo Kier [Hans], Michael Parker [Digger], River Phoenix [Mike Waters], Keanu Reeves [Scott Favor], William Richert [Bob Pigeon], James Russo [Richard Waters]
Awards: Venice Festival Award 1991: Volpi Cup for Best Actor (Phoenix)
Genre: A road movie about a young hustler searching for love and his long lost mother in the Pacific North West.
Plot: Mike (Phoenix) is a teenage hustler on the streets of Seattle and Portland. A narcoleptic, he was abandoned many years previously by his mother. His best friend on the street is Scott Favor (Reeves), the son of the mayor of Portland. Scott is slumming, rebelling, calculatedly thumbing his nose at his straight-laced father before returning to the fold of wealthy respectable society.

Mike is on a quest to find his mother. Both have come temporarily under the benevolent wing of Bob Pigeon (Richert), an older Shakespeare-quoting denizen of the streets who, while not apparently pimping, does keep a protective watch out for his boys.

Mike's quest takes him and Scott first to Idaho and the home of his brother and then to Italy as they follow tenuous leads. Along the way, in a poignant scene which was reportedly improvised by the two young leads rather than being carefully scripted, Mike declares his love for Scott while the two sit beside an open camp fire.

As Scott's twenty-first birthday approaches, he increasingly distances himself from life on the streets, returning to his father's world of limousines and high finance. In the end he is able to publicly deny his erstwhile companion Bob.

MPAA: Rated R. Includes a large amount of sexual content. Several young hustlers discuss their trade and their tricks. Early in the film, Mike is seen in a non-explicit scene as a customer gives him a blow job.

While in Italy, Scott and Carmella engage in a sexual encounter, seen as a series of static images during which we are treated to a certain amount of on-screen nudity. And in one of the film's more memorable images, the cover boys of a number of hard-core gay publications come to life to discuss their lives.

MY SIDE OF THE MOUNTAIN

★★

Credits: VHS/1969/USA, Canada/Colour/100 minutes
Director: James B. Clark
Screenplay:
Ted Sherdeman, Jane Klove, Joanna Crawford
Based on the novel by Jean Craighead George.
Cast: Theodore Bikel [Bando], Teddy Eccles [Sam Gribley], Cosette Lee [The Apple Lady], Tudi Wiggens [Miss Turner]
Genre: A far-fetched children's adventure tale of a twelve-year-old boy who leaves home to spend a year in the woods in emulation of Henry David Thoreau.
Plot: Twelve-year-old Sam (Eccles), upset when his

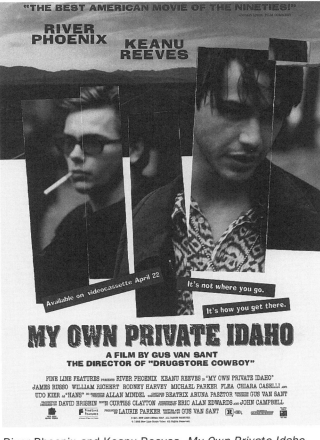

River Phoenix and Keanu Reeves, *My Own Private Idaho* (1991)

father is unable to take him on a long promised backpacking trip, decides to head off to the Quebec woods by himself. Travelling alone by bus from Toronto, he reaches the town of Knowlton. Here he hikes off into the Laurentian Mountains in search of a place to spend the winter and conduct his experiments into the life cycle of pond algae. This kid is twelve-years-old?

Altogether far too solemn and earnest a kid who seemingly never smiles, Sam nonetheless manages to befriend an itinerant musicologist named Bando (Bikel) and Miss Turner (Wiggens), the Knowlton librarian. Neither of these apparently sane and responsible adults seems to question the idea of a twelve-year-old boy living alone in a hollow tree with his pet raccoon and the peregrine falcon he has managed to capture and train single-handedly. This despite knowing that there is a search underway for the boy.

A series of adventures, misadventures and near disasters ensues before Sam, snow bound and nearly suffocating in his tree, decides to cut short his experiment and return home shortly after Christmas.

MPAA: Rated G. Eccles appears nude once when Sam strips down to go skinny-dipping. This is quite a distant shot, and Eccles is only briefly seen from the rear as he runs into the water. This is also almost the only truly natural, kid-like thing Sam does throughout the film!

N

THE NAME OF THE ROSE ★★★★

Credits: VHS/1986/Italy-Germany-France/Colour/ 128 minutes

Director: Jean Jacques Annaud

Screenplay: Andrew Birkin, Gerard Brach, Howard Franklin, and Alain Godard. Based on the novel by Umberto Eco.

Cast: F. Murray Abraham [Bernardo Gui], Elya Baskin [Severinus], Feodor Chaliapin, Jr. [Jorge], Sean Connery [William of Baskerville], William Hickey [Ubertino], Michael Lonsdale [the Abbot], Ron Perlman [Salvatore], Christian Slater [Adso of Melk], Valentina Vargas [the girl]

Awards: Won several awards in Europe, including acting awards for Connery in Germany and Britain, and cinematography awards in Italy.

Devon Sawa (left), *Now And Then* (1995)

Genre: A medieval mystery drama which tells of murder, intrigue, religious fervor, love, sex, duty and desire within the walls of a fourteenth-century Benedictine abbey.

Plot: In the year 1327 William of Baskerville (Connery), a Franciscan friar and former Inquisitor, and his teenage novice, Adso of Melk (Slater), arrive at an isolated Benedictine monastery in the mountains of northern Italy. Although there for an important religious debate, William and Adso quickly get caught up in the investigation of a series of mysterious deaths of handsome young monks.

The devil, it is claimed, is hurling beautiful boys from the windows of the abbey. Young Adso must simultaneously face a very different crisis when he meets a beautiful and mysterious young peasant woman (Vargas) in an abbey storehouse. After she seduces him, he begins to question his religious vocation. His doubts are intensified when she is one of three people convicted of heresy and witchcraft by the Papal Inquisitor Bernardo Gui (Abraham) and sentenced to be burned at the stake.

MPAA: Rated R. Vargas and Slater both appear nude in the surprisingly frank love making scene in the storehouse.

This includes very brief full-frontal exposure of the then sixteen-year-old Slater. There are also suggestions that Adso is attracting the attention of some of the monks in the abbey, especially as homosexual intrigue may have been a factor in some of the mysterious deaths.

NEA ★★

Credits: VHS/1976/France/Colour/103 minutes

In French with English subtitles.

Director: Nelly Kaplan

Cast: Heinz Bennent, Francoise Brion, Sami Frey [Axel Thorpe], Micheline Presle, Ann Zacharias [Sybille]

Genre: A satiric sex comedy.

Plot: What do you do if you are a sixteen-year-old virgin schoolgirl with a great deal of sexual curiosity and imagination? Why, secretly write a best selling erotic novel, of course. That's just what Sybille (Zacharias) does in Nea.

While engaged in this task, she feels it necessary to do a lot of research on her subject matter. When spying on others or when a clinical examination of the genitalia of a teenage boy no longer suffice, she seduces Axel Thorpe [Frey], her publisher.

MPAA: Rated R. This film is concerned entirely with sexual questions, and there are a great many sexual scenes throughout the film: Sybille and Axel, Sybelle's mother and her aunt, Axel and her mother, Axel and her sister.... Much more, and this film would have been pushed over the line into pornography. As it is, it is merely second rate.

NOT ANGELS BUT ANGELS ★★★

Credits: VHS/1994/Czech Republic-France/Colour/80 minutes. In Czech with English subtitles.

Writer/Director: Wiktor Grodecki

Genre. A documentary about juvenile male prostitution in Prague.

Plot: For this absorbing but frequently uncomfortable film, the producers interviewed some eighteen or so teenagers working in the sex trade in the bars, clubs and public places of Prague.

The boys, some as young as fourteen, discuss their past, their present and their future. Most of them runaways, the boys seem universally to have been driven to prostitution by economic necessity. Unable to support themselves with regular jobs, they market their most obvious assets, their youth and their bodies.

The filmmakers have allowed the boys to speak for themselves without judging them or their trade. They answer questions about their background, their start in prostitution, their customers, what they will, or won't do, their knowledge of AIDS and condoms, their personal sexual orientation, their fears, their desires and their vision of their personal future.

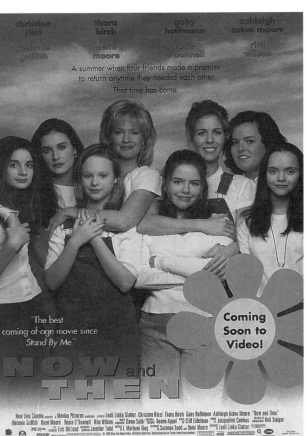

Now And Then (1995)

When the filmmakers interview the boys, one sees the loneliness, the desperation, the poverty which drove some of them to the trade. One may not agree with their choices, but at least one sees that these boys are very real people with very real personalities.

MPAA: Not rated. The entire film is concerned with discussion of sexual matters. At several points in the film optically altered stills from hard-core pornography have been inserted.

NOW AND THEN ★★★★★

Credits: VHS/1995/USA/ Colour/97 minutes

Director: Lesli Linka Glatter

Screenplay: I. Marlene King

Cast: Thora Birch [Teeny, age 12], Bradley Coryell, Melanie Griffith [adult Teeny], Gaby Hoffmann [Samantha, age 12], Justin Humphrey, Cloris Leachman [Grandma Albertson], Ashley Ashton Moore [Chrissy, age 12], Demi Moore [adult Samantha], Rosie O'Donnell [adult Roberta], Christina Ricci [Roberta, age 12], Travis Robertson, Devon Sawa [Scott Wormer], Walter Sparrow [Crazy Pete], Rita Wilson [adult Chrissy]

Genre: One of the few really good coming of age stories that looks at life from a girl's point of view, *Now And Then* is a nostalgic drama about four women, reunited after many years, reminiscing about the summer they were twelve-years-old.

Plot: There is something very special about being twelve-years-old. No longer a small child, yet not quite a teenager. Still having the innocence and imagination of a child but beginning to feel the pressures and needs of a young adult.

Teeny (Birch), Samantha (Hoffmann), Chrissy (A. A. Moore) and Roberta (Ricci) are the four girls. Growing up in a new, planned community near Shelby, Indiana, they are struggling with puberty and the growing independence which adolescence brings, while attempting to bring some understanding to the adult turbulence in their lives. They must also deal with the Wormers (Coryell, Humphrey, Robertson, and Sawa as Scott, the oldest). These four brothers have one purpose in life: to torment the four girls.

During a midnight seance in the local cemetery, the girls become intrigued by the tombstone of Dear Johnny, a twelve-year-old boy who died twenty five years previously. While trying to learn more about the boy, the girls must come to grips with the tragedies in their own lives. Roberta's mother died many years earlier in a car accident. Samantha's parents have just separated and are getting a divorce. Teeny's parents are conspicuous by their frequent absences. And Chrissy's mother has obvious limitations. To help themselves cope, the four girls make a pact to always be there for each other in times of need.

MPAA: Rated PG-13. Canadian Home Video rated PG. There is a lot of talk about sex amongst the four twelve-year-old girls, as well as a painfully hilarious sex lecture given to Chrissy by her mother, who can't quite get herself to actually say the word, let alone discuss the act itself.

There is also an extended nude scene involving all four Wormer boys. The girls, on their way to the county library, come across the four boys skinny-dipping. Getting back at them for all the tricks the boys have played on them, the girls steal the boys clothes.

All four boys are seen in extended full length rear shots, running through the woods, and down the road in an effort to retrieve their clothes. In all the shots where the boys face the camera, they are hidden by hands or various other strategically placed objects.

ODE TO BILLY JOE ★★★

Credits: VHS/1976/USA/Colour/106 minutes
Director: Max Baer
Screenplay: Herman Raucher
Based on Bobbie Gentry's song of the same title.
Cast: Robby Benson [Billy Joe McAllister], James Best [Dewey Barksdale], Terence Goodman [James Hartley], Simpson Hemphill [Brother Taylor], Joan Hotchkiss [Mama], Sandy McPeak [Papa], Glynnis O'Conner [Bobby Lee Hartley]
Genre: A dramatization of the events of the song written and sung by Bobby Gentry, but which goes beyond the music to explain why Billy Joe McAllister jumped off the Tallahatchie Bridge.
Plot: Growing up in rural Mississippi in 1953, fifteen-year-old Bobby Lee (O'Conner) has very strict parents, even for that time and place. She wishes to be allowed to receive 'gentlemen callers' at home. Specifically, she wishes for Billy Joe McAllister (Benson) to be allowed to come calling on her but Papa (McPeak) won't hear of it. Both Billy Joe and Bobby Lee are filled with desires. Billy Joe in particular is eager to test his manhood and lose his virginity.

After the night of the Jamboree, during which Billy Joe gets royally drunk, the boy disappears. When Bobby Lee finds him in the woods two days later, he is in a state of anguish. He is desperate to 'have' Bobby Lee, but she won't give in to his pleadings. Then the truth comes out. When he got drunk at the Jamboree, he "went" with a man. Bobby Lee tries to rationalize his actions, saying he was drunk at

the time and didn't know what he was doing. Billy Joe refutes this saying he wasn't that drunk. He was well aware of what he was doing.

It is never clearly stated whether this was a question of his own sexual orientation or just a one time experiment. But to Billy Joe the experience is to have devastating consequences. In his anguish, the boy castigates himself as a sinner, an abomination, a trespasser against the laws of God and of nature. Later that night, in a state of turmoil,

The Outsiders (1983)

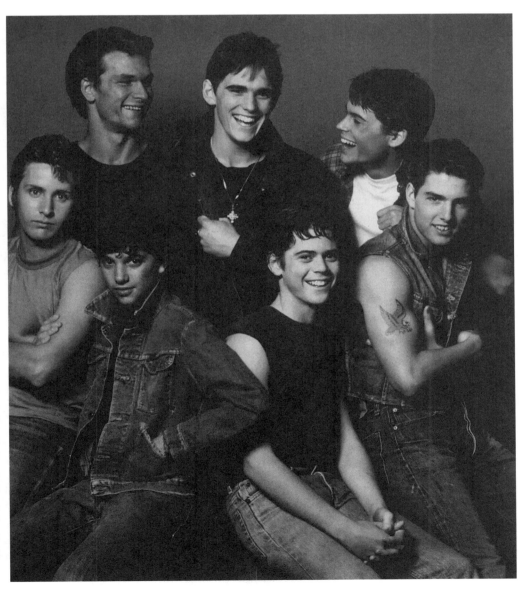

he throws himself from the bridge.

The people in the community, aware of the relationship between Billy Joe and Bobby Lee, assume that she is pregnant. In order to protect Billy Joe's good name, she encourages the fallacy by leaving town. On her way to catch the bus she meets Mr. Barksdale (Best), the local mill owner and Billy Joe's former employer. When he admits to being the man Billy Joe was with, Bobby Lee persuades him to remain silent, again to protect Billy Joe's reputation.

The film should be lauded for trying to take a stand against a society which is so homophobic that even a single same sex encounter, regardless of the actual orientation of the youth involved, can drive a boy to suicide. Unfortunately the answer presented here, while probably accurate for the film's setting and time, leaves a lot to be desired. Surely combatting the homophobia rather than denying the sexuality is the better way to end the obscenely high suicide rate amongst gay teenagers which still exists.

MPAA: Rated PG. Canadian Home Video rated PG. There are several static, tableau style sex scenes as Billy Joe and another teenager walk through a makeshift brothel at the Jamboree looking at and commenting on the various men who are with the hookers. One of the women bares her breasts for the boys in a very, very brief sequence.

OLIVIER OLIVIER ★★★★

Credits: VHS/1992/France/Colour/110 minutes
In French with English subtitles.
Writer/Director: Agnieszka Holland
Based on a 1984 French newspaper story.
Cast: Florian Billion [Paul], Francois Cluzet [Serge], Gregoire Colin [Olivier], Faye Gatteau [young Nadine], Marina Golovine [Nadine], Emmanuel Morozof [young Olivier], Frederic Quiring [Marcel], Brigitte Rouan [Elizabeth], Jean-Francois Stevenin [Inspector Druot]
Awards: Los Angeles Film Critics Association Awards 1993: Best Score.
Genre: A fact-based drama about the disappearance of a nine-year-old boy and his apparent return six years later.
Plot: When nine-year-old Olivier (Morozof) disappears without a trace while riding to his grandmother's house his family falls apart. Somewhat dysfunctional prior to the boy's disappearance, individually and collectively they disintegrate afterwards. Father (Cluzet) takes a job in Africa leaving his wife and daughter behind. Mother (Rouan) retreats into a form of madness. Sister Nadine (Gatteau) begins to practice arcane occult rituals in the attic, eventually developing telekinetic abilities. The only apparent note of sanity is Marcel (Quiring), a bachelor

neighbour who more and more becomes a source of practical assistance to Elizabeth and Nadine.

Six years later, a fifteen-year-old boy is picked up in Paris. A drug user, and a juvenile prostitute with no apparent past, he is identified by the police inspector who investigated Olivier's disappearance as being the missing boy. Reunited with the family, Olivier (now played by Colin) is accepted by the family as their missing son. He seems to remember details which only Olivier could remember. Eventually even the skeptical Nadine (now played by Golovine) accepts him as her long lost brother when she hears Olivier teaching a neighbourhood boy, Paul (Billion), a song he used to sing as a boy when he engaged in peeing contests with Marcel.

But is he really Olivier? The truth becomes known when Olivier walks in on Marcel while the man is in the act of raping Paul. Now both Olivier and the rest of the family must come to terms with the realities of their situation.

MPAA: Rated R. Canadian Home Video rated 18-A. There is some minor nudity involving several male characters, all of it side or rear shots. There is one scene portraying the rape of a young boy. After his return from Paris, Olivier and Nadine become involved sexually on one occasion in what is apparently a case of sibling incest.

ORDINARY MAGIC ★★★

Credits: VHS/1993/Canada/Colour/96 minutes
Director: Giles Walker
Screenplay: Jefferson Lewis
Based on the novel by Malcolm Bosse.
Cast: Paul Anka [Joey Dean], David Fox [father/Warren], Glenne Headly [Charlotte], Heath Lamberts, Ryan Reynolds [Ganesh/Jeffrey]
Genre: A drama about family ties, culture clash, traditional values and prejudice played out when a teenage boy returns to his father's birthplace in Canada after growing up in India.
Plot: When his father Warren (Fox) dies in India, fifteen-year-old Jeffrey (Reynolds) must leave the culture in which he has been raised and move to Canada to live with his aunt Charlotte (Headly). Here he must learn to deal with culture shock, cold weather and social isolation. Although fair haired and fair skinned, Jeffrey is thoroughly Indian in culture and social outlook, a fact that does not sit easily with many of the residents of Paris, Ontario where he now lives with his aunt.

While still acclimatizing himself to the differences, he is faced with a more serious problem: the town council, in partnership with a wealthy, unscrupulous developer (Anka), has plans to develop a "world class" resort in the town. The family home, built by Jeffrey's great-grandfather, stands on land the developer wants to include in the project.

Facing down the developers and the town council when served with notices of expropriation and eviction, Charlotte and Jeffrey refuse to move. Drawing on Jeffrey's Indian upbringing, aunt and nephew begin a hunger strike to bring attention to their situation. They refuse to back down, and though initially alone against the town, eventually the two garner enough support to keep their

Matt Dillon, *The Outsiders* (1983)

home and kill the project.

MPAA: Not rated. There is one sex scene involving Charlotte and her boyfriend, a scene witnessed by Jeffrey when he comes to investigate what he assumes to be screams of pain emanating from his aunt's bedroom. This is just the first of several mystifying encounters with western sexuality and male-female relationships the boy will face in the days ahead.

ORPHANS ★★★

(Also known as *Shaken But Not Crushed* or as *Podranki*)

Credits: VHS/1976/USSR/Colour/105 minutes
In Russian with English subtitles. Also available dubbed.
Writer/Director: Nikolai Gubenko
Cast: Yuosas Budraitis, Georgyi Burkov, Aliosha Cherstvov, Alexander Kaliagin
Genre: A nostalgic drama about a family of orphans in the post World War II era in the Soviet Union, seen through the eyes of the youngest.
Plot: Natalia, Alexei, Denis and Sergei have been orphaned by the war. Their father was a battle casualty, their mother died when Alyosha (as Alexei is known) was only a year old. Natalia, the oldest, dies when she is only fourteen. Denis and Sergei are adopted by two different families, but Alyosha, the youngest, is placed in an orphanage after a brief, unsuccessful stay in a foster home. Although the staff are not uncaring, like any other institution this one tends to be impersonal.

Among the teaching staff, Alyosha is fortunate to find a man who encourages the boy in his writing. What is missing from Alyosha's life, however, is a sense of family. He and his brothers were separated when very young and Alyosha has no memories of them, nor they of him. It is not until thirty years later, as adults, that they become re-acquainted. In an attempt to find that missing sense of family, Alyosha, now a published author, tracks down Denis, now a successful architect and Sergei, now a prisoner behind bars.
MPAA: Not rated. There are several scenes which seem to indicate that Alyosha, as young as he is, is beginning to feel some fundamental sexual desires. There is a teacher he is particularly attracted to and a statue of a nude woman in the orphanage grounds which constantly attracts his eyes.

There is one scene of a woman sunning herself topless on the school roof. There are also several scenes of pre-teen boys in the nude, including some brief full-frontal shots. Several young boys are seen being bathed in the orphanage. A large group of nude pre-adolescent boys is seen on a beach running down the sand and into the water.

OUTCASTS ★★★

(Also known as *The Outsiders*)

Credits: VHS/1986/Taiwan/Colour/102 minutes
In Mandarin with English subtitles.
Director: Yu Kan-Ping
Based on the novel "The Outsiders" by Shiang Yeong.
Cast: Lee Tai Ling, Shao Hsin, Su Ming-Ming, Sun Yueh
Genre: A ground-breaking film, this drama from Taiwan,

the first gay-themed film from China's island province, explores the life of a gay high school student after he is sent packing by his father.

Plot: When Ah-Ching is caught in his high school's science labs engaged in sex with an adult, the school, ever mindful of its own reputation, expels the boy. His father likewise gives the boy the boot, beating him severely and tossing him into the street. Homeless, Ah-Ching gravitates to the park, "The Office" as it is known in Taipei's gay community. Here in the cruising grounds, Ah-Ching is befriended by Master Yang, an aging photographer.

Taken to Yang's home, Ah-Ching becomes a member of a surrogate family of gay youths which includes Jade, Mouse and Wu-Ming, all of whom have been thrown out of their family homes and all of whom now call Yang's apartment home.

Ah-Ching is also introduced to a larger gay community where handsome youths become the ornamental accompaniment to wealthy and powerful middle aged men. (One might compare this with the films of Eloy de la Iglesia, or the Australian *Everlasting Secret Family*.) It is also, unfortunately, a world of juvenile prostitution, police shakedowns and physical abuse. But on a more positive note, it is also a world where Yang and his landlady can provide some small measure of stability and security to these outcasts. They are also able to provide employment when they open the "Blue Angel," a gay bar.

Interestingly, all of the gay youths in this film are shown as coming from broken homes. Is this coincidence? Or is this seen by the writers as a contributing factor in questions of sexual orientation? Ah-Ching's own broken home is an on-going sub theme in the film, with several lengthy flashbacks to his past, his relationship with his mother, and his relationship with his younger brother, Ti-Wa, who died of pneumonia as a child.

MPAA: Not rated. Although dealing with gay themes and beginning with the expulsion of Ah-Ching from his school when he is caught engaged in a sexual act at school, the sex in this film is all implied, not explicitly shown.

Some North American audiences might be uncomfortable with the prevalence of a convention which sees a gay version of a December-May relationship as the norm.

THE OUTSIDERS ★★★

Credits: VHS/1983/USA/Colour/91 minutes
Director: Francis Ford Coppola
Screenplay: Kathleen Knutsen Rowell
Based on the novel by S. E. Hinton.
Cast: Tom Cruise [Steve Randle], Matt Dillon [Dallas Winston], Emilio Estevez [Two-Bit Matthews], Leif Garrett [Bob Sheldon], C. Thomas Howell [Ponyboy Curtis], Diane Lane [Cherry Valance], Rob Lowe

[Sodapop Curtis], Ralph Macchio [Johnny Cade], Patrick Swayze [Darrel Curtis]

Genre: A melodramatic tale with an outstanding cast that deals with questions of rich and poor, gangs and friendships, neglect and abuse, and acts of selfless heroism.

Plot: It's the early sixties in the Midwestern United States. The teenagers of one small town are split through the middle. The poor, neglected, working class, but ultimately noble Greasers, are pitted against the rich-kid Soc. When two sixteen-year-old Greasers, Ponyboy (Howell) and Johnny Cade (Macchio) kill Bob Sheldon (Garrett), leader of the Soc, in the park one night they flee to the countryside to an abandoned church to hide from the law.

A group of young children get caught in the building when it starts to burn. Ponyboy and Johnny become heros by carrying them to safety, risking their own lives for the sake of others. Johnny is badly burned in the rescue efforts and paralyzed from the waist down, his injuries ultimately proving fatal.

The film suffers badly from melodramatic, overblown performances by many of the young cast members, most of whom were at the beginnings of their careers when this film was made. It suffers as well from a fairly transparent plot and many cardboard characterizations. It also reeks of a comfortable, patronizing middle class romanticism about the nobility of poverty. It is, however, redeemed by Coppola's sure hand with visual imagery, and despite all the film's faults, one can't help but get caught up in the story, especially the plight of Johnny and Ponyboy, the two young friends at its heart.

MPAA: Rated PG. As might be expected in a story dealing with gangs, there is considerable violence on screen, including the murder of Bob Sheldon and a choreographed rumble between the Greasers and the Soc. There is also one very brief nude scene involving a side shot of Sodapop (Lowe) as he steps out of the shower.

OVER THE EDGE ★★★★★

Credits: VHS/1979/USA/Colour/91 minutes
Director: Jonathan Kaplan
Screenplay: Charlie Haas and Tim Hunter
Cast: Matt Dillon [Richie White], Tom Fergus [Claude], Ellen Geer [Sandra Willet], Kim Kliner [Abby], Michael Kramer [Carl], Erich Lalich [Tip], Pamela Ludwig [Corey], Harry Northup [Doberman], Julia Pomeroy [Julia], Andy Romano [Fred Willet], Vincent Spano [Mark], Tiger Thompson [Johnny]

Genre: Not as well-known as it should be, this drama is probably one of the best yet made about teenage alienation and rebellion in the suburban wasteland. Although set and filmed in the seventies, it still works as a powerful tale of kids on the rampage.

Plot: New Granada is a planned community. Attracting industry and real estate resale values are more important than the youth of the community. Carl (Kramer) is the fourteen-year-old son of the local Cadillac dealer. Richie (Dillon), his best friend, is the son of a single mother. The local police force, particularly in the person of officer Doberman (Northup), have picked out these two boys for particular attention, and in a community where family communication is non-existent, parents are more likely to listen to Doberman than to their sons.

After the town tries to shut down the teens' only re-creational outlet, a bare Quonset hut with a static play-ground, things go from bad to worse. When a town meeting is called to discuss even further restrictions on the teens after Richie is shot and killed during a police chase, the kids go on a rampage, trashing the local school and setting fire to the cars in the parking lot.

This film marked the then fourteen-year-old Matt Dillon's screen debut but was not released until several years after it was produced: not until after Dillon had become a major figure.

MPAA: Rated PG. Primarily a tale of bored teenagers in revolt against increasing restrictions, there is little overt sexual behaviour in this film. Beyond some talk and several instances of boys putting each other down by calling each other "faggot," the closest we get to sex occurs when Carl and Corey (Ludwig) spend the night together while Carl is on the run. However, this is no more than implied: we see Carl and Corey getting into a sleeping bag together and then getting up again in the morning.

P, Q

PARADISE ★

Credits: VHS/1982/USA/ Colour/100 minutes
Writer/director: Stuart Gillard
Cast: Willie Aames [David], Phoebe Cates [Sarah], Richard Curnock [Geoffrey], Aviva Marks [Rachel], Joseph Shiloach [Ahmed], Tuvia Tavi [the Jackal], Neil Vipond [the Reverend]
Genre: A romantic adventure tale which is a blatant copy of *The Blue Lagoon* format of two teenagers discovering love and sex in an isolated locale. This time the deserts of the Middle East.
Plot: The film opens in Baghdad, in the year 1823. Sarah (Cates) and her guardian Geoffrey (Curnock) have engaged a small caravan to take them to Damascus, the first stage on a trip home to London. They are joined by David (Aames) and his missionary parents (Vipond and Marks).

A randy teenager, despite the lectures from his puritanical father, David is immediately swept off his feet by the beautiful young girl. Unfortunately, so is the Jackal (Tavi), a lecherous slave trader who would have her for his own.

The caravan sets off across the desert with the Jackal and his men in hot pursuit. The Jackal's men waste little time in killing off everybody in the caravan, other than David and Sarah. The teenagers survive by finding a seemingly endless string of lush, uninhabited oases where they learn about love and sex, mostly by watching a pair of chimpanzees. In the desert? Well, that's no more ludicrous than anything else in this film.

Actually, the director should have stuck to chimps. They're more fun than the kids. Absurd dialogue badly delivered doesn't help, either. Cates is simply not believable as a well brought up middle class English girl. But then, given the dubious premise of the film to begin

Academy Award® Winner
Best Foreign Language Film 1988
"The Year's Best Film!"
L.A. TIMES

MAX von SYDOW
PELLE THE CONQUEROR
Dubbed by Max von Sydow

Pelle Hvenegaard and Max von Sydow, *Pelle The Conqueror* (1988)

with, who cares?
MPAA: Rated R. The film includes a great many sexual situations as the two teenagers go through the discovery of sex, helped along the way by a medical text book which had once belonged to Sarah's father. They talk about it, agonize about it and finally do it. There is even a scene of a monkey masturbating, giving Sarah an excuse to speculate on whether David does.

There are also a great many nude scenes. Many of these involve Cates. The camera spends a lot of time caressing her body. Aames is not neglected, however, and his scenes include some full-frontal underwater scenes as David and Sarah swim in one of the oases they stumble across.

Shortly after the film's original release Aames attempted to disavow these scenes, claiming they were done by a body double and inserted later. Judge for yourself. There are also a great many shots of both principals in more or less revealing loincloths.

PELLE THE CONQUEROR ★★★★★

(Also known as *Pelle Erobreren*)

Credits: VHS/1988/Denmark-Sweden/Colour/138 minutes. In Danish and Swedish with English subtitles.
Writer/Director: Billy August
Based on the novel by Martin Anderson Nexo.
Cast: Pelle Hvenegaard [Pelle], Max von Sydow [Lasse Karlsson]
Awards: Academy Awards 1988: Best Foreign Film; (nomination) Best Actor (von Sydow). Cannes Film Festival 1988: Best Film. Golden Globe Awards 1988: Best Foreign Film. National Board of Review: five best foreign films. European Felix Awards: (nomination) Best

Film; Best Actor (von Sydow); Best Debutante Performer (Hvenegaard). The film also won numerous other awards in Europe, including Best Film and Best Actor (von Sydow) awards in both Sweden and Denmark.

Genre: A drama about an innocent and rather gullable farm boy and his widower father, a well-meaning but weak, uneducated dreamer.

Plot: Lasse Karlsson (von Sydow) leaves Sweden and travels to Denmark with his son Pelle (Hvenegaard) to look for work and a better life. What they find is the Stone Farm and its owner Kongstrup. Lasse is hired on as a stable hand to care for the cows and Pelle is given work as a cow herd.

The work is hard, the living conditions poor, the farm manager harsh and the wages low. Also, as Swedes in Denmark, Lasse and his son are subjected to abuse and discrimination. Pelle is constantly picked on by the other children when he goes to school, both for being Swedish and because his father is courting Madame Olsen, whose husband is presumed to have been lost at sea.

Pelle's only friend is Kongstrup's illegitimate son Rud, a mentally deficient and physically deformed boy. Others in the area constantly taunt Pelle, especially the young Trainee on the farm. Despite his treatment, Pelle is irrepressible and never loses sight of his dream to see the world.

This film is reported to have been cut from 160 to 138 minutes for its North American distribution. The VHS tapes I have seen appear to have been printed from this shortened version.

MPAA: Rated PG-13. Hvenegaard is seen in several nude scenes including a number involving full-frontal exposure. The most noteworthy occurs when the Trainee lures Pelle into a barn with tales of hidden gold coins. Instead, however, Pelle finds humiliation. The Trainee pulls the boy's pants off and forces him into the yard where many of the farm hands are working.

LE PETIT AMOUR ★★★★

(Also known as *A Little Love*, or as *Kung Fu Master*)

Credits: VHS/1987/France/ Colour/80 minutes
In French with English subtitles.
Director: Agnes Varda
Cast: Jane Birkin [Mary Jane], Mathieu Demy [Julien], Lou Doillon [Lou], Charlotte Gainsbourg [Lucy]
Genre: Frama about an intergenerational love affair between a forty-year-old divorcee and a teenage boy.
Plot: Mary Jane (Birkin) meets fourteen-year-old Julien (Demy), a classmate of Mary Jane's daughter Lucy (Gainsbourg), at Lucy's birthday party when the boy gets drunk and sick. Despite herself, Mary Jane finds herself attracted to the boy. For reasons of his own, Julien responds to her overtures. He visits Mary Jane when he knows Lucy will be out of the house and engineers a rendezvous in a hotel.

When Mary Jane and her two daughters travel to London to visit her family for Easter vacation, Julien is invited to accompany them. After Lucy discovers her mother kissing Julien in the garden, Mary Jane and the boy go off alone to a small island for a few days of bliss. On their return to Paris, Mary Jane's life falls apart. As a result of the affair with Julien, Lucy's father takes custody of their daughter, and Julien's family forbid them meeting again.

The film is told from Mary Jane's point of view, and it is clear that at first she is uncomfortable with her own feelings towards Julien. It is also clear that Julien, despite his age, is a fully consenting partner to the relationship: he pursues Mary Jane as actively as she pursues him.

Mathieu Demy, who plays Julien, is the son of director

Bernard Brieux (left), *Petit Con* (1984)

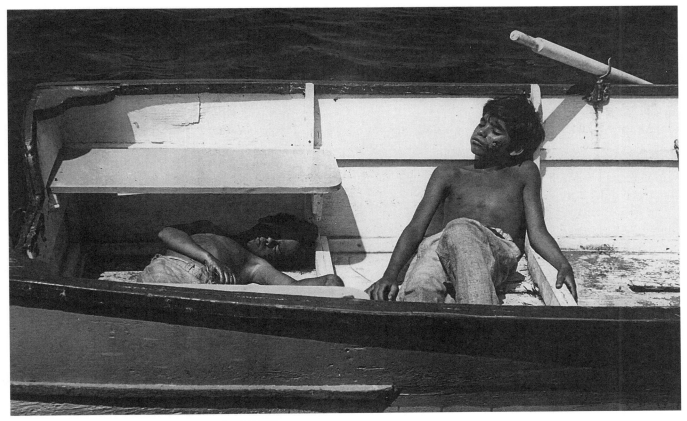

Ruben Figueroa and Miguel Alejandro, *Popi* (1969

Agnes Varda and her husband, renowned French director Jacques Demy. Jane Birkin and Charlotte Gainsbourg, who play mother and daughter in this film, are in real life mother and daughter as well.

MPAA: Rated R. Despite the controversial nature of the subject matter, the treatment of the material is not the least exploitive. Although it is made clear that Mary Jane and Julien share a bed on the island, nothing more explicitly sexual than a kiss is portrayed on screen.

In addition to the relationship between Julien and Mary Jane, there is also a lot of teenage sex talk on-screen: AIDS, condoms, safe sex, have you done it, and so on.

PETIT CON ★★★★

(Also known as *P'tit Con*, as *Little Schmuck*, as *Little Jerk* or as *Little Nutter*)

Credits: VHS/1984/France/Colour/90 minutes
In French with English subtitles.
Writer/Director: Gerard Lauzier. Based on the French comic *Souvenirs d'un Jeune Homme*, by Lauzier.
Cast: Souad Amidou, Bernard Brieux [Michel], Caroline Cellier, Guy Marchand
Genre: Comic drama about a teenager in search of himself.

Plot: Michel (Brieux) is an altogether far too serious and pretentious eighteen-year-old whose bourgeois roots have a bad habit of getting in the way of his professed Marxist principles and whose emotions smack more of a how-to text book than truly experienced passions.

He has, he complains to his diary, been eighteen for an entire month. And what has he done with his life? NOTHING! Life, it seems, has been a series of failures for poor Michel. "If only ... If only ... If only ..." he laments. He therefore resolves: 1. To combat his unhealthy sensitivities. 2. To combat despair and break the vicious circle of euphoria and depression that keeps him from any constructive action. 3. To overcome pride and loneliness. 4. To solve the PROBLEM at any cost.

The PROBLEM is that he is a very horny virgin. Replete with smug and romantic middle class notions about the nobility of the downtrodden poor, Michel heads out to do his part. He soon finds the truth may be neither so romantic nor so noble.

The old drunk he helps home from the bar is an ignorant, racist slob who makes a pass at the boy in the dark. The drunk's stepdaughter Salina is quite prepared to cure Michel's virginity problem, but she is also quite prepared to use him for her own ends. She moves into his tiny rented room and brings her fresh-out-of-jail boyfriend with her.

The only sympathetic hearing Michel gets is in the home of some aging hippies cum artists whose pretensions are every bit as bad as Michel's. Furthermore, from a fourteen-year-old girl through middle-aged women to a gay teenager virtually every member of this household has designs on Michel's body. In turn, each tries to seduce the youth.

As for Michel's own family, it isn't until the boy's failed suicide attempt that his own father is able to make any inroads into building a truly understanding relationship with his estranged son. By the closing frames of the film this is still a very shaky proposition.

Bernard Brieux's portrayal of the confused, pretentious youth is close to perfection. Haven't we all known somebody just like Michel? The teenage expert on life whose experience with the subject comes from the printed page not the reality of the world beyond his bedroom door.

MPAA: Rated R. A number of sexual situations occur throughout the film, including scenes of masturbation, gay advances, intergenerational sex (Michel with an older woman, Maryse) and the night Michel spends with Salina. There are also several shots of bare breasted women including Maryse and Salina.

PIXOTE ★★★★★

Credits: VHS/1981/Brazil/Colour/127 minutes
In Portuguese with English subtitles.
Writer/Director: Hector Babenco
Based on the novel *Infancia dos Mortos* by Jose Louzeiro.
Cast: Claudio Bernardo [Garotao "Big Boy"], Fernando Ramos da Silva [Pixote], Rubens de Falco [Juiz], Jose Nilson Martin Dos Santos [Diego], Jardel Filho [Sapatos Brancos], Jorge Juliao [Lilica], Edilson Lino [Chico], Gilberto Moura [Dito], Marilia Pera [Sueli], Zenildo Oliveira Santos [Fumaca], Tony Tornad [Cristal]
Awards: New York Film Critics 1981: Best Foreign Film. Los Angeles Film Critics 1981: Best Foreign Film. National Society of Film Critics 1981: Best Actress (Pera). The National Board of Review: five best foreign films.
Genre: Brilliant. Gritty. Disturbing. Hard-hitting. This dramatic film is a must-see for anybody interested in or concerned about street kids and children at risk anywhere in the world. Fortunately, this film, which has been out of print on video for some time, has recently been re-released.
Plot: Pixote (da Silva) is a homeless ten-year-old boy living on the streets of Sao Paulo. He is picked up by the police and sent to an overcrowded and brutal reform school. At the school he witnesses the brutal gang rape of a young boy, becomes involved with drugs and glue sniffing, and learns important lessons about crime.

After several boys in the school die at the hands of the police and the school authorities, Pixote and several other boys escape. Pixote, a cross-dressing gay teenager named Lilica (Juliao), Dito (Moura) and Chico (Lino) go to Rio de Janeiro to sell drugs. After several setbacks, the four boys take up with an aging alcoholic prostitute, Sueli (Pera), robbing her johns at gunpoint, eventually murdering one. After Chico and Dito are killed, Lilica leaves. Sueli then kicks Pixote out onto the street again, leaving him with nothing but the clothes on his back and a handgun.

One should compare this film with the somewhat later Indian film *Salaam Bombay!* which deals with children in similar circumstances and likewise employed real street children on-screen. All of the principal juvenile roles in Pixote were played by boys who were themselves street kids or from destitute families. On August 25, 1987, while still a teenager, da Silva was shot and killed by the Brazilian police while committing a robbery.
MPAA: Rated R. Gang rape, gay sex, masturbation, shower scenes, intergenerational straight sex: the film features several nude scenes and sexual situations, both gay and straight.

Most of the young actors in lead roles appear at least once in full-frontal nude scenes. The most noteworthy is a group shower scene at the detention centre. Da Silva is seen nude when Pixote hallucinates about running down the street nude after he indulges in glue sniffing.

POPI ★★★★

Credits: VHS/1969/USA/Colour/115 minutes
Writer/Director: Arthur Hiller
Screenplay: Tina and Lester Pine
Cast: Miguel Alejandro [Junior], Alan Arkin [Abraham "Popi"], Ruben Figueroa [Luis], Rita Moreno [Lupe]
Genre: A touching, sometimes comic drama about a poor widower trying to better the lives of his two sons.
Plot: Abraham Rodriguez (Arkin), a single Puerto Rican father, is trying to survive in a shabby one-room apartment in New York City. He is providing as best he can for his two sons by holding down three jobs. But he wants the good life for eleven-year-old Junior (Alejandro) and nine-year-old Luis (Figueroa). If you can provide for them, he tells us, he'll give the boys to you. Sign the papers and everything. They're good kids, good in school, he assures us.

The violence and dirt in New York finally get too much for Abraham and he concocts a far fetched scheme to get the boys adopted by a wealthy family. He'll put them adrift off the coast of Florida in a small row boat. When they are picked up, Junior and Luis are to tell the authorities they are Cuban refugees. Although the boys are very reluctant to take part in this scheme, Abraham sets it in motion anyway, casting the boys adrift off Miami.

After several days of panic when there is no word of the boys, he finally hears the news. They have been found but are in serious condition in the hospital suffering from heat stroke and dehydration. Thus begins a series of comic escapades while Abraham tries to keep a watchful eye on his boys who have become national heroes for their daring escape from Cuba. They even get an invitation to the White House!

Inevitably, of course, the truth will out and the boys, to their everlasting joy, are reunited with their "Popi", proving yet again that be it ever so humble, there's no place like home.

James Lyons (right), *Postcards From America* (1994)

MPAA: Rated G. That this film would be given a "G" rating in 1969 is an indication of how much the criteria used by the MPAA to assign ratings have changed over the years.

There are several scenes of violence in the film, including Abraham slapping his sons around. There is also a shot of a teenage punk decapitating a live pigeon.

Both Alejandro and Figueroa have several nude scenes, including some very brief full-frontal shots of both boys. They are beaten and left naked in an alley by a gang of young teenage toughs. Both boys are seen in the bathtub. The boys play nude on the beach in Florida. They are seen running around the halls of the hospital in Miami wearing backless hospital gowns.

PORKY'S ★★

Credits: VHS/1981/Canada/Colour/99 minutes
Writer/Director: Bob Clark
Cast: Kim Cattrall [Miss Honeywell], Susan Clark [Cherry Forever], Scott Colomby [Brian Schwartz], Tony Ganios [Meat], Mark Herrier [Billy], Art Hindle [Ted Jarvis], Kaki Hunter [Wendy], Alex Karras [The Sheriff], Wyatt Knight [Tommy], Wayne Maunder [Cavanagh], Chuck Mitchell [Porky], Dan Monahan [Pee Wee], Jack Mulchahey [Frank], Cyril O'Reilly [Tim], Nancy Parsons [Miss Balbricker], Roger Wilson [Mickey]
Genre: *Porky's* is the quintessential teenage sex comedy and though mindless, is not without a few belly laughs.

Plot: Six teenage boys in the small Florida town of Angel Beach have one thing one their minds and it's not school work. How could it be? The only course this school seems to offer is gym class. Or is that only to enable the director to set up lots of shots of young bodies in shorts and T-shirts? Followed, of course, by the inevitable locker room and shower scenes.

Am I too cynical? In a farce where half the characters have names with sexual overtones? SEX! That is what motivates these boys. Especially the butt of everybody's jokes, Pee Wee (Monahan), a virgin with a burning desire to alleviate his condition.

After a visit to local hooker Cherry Forever (Clark) turns out to be a set up for a practical joke which leaves Pee Wee running naked down the highway, the boys decide to cross the county line to pay a visit to Porky's, a bar and brothel deep in the everglades. When the boys are swindled and tossed out of the bar by owner Porky (Mitchell), they plot revenge. Aided by a young gym teacher, they trash the establishment, leaving Porky humiliated and itching for revenge.

One of the most financially successful Canadian productions of all time, this film was followed by no less than two sequels, *Porky's 2; The Next Day*, and *Porky's Revenge*, neither of which comes up to the minimal standards of the original.

MPAA: Rated R. Although a few socially redeeming subplots have been thrown in concerning physically abused teens and anti-semitism, essentially Porky's is about sex. Implied sex, sex talk, sex humour, sexual situations, sexual frustrations, it's all there, and then some.

There is also a great deal of nudity, both male and female. Most of the young leads appear in full-frontal nude shots, the boys in the rout as they leave Cherry Forever's home in a panic, the girls in the well-known shower scene as the boys watch through a hole in the wall.

LES PORTES TOURNANTES
★★★★

(Also known as *The Revolving Doors*)

Credits: VHS/1988/Canada, France/Colour/100 minutes
In French with English subtitles.
Director: Francis Mankiewicz
Screenplay: Jacques Savoie and Francis Mankiewicz
Based on a novel by Jacques Savoie.
Cast: Gabriel Arcand [Madrigal], Francois Methe [Antoine], Miou Miou [Lauda], Jacques Penot [Pierre], Monique Spaziani [Celeste]
Awards: Canadian Genie Awards: ten nominations.
Genre: A drama about three generations of one francophone family from New Brunswick and their search for roots and family ties.
Plot: Sometimes confusing temporally, *Les Portes Tournantes* tells the story of pre-teenager Antoine (Methe) and his search, both spiritually and physically, for his paternal grandmother.

Living alone with his artist father Madrigal (Arcand), Antoine stumbles upon a journal in a suitcase full of mementos recently sent to the man. As he reads the journal the film flashes back to the youth of the writer, Celeste (Spaziani), the grandmother Antoine has never met.

Like Antoine himself, his grandmother is a piano player. Through his reading of the journal the boy learns some of the secrets buried in his family's past: Celeste's poor rural roots; her years as a silent film pianist in Campbelltown; her marriage to the wealthy Pierre (Penot); her life after Pierre's death in World War II; where she is now; how she got there; why Madrigal never knew her. Eventually, obsessed by a desire to meet his grandmother and armed with little more than an old nightclub poster, Antoine sets out alone to track her down in New York City.

Much of the story is told through the use of flashbacks as Antoine reads his grandmother's journal. Another recurring storytelling device involves Antoine taping letters to his mother Lauda (Miou Miou), explaining his thoughts and mulling over events. As Antoine is an appealing mix of wide-eyed innocence and wisdom beyond his years, this device works much

better than one might assume.
MPAA: Not rated. Strictly PG level material. The only "questionable" scene occurs when young Antoine, evidently having heard his father use the term to disparage Lauda, announces to his mother that when he grows up, he too wants to be a lesbian.

POSTCARDS FROM AMERICA
★★★★

Credits: VHS/1994/Great Britain, USA/Colour/93 minutes
Writer/Director: Steve McLean
Based on *Close To The Knives* and *Memories That Smell Like Gasoline*, autobiographical writings by David Wojnarowicz.
Cast: Michael Imperioli [the hustler], Maggie Low [mother], James Lyons [adult David], Michael Ringer [father], Michael Tighe [teenage David], Olmo Tighe [young David]
Genre: A non-linear drama about the life of writer and AIDS activist David Wojnarowicz who died in 1992. This film is biographical without being truly a biography. *Postcards From America* covers three periods in the life of the writer: pre-adolescence, his teenage years and his young adulthood.
Plot: David as a young boy (Olmo Tighe) is physically and psychologically abused by his alcoholic father (Ringer), a man who "hated women, hated children, hated animals and obviously hated himself."

Looking for love in Times Square, trying to find the hugs and kisses he never got from mom and dad, David is

Olmo Tighe, *Postcards From America* (1994)

being sexually abused and posing for nude photographs by the age of ten. By his teenage years, David (Michael Tighe) is struggling with his sexuality, selling his body on the streets and in the washrooms of New York, shoplifting for food and clothing, living on the edge.

For a while, a married lawyer gives him back his sense of self worth in a relationship which survives the end of sex. As a young adult (Lyons), David hits the road, hitchhiking around the country, taking whatever comes his way, including rape in the back of a van.

Christian Tapdrup (right), *Pretty Boy* (1993)

This beautifully photographed film slides effortlessly back and forth from one period in David's life to the other as we see in a series of snapshots, or postcards, significant episodes in the writer's memory. Mugging people in New York. His mother crouching protectively over him while his father brandishes a revolver. Staring at his uncle lying on the back lawn in the first stirrings of his sexuality. Being beaten by his father for not crying when Kennedy's killed. On the road in the west.

Like so many films which are presented in a non-linear, non-narrative fashion, this one perhaps gives us a better picture of David's life than a more traditional technique might have. I think a comparison with *The Long Day Closes*, or the Canadian film *32 Short Films About Glenn Gould* or Derek Jarmon's *Wittgenstein* would be justified. Definitely this is one not to be missed.
MPAA: Not rated. Contains several scenes of domestic violence and abusive behaviour.

PRAYER OF THE ROLLER BOYS ★★★

Credits: VHS/1991/USA, Japan/Colour/94 minutes
Director: Rick King
Screenplay: W. Peter Iliff
Cast: Corey Haim [Griffin], Patricia Arquette [Casey], Christopher Collet [Gary Lee], Julius W. Harris [Speedbagger], J. C. Quinn [Jaworski], Jake Dengel [Tyler], Devin Clark [Miltie], Mark Pellegrino [Bango], Morgan Weisser [Bullwinkle]
Genre: An action-adventure tale set in some not-too-distant future where, in time-honoured fashion, a few good men and women defeat the forces of evil.

Plot: Brothers Griffin (Haim) and Miltie (Clark) are scraping along, living in a tent and delivering pizzas to make ends meet. Around them, the world has gone to pieces. The United States economy is now foreign owned. Chaos rules the streets. Gangs abound. One above all seems to hold sway: the Rollerboys. They are a group of clean cut, well dressed, drug-dealing, racist, violent, patriotic bully boys on in-line skates.

Under the leadership of Gary Lee (Collet), they are also very wealthy, controlling the market for drugs, especially the highly addictive Mist, which they manufacture. Gary Lee is also a boyhood friend of Griffin.

When circumstances bring the two together again, Griffin is persuaded by police officer Jaworski (Quinn) to join the Rollerboys as an undercover agent. Although at first reluctant, Griffin's realization that his little brother Miltie is becoming addicted to Mist and his feelings towards Casey (Arquette), herself an undercover cop, convince him, setting up a series of violent confrontations before the happy ending.

MPAA: Rated R. A great deal of violence occurs in this film. There is also some minor partial nudity, mostly bare breasts. As well, Arquette and Haim have a romantic encounter, mostly off screen during which it is implied that Haim loses his clothes.

Christian Tapdrup and Benedicte W. Madsen, *Pretty Boy* (1993)

PRETTY BABY ★★★★

Credits: VHS/1978/USA/Colour/109 minutes
Director: Louis Malle
Screenplay: Polly Platt
Cast: Keith Carradine [E. J. Bellocq], Antonio Fargas [Professor], Frances Faye [Nell], Susan Sarandon [Hattie], Diana Scarwid [Frieda], Brooke Shields [Violet]
Genre: An historical romance set in the Storyville district of New Orleans which details the relationship between photographer E. J. Bellocq and a twelve-year-old prostitute.
Plot: New Orleans! What wonderfully romantic notions that name brings to mind. Bourbon Street. The French Quarter. Ragtime and Jazz. Great food. Great Music. For twelve-year-old Violet (Shields), however, life is not so romantic. In 1917 she is one of several resident children who live with their "working girl" mothers in the Story-ville brothel run by Madame Nell (Faye). She sleeps in a garret with the rats. She wanders in and out of the rooms where the women ply their trade. She runs errands for the whores, performing little services for them. She is also old enough to start attracting the eye of some of the paying customers.

Into this setting steps E. J. Bellocq (Carradine) who arranges to photograph some of Nell's "girls," especially Violet's mother Hattie (Sarandon). At first Violet is little more than a nuisance for the photographer, who declares he has no time for hate or love. But life is changing rapidly for Violet. Her mother marries a john and, leaving her daughter in Madame Nell's House, departs for Saint Louis.

Violet herself is initiated into the trade, her virginity auctioned off to the highest bidder. Then the House is shut down by economic pressures brought on by morality crusaders driving customers away. Violet, fearful of being placed in an orphanage, finds her way to Bellocq's home where their relationship begins to change.

Having never known anything else, at first Violet is unable to be anything but a whore. Eventually, however, Bellocq asks the girl, still only thirteen-years-old, to marry him. But there is to be no romantic ending to the story for Violet, for Hattie reappears and claiming that the marriage is not legal without her consent, takes Violet away with her. As Hattie, her husband and Violet leave on the train, you realize that the girl will need to mature a great deal as she leaves her whoring past behind and grows into a normal young teenager.

This film was extremely controversial when first produced, and many censorship authorities outside the United States demanded major cuts to the film, or else banned it outright. Fortunately, what could have been a horrendous, sleazy, exploitive look at the problem of juvenile prostitution has been sensitively handled by Malle who has shown not only the sensational, but also the grit behind the scene, not so much the sex, but the personalities of the people who ply the trade.

MPAA: Rated R. The film is concerned in large measure with questions of prostitution, child prostitution and sexual relations between men and young girls. Violet is the only child prostitute in Nell's house at the time of the story, but it is clear that several of the others began their careers in their early teens.

Both Hattie and Violet are seen nude: Hattie poses bare breasted for Bellocq, and Violet is seen nude several times, including bare buns and bare breasts, though Shields was very obviously still pre-adolescent at the time the film was made.

PRETTY BOY ★★★

(Also known as *Smukke Dreng*)

Credits: VHS/1993/Denmark/Colour/82 minutes
In Danish with English subtitles.
Writer/Director: Carsten Sonder
Cast: Brigit Bruel [grandmother], Kit Goetz [Mother], Stig Hoffmeyer [Ralph], Niels Jorgensen [Mortensen], Benedicte W. Madsen [Renee], Rami Nathan Sverdlin [Max], Christian Tapdrup [Nick]
Genre: A drama about a teenage runaway on the streets of Copenhagen.
Plot: When thirteen-year-old Nick (Tapdrup) first arrives in Copenhagen he has no place to spend the night. Like many young runaways, the teenager is fleeing a home situation which, if not physically abusive, is psychologically so. And like so many other young runaways with no legitimately marketable skills or assets he is soon trading the use and abuse of his body for food and a bed.

His blond good looks prove no hindrance in this endeavour: he is not called Pretty Boy for nothing. Nick soon falls in with a crowd of other young prostitutes and petty thieves under the leadership of Renee (Madsen), a sexually ambivalent girl who is known to the others as "one of the lads."

Although Nick and Renee make love several times, Nick also maintains an ongoing relationship with Ralph (Hoffmeyer), an astronomer and academic who is prepared to provide bed and breakfast in exchange for sex. The other ongoing adult presence in the lives of these youths is Mortensen (Jorgensen), a pudgy car dealer known to the boys as Mrs. Mortensen. His pleasures seem to come from dressing up in a french maid's uniform and being humiliated and degraded by the young hustlers.

Although Nick is evidently searching for stability and love in his life, he cannot find it anywhere. His mother's home is unbearable. The other hustlers may provide short-term companionship but not lasting stability. Mortensen is hardly what he is looking for. Ralph feels free to throw him back out on the street when the boy's presence is inconvenient. Is it any wonder that by the end of the film Nick has become increasingly violent, to the point where he is capable of killing?
MPAA: Not rated. The film has several scenes of violence both directed against Nick and perpetrated by him.

There are also a number of nude scenes involving Tapdrup. He is seen in several bare butt shots running around Ralph's apartment. He also appears in a full-frontal shot when Ralph throws him, nude and still wet from the shower, down the back stairs of his apartment when his girl friend Camilla shows up unexpectedly.

Madsen is also seen bare-breasted. Nick's mother (Goetz) is seen engaged in sex with one of her many male visitors.

PRIVATE LESSONS ★★★

Credits: VHS/1981/USA/Colour/83 minutes
Director: Alan Myerson
Screenplay: Dan Greenburg, based on his novel *Philly*.
Cast: Meredith Baer [Miss Phipps], Ed Begley, Jr. [Jack Travis], Eric Brown [Philly Fillmore], Howard Hesseman [Lester Lewis], Sylvia Kristel [Nicole Mallow], Patrick Piccininni [Sherman]
Genre: A romantic comedy about many a fifteen-year-old boy's wildest erotic dreams: being alone for several weeks with a beautiful, sexy and willing older woman who will transform him from an awkward, gawky puppy into a sexy, sophisticated young man.
Plot: Philly (Brown) is the bored rich kid with too many toys who has been left alone in the family mansion while dad is away on a three week business trip. Well, almost alone. Lester (Hesseman) the chauffeur and Nicole (Kristel) the new housekeeper are there to look after his needs.

Eric Brown and Sylvia Kristel, *Private Lessons* (1981)

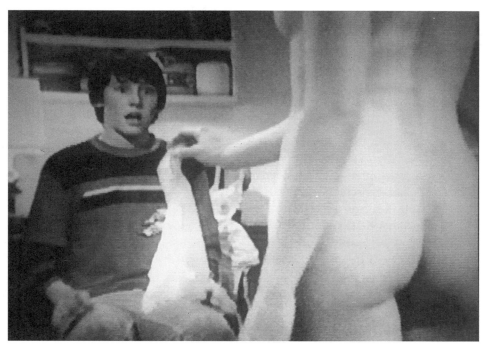

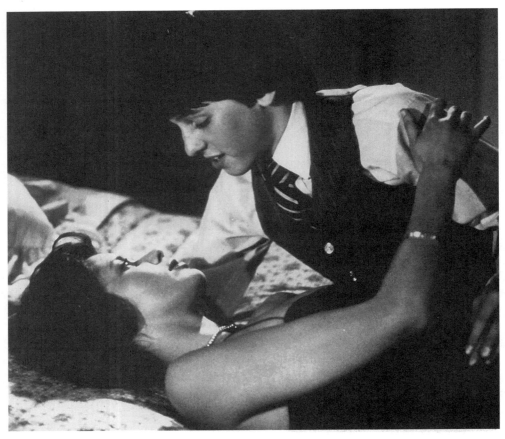

Eric Brown and Sylvia Kristel, *Private Lessons* (1981)

Brown appears nude in a full length butt shot after jumping out of the bath Philly has been sharing with Nicole. Nicole urges him to join her in the tub, he insists on wearing his swim suit. Once in the tub, she persuades him to take it off but when her hands stray to areas he wasn't anticipating, he panics and jumps out of the tub.

PUBERTY BLUES
★★★★

Credits: VHS/1981/Australia/ Colour/86 minutes
Director: Bruce Beresford
Screenplay: Margaret Kelly
Cast: Leander Brett [Cheryl], Jad Capelja [Sue], Jay Hackett [Bruce], Tony Hughes [Danny], Sandy Paul [Tracy], Geoff Rhoe [Garry], Tina Robinson [Freda], Nell Schofield0 [Debbie]
Genre: A romantic tale about a group of surfers on Manly Beach in Sydney, Australia, seen, for a change, through the eyes of a girl.
Plot: Ain't life grand when you're a surfer chick and part of the in crowd? Once you get accepted you get to do fun things like smoke in the washroom, hang out at the paddock, lie around the beach all day in your bikini watching your guy surf, wear his friendship ring, fetch his food, hand him his towel and generally be his cheerful girl Friday and head cheer-leader. Most important, you get to put out for him when he wants to "root."

Forget romance, sex is mechanical. And don't even think about admitting that you are a virgin. This is the life of bliss that Debbie (Schofield) and Sue (Capelja) long for and attain in this perceptive coming of age film which, unusually, especially for its time, is told from a girl's point of view.

What a bleak point of view it is, despite Debbie and Sue's insistence that this is nothing short of heaven on earth. Eventually, even Debbie and Sue see through the surface to the pain lying beneath. Why can't we do what I want sometimes? Because I'm your guy and I don't want to. Why can't a girl surf? Because chicks don't surf! Why can't we be friends with Freda (Robinson) Because she's a homely, red-headed moll.

MPAA: Rated R. This film is primarily Debbie's story

What Philly doesn't know is that Nicole and Lester are plotting to blackmail him. The plot requires Nicole to seduce Philly and then, because she is supposed to have a weak heart, to fake her own death. Unfortunately for the plotters, Nicole finds herself attracted to the boy and ends up turning the tables on Lester.

Philly falls big time for Nicole, though he has an annoying habit of running to his best friend Sherman (Piccininni), the fat kid next door, after every new move in order to spread the news. And the moves come thick and fast as Philly changes in three weeks from the awkward kid who stares wide-eyed with wonder and embarrassment at Nicole when she does a strip tease for him, into a super sophisticated young stud at the end of the film.

Author and screenwriter Dan Greenburg appears in a small role as the owner of a run down hotel. The film was re-made in 1993 in Japan, with Greenburg once again providing the screenplay.

MPAA: Rated R. Brown and Kristel have two sensuous but not very explicit sex scenes. Kristel appears nude several times, including topless and bare buns shots during the strip-tease and sex scenes.

Puberty Blues (1981)

and she gets involved sexually a number of times with different boys. Once with Bruce (Hackett) in the back of a van at the drive-in. Once with Garry (Rhoe) in an abandoned house. Freda is tricked into allowing three boys to abuse her late at night.

As well as the sex, we are treated to a number of bare bodies. Hackett and Rhoe and an unknown lifeguard show off their buns and several women are seen topless on the beaches.

RAMBLING ROSE ★★★★

Credits: VHS/1991/USA/Colour/115 minutes
Director: Martha Coolidge
Screenplay: Calder Wallingham, based on his novel.
Cast: Laura Dern [Rose], Robert Duvall [Daddy], Lukas Haas [Buddy], Lisa Jakub [Dolly], Diane Ladd [Mother], Evan Lockwood [Waski]
Awards: Academy Awards 1991: (nomination) Best Actress (Dern); (nomination) Best Supporting Actress (Ladd). Independent Spirit Awards 1992: Best Director (Coolidge); Best Film; Best Supporting Actress (Ladd).
Genre: Presented as a look back at the year he was thirteen, this nostalgic drama is one man's memories of his first love.

Plot: In the midst of the Great Depression, Rose (Dern) a young woman with a "past" is hired sight unseen by an eccentric southern family to be a live-in cook and maid. Thirteen-year-old Buddy (Haas, in yet another fine screen appearance), a quiet, brilliant boy with, to quote his mother (Ladd), an "evil streak," is quickly smitten by the sexy, free-wheeling and somewhat unstable Rose. She, on the other hand, has fallen for Daddy (Duvall) and tries, nearly successfully, to seduce him.

Having witnessed this scene while peeping through a key hole, Buddy begins to fantasize about Rose. When Rose comes into his bedroom late that night to unburden her mind Buddy finds his fantasies turning into reality. The reality is far better than any of his "dirty little comic books!" After a series of amorous adventures and

James Dean (right), *Rebel Without A Cause* (1955)

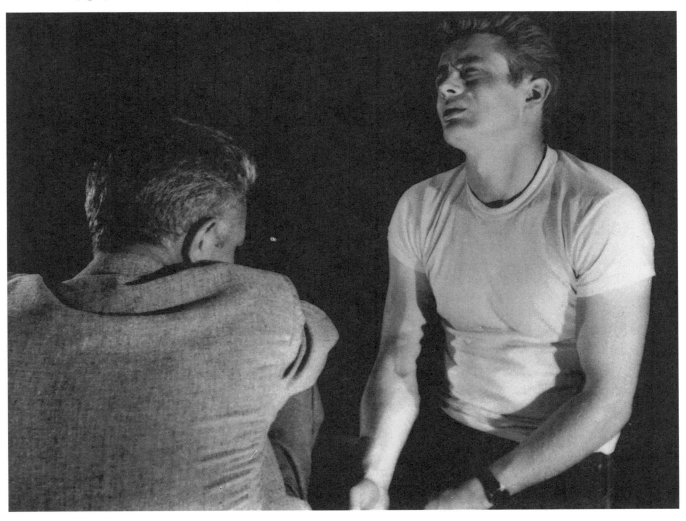

misadventures, when Rose finally meets Mr. Right, Buddy is reduced to tears at the wedding.

MPAA: Rated R. The film includes some minor nudity, principally bare breasts in the scene where Rose tries to seduce Daddy.

Sex plays a larger role in the story: the seduction scene and the scene where Buddy experiences what he claims is "without a doubt the most fascinating experience" of his life are the two of the most important. Rose's sexuality permeates the entire film.

THE RASCALS ★★★★

(Also known as *Les Turlupins*)

Credits: VHS/1981/France/Colour/93 minutes
In French with English subtitles.
Also Available in a dubbed version.
Writer/Director: Bernard Revon
Cast: Bernard Brieux [Bernard], Thomas Chabrol [Didier], Sebastien Drai-Dietrich [Vincent], Pascale Rocard [Marie-Helene]
Genre: A comedy about a pair of unstoppable teenagers at a French boarding school for boys during World War II.
Plot: The Germans are occupying France. Food is scarce. Air raids and shelters are a constant fact of life. Resistance fighters and collaborators are everywhere. But teenagers Bernard (Brieux) and Didier (Chabrol) have more vital things on their minds. The girls at Ste. Clothilde school just down the road, for a start.

When they discover a note from "two pretty girls" hidden in a text book shared between the two schools, things start to look up. A clandestine meeting in the park leads to romance for Bernard and Marie-Helene. Meanwhile, Didier has pressed Vincent (Drai-Dietrich) into service to arrange a meeting with the younger boy's sister.

Nothing can stop these boys in their search for romance. Not the arrest of a teacher for his work in the resistance. Not the suicide of a class mate depressed by the war situation. Not Christian's unceasing and sometimes farcical attempts to get expelled from the school. Not the death of Bernard's grandfather.

Nor will the boys stop at anything in their efforts to arrange meetings between Bernard and Marie-Helene. A false air raid warning can lead to a meeting in the shelters. An engineered detention can lead to sex in the dormitories. But in the end the two must part, Marie-Helene going to a marriage with her cousin, the boys to an uncertain future in the resistance.

Compare the difference in tone and outlook with that other great French war time story set in a boys boarding school, *Au Revoir Les Enfants*.

MPAA: Rated R. There are constant sexual undercurrents to almost everything these boys do. Bernard's desire to make love to Marie-Helene becomes an obsession and the antics he and Didier pull in order to finally reach his goal border on the farcical.

In the scene where Bernard and Marie-Helene do finally make love, both young performers are seen nude including frontal-exposure of Brieux.

Rocard is seen bare-breasted in an earlier scene in an air-raid shelter, when Marie-Helene unbuttons her blouse for Bernard. Both Brieux and Chabrol are seen nude in a shower scene. A large number of young teens are in this scene, which includes full-frontal shots of several boys, though it is difficult to pick out Brieux and Chabrol. They are clearly seen in a rear shot as they walk away from the showers.

Young Drai-Dietrich is seen nude, including a brief frontal-shot while Vincent is subjected to a medicinal bath in the school infirmary.

REBEL WITHOUT A CAUSE ★★★★★

Credits: VHS/1955/USA/Colour/111 minutes
Director: Nicholas Ray
Screenplay: Stewart Stern
Inspired by the story *The Blind Run* by Dr. Robert M. Lindner.
Cast: Corey Allen [Buzz], Jim Backus [Franck Stark], James Dean [Jim Stark], Ann Doran [Mrs. Stark], William Hopper [Judy's Father], Frank Mazzola [Crunch], Sal Mineo ["Plato" John Crawford], Edward Platt [Ray], Natalie Wood [Judy]
Awards: Academy Awards 1955: (nomination) Best Supporting Actress (Wood); (nomination) Best Supporting Actor (Mineo).
Genre: Perhaps the quintessential drama about teenage rebellion and alienation.
Plot: A classic which appears on many a writer's list of the best films of all time, *Rebel Without A Cause* follows one day in the life of three troubled teenagers, Jim Stark (Dean), Judy (Wood) and Plato (Mineo). Jim is torn apart and turning to alcohol by what he sees as an unhealthy home life. His emotionally weak father (Backus) is totally under the thumb of his shrill, domineering mother (Doran). Judy is on the run from an unsympathetic, seemingly uncaring and unloving father. Plato's parents are divorced and he spends most of his time in the care of his mother's black maid, never seeing his father, rarely seeing his mother.

In a single long day that begins with Jim picked up for being drunk and disorderly, the three teens, all from respectable middle class families, must fight their various personal demons. Jim, new at Dawson High School, is immediately set upon by Buzz (Allen), Crunch (Mazzola) and the other members of their gang. Taunted for being a chicken, Jim accepts a challenge from Buzz to take part in a "Chickie Run" in stolen cars at the top of the bluffs. When the challenge turns tragic, Jim is faced with a moral dilemma. Although urged by his parents not to do so he decides, for the sake of his own honour, to speak to Ray (Platt), a Juvenile Officer with the local police and truly the only sympathetic adult character in the film.

Rebecca DeMornay and Tom Cruise, *Risky Business* (1983)

Unable to locate Ray and being chased by Crunch and the rest of the gang, Jim, Judy and Plato hide out in an abandoned mansion. There they become, in Plato's mind, a family to take the place of the one he has never known. Unfortunately, Plato has brought a handgun with him and injures one of the gang. The police also being on the scene, the stage is set for the final tragedy.

One of the first films to look seriously at the question of teenage alienation and the generation gap, *Rebel Without A Cause* still packs a powerful message despite its age.

MPAA: Not rated. Although violence and sexual tension run rampant beneath the surface of this film, thanks to the vigilance of the Breen office and the Hayes code in effect when the film was produced, little is shown on-screen. If rated today, I doubt that it would be given more than a PG-13 rating, more likely PG.

Jim and Judy probably make love during the night in the abandoned mansion, but this is left entirely to one's imagination. Indisputably Plato is gay, but in 1955 this was decidedly a love that dared not speak its name and nothing could be shown or even openly implied. However, the look that Plato gives Jim when they first meet in the Planetarium is nothing less than love at first sight.

THE REFLECTING SKIN ★★★★

Credits: VHS/1991/Great Britain-Canada/Colour/95 minutes

Writer/Director: Philip Ridley

Cast: Jeremy Cooper [Seth Dove], Lindsay Duncan [Dolphin Blue], Duncan Frazer [Luke Dove], Evan Hall [Kim], Robert Koons [Sherriff Ticker], David Longworth [Joshua], Sheila Moore [Ruth Dove], Viggo Mortensen [Cameron Dove], Codie Lucas Wilbee [Eben]

Genre: A thriller about the serial killings of young boys and the effect this has on one overly imaginative eight-year-old.

Plot: The setting is rural Idaho in the early 1950s. Eight-year-old Seth Dove (Cooper) lives with his overwrought mother and distant father. Because of his geographic isolation Seth has few friends and his imagination has plenty of room to roam. He thinks Dolphin Blue (Duncan), the young widow down the road, is a vampire. The dead baby he finds must be an angel. And the big, black Cadillac which mysteriously appears must be sinister.

When Seth's few friends start to disappear, panic ensues in the neighbourhood. And when the body of young Eben (Wilbee) is found in the Dove family's well, dark secrets from the past come back to haunt Luke Dove (Frazer), Seth's father.

Years ago, Luke was found in a barn in an amorous embrace with a seventeen-year-old boy. Sherriff Ticker

(Koons), stating that it's only a short step from kissing boys to killing them, accuses Luke of the murder of Eben. Unable to take the shame of the accusations or to deal with his past homosexual activity, Luke commits suicide. A horrified Seth watches. But the killings don't stop and first young Kim (Hall) and then Dolphin Blue become victims.

This visually stunning film is filled with shot after carefully crafted shot which will linger in your memory long after the lights come on again. In its purely visual effects, it is on a par with *The Long Day Closes*. David Pope's cinematography is some of the finest to be found in any of the films in this book.

MPAA: Rated R. The film has a number of scenes of graphic violence and one nude shot of Mortensen. After Cameron and Dolphin Blue make love, Seth spies them lying together in an upstairs room, Cameron cuddled in her arms as he lies on the floor. This is a full-length rear shot.

RETURN TO THE BLUE LAGOON ★

Credits: VHS/1991/USA/Colour/102 minutes

Writer/Director: William A. Graham

Screenplay: Leslie Stevens

Based on the novel *The Garden Of God*, by Henry Stacpoole.

Cast: Nana Coburn [Sylvia], Peter Hehir [Quinlan], Milla Jovovich [Lilli], Brian Krause [Richard], Lisa Pelikan [Sarah], Courtney Phillips [young Lilli], Garette Patrick Ratliff [young Richard]

Genre: The sequel to the 1980 version of *The Blue Lagoon*. This time around we follow the romantic adventures of Richard and Emma's son while he and a female companion cavort in loincloths on exotic tropical beaches.

Plot: The infant Richard is picked up in a row boat, drifting on the ocean. As both his parents have died he is cared for onboard ship by Sarah (Pelikan), the widow of a missionary who is returning home with her infant daughter, Lilli. Some days later, Sarah, Richard and Lilli are set adrift in a small boat when the ship's crew begins to succumb to cholera. By an amazing coincidence, they land on the exact same beach that had formerly been home to Richard's young parents. The life of a castaway begins anew and we are treated to many idyllic scenes of carefree

life on the island as Richard (first Ratliff, then Krause) and Lilli (Phillips and Jovovich) grow up in paradise.

Their happiness is shattered, first by the death of Sarah, then by the arrival of a ship seeking fresh water. Richard is smitten by Sylvia (Coburn), the captain's daughter. Lilli is sexually assaulted by sea man Quinlan (Hehir). When the ship prepares to leave the island the young couple must decide whether to go with them, or stay on the island.

Although the settings and the photography are wonderful, the film as a whole is a waste of time. Barely

Tom Cruise, *Risky Business* (1983)

tolerable while Richard and Lilli are pre-teens, it rapidly degenerates into silliness once they reach puberty, too coy to deal with the obvious sexuality in anything other than a sniggering nudge-nudge, wink-wink fashion.

As a parting request, I would ask that somebody please keep all future generations of this family well away from exotic tropical islands so we may be spared any further sequels.

MPAA: Rated PG-13. There is a lot of sex talk in the film, particularly when Richard and Lilli reach their teenage years. There are also a number of scenes where the two teens spy on each other: Richard is excited by Lilli's breasts, Lilli fascinated and astonished to see Richard with an erection.

Other than a brief glimpse of Lilli's breasts, however, the only on-screen nudity is the infant Richard when he is first found drifting in the boat. Despite the fact that, when the three are bathing together below the waterfall, Sarah comments that she had long ago given up trying to get the two young children to wear clothes, at no point does either Richard or Lilli actually appear nude on-screen. As befits a good Victorian woman Sarah bathes in a dress.

LA REVOLTE DES ENFANTS ★★★

Credits: 1991/France/Colour/127 minutes
French language only.
Director: Gerard Poitou-Weber
Cast: Andre Wilms, Michel Aumont, Clementine Amouroux, Robinson Stevenin, Nadia Strancar, Daniel Laloux, Dominique Reymond
Genre: A period drama about abused and incarcerated youth in revolt against an uncaring and dehumanizing penal system.
Plot: The setting is France in the year 1847 just prior to the Paris uprisings celebrated in *Les Miserables*. A beautiful young duchess who is working as a journalist in Paris travels to a tiny off-shore island where there is a prison colony for juvenile offenders, invited there by a staff member intent on reform. The boys range in age from eight or nine years old to their late teens. Theoretically they are receiving an education and vocational training during their incarceration but in truth this amounts to little more than long hours employed in boring, menial tasks. Coupled with uncaring and frequently brutal guardians under the direction of a cruel governor known as Uncle, the situation is ripe for revolt.

When the boys do finally rise up and take control, a series of protracted negotiations with the governor of the prison take place. Eventually the boys' demands are met and an accord is signed. Unknown to the boys, however, the military have been notified. Just as the inmates are surrendering their weapons the soldiers arrive and a massacre ensues.

To the best of my knowledge, this film has is not available on tape in North America. I came across it quite by accident on the Canadian Broadcasting Corporation's French language television services one evening.
MPAA: Not rated. There are a number of scenes suggesting gay sexual activities in the prison, both between the prisoners themselves and between the prisoners and the guards. In one instance a guard disappears into a private room with one of the boys and in another two boys in a cell are interrupted as they are obviously preparing for sexual activity.

A small amount of nudity, including some full-frontal shots of a number of young boys and teenagers occurs as well, principally in an early scene where some new arrivals to the prison are required to strip and shower before being issued uniforms.

RICH KIDS ★★★

Credits: VHS/1979/USA/Colour/97 minutes
Director: Robert M. Young
Screenplay: Judith Ross
Cast: Trini Alvarado [Franny Philips], Paul Dooley [Simon Pieterfreund], Terry Kiser [Ralph Harris], Jeremy Levy [Jamie Harris], John Lithgow [Paul Philips], Roberta Maxwell [Barbara Pieterfreund], David Selby [Steve Sloan], Kathryn Walker [Madeline Philips], Irene Worth [Madeline's mother]
Genre: A romantic comedy about two twelve-year-olds from wealthy New York professional families coping with the stress of divorce and their new found feelings for each other.
Plot: In this sometimes overly leisurely tale, Franny (Alvarado) begins to realize that her parents (Walker and Lithgow) are separating. She turns to classmate Jamie (Levy) for comfort and advice. His parents (Maxwell and Kiser) divorced some years earlier and so is able to tell his friend what she may expect in the days and weeks ahead.

As the stress in Franny's life increases she spends more time with Jamie, including a sanctioned sleep over at his father's apartment. When the animosity between her parents increases to the point of being unbearable, the two kids run away to Jamie's father's apartment which is empty for the weekend.

When the parents finally realize where they are, a total of eight adults descend on the place to find the two children together in the bathtub. While the various parents scream mutual recriminations at each other, Franny and Jamie calmly leave the apartment. Reasoning that they can't be totally separated as they will still see each other at school (their parents, after all, have already paid for the full term), Franny goes home to bed and Jamie returns to his father, the only adult who really seems to care how the children feel about each other.
MPAA: Rated PG. There is a small amount of sex talk and some implied sexual situations. Franny and Jamie share a bath with the implication that they are nude together in the tub. There are some extremely brief shots of the two kids as they are being pulled from the bathtub by the angry adults. Levy's buns appear to be seen in a very brief side shot as he gets out, however there are so many soap suds both in the tub and on their bodies that nothing is actually visible.

RISKY BUSINESS ★★★★

Credits: VHS/1983/USA/Colour/99 minutes
Writer/Director: Paul Brickman
Cast: Curtis Armstrong [Miles], Tom Cruise [Joel], Rebecca DeMornay [Lana], Shara Denise [Vicki], Richard Masur [Rutherford], Joe Pantoliano [Guido], Bronson Pinchot [Barry], Raphael Sbarge [Glenn], Bruce A. Young [Jackie]
Genre: A teen sex comedy, better and more intelligent than your average example of the genre.
Plot: If you're a fairly straight-laced high school senior in an upper class Chicago suburb, what do you do if your parents go away for a week? After you've dropped daddy's Porsche into Lake Michigan, that is.

If you are Joel (Cruise), you go looking for a little sex. Best buddy Miles (Armstrong) calls up Jackie (Young), having obtained her number from an ad. When Jackie turns out to be far less than Joel's dream date (Jackie is a black cross-dresser), Joel decides to try another name. Lana (DeMornay) seems to be everything a teenager could want in a girl. Until she presents the bill, that is. Taking one of Joel's mother's prized possessions as security while Joel's at the bank cashing in a bond, she secretly leaves. When Joel tracks her down, he winds up in even bigger financial problems and at odds with Lana's pimp, Guido (Pantoliano).

To pay off Joel's mounting debts (he has to get the Porsche cleaned up, after all, as well as paying Lana), teenager and call girl set up a wildly successful bordello in his home. A lot of local boys with a lot of money are prepared to part with some of it in order to get some sexual experience before they head off to college in the fall.

Unfortunately for Joel, Guido figures he's entitled to this cash because they are his "girls." To ensure he gets his money, just hours before Joel's parents return home Guido strips the house bare while the boy is off retrieving the car. He then offers to "sell" the goods back to him.
MPAA: Rated R. There are several scenes of female nudity. (Joel has a recurring fantasy about women in the shower.) Joel and Lana are seen in a number of sexual encounters, though none are overly explicit. Cruise also has a couple of scenes where he is wearing only a pair of briefs. There is also a certain amount of sex talk and sexual innuendo.

ROMEO AND JULIET ★★★★★

Credits: VHS/1968/Italy/Colour/138 minutes
Director: Franco Zeffirelli
Screenplay: Franco Brusati, Masolino D'Amico, and Franco Zeffirelli
Based on the play by William Shakespeare.
Cast: Pat Haywood [the nurse], Olivia Hussey [Juliet], John McEnery [Mercutio], Milo O'Shea [Friar Lawrence], Natasha Parry [Lady Capulet], Bruce Robinson [Benvolio], Robert Stephens [The Prince], Leonard Whiting [Romeo], Michael York [Tybalt]
Awards: Academy Awards 1968: Best Cinematography; Best Costume Design; (nomination) Best Picture; (nomination) Best Director (Zeffirelli). Golden Globe Awards 1968: Best Foreign Film; Best Newcomer (Whiting); Best Newcomer (Hussey). National Board of Review Awards: Best Director (Zeffirelli); Ten Best Films of the Year. *Romeo And Juliet* also received awards in Italy, Great Britain, Greece and Japan.
Genre: The quintessential romantic drama and one of the great cinematic renditions of any of the Bard's plays.
Plot: The story of the star-crossed young lovers from feuding families surely needs no introduction. In bringing the story to film, Zeffirelli has kept close to the original script while filling the screen with vibrant colour, gorgeous costumes and handsome young men in tights. Unique among cinematic renditions of this play, Zeffirelli chose to cast two teenagers in the title roles: seventeen-year-old Whiting as Romeo and fifteen-year-old Hussey as Juliet.

In addition to being more faithful to the original play (Shakespeare says Juliet is not yet fourteen), in my opinion it renders the story more believable. Surely it is teenage impetuousness which drives this tale of feuding retainers and tragic love.
MPAA: Rated PG. Canadian Home Video rated PG. Despite the liberal rating the film includes the well known nude love scene involving Whiting and Hussey. The nudity is primarily full-length rear shots of Whiting, either lying on the bed beside Hussey or standing before an open window.

We get only a very brief glimpse of Hussey's breasts in one shot. That Romeo and Juliet have been sexually involved is really only implied in this scene. It opens with the two principals lying on the bed after having spent the night together before they dress, and Romeo climbs out from Juliet's chamber.

SALAAM BOMBAY! ★★★★★

Credits: VHS/1988/India/Colour/114 minutes
In Hindi with English subtitles.
Director: Mira Nair
Screenplay: Sooni Taraporevala
Cast: Aneeta Kanwar [Rekha], Nana Patekar [Baba], Chanda Sharma [Solasaal "Sweet Sixteen"], Shafiq Syed [Krishna "Chaipau"], Hansa Vithal [Manju], Raghuvir Yadav [Chillum]
Awards: Montreal Film Festival 1988: Jury Award; Ecumenical Jury Prize; Most Popular Film Award. Cannes Film Festival 1988: Camera D'Or. Academy Awards 1988: (nomination) Best Foreign Film.
Genre: A drama about homeless street children and child prostitution in Bombay. Like the earlier Brazilian film *Pixote, Bombay* features real-life street children among the cast members.
Plot: Krishna (Syed) is a ten-year-old boy who has been abandoned by his mother because she believes he owes his brother 500 rupees as a result of damaging a motorcycle. Sent into town to make a purchase for the owner of the circus where he has been working, Krishna returns to find the circus has departed and he has been left alone.

With the little money he has left to him, the boy buys a train ticket to the nearest city, Bombay. Homeless and penniless he is forced to live on the streets associating with pimps, prostitutes, drug dealers and petty criminals, earning money however he can. He finds employment as a Chaipau (tea boy), cleaning chicken cages, plucking chickens, washing dishes at a

School Ties (1992)

wedding banquet and through petty theft.

Among the many residents of the street where he lives are Baba (Patekar), the local crime lord, drug dealer and pimp; Sweet Sixteen (Sharma), a beautiful young Nepali girl who has been sold into prostitution and whose virginity will earn a fortune for the brothel; Chillum (Yadav), a small time drug dealer and addict who takes the young street boys under his wing and Chacha, the tea seller who employs Krishna but takes every advantage he can of the boy.

At every turn Krishna is subjected to lies, deceptions, blows, beatings and even incarceration after he is picked up by a policeman while walking home late at night. When Chillum, who has become a surrogate father figure for Krishna, dies, the boy's world crumbles even further.

After the theft of the money he has been saving to repay his brother the 500 rupees and his spur of the moment murder of Baba the pimp, Krishna is reduced to tears as he realizes that he is never going home; that this street is his home.

I have also long suspected that the producers of the film have tried to imply a sexual relationship between Chillum and the group of young street boys who come under his wing. There are several scenes of physical closeness between Chillum and Krishna including a couple of tickling sessions and a long sequence in a graveyard which ends with Krishna and Chillum falling asleep with their arms and legs entwined.
MPAA: Not rated. The film deals with questions of prostitution, especially juvenile prostitution, however there is nothing overtly sexual portrayed on screen.

William Hurt and Chris Cleary Miles, *Second Best* (1993)

SCHOOL TIES ★★★★

Credits: VHS/1992/USA/Colour/107 minutes
Director: Robert Mandel
Screenplay: Dick Wolf and Darryl Ponicsan
Based on a story by Dick Wolf.
Cast: Ben Affleck [Chesty Smith], Randall Batinkoff [Rip Van Kelt], Matt Damon [Charlie Dillon], Peter Donat [Headmaster Dr. Bartram], Brendan Fraser [David Greene], Cole Hauser [Jack Conners], Zeljko Ivanek [Cleary], Amy Locane [Sally Wheeler], Andrew Lowery [McGivern], Chris O'Donnell [Chris Reece], Anthony Rapp [McGoo], Kevin Tighe [Coach McDevitt]
Genre: A drama about class differences and anti-Semitism played out within the walls of an exclusive New England boarding school for boys.
Plot: It's 1955. David Greene (Fraser) a poor, but bright boy from a working class neighbourhood in Scranton, Pennsylvania receives a scholarship from St. Matthew's Academy, normally the exclusive preserve of New England's financial aristocracy.

St. Matthew's has not won a football game for several years and David is an outstanding quarterback. David is also Jewish, something the alumni, the headmaster and the coach are willing to overlook. David's father and the coach both advise him to conceal this information. Eventually, however, it comes out when Dillon (Damon) overhears a conversation between two men at dinner. Dillon, already jealous that David has taken the quarterback slot, spreads the news.

The casual non-specific anti-Semitism and racism rampant among his classmates is now turned directly on David. His roommate (O'Donnell) won't speak to him. His girlfriend Sally (Locane) turns away from him. An anonymous swastika appears over his bed.

The issue comes to a head when a crib sheet is discovered on the floor of an exam room. Following the school's traditional honour code, the boys are left to discover the culprit or risk failing grades for the entire class. When confronted with a choice of offenders, David or Collins, the student body decides to pin the blame on David, the outsider, the Jew, the boy from a different world, despite the fact that some of them know Collins to be the guilty party.

MPAA: Rated PG-13. There are several fist fights in the film. As well, there are innumerable instances of racial slurs and epithets. These range from the French teacher telling the boys they may not play jazz in the dorms because he "doesn't want the jungle in here" to a red swastika anonymously pinned over David's bed in the dorms.

As in any film about teenage boys, there is a certain amount of sex talk, though perhaps not as much as one might expect. There are also a couple of nude scenes set in the dormitory showers. In one, Fraser, Damon and O'Donnell are all seen, in rear shots only.

SECOND BEST ★★★★★

Credits: VHS/1993/USA/Colour/105 minutes
Director: Chris Menges
Screenplay: David Cook, adapted from his own novel.
Cast: Keith Allen [John], Alan Cumming [Edward], Jane Horrocks [Debbie], John Hurt [Uncle Turpin], William Hurt [Graham], Chris Cleary Miles [James], Prunella Scales [the Social Worker]
Genre: A beautiful, gentle drama about a quiet, introverted middle-aged bachelor and the disturbed ten-year-old boy he wishes to adopt.
Plot: Graham (William Hurt) is an unassuming postmaster in a small Welsh village. James (Miles in a standout performance) is a moody, manipulative young boy prone to deal-making and self-mutilation in order to get what he wants in life. When he doesn't get his way, James takes to his heels.

Second Best is the story of their relationship from first encounter to final acceptance of each other. Along the way both man and boy must come to terms with the ghosts and skeletons in their respective closets, including Graham's feelings towards his dead mother and bedridden father. Graham must also deal with the questioning of his masculinity and sexual orientation by the social worker (Scales). Why does a single man of his age want to adopt a little boy?

James must overcome his mother's suicide and his father's incarceration and earlier dealings with the boy. When James' father John (Allen) does show up, he reveals that he has AIDS and has only a short time to live. Graham insists that he must deal openly and honestly with James, both about his illness and about his feelings towards James.

MPAA: Rated PG-13. There is no open sex in *Second Best* and it becomes obvious, despite the social worker's queries, that Graham has no sexual interest in the boy. But probe she must.

James also insists that one of his earlier caseworkers must have been a lesbian because she's overweight and a poor housekeeper, hence not a proper woman. There is no nudity in the film. The closest we come to bare skin is a few shots of James in his underwear, sometimes running through the woods and once, in a deliberate attempt to shock, walking into Graham's store during business hours.

THE SECRET OF ROAN INISH ★★★★★

Credits: VHS/1994/USA/Colour/102 minutes
Writer/Director: John Sayles
Based on the book *Secret Of The Ron Mor Skerry* by Rosalie K. Fry.
Cast: Cillian Byrne [Jamie], Eileen Colgan [Tess], Jeni Courtney [Fiona], Mick Lally [Hugh], John Lynch [Tadhg], Susan Lynch [the Selkie], Fergal McElherron [Sean Michael], Gerard Rooney [Liam], Richard Sheridan [Eamon]
Awards: Independent Spirit Awards 1996: (nomination) Best Director (Sayles); (nomination) Best Film; (nomination) Best Screenplay.
Genre: An Irish fairy tale about a ten-year-old girl who, with her teenage cousin and grandparents, learns about the

Brad Renfro (left), *Sleepers* (1996)

importance of family and place while listening to the tales of her forebears and their ancestral home.

Plot: When her single father can no longer care for her by himself in the city, ten-year-old Fiona is sent to live with her grandparents Hugh (Lally) and Tess (Colgan) and teenage cousin Eamon (Sheridan) on the west coast of Ireland. From her grandfather, from Eamon and from Tadhg (John Lynch), a distant relative living in the area, Fiona hears the stories of her family's past and their mysterious relationship with the local seals. She hears of Sean Michael (McElherron), her grandfather's great grandfather who was rescued from the sea by a mysterious seal. She learns of Liam (Rooney), who is said to have married a selkie (Susan Lynch), a mythical creature part seal part beautiful woman and of Jamie (Byrne), her long lost baby brother who drifted out to sea in his cradle the day the family abandoned their ancestral home on the tiny island of Roan Inish.

While on a visit to the island with Eamon, Fiona sees a naked toddler running through the meadows. Convinced that it is Jamie who has survived the intervening years being cared for by the seals, she persuades Eamon to take her back to the island. Together they secretly repair the old cottages, cleaning, whitewashing and re-thatching them. On the night of an approaching storm Fiona accidentally lets slip that she has seen the boy. No force on earth can hold her grandmother back from heading immediately to

the island to look for the boy. That night in the dark he appears, pushed to shore and into the woman's arms by the seals.

MPAA: Rated PG. Canadian Home Video rated G. As the young Jamie, Cillian Byrne has numerous nude scenes: until the closing moments of the film he is always nude when on screen. This involves frequent full-frontal exposure of the toddler.

A SEPARATE PEACE ★★★

Credits: VHS/1973/USA/ Colour/104 minutes
Director: Larry Peerce
Screenplay: Fred Segal
Based on the novel by John Knowles.
Cast: Victor Bevine [Brinker], Peter Brush [Leper], John Heyl [Finney], William Roerick [Mr. Patchwithers], Parker Stevenson [Gene]
Genre: A drama about friendship, proving oneself, conflict and tragedy set within the grounds of an exclusive New England boarding school for boys during World War II.
Plot: Gene (Stevenson) and Finney (Heyl) are seniors at Devon Academy, an old New England school. They are also roommates, best friends and complete opposites. Gene is a serious straight-A student. Finney is a vibrant, charismatic athlete who is only just able to pull down a C average. The war is in full swing and obviously much on the minds of these boys. Within a year most of them will have enlisted. Much of their day seems to be taken up with proving themselves through increasingly dangerous stunts.

When Finney is seriously injured in a fall from a tree, an accident for which Gene blames himself, the relationship between the two boys becomes strained for a while. When Finney returns to school in the fall, he is confined to crutches, but seems to take his situation well. He won't hear of anything spoken against Gene or Gene's possible role in the accident. Not until, that is, the other boys, under the leadership of Brinker (Bevine) put Gene on trial.

Leper (Brush), a former

Jonathon Tucker, Joe Perrino, Geoffrey Wigdor and Brad Renfro, *Sleepers* (1996)

classmate who is AWOL from the army and facing the threat of a Section 8 discharge, presents evidence that in fact the accident may have been Gene's fault. Finney storms from the room, re-fracturing his leg in a fall down the stairs. Although a clean break, Finney mysteriously dies in the operating room, a loss which will affect Gene for the rest of his life.

Although it is clear that there is a great deal of love involved in the relationship between Gene and Finney, it is never stated and never acted upon, at least not on screen. The relationship is strictly platonic, though at one point Gene, obviously upset about something, tries to begin a seri-ous conversation with Finney about something. Is he about to deal with his feeling towards Finney? We'll never know. Although not acknowledging their feelings for each other is consistent with Knowles original novel, perhaps the story is weakened by this head-in-the-sand attitude.

MPAA: Rated PG. There is no nudity in the film but these boys spend a considerable amount of time wearing nothing but shorts of either the gym or boxer variety.

Geoffrey Wigdor, Joe Perrino and Jonathon Tucker, *Sleepers* (1996)

SHAG: THE MOVIE ★★★

Credits: VHS/1989/USA/Colour/96 minutes
Director: Zelda Barron
Screenplay: Robin Swicord, Lanier Laney and Terry Sweeney
Cast: Phoebe Cates [Carson McBride], Scott Coffey [Chip], Bridget Fonda [Melaine Buller], Annabeth Gish ["Pudge" Carmichael], Page Hannah [Luanne Clatterback], Tyrone Power, Jr. [Harley], Robert Rusler [Buzz], Jeff Yagher [Jimmy Valentine]
Genre: A girl's version of *American Graffiti* in which four friends have one last fling together the summer after high school graduation.
Plot: Definitely not as good a film as *American Graffiti* from which it obviously derives a great deal, *Shag* follows Luanne (Hannah), "Pudge" (Gish), Melaine (Fonda) and Carson (Cates) on a wild weekend in Myrtle Beach just before the summer of 1963 ends and the four girls are slated to go their separate ways.

Intended as a last fling before Carson marries staid and respectable Harley (Power), the son of a local tobacco mag-nate, as the weekend progresses it develops in ways which none of the girls could have anticipated. New guys, new loves, new adventures, new places, new ideas intrude on the lives of the four girls as they party, fall in and out of love and come to deeper understandings of themselves.

After a weekend of beauty contests, dance contests, house parties and soul searching, their lives have been changed forever, mistakes avoided and new alliances forged. Carson meets Buzz (Rusler) and begins to question her relationship with Harley. "Pudge" meets Chip (Coffey) who is about to enter Annapolis and sees herself in a whole new light. Melaine meets the singer Jimmy Valentine (Yagher) and begins to see Hollywood as a definite alternative to the preacher's manse in Spartanburg. Luanne and Harley begin to see each other through new eyes.

MPAA: Rated PG. A lot of sex talk but little action. When Carson and Buzz spend the night together on the senator's yacht, the sex is merely implied and talked about afterwards.

There is no on-screen nudity, though Fonda has a bathtub scene washing up after being attacked with shaving cream by two local girls. Throughout this scene only her head and shoulders are seen above the water.

SLEEPERS ★★★★

Credits: VHS/1996/USA/ Colour/148 minutes
Writer/Director: Barry Levinson
Based on the book by Lorenzo Carcaterra.
Cast: Kevin Bacon [Sean Nokes], Billy Crudup [Tommy], Robert De Niro [Father Bobby], Minnie Driver [Carol], Ron Eldard [John], Vittorio Gassman [King Benny], Dustin Hoffman [Danny Snyder], Terry Kinney [Ferguson], Bruno Kirby [Shake's father], Jason Patric [Lorenzo "Shakes"], Joe Perrino [young Shakes], Brad Pitt [Michael], Brad Renfro [young Michael], Jonathon Tucker [young Tommy], Geoffrey Wigdor [young John]
Genre: A gripping, gritty drama about a friendship which runs deeper than blood and about revenge for past violations.
Plot: In the late 1960s, the Hell's Kitchen neighbourhood of Manhattan was an inward-looking community which took care of it's own and whose heroes were gangsters like King Benny (Gassman). In the summer of 1967 four young friends from this community pull a prank that turns sour. After stealing a hot dog vendor's cart on a lark, Lorenzo, or Shakes (Perrino), Tommy (Tucker), John (Wigdor) and Michael (Renfro) accidentally injure a man in a subway station. With the victim near death, the four boys are sentenced to periods of up to eighteen months in the Wilkinson Home For Boys.

At Wilkinson they are among the youngest and the smallest of the inmates and are almost immediately singled out for harassment by the older inmates. They are also singled out for special treatment by several of the guards, a special treatment which involves physical, psychological and sexual abuse.

During their first minutes at Wilkinson the guard Sean Nokes (Bacon) ogles Shakes while he undresses to change into his uniform. On Shakes's last night in the institution, on his fourteenth birthday, Nokes viciously rapes the boy. During the intervening period they are subjected to daily abuse. At times the physical abuse is so severe that it requires hospitalization.

One of the other inmates is beaten to death for daring to beat the guards in a football game, a death which goes on the record as pneumonia. Despite the severity of the abuse, however, as they leave Wilkinson the boys agree not to discuss their treatment, even amongst themselves. After all, who would believe them? As one might expect, however, the experience has left each of the four emotionally scarred for life.

Thirteen years later, in the fall of 1981, John (Eldard) and Tommy (Crudup), by now hardened criminals, chance upon Nokes in a restaurant, killing him on the spot. The Hell's Kitchen support system closes ranks behind them. Michael (Pitt), now a junior prosecutor, takes on the case.

With support from Shakes (Patric), King Benny and a docile alcoholic defense lawyer, Danny Snyder (Hoffman), Michael conspires to lose the case while exposing the tortures the four boys suffered at Wilkinson.

The strategy for truly losing the case hinges, however, on getting a believable witness to perjure himself on the stand. For this they turn to the neighbourhood priest, Father Bobby (De Niro), himself a product of Hell's Kitchen and Wilkinson and a stabilizing fixture in the lives of the four friends from their earliest childhood.

Levinson has managed to draw first-class performances from Perrino, Renfro, Tucker and Wigdor as the four young friends subjected to vicious abuse in the reform school. Among the adults, only De Niro and Hoffman really stand out, De Niro proving once again that he is one of America's finest screen performers.

Although the claim that this is a true story has been strongly disputed, it really matters little. There have been so many verified instances of torture and abuse, both physical and sexual, in juvenile detention centres and residential care facilities that the spirit of this story is fact even if the details are fiction.

Useful comparisons might be made with several other films. Two which spring most immediately to mind are the Canadian films *The Boys Of St. Vincent* (which is based on verified cases of abuse) and *Lilies* (which likewise deals with long delayed revenge).
MPAA: Rated R. Canadian Home Video rated 14-A. Frequent coarse language and explicit violence including vicious attacks on young teenagers, fist fights and cold blooded murder. The sexual assaults are depicted mostly by inference and sound. It is clear what is happening to the boys, but it is not shown on-screen. Among other indignities, they are sodomized and forced to perform oral sex on various guards.

THE SLINGSHOT ★★★★

Credits: VHS/1994/Sweden/Colour/102 minutes
In Swedish with English subtitles.
Writer/Director: Ake Sandgren
Based on a book by Roland Schutt.
Cast: Reine Brynolfsson [Hinge Bergegren], Basia Frydman [Zipa Scutt, the mother], Ernst Gunther, Ernst-Hugo Jaregard [Lundin], Niclas Olund [Bertil Schutt], Jesper Salen [Roland Schutt], Stellan Skarsgard [Fritiof Schutt, the father], Jakob Leygraf [Stickan]
Genre: A drama about a young boy growing up an outsider in Stockholm in the 1930s, set upon by other children and by his teachers because of his parents.
Plot: Twelve-year-old Roland (Salen) is seemingly the victim of everybody's anger. He is picked on by other boys in the neighbourhood, and singled out for frequent and

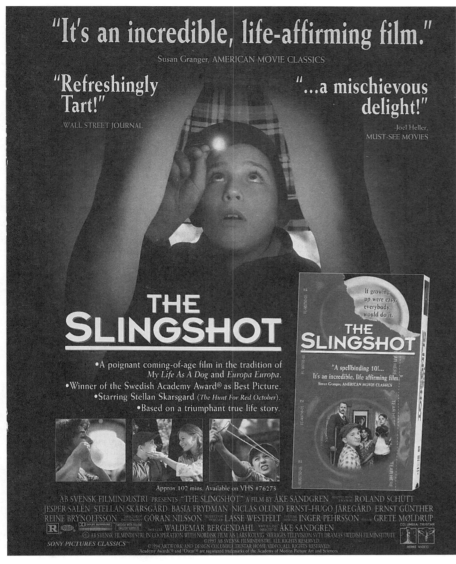

"It's an incredible, life-affirming film."
Susan Granger, AMERICAN MOVIE CLASSICS

"Refreshingly Tart!"
WALL STREET JOURNAL

"...a mischievous delight!"
-Joel Heller,
MUST-SEE MOVIES

THE
SLINGSHOT

•A poignant coming-of-age film in the tradition of *My Life As A Dog* and *Europa Europa*.
•Winner of the Swedish Academy Award® as Best Picture.
•Starring Stellan Skarsgard (*The Hunt For Red October*).
•Based on a triumphant true life story.

Approx.102 mins. Available on VHS #76273

AB SVENSK FILMINDUSTRI PRESENTS "THE SLINGSHOT" A FILM BY ÅKE SANDGREN ROLAND SCHÜTT
JESPER SALEN STELLAN SKARSGARD BASIA FRYDMAN NICLAS OLUND ERNST-HUGO JÄREGÅRD ERNST GÜNTHER
REINE BRYNOLFSSON GÖRAN NILSSON LASSE WESTFELT INGER PEHRSSON GRETE MØLDRUP
WALDEMAR BERGENDAHL ÅKE SANDGREN

SONY PICTURES CLASSICS

Jesper Salen, *The Slingshot* (1994)

sometimes vicious punishment at school. His sin? He is different. His mother (Frydman) is a Russian Jew who illegally promotes the use of condoms. His disabled father (Skarsgard) is a poor revolutionary socialist who runs a tobacco shop where condoms are sold under the counter and fellow Marxists meet.

Roland just wants to fit in, to prove that he is as Swedish as everybody else. He also desperately wants a bicycle and will go to almost any length to raise the money to buy one. Unfortunately most of his schemes prove to be risky. He sells slingshots made from scrap metal and condoms, but the condoms are illegal. As are the "balloons with a knob" that he sells to the neighbourhood children.

Then Stickan [Leygraf] suggests that Roland repair and paint bicycles for his friends. What Roland doesn't known is that the bicycles are stolen. When the police

catch up with Stickan and his friends, Roland's ignorance of the facts doesn't save him. He is forced to sign a confession and is sent to a reform school.

This film is a tribute to the undying optimism of a child. No matter how savagely he is beaten, no matter how bleak things may seem to the adults around him, Roland never gives up hope. Life is wonderful and he means to live it to its fullest. Even being sent to a reform school holds no terrors for the boy. He is even looking forward to it. As he tells his teacher in front of the whole class, at the reform school the teachers will be competent.

MPAA: Rated R. There is a great deal of violence directed against Roland in this film, both from other boys and from the teachers at his school, including one savage beating with a wooden paddle.

Salen has a couple of nude scenes where he bares his buns for the camera, once just before his teacher beats Roland and again at home when his furious parents examine the boy's injuries. Skarsgard also has a couple of bare buns shots while the father receives morphine injections to relieve the pain of his sciatica.

At the reform school, several boys appear in full-frontal nude shots diving into the lake after being deloused and scrubbed clean on the dock. Salen is in the scene but only appears fully nude in a distant shot where he can't be clearly identified.

The film also includes some sex talk, both the mother's lectures about the use of condoms and the boys talking about sexual matters. As well several boys, including Roland, are involved with a teenage girl in the park who for a fee will let them look up her skirt and finger her under a blanket.

SON OF THE SHARK ★★★★

(Also known as *Le Fils du Requin*)

Credits: VHS/1994/France/Colour/85 minutes
In French with English subtitles.
Writer/Director: Agnes Merlet
Based on a true story.
Cast: Sandrine Blancke [Marie], Erik Da Silva [Simon Vanderhoes], Maxime LeRoux [the father], Ludovic

River Phoenix and Wil Wheaton, *Stand By Me* (1986)

Vandendaele [Martin Vanderhoes]

Awards: Venice Film Festival (1993): Prix de la Critique Internationale.

Genre: A chilling fact-based drama about two anti-social young brothers caught in the cycle of domestic violence.

Plot: Simon (Da Silva) and Martin (Vandendaele) are brothers with only each other for support. Their father (LeRoux) physically abuses them. They feel abandoned by their mother who left the family many years ago. Foster homes and group care do nothing for them. They escape as quickly as they are placed. They steal. They vandalize. They are abusive to others. They play disgusting tricks on unsuspecting townspeople.

Having never received love or tenderness they are incapable of giving it. The older brother, Martin, seems to care for his one-time classmate Marie (Blancke), but he is unable to express his feelings. The only way the brothers know of showing care is through violence. They force Marie to strip to her underwear with every expectation on her part that she will be ravaged. Martin at one point even tries to get her to join him in drowning themselves. (He has an ongoing fantasy of disappearing into the ocean in fulfillment of his notion that he is the son of a shark.)

Even with each other, as often as not Simon and Martin display their bonding and commitment through violent actions: fist fights, shoving and punching. Truly it is only each other that these boys care for. And it is their love for each other which causes them time and time again to run away from group homes, reform schools and foster homes, always working to be together, always drawn inexorably together as if by some magnetic force.

A sobering indictment of the effects of the physical abuse of children, this chilling depiction of boys out of control engaging in vandalism and mayhem for its own sake is made even more chilling by the realization that it is based on a true story.

MPAA: Not rated. Frequent coarse language and violence with Martin and Simon as both victims and perpetrators. On two occasions the boys force young girls to strip to their underwear.

There is one minor incident of nudity. The two boys return to their school one day and while one tries to attract Marie's attention the other moons the class through the windows.

SOUP AND ME ★★★

Credits: VHS/1978/USA/Colour/24 minutes
Director: Dennis Donnelly
Screenplay: Mark Fink
Based on the stories by Robert Newton Peck.
Cast: Christian Berrigan, Owen Bush, Frank Cady, Kathleen Freeman, Mary Margaret Patts, Shane Sinutko
Awards: Columbus Film Festival.
Genre: Originally an ABC Television special, this fun little comedy about two boys getting into mischief while growing up together in a farming community has been made available on video tape.
Plot: Rob and Soup are two pre-teens growing up together in the country. They spend their days antagonizing Mr. Sutter and feuding with Janice Riker.

When Janice discovers the two boys skinny-dipping, she tosses all their clothes into the water. Unable to retrieve any of their clothes, the boys are forced to make their way home au naturel.

When they come across a church rummage sale, they think they are in luck until they find there is nothing but dresses on the racks behind the church. Fortunately it's Halloween — they have just found their costumes!
MPAA: Not rated. While most of the nude sequence is simulated with lots of shots of bare torsos and bare legs as they run across open fields, there are a couple of full length bum shots of both boys when they first come out of the water.

STAND BY ME ★★★★★

Credits: VHS/1986/USA/Colour/87 minutes
Director: Rob Reiner
Screenplay: Raynold Gideon and Bruce A. Evans
Based on the novella *The Body* by Stephen King.
Cast: John Cusak [Denny Lachance], Richard Dreyfuss [the writer], Corey Feldman [Teddy Duchamp], Jerry O'Connell [Vern Tessio], River Phoenix [Chris Chambers], Casey Siemaszko [Billy Tessio], Kiefer Sutherland [Ace Merrill], Wil Wheaton [Gordie Lachance]
Awards: The National Board Of Review: Ten Best Films in English list. Kinema Jumpo (Japan) 1987: Ten Best Foreign Films list; Readers' Choice Award. Academy Awards 1986: (nomination) Best Adapted Screenplay.
Genre: A drama about four young friends bonding together in the last summer before they enter high school. This film has become the standard against which every other coming of age film has since been judged, and rightly so.
Plot: The summer of 1959 in Castle Rock Oregon. Four twelve-year-old boys hear rumours that the body of a another boy missing from a neighbouring town is lying on the bank of a river some miles away. Pulling the time-honoured ruse, each tells his parents he will be sleeping over at another's house. The four boys set off on foot to find the body, satisfy their curiosity and hopefully become heroes. Through a series of adventures along the way involving junk yard dogs, trains, bridges, leeches and stories told 'round the campfire, the film draws finely lined portraits of the four boys, and their relationships with each other.

Teddy (Feldman), a victim of past physical abuse, is the crazy one given to fits of blinding rage and violent fantasies, constantly testing himself. Vern (O'Connell) is a chubby exuberant bundle of nerves who sometimes has difficulty keeping up with his brighter buddies. Chris (Phoenix), the leader of the group and the peace maker, is the misunderstood good kid from a bad family who can't live down the preconceptions that precede him. Gordie (Wheaton) is the storyteller, the quiet intellectual, who will never match the place his football star older brother Denny (Cusak) held in his father's heart. A situation only made worse by Denny's recent death in a car accident.

The four boys are still at an age when TV westerns and cartoon characters seem more important than the girls they are just starting to notice. Over a mere two days on the road, however, they will grow, mature and draw closer to each other. Though it is obvious that as high school looms around the corner their different personalities will lead them down different roads, for one brief moment in time they come together. After being gone only two days, they return to a town that seems somehow different, smaller. And with this comes the realization that they will never again have friends like the ones they had when they were twelve.
MPAA: Rated R. There is a considerable amount of coarse language throughout the film as well as some fairly juvenile sex talk.

STOLEN CHILDREN ★★★★

(Also known as *Il Ladro Di Bambini*)

Credits: VHS/1992/Italy/Colour/116 minutes
In Italian with English subtitles.
Director: Gianni Amelio
Screenplay: Gianni Amelio, Sandro Petraglia and Stefano Rulli
Cast: Fabio Alessandrini [Grignani], Giuseppe Ieracitano [Luciano], Florence Darel [Martine], Marina Golovine [Nathalie], Enrico Lo Verso [Antonio], Valentina Scalici [Rosetta]

Awards: Cannes Film Festival 1992: Grand Jury Prize; (nomination) Best Film.

Genre: A drama about two pre-teens and their changing relationship with the young Carabiniere officer detailed to deliver them to a Children's Home in Sicily after their mother is jailed.

Plot: Eleven-year-old Rosetta (Scalici), her mother and her younger brother Luciano (Ieracitano) live in a Milan housing development. Money is short, but the family has other income. Mom has been forcing Rosetta into prostitution for the past two years. When the mother is arrested, Luciano and Rosetta are taken into care and sent to a Children's Home in another city.

The first Home, citing technicalities, refuses the children because of Rosetta's past. They are to be sent instead to a Home in Sicily. Antonio (Lo Verso), a young Carabiniere officer is assigned the task of delivering them. Despite his misgivings, despite Rosetta's difficult ways, despite Luciano's asthma and sullen silence, the young man sets out with the children.

What begins as simply an assignment, however, soon becomes something more as Antonio starts to care about the children as individuals. He attempts to protect Rosetta from those, including his own family, who would hold her past against her. He breaks through Luciano's shell, becoming a hero and role model for the boy, especially after an impromptu swimming lesson at a roadside beach. In fact, the formerly withdrawn little boy is looking forward to regular visits from Antonio and talks of becoming a Carabiniere officer himself.

Unfortunately, reality sets in. The children are late arriving at the Sicilian Home. Antonio is accused of kidnapping the children and his future with the force is in jeopardy. At the end, the children, disillusioned and alone, are left with only each other for support.

MPAA: Not rated. Canadian Home Video rated 14-A. Although dealing with the question of child prostitution, there are no overtly sexual scenes in the film, nor is there any nudity. We are shown a john entering the apartment in Milan and being led away again by the police. What takes place between the man and the girl is left to the viewer's imagination. The closest we get to nudity is several shots of Luciano in his underwear on the beach and in the water.

STREET KID ★★★

(Also known as *Gossenkind*)

Credits: VHS/1991/Germany/Colour/89 minutes
In German with English subtitles.
Director: Peter Kern
Screenplay: Susanne Glaser
Cast: Daniel Aminathey [Jimmy], Daniel Berger [Albert],

Christoph Elbsloh [Felix], Winfried Glatzeder [Karl Heinz], Max Kellermann [Axel Glitter], Philip van der Wingen [Paul], Nicole Weber [Elizabeth]

Genre: A comic drama about a fourteen-year-old street hustler and his relationship with a middle-aged businessman.

Plot: Abused at home and hassled by the police on the streets of Dusseldorf, fourteen-year-old Axel Glitter (Kellermann) is a street kid with an attitude and an outrageous pompadour.

Although banned from the railway station, the hustlers' prime hunting ground, the boy tells the police they can't get rid of juvenile prostitution. "There are," he tells them, "dozens of men out there who want me." Following yet another row with his mother and his stepfather, Axel runs away from home. His stepfather, upset that Axel doesn't turn over the money he makes hustling, rapes the boy in front of his mother.

Out on the street again, Axel meets Karl Heinz, a married man with a son and problems of his own. After a series of escapades which begin to border on farce, Karl Heinz, who is wrongly suspected of molesting Felix (Elbsloh), a young boy he has been babysitting, makes plans to leave town. He closes out his bank accounts telling the startled clerk he is driving away with his fourteen-year-old boyfriend.

Together, businessman and street kid head towards the country estate where Karl Heinz's wife and son have been staying. Unbeknownst to Karl Heinz, however, his wife's current lover is also there. And his son Paul (van der Wingen) has been forming a loving relationship with one of the farm hands.

MPAA: Not rated. A great deal of sexual dialogue occurs throughout the film. Axel and Karl Heinz kiss several times. There is a very dark full-frontal nude shot of Ramon, the current boyfriend of Karl Heinz's wife. There is also a brief, very dark shot of Axel's bare buns when his stepfather rapes him.

STREETWISE ★★★★★

Credits: VHS/1984/USA/Colour/92 minutes
Director: Martin Bell
Developed from *Streets of the Lost*, a Life Magazine story.
Genre: A candid documentary about kids, some as young as thirteen or fourteen, living on the streets of Seattle.

Plot: For several weeks in the early fall, a film crew followed the lives of a number of young homeless street dwellers in downtown Seattle, recording their lives, their thoughts, their memories, their dreams. Speaking to each other and to the camera they tell us how they came to be on their own, fending for themselves.

A history of broken homes and physically, sexually and psychologically abusive parents has driven most of these teenagers to the streets. Once on the streets, they survive by "spare changing," scamming, selling blood, drug dealing, dumpster diving, petty crime and prostitution.

Though some still live in a family home, most sleep in abandoned buildings or run-down hotels. In and out of detention, relying on free clinics and handouts, underfed, with the eternal optimism of youth, many of these kids, most of them school dropouts, can still dream of a better future, of living in a nice suburban home with a regular nuclear family.

Though they may live on the street, their lives are not totally bleak: there are moments of caring tenderness, of

Gary Grimes and Jennifer O'Neill, *Summer of '42* (1971)

love, of joy and of humour, however fleeting, before moving on, hitchhiking or hopping a freight to somewhere else, whether that be Alaska or Florida, New York or California. The truth of their existence, however, is more likely to be seen in the suicide in a juvenile detention centre of Dewayne while facing charges of drug dealing.

This is a must-see film for anybody concerned about the plight of youth at risk. It has not lost an ounce of its

power or relevance in the intervening years. In fact, in today's get tough atmosphere it may even be more vital than it was in the early 1980s.

Nearly a decade after *Streetwise* was released, director Martin Bell returned to the streets of Seattle for the fictional film *American Heart*. The latter film owes a great deal to the documentary: many of the situations and characters grow directly from the situations seen in *Streetwise*.

MPAA: Not rated. A great deal of coarse language as well as talk of drugs, sexual matters and prostitution. There is one instance of nudity: two homeless people, a teenage boy named Rat and a young adult named Jack, share a cold shower. There is also a certain amount of casual violence, fist fights and abusive behaviour.

SUMMER OF '42
★★★★

Credits: VHS/1971/USA/Colour/ 102 minutes
Director: Robert Mulligan
Screenplay: Herman Raucher
Cast: Katherine Allentuck [Aggie], Oliver Conant [Benjie], Gary Grimes [Hermie], Jerry Hauser [Oskie], Christopher Norris [Miriam], Jennifer O'Neill [Dorothy]
Awards: Academy Awards 1971: Best Original Score; (nomination) Cinematography; (nomination) Film Editing; (nomination) Story and Screenplay.
Genre: One of the classic coming of age dramas, *Summer Of '42* is a nostalgic look at world which may never have existed—the wonderful, frightening, confusing summer when three boys turn fifteen and experience their first real loves and sexual urgings.
Plot: The Terrible Trio are Hermie (Grimes), the good-looking but awkward kid trying almost too hard to be the sophisticated young man he isn't, Oskie (Hauser), the chubby would-be womanizer and Benjie (Conant) the glasses wearing, naive, slightly nerdy young teen. They are spending their summer on The Island trying to pick up the girls and make sense of their adolescent longings. Longings which are only heightened by Benjie's discovery of an illustrated medical cum sexual text and Hermie's falling for an older woman, Dorothy (O'Neill), the young

war widow in the isolated house by the beach.

While Oskie is making "progress" with the beautiful Miriam (Norris), Hermie's relationship with Dorothy moves from carrying her groceries home through assisting her with household chores to a sexual liaison.

The film is well worth seeing, and includes a number of classic scenes. The scene where Hermie is urged on by Oskie to make his first painful foray into the drug store to buy a box of condoms, is priceless.

Summer Of '42 was followed by the less satisfactory sequel, *Class Of '44*, involving some of the same cast members. Several other filmmakers have drawn on *Summer of '42* for inspiration. Echoes of this film can be found in the Israeli film *Lemon Popsicle* and its American remake *The Last American Virgin*, as well as the more recent film *The Inkwell*.

MPAA: Rated PG. Canadian Home Video rated 14-A. In a reflection of the inconstant nature of the MPAA rating system, *Summer of '42* was originally rated R but this was later revised.

The sexual encounter between Oskie and Miriam is played out entirely off-screen, except for Oskie's frequent running back to the bonfire on the beach to ask for further pointers from the step-by-step guide to sex the boys have written down.

The affair between Dorothy and Hermie, while again mostly implied, is a beautifully sensual scene.

SUNDAY'S CHILDREN
★★★★★

Credits: VHS/1992/Sweden/Colour/116 minutes
In Swedish with English subtitles.
Director: Daniel Bergman
Screenplay: Ingmar Bergman
Based on Ingmar Bergman's childhood memories.
Cast: Thommy Berggren [Erik], Lena Endre [Karin], Jakob Leygraf [Dag], Henrik Linnros [Pu]
Genre: A biography of well-known Swedish film director Ingmar Bergman.
Plot: In a film which brings to mind the paintings of Carl Larsson, director Daniel Bergman, through a screenplay by his father, examines the latter's boyhood summers in rural Sweden in the 1920s. Looking at some of the events

which were to affect Ingmar Bergman for the rest of his life, the film is primarily the chronicle of a father-son relationship.

Eight-year-old Pu (Linnros), as the future director was nicknamed, is witness to the tensions between his mother (Endre) and father (Berggren), overhearing one night talk of their possible separation. Pu is on the receiving end of both harsh and severe discipline and exquisite tenderness and understanding from his father, the dichotomy affecting the ambivalent relationship between the two for the next forty years.

The love-hate relationship spills over into Pu's other family ties. His mother, his grandmother, his uncle Carl, his brother Dag (Leygraf): Pu's relationship with each seems at times to mirror that with his father. This is most clearly the case with Dag who can one day share forbidden secrets with his younger brother and the next trick him into eating a live earthworm.

The film makes use of several jumps forward to 1968 to show the lifelong effects of the young Bergman's childhood on his later relationships with his father. As such it is one of a very few films which attempts to show clearly that, as the cliche goes, the child is father of the man.

Overhearing your parents discussing separation and divorce can affect one for life. Being savagely slapped in public by your father when you are eight may well affect your feelings for him when you are fifty. But so can a warm hug and a kiss at the railway station, or an affectionate embrace sitting naked in the sun after skinny-dipping together in a cold lake.

MPAA: Not rated. There is some minor incidental nudity: Dag and Pu looking at a book of photographs of nude women, a woman breast-feeding her children, Pu dropping his pants just before an attack of diarrhea and Pu and his father skinny-dipping together on their way home from preaching in a neighbouring town.

The last scene includes brief full-frontal exposure of Linnros. There is almost nothing sexual in the film beyond one instance of Pu watching Dag masturbate late one night in their shared bedroom. It's a scene in which the camera is more concerned with Pu's reactions than Dag's behaviour, which is portrayed almost entirely by sound effects: squeaking bed springs and heavy breathing.

T

36 FILLETTE ★★★

Credits: VHS/1988/France/Colour/88 minutes
In French with English subtitles.
Director: Catherine Breillat
Screenplay: Catherine Breillat and Roger Salloch
Cast: Etienne Chicot [Maurice], Jean-Pierre Leaud [Boris Golovine], Stephane Moquet [Gi-Pe], Oliver Parniere [Bertrand], Delphine Zentout [Lili]
Genre: Billed as "A French Lolita," this is a comedy told from a feminine point of view about a precocious fourteen-year-old brat set on losing her virginity.
Plot: Lili (Zentout) has one principle goal to reach during her summer vacation in Biarritz with her family. She is intent on losing her virginity. While on the way to a disco with her older brother Jean-Pierre (Moquet) she makes the acquaintance of a middle-aged playboy named Maurice (Chicot). She immediately sets her sights on him as the person who will help her accomplish her goal. She is also aided in her quest by a well developed body, her precocity and her seemingly adult sexual knowledge.

Beneath the skin, however, she is basically still a very naive little girl. She is also a fundamentally obnoxious person, a demanding little brat who sees no further than the tip of her own nose. The only person who matters in Lili's life is Lili. Everybody else exists solely for the purpose of fulfilling her needs, whether it's her parents, her brother, Maurice or Bertrand (Parniere), the teenager in the next campsite. Zentout's portrayal of this very confused and basically unlikable teenager is superb.

Watch for Truffaut star Jean-Pierre Leaud in a small role as the musician Lili meets in a bar. The title is a reference to Lili's clothing size, a size which she is rapidly outgrowing.
MPAA: Not rated. There are several nude and partially nude scenes including shots of Zentout topless, and unrevealing shots of Chicot and Parniere.

There are also a number of sexual encounters shown, all involving Lili with various male characters: with Maurice, making love; with Maurice, performing oral sex on the man; with Bertrand, making love.

Valerie Dumas and Thierry Tevini, *Tendres Cousines* (1983)

TENDRES COUSINES ★★★

Credits: VHS/1983/France/Colour/90 minutes
Dubbed in English.
Director: David Hamilton
Screenplay: Pascal Laine, based on his own novel of the same name.
Cast: Elisa Cervier [Claire], Pierre Chantepie [Mathieu], Jean-Yves Chatelais [Charles], Valerie Dumas [Poune], Hannes Kaetner [Professor Schonberg, the scientist], Catherine Rouvel [Madame Lacroix], Anja Shute [Julia], Thierry Tevini [Julien], Pierre Vernier [the father]
Genre: A beautifully photographed nostalgic comedy of

Tendres Cousines (1983)

manners with a teenage protagonist.

Plot: Poor Julien (Tevini). He's a cute schoolboy with a problem. He's going on fifteen and back home from school for a summer on the family estate. It's the summer of 1939 and "all's quiet as can be." Even radio reports from Hitler's Germany seem far away and unreal.

Julien's biggest problem is rampant puberty. He's in love. With his cousin Julia, two years his senior. Only one problem. Julia is in love with Charles (Chatelais), the boorish fiance of Julien's sister Claire (Cervier). And Julia's little sister Poune (Dumas) is in love with Julien. So devoted is his younger cousin that poor Julien "can't even get five minutes alone to take a pee."

Then there are all the beautiful young serving girls on the estate. Every one of them is only too willing, it would seem, to take the young master of the house in hand, and give the schoolboy a few practical lessons in what really matters in life.

The adults in this household all have problems of their

own and no time for the teenagers. Julien's mother has financial worries so she has taken in boarders. The only advise to his son from dapper dad (Vernier) is "next time, don't get caught." The only sympathetic and practical counsel for the confused young people comes from the eccentric boarders: the fading actress who is perpetually just on the brink of a comeback, and the mad German scientist (Kaetner) who captures souls in white and orange balloons.

Like any film from David Hamilton, this one is visually a treat. It even has a better story line than most of his films, though typical of this director the story is clearly of secondary importance. This is primarily beautifully photographed soft-core erotica.

MPAA: Not rated. Typical of David Hamilton's films and still photography, *Tendres Cousines* has lots of young female bodies on view, though perhaps fewer than in some of his other films.

Unlike most of his films, the boys get their clothes off as well, even if it is only one boy (Tevini), only rear shots and only partially seen. Several of the young actresses appear in full-frontal nude shots. Most appear topless.

Julien is seen in a number of bare butt shots. A great many sexual situations occur, though unlike other David Hamilton films there are almost no girl with girl situations. Julien has several sexual encounters: with Mathilde, with Madelaine, with Madame Lacroix (Rouvel) and with his cousin Julia. Julien's father is clearly having a sexual affair with the teenage farm hand Mathieu (Chantepie), but nothing of this is shown on-screen.

LA TETA Y LA LUNA ★★★★

(Also known as *The Tit And The Moon*)

Credits: VHS/1994/Spain-France/Colour/87 minutes
In Spanish with English subtitles.
Director: Bigas Luna
Cast: Gerard Darmon [Maurice], Biel Duran [Tete], Abel Folk [the father], Laura Mana [the mother], Mathilda May [Estrellita], Miquel Poveda [Miguel], Genis Sanchez [Stallone]
Genre: A dark comedy that looks at life and the eccentric people who reside in a Spanish seaside town, as seen through the eyes of a young boy with an obsession for breasts.
Plot: Nine-year-old Tete (Duran), is a boy with a mission. Jealous of his newborn brother breast feeding, he sets out to find a breast of his own. Along the way he encounters a host of people, each with their own obsession.

Maurice (Darmon) is a professional entertainer. His speciality? Farting. His problem? Impotence. His solution? Loaves of french bread. Estrellita (May), his wife, is a dancer with a passion for tears and smelly feet. The former she keeps in a bottle, the latter send her into orgasmic frenzies. Miguel (Poveda) is a young man with smelly feet and a passion for Estrellita. He serenades her at all hours of the night and day. Tete's father (Folk) directs the making of human castles in competition with other towns, and calls upon the spirits of the ancient Romans to assist them in their endeavours.

Tete just wants a breast full of milk, preferably Estrellita's, to call his own. When not devising schemes to get what he wants, he fantasizes about landing on the moon to plant the flag of Catalonia, about marching with the Roman legions, about breasts. In fact, when he finally achieves his goal, one wonders. Is this just another fantasy or is this one that comes true?

MPAA: Not rated. Canadian Home Video rated 18-A. The film includes a number of sex scenes, mostly involving Estrellita. She is seen with Maurice on a number of occasions as well as with Miguel. There is also a sex scene with Tete's parents.

During many of these sex scenes, Tete is our witness, telling us his wry, innocently fantastic thoughts as he watches the proceedings. He views intercourse as a means by which the man can fill the woman up with the milk he so desperately desires. Near the end of the film nine-year-old Tete is seen sucking on the breasts first of Estrellita then of his mother. In addition to this scene, there are a large number of other shots of bare breasts throughout the film, including one where Estrellita directs a stream of milk into Tete's mouth.

There is also a shot of Poveda nude as Miguel, distraught when Estrellita and Maurice suddenly leave town, strips naked and walks into the sea in an unsuccessful attempt to commit suicide. This is a dark shot, and Poveda is seen from the rear only.

THIS BOY'S LIFE
★★★★★
Credits: VHS/1993/USA/Colour/115 minutes
Director: Michael Caton-Jones
Screenplay: Robert Getchell
Based on the autobiography of Tobias Wolff.
Cast: Zack Ansley [Skipper], Ellen Barkin [Caroline], Jonah Blechman [Arthur Gale],

Chris Cooper [Roy], Robert De Niro [Dwight], Leonardo DiCaprio [Toby], Eliza Dushku [Pearl], Carla Gugino [Norma]
Genre: The biography of the teenage years of American writer Toby Wolff.
Plot: When Caroline (Barkin) breaks up with her boyfriend Roy (Cooper), she and her son Toby (DiCaprio) head west to Utah. Dreams of making a fortune prospecting for uranium soon prove a fantasy which becomes a nightmare when Roy arrives on the scene.

Caroline and Toby pack their bags and move on to

Leonardo DiCaprio, *This Boy's Life* (1993)

Seattle. There Toby, now calling himself Jack, finds himself in trouble with the school authorities and the police. At her wits end, Caroline takes up the suggestion of her new boyfriend Dwight (De Niro) and sends her son to live with him and his three children (Ansley, Dushku and Gugino) in the Cascades town of Concrete. Although promising himself, his mother and Dwight that he will clean up his act, Jack seems to run afoul of Dwight every time he so much as turns around.

The friction between man and boy is only made worse by Dwight's violent mean streak coupled with a hair trigger fuse. Jack is abused physically and psychologically from day one. Dwight beats him and puts him down. The man is consistently sarcastic to the boy. He gets Jack a paper route, then spends the money himself. He trades Jack's much prized rifle for a dog the boy neither wants nor likes. And Dwight's marriage to Caroline does not improve Jack's lot for she refuses to take sides in their constant fighting.

In the whole town of Concrete there is seemingly only one person who really understands Jack, and is able to be a friend. This one real friend is Arthur Gale (Blechman). Like Jack, Arthur is somebody who doesn't really belong in the backwoods of Washington state, for Arthur is gay.

Eventually Jack conceives a plan to escape from Concrete. With a great deal of skulduggery, several forged documents and a little luck he gets accepted at a prestigious Eastern prep school with a full scholarship.

Anchored by superb performances from De Niro and DiCaprio, two of the finest and most versatile actors in Hollywood today, this horrific true story of child abuse is one that should not be missed.

MPAA: Rated R. Canadian Home Video rated 14-A. Frequent scenes of violence and physical abuse as well as a great deal of coarse and suggestive language.

Sexual scenes include Caroline with Roy and Caroline with Dwight. In both instances the sex borders on being abusive.

Although Arthur Gale is clearly gay and probably very much in love with Jack, there is nothing sexual in their relationship, though Arthur does give Jack a kiss when the two are playing the piano together in Arthur's home.

THIS SPECIAL FRIENDSHIP
★★★★

(Also known as *Les Amities Particulieres*)

Credits: VHS/1967/France/B&W/99 minutes
In French with English subtitles.
Director: Jean Dellanoy
Screenplay: Jean Aurenche. Dialogue by Pierre Bast Based on the novel by Roger Peyerfitte.

Cast: Michel Bouquet [Father Trennes], Didier Haudepin [Alexandre Motier], Francis Lacombrade [Georges de Sarre], Francois Leccia [Lucien Rouvere], Dominique Maurin, Lucien Nat [the Father Superior], Louis Seigner [Father Lauzon]

Genre: An indictment against those who would force apart two boys in love, this is a tragic drama about friendship, love and the repression of feelings set within the walls of an austere Catholic boarding school for boys in 1920s France.

Plot: Sixteen-year-old Georges (Lacombrade), the son of the Marquis de Sarre, has arrived at his new school, a strict Catholic boarding school. From the moment he sets foot on the grounds, he is warned about the dangers of forming impure, special friendships with other boys. He is warned during the sermons at Mass. He is warned in the confessional. He is even warned by his fellow students.

When he becomes aware of the existence of such a relationship involving his best friend Lucien Rouvere (Leccia) and fellow student Andre Ferron, he anonymously brings it to the attention of the Father Superior (Nat). Georges's motives in doing so are not clear, even to himself. Does he wish to protect the two from sin? Or is he jealous and wishes to ensure Andre is removed from the scene? Then one day, during Mass, Georges is smitten by a pretty face. Alexandre (Haudepin) enters the church, symbolically carrying a lamb.

Four years younger than Georges and a vivacious imp with an infectious grin, Alexandre is the younger brother of one of Georges's classmates. The obstacles against their friendship are severe. At least one priest, Father Trennes (Bouquet) suspects the truth and threatens Georges with exposure. Georges retaliates by telling the Father Superior that Father Trennes is entertaining boys in his private quarters late at night, providing them with cigarettes and wine. As a result, Trennes is dismissed.

Through all this, Georges and Alexandre persevere, slipping notes to each other at Mass, writing love poems to each other, exchanging gifts and meaningful glances in the dining hall, meeting secretly in a disused greenhouse on the school grounds. Then disaster strikes. The two boys are caught together by Father Lauzon (Seigner), confessor to both boys.

Trying to break up the friendship without causing a scandal, the priest demands Georges return all the letters he has received. Georges is unable to explain the true situation to Alexandre and the younger boy is heartbroken, thinking Georges has abandoned him. In a fit of despondency on the way home for the holidays, Alexandre rips up the letters Georges has returned then jumps from the speeding train.

MPAA: Not rated. Although the implication is that several of the boys in this school are involved in "special friendships" and certainly the priests fear the existence of sexual liaisons, consistent with Peyerfitte's original novel, nothing sexual occurs in the relationship between Georges and Alexandre.

Alexandre gives Georges a quick, chaste kiss on the cheek during one of their greenhouse meetings and when Father Lauzon breaks in on them, they are wrestling together in the straw in what appears to the priest to be a compromising position but the relationship in fact is chaste.

David Thewlis and Leonardo DiCaprio, *Total Eclipse* (1995)

TO PLAY OR TO DIE ★★★★

(Also known as *Spelen Of Sterven*)

Credits: VHS/1990/Netherlands/Colour/50 minutes
In Dutch with English subtitles.
Director: Frank Krom
Screenplay: Anne Van De Putte and Frank Krom
Based on a story by Anna Blaman.
Cast: Tjebbo Gerritsma [Charel], Geert Hunaerts [Kees]
Genre: A dark, psychological thriller about a gay youth in love with an abusive straight boy.
Plot: On the surface, Kees (Hunaerts) is every parent's ideal son. He is a handsome but shy, quiet, academically inclined high school student. Beneath this pleasant surface, however, lie some serious psychological problems.

Kees is obviously in love with his classmate Charel

(Gerritsma). He will do almost anything to attract Charel's attention. He lends the other boy his homework. He refuses to name Charel as the ringleader when he gets locked in a toilet at school. He tolerates any amount of abuse, both physical and psychological, from Charel just to be with him. In fact he seems to find the abuse he receives to be sexually stimulating. After being beaten to a bloody pulp by Charel, Kees masturbates while fantasizing about the other boy.

Finally, in desperation, Kees invites Charel home after school. The ensuing confrontation is both verbally and physically bloody and leads almost inevitably to tragedy.

Kees is clearly gay and in love with Charel. What is not explained is the evident sexual stimulation Kees receives from Charel's abusive behaviour. Nor is Charel's behaviour explained. Is he merely uncaring? Is he habitually abusive to everyone? Or is he homophobic and responding violently, perhaps even unconsciously, to Kees's obvious but unspoken attraction to him?
MPAA: Not rated. Kees, along with several other boys, is seen nude in the school locker rooms. After Kees has named four of the boys who locked him in the toilet they get their revenge by stripping him naked, forcing him to run around the room as they toss his underwear back and forth.

During this sequence Hunaerts appears in several full-frontal nude shots. Several other boys are seen in the showers, obscured slightly by a sheet of textured glass. Kees is seen masturbating after he has just been physically assaulted by Charel.

TOM SAWYER ★★★★

Credits: VHS/1973/USA/Colour/102 minutes
Director: Don Taylor
Music, Lyrics and Screenplay: Richard M. Sherman and Robert B. Sherman. Novel by Mark Twain.
Cast: Lucille Benson [the Widow Douglas], Jeff East [Huckleberry Finn], Jodie Foster [Becky Thatcher], Kunu Hank [Injun Joe], Joshua Hill-Lewis [cousin Sidney], Celeste Holm [Aunt Polly], Susan Joyce [cousin Mary], Warren Oates [Muff Potter], Johnny Whitaker [Tom Sawyer]
Awards: Academy Awards: (nomination) Best Art Direction; (nomination) Best Musical Score; (nomination) Best Costumes.

Genre: A musical comedy and like any other musical comedy, this film should not be taken too seriously. Nevertheless, an infectious score and a cast obviously enjoying themselves make this a fun adaptation of the Mark Twain classic and a personal favourite among the many Mark Twain adaptations I have seen.

Plot: *Tom Sawyer* is a paean to the freedoms of childhood and the inevitability of growing into the responsibilities of the adult world. It is a transformation Tom Sawyer enters eagerly into but which Huck Finn, the eternal child in all of us, turns his back on.

The story should need little or no introduction, and the producers have managed to follow the original material fairly well, considering the undoubted difficulties involved in translating a novel into musical theatre. I believe that most of the major scenarios Mark Twain presents in the book have been retained in the film, though there have inevitably been some modifications. There is great pleasure to be found in re-acquainting oneself with this old friend in a new costume.

The casting in this film is superb: Whitaker as Tom Sawyer, East as Huckleberry Finn and Foster as Becky Thatcher are wonderful and obviously enjoying every minute of the production, as indeed are the majority of the cast. They are helped immensely by the lyrics and the score.

Tom Sawyer was followed a year later by a very disappointing musical version of *Huckleberry Finn* from the same writing team and featuring several of the same cast members, a version which commits the unpardonable sin of making *The Adventures Of Huckleberry Finn* boring.

MPAA: Rated G. Despite the G rating, there is a nude scene involving East and Whitaker. After running away to the island to hide from Injun Joe (Hank) after Tom has accused him of the murder of Doc Robinson, Tom and Huck go skinny-dipping.

All that is seen is a couple of flashes of bare bums above the very muddy waters of the Mississippi. This scene is remarkable for being the only skinny-dipping scene that I am aware of in any filmed adaptation of any of Mark Twain's Tom Sawyer or Huckleberry Finn stories.

Can you imagine Twain's reaction if he knew his young heroes no longer go skinny-dipping?

TOTAL ECLIPSE ★★★

Credits: VHS/1995/France-Great Britain-Belgium/Colour/110 minutes
Director: Agnieszka Holland
Screenplay: Christopher Hampton
Cast: Dominique Blanc [Isabelle Rimbaud], Romane Bohringer [Mathilde], Leonardo DiCaprio [Arthur Rimbaud], David Thewlis [Paul Verlaine]
Genre: A biography.
Plot: In 1871 the young French poet Paul Verlaine (Thewlis) receives several original poems from a previously unknown poet. Inviting the young man to Paris, Verlaine is astounded to find that far from being twenty-one, as his letter indicated, Arthur Rimbaud (DiCaprio) is only sixteen.

For someone of twenty-one, Verlaine tells Rimbaud, the poems are remarkable. For someone of sixteen they are unprecedented. Verlaine quickly takes Rimbaud in hand, supporting him financially and introducing him to Parisian literary circles.

The relationship which develops between man and boy is mutually self destructive. It is also sexual, and though Verlaine is married and a new father, the older man's sexual energy is soon directed primarily towards the boy rather than his teenage wife (Bohringer). This may not be such a loss for Mathilde, however, as more frequently than not, Verlaine's actions towards her are abusive.

Over a period of three years, the love-hate relationship between Verlaine and Rimbaud takes the two of them through ecstasy and hell. One goes into this film with great expectations. Agnieszka Holland directing Leonardo DiCaprio in a gay love story which involves the young superstar in several nude scenes, including full-frontal

David Thewlis and Leonardo DiCaprio, *Total Eclipse* (1995)

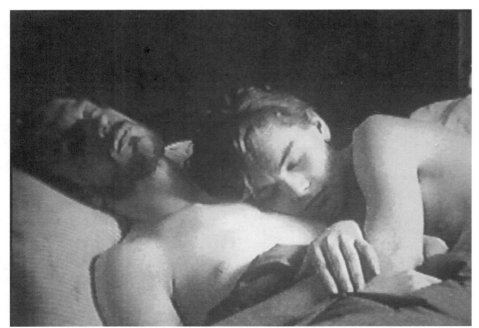

shots, as well as gay sex scenes.

Unfortunately, the combination doesn't quite hit. DiCaprio's Rimbaud smacks too much of 1990's California and not enough of 1870's Paris. Christopher Hampton's script doesn't give us sufficient reasons for Verlaine to fall for this manipulative and unlikable boy. We hear he is a poetic sensation. All we see on screen is an egocentric brat. Nor do we see reasons for Rimbaud to have chosen Verlaine as his mark.

MPAA: Rated R. Canadian Home Video rated R. There are several nude and sexual scenes. These include full-frontal shots of both DiCaprio and Thewlis, as well as rear and bare breast shots of Bohringer.

Sexual scenes include gay kissing and lovemaking between Rimbaud and Verlaine as well as straight sex between Verlaine and Mathilde and between Rimbaud and an African woman. The straight sex of Verlaine and his wife is frequently abusive.

TRAIN OF DREAMS ★★★

Credits: VHS/1987/Canada/Colour/90 minutes/Drama.
Director: John N. Smith
Screenplay: Sally Bochner, John N. Smith and Sam Grana
Cast: Christopher Neil [Nicky], Jason St. Amour [Tony], Marcella Santa Maria [Tony's Mother], Fred Ward [the teacher].
Genre: Another look at institutionalized youth from the director of the much acclaimed *Boys Of St. Vincent,* this time a drama about teens in detention.
Plot: Tony (St. Amour) is a sixteen-year-old English-speaking, Italian Canadian high school dropout from a broken home growing up in a poor neighbourhood in Montreal. An out of control angry young man unable to take responsibility for his own actions, Tony fights constantly with his hard-pressed mother (Santa Maria). In trouble with the law, he is sentenced to two years in a Juvenile Detention Centre when he violates the conditions of his parole. Inside, he learns some hard truths. Perhaps he is not as tough as he would like to think he is. Perhaps his own situation isn't as bad as he thought it was. Perhaps a smart mouth isn't going to get him any place he wants to be.

Befriended by a understanding, unflappable, unshockable teacher (Ward) who successfully makes these tough-acting young offenders write poetry, Tony gradually takes control of his life. Coming home on a weekend pass, Tony is dismayed to find his ten-year-old brother (Neil) starting down the same path he himself has walked: sniffing glue, stealing from his mother's purse, fighting with his mother.

A product of Canada's National Film Board, much of this film was shot on location at the Bluewater Correctional Centre in Ontario. *Train Of Dreams* has been released on video tape, but even in Canada can be difficult to find.

MPAA: Not rated. As might be expected from a group of incarcerated teenage boys, there is a great deal of sex talk, though it seems to be all talk and no action. Most of their poetry and much of their casual conversation involves sexual yearnings: how much they miss it, how much they want it, how much they are going to get when they finally get out.

St. Amour has one lengthy nude scene, including frank full-frontal exposure when Tony is strip-searched on his arrival at the detention centre.

TU SOLO ★★★

(Also known as *On Your Own*)

Credits: VHS/1986/Spain/Colour/96 minutes
In Spanish with English subtitles.
Writer/Director: Teo Escamilla
Cast: Students of La Escuela De Tauromaquia De Madrid who are not individually credited.
Genre: A drama about the ups and downs of a group of teenage and even pre-teen boys who are training to be bull fighters.
Plot: Set in a school for boys who would be bull fighters, *Tu Solo* examines the trials and tribulations of these young hopefuls. Although set among bull fighters, many aspects of the story are universal to any professional sport. Teenagers who feel passionately about the game. The long hours of training necessary to perfect their skills. The conflict with parents concerned about their son's future and education, lest he have no other skills to fall back on should he fail in his chosen sport.

The passionate, dedicated youngster who will give up everything—home, family and old friends—to follow his dreams of a professional sports career. The vultures: the promoters, the agents, the owners, the gamblers, the pundits and the punters who hang around the perimeter of the arena, each out to make his own peseta from the boy's skills. The unforgiving crowds who care only for the spectacle.

But also there are high points for the boys. The passion, the intensity, the adrenaline rush from the freely admitted dangers of the sport. The friendships formed. The unsanctioned village fights. The nude rite of passage inspired by the autobiography of one of the sports legends. The triumph of the first real fight before a real crowd in a real arena with a real bull.

Regardless of one's own feelings about bull fighting,

there can be no denying the intensity of the feelings of these boys for their chosen sport. In this respect, I would suggest that one ought to compare this film with some other sports films: *Rudy, Hoop Dreams, Hoosiers* and *American Flyers* come immediately to mind.

Unfortunately, some of the production values of this film are not quite what one could wish for. And it is quite evident that most of the boys were cast for their abilities in the bull ring, not for their acting skills. Given the nature of the sport, this is, of course, inevitable. It also tends to make the bull fighting sequences the highlights of the film.

MPAA: Not rated. Includes an extended nude sequence featuring six boys, ages about twelve to sixteen, all of whom are seen in frequent full-frontal shots as they challenge a young bull in the grey light of pre-dawn. This rite-of-passage sequence includes the most unself-conscious and unaffected juvenile nudity I have seen on-screen in a long time. Once these boys enter the ring to challenge the bull, it is obvious that they lose all awareness of both the camera and their nudity.

This sequence is played out as a series of pas-de-deux as the six boys separately take their turns against the young bull with all the grace and beauty of a ballet. Sensuous and sensual without being erotic, for both the boy and the viewer the nudity only serves to accent the balletic qualities and seems to further increase the boy's sensitivity to the bull.

THE TWO OF US ★★★

(Also known as *Le Vieil Homme Et L'Enfant*, as *Claude*, and as *The Old Man And The Boy*)

Credits: VHS/1968/France/B&W/86 minutes
Dubbed in English.

Writer/Director: Claude Berri
Cast: Roger Carel [Victor], Alain Cohen [Claude Langmann], Charles Denner [the father], Luce Fabiole [Meme], Paul Preboist [Maxime], Michel Simon [Pepe]
Genre: A comedy about a French Jewish boy sent to the countryside for safety during World War II.
Plot: In 1943 being a Jew in France means a life of constant fear of being denounced by neighbours and a life of constantly moving from town to town. When the parents of young Claude (Cohen) are offered the chance to send the boy into hiding in the country they jump at it. And what an ideal cover they are offered: the home of the mildly eccentric elderly anti-semitic supporter of Marshal Petain!

From the moment of his arrival in the home of "grandpapa" (Simon) it becomes a gentle battle of wits for the young refugee to conceal his Jewishness from the old man, his wife [Fabiole] and the neighbours. Over the course of a year a genuine love develops between the two while the boy, through a variety of stratagems, manages to conceal his true identity.

However, being a city kid in a country school causes other problems for Claude, problems which he can't escape quite so easily. In the end, with the Germans being pushed out of France, Claude's parents are able to safely retrieve their son. In a tearful farewell, Claude and the old man part company, "grandpapa" still unaware that he has harboured a Jewish fugitive.

MPAA: Not rated. As the young Claude, Cohen appears in a couple of nude shots including one full-frontal scene. Both revolve around his difficulty in concealing the fact he is circumcised when he must bathe in a portable tub in the middle of the kitchen floor with his elderly foster mother hovering around convinced he needs assistance.

VITO AND THE OTHERS ★★★

(Also known as *Vito E Gli Altri*)

Credits: VHS/1992/Italy/Colour/90 minutes
In Italian with English subtitles.
Writer/Director: Antonio Capuano
Cast: Giovanni Bruno [Gaetano], Antonio Farak [Lino], Giuseppina Fusco [Alba], Antonio Jaccarino [Formaggino], Mario Lenti [Aniello], Pina Leone [Miriam], Nando Triola [Vito]
Genre: A drama about young street children in Naples.
Plot: Twelve-year-old Vito (Triola) and his friends are angelic-looking children living on the anything but heavenly back streets of Naples. They want respect in a world which seemingly has none to give to the poor and the young. How do you get ahead in the shit-pile that is life? You accumulate money and power.

Vito and the others find power in their numbers and in the barrel of a handgun. Money is accumulated by purse snatchings, theft, shakedowns and intimidation. Dealing drugs and selling your body to wealthy pedophiles helps to bring in the money as well.

A period of incarceration is not a major set-back for Vito. While in the borstal he may be raped, tattooed, beaten and bullied by the much older boys who surround him, but he emerges from the experience tougher, harder and even more determined, even less concerned for those around him.

The total portrait of these cynical pre-teens who are experienced, despairing and crudely knowledgeable beyond their years is chilling and disturbing. Unfortunately the messenger is flawed. The film is disjointed, uneven and at times very confusing. At the end of the film one is left with a feeling of never having got to know these children. This lack of knowledge leads to lack of any real caring or sympathy for their plight. It's too bad. With a little better treatment from the director and producer this could have been a much more powerful film. It is still worth seeing, but it doesn't have the immediacy and impact of other films about street kids such as *Streetwise, Pixote*, or *Salaam Bombay*!
MPAA: Not rated. A great deal of coarse language and many sexual situations, scenes of drug dealing and violence. These include rape, juvenile prostitution and brutal, casual murder.

Lucien John and David Gumpilil, *Walkabout* (1971)

WALKABOUT ★★★★★

Credits: VHS/1971/Australia/Colour/100 minutes
Director: Nicolas Roeg
Screenplay: Edward Bond
Based on the novel by James Vance Marshall.
Cast: Jenny Agutter [the girl], Lucien John [the white boy], David Gumpilil [the black boy], John Meillon [the father]
Genre: A drama about two English children lost in the Australian Outback who are assisted in their trek by a teenage aborigine.
Plot: After many years of requests from film buffs, this film has finally made it to video in a letterboxed tape from Public Media Home Vision Cinema/Janus Films. The tape is a director's cut which includes scenes not in the original theatrical release. The wait has been worth it.

On a trip into the Australian bush with their father (Meillon), two English children, a teenage girl (Agutter) and a young boy (John), are suddenly stranded miles from civilization. Their distraught father fires at the children then commits suicide, setting fire to the car. With little food and ill prepared for such an ordeal, the two children head into the wilderness. Scrub lands become rocky hillsides which soon turn into open desert. Their meagre food supplies quickly run out and the one water source they are able to locate disappears in the heat of the sun.

When things seem at their bleakest, a teenage aborigine boy (Gumpilil) on his rite-of-passage Walkabout appears on the scene. He supplies them with food, shows

War Of The Buttons (1994)

great disservice, for this film is much more, much deeper than a simple adventure tale. Throughout, in the juxtaposition of the twentieth century and the stone age, the film poses questions. What is civilization? What is dignity? What is friendship? What are man's true needs? What is nobility of character? In truth, how far are we from the seemingly primitive and alien world of the aborigine?

MPAA: Canadian Home Video rated PG. Gumpilil is partially or completely nude throughout the film, never wearing more than a brief loincloth.

Agutter has an extended nude swimming scene. All three of the principal actors appear in full-frontal nude shots in the closing minutes of the film while swimming in a desert pond. There are also several shots of nude and partially nude aborigines of all ages.

THE WAR OF THE BUTTONS ★★★★

(Also known as *La Guerre Des Boutons*)

Credits: VHS/1962/France/B&W/88 minutes
In French with English subtitles.
Director: Yves Robert
Based on the novel by Louis Pergaud.
Cast: Jacques Dufilho [Aztec's father], Yvette Etievant [Lebraque's mother], Michel Galabru, Michel Isella [Aztec], Martin Lartique [petit Gibus], Jean Richard [Lebraque's father], Pierre Trabaud [the teacher], Andre Treton [Lebraque]
Genre: A comedy about warring gangs of young boys from neighbouring French villages.
Plot: Long-standing rivals, the boys from the villages of Longeverne and Velrans are sworn enemies. Fighting it out in the woods with insults, epithets, sticks and slingshots, the boys' war mirrors the rivalry of the village elders.

As the battles escalate, the Longeverne boys under the leadership of Lebraque (Treton) capture Aztec (Isella), the Velrans leader. Saying that the most important thing a man has is his honour, Lebraque cuts off all the other boy's buttons, taking them as trophies of war and leaving the boy to struggle home clutching his clothes and his dignity as best he can.

The Velrans boys waste no time retaliating in kind. Their copy-cat treatment of Lebraque earns him a severe beating by his father. To prevent the taking of their buttons, the Longeverne boys charge into their next fray stark naked, a ploy that disconcerts their opponents, though is not repeated. The nude warriors complain that it was too cold.

Escalation of the war continues, however. Lebraque

them how to find water, then proceeds to guide them through the wild lands to the outskirts of a white mining settlement.

During the several days of their trek with the aborigine, a mutual sexual attraction between the two teenagers develops, though it remains unspoken as neither speaks the other's language nor makes any attempts to learn. On their last night together, as the two white children bed down in a long abandoned settler's house, the aborigine performs a ritual dance outside. The meaning of the dance is never made clear, but the boy is found dead in a tree in the morning as the two English children begin the last stages of their journey back to the city and, for the girl, a lifetime of contemplating "What if?"

This film is one of the yardsticks against which all "kids against the wilderness" films must be measured, though to categorize *Walkabout* in this way is to do it a employs cavalry: a tired draught horse and a stubborn donkey. Aztec calls in the armoured division: his father's brand new tractor. The parents, however, move to bring the war to an end.

When Macailler, one of the Longeverne boys, is punished by the rest as a traitor. His punishers are in turn punished by their parents. All the boys earn sound thrashings. Lebraque, to escape this treatment, runs away, hiding out in the forest for several days before he is found and sent to a boarding school.

On his first day there, he discovers that one of his dorm-mates is none other than his old adversary Aztec, who is now welcomed as a long lost friend.

This film was remade in a colour version in 1994, reset in Ireland. The 1962 version is in fact the second film version of the novel. It was previously brought to the screen in the 1930s in a version generally known in English as *Generals Without Buttons*. I know nothing about the current state of this earlier version and I have found no evidence that it has ever been made available on video tape in North America.

MPAA: Not rated. All of the boys from the village of Longeverne are seen nude during the battle scene. However, with the exception of petit Gibus (Lartique), the nudity is strictly bare bums and shot in such a way that it is difficult to distinguish individual characters.

Petit Gibus, the youngest of the boys, is seen running alone down a country lane, his only covering a judiciously placed hand as he complains "I knew I shouldn't have come."

WAR OF THE BUTTONS
★★★★

Credits: VHS/1994/Great Britain-France/Colour/95 minutes
Director: John Roberts
A remake of the 1963 French Film *La Guerre des Boutons,* by Yves Robert, based on the novel by Louis Pergaud.
Cast: Paul Butt [Gorilla], John Coffey [Geronimo], Liam Cunningham [the Master], Gregg Fitzgerald [Fergus], Thomas Kavanagh [Rilley], Colm Meaney [Geronimo's Dad]
Genre: A comedy about two groups of young boys from neighbouring villages battling for their honour and their buttons.
Plot: This film is much better than your average remake, the story having been successfully shifted from the French countryside to the west of Ireland. The boys from the neighbouring villages of

Carrickdowse and Ballydown are bitter rivals. Their battles escalate from name calling and pushing and shoving, to graffiti and sling shots. Then the Ballies, under their leader Fergus (Fitzgerald), capture Gorilla (Butt), one of leaders of the Carricks. They cut off his buttons, his shoelaces, his tie and his belt as trophies of war.

When the Carricks retaliate in kind, Fergus is beaten by his father, but he conceives a brilliant plan. In the next skirmish the Ballies charge into battle nude, so disconcerting the Carricks that they turn and flee. The war continues to escalate until a brand new tractor is destroyed.

Fergus and Geronimo (Coffey), the leader of the Carricks, are unjustly blamed for the damage and flee into the hills. When they are eventually taken by the authorities, they are sent to the same reformatory where they

Heather Matarazzo, *Welcome To The Dollhouse* (1996)

become lifelong friends.

MPAA: Rated PG. There is nothing overtly sexual in this film. About a dozen boys, most of them preteens, appear nude in the battle scene primarily in rear shots. There is brief frontal exposure as well. Fergus, the oldest, appears not the least disconcerted when the boys realize that the village girls are watching: the other boys turn tail and run.

WEDDING IN WHITE ★★★★

Credits: VHS/1972/Canada/Colour/103 minutes
Writer/Director: William Fruet
Cast: Paul Bradley [Jimmie], Bonnie Carol Case [Dolly], Carol Kane [Jeannie], Doug McGrath [Billy], Doris Petrie [Mary], Leo Phillips [Sandy], Donald Pleasence [Jim

Jeff Bridges (centre) and Caroline Goodall, *White Squall* (1996)

Dougal], Christine Thomas [Sarah]
Genre: A hard hitting drama about rape, teenage pregnancy, family honour and forced marriage set in a small Canadian town during World War II.
Plot: Looking for a light pick me up after a hard day at work? If so, avoid this film. If, on the other hand, you are in the mood for something sad, depressing, bleak, bitter and gritty which is guaranteed to infuriate you, consider it.

In the middle of World War II, young Jimmie (Bradley) comes home on leave with his buddy, Billie (McGrath). That night Billie rapes Jimmie's younger sister

Jeannie (Kane) who has always played second fiddle to her older brother in the eyes of their father (Pleasence).

When dad discovers that his sixteen-year-old daughter is pregnant, he refuses to believe that Billie, a soldier and therefore a man of honour, could have been responsible. Feeling that his own honour is at stake in his daughter's pregnancy—she must, after all, be a slut and a whore—he tries to disown her and force her out of the family home. When Sandy (Phillips), one of his old army buddies and an aging bachelor with a serious drinking problem, offers to marry Jeannie, dad forces the loveless union on the girl.

Although the portrayal of some of the minor characters is a bit two-dimensional and tends in some cases towards caricature, Kane and Pleasence make this film well worth watching.

MPAA: Rated R. Other than the rather disturbing rape scene early in the film and a certain amount of sex talk, there is little overtly sexual in *Wedding In White*.

WELCOME TO THE DOLLHOUSE ★★★★

Credits: VHS/1996/USA/Colour/87 minutes
Writer/Director: Todd Solondz
Cast: Bill Buell [Mr. Weiner], Matthew Faber [Mark Weiner], Dimitri Iervolino [Ralphy], Daria Kalinina [Missy Weiner], Eric Mabius [Steve Rogers], Rica Martens [Miss Grissom], Heather Matarazzo [Dawn Weiner], Angela Pietropinto [Mrs. Weiner], Brendan Sexton, Jr. [Brandon McCarthy]
Genre: A drama about the pain of being an outcast seventh grader.
Plot: Dawn (Matarazzo) is living a life of hell. She is a plain, unassertive girl who has one goal in life. She wants to be popular. Unfortunately, she is the object of everybody's derision. Nicknamed Weiner Dog at school, she is ignored at home.

Her parents (Pietropinto and Buell), who lack some very basic parenting skills, care more for her computer-nerd brother Mark (Faber) and too cute to be true little sister Missy (Kalinina). Her social problems aren't helped in the vicious atmosphere of the seventh grade by her severe, unflattering hair style, her less-than-fashionable clothes, her heavy glasses or her friendship with the much younger Ralphy (Iervolino).

In the way that young adolescents can be, her classmates are cruel beyond belief. Unable to see beneath the clothes and the hairstyle, they tag her as ugly. Desperate for social acceptance, Dawn first sets her sights on Steve (Mabius), a high school student who joins Mark's band in exchange for help with his homework.

When Steve turns his back on Dawn, she falls for Brandon (Sexton). Brandon, the class tough from a poor family, at first threatens to rape her in retaliation for a detention he feels was her fault. Perhaps because any attention is better than none, Dawn begins to spend time with him, eventually becoming a friend.

The relationship doesn't last, however. Brandon runs away rather than face being institutionalized for a drug offense. It is an offense which he probably didn't commit, though he will be blamed for it anyway. Like Chris Chambers in *Stand By Me*, Brandon's family's reputation precedes him.

Shortly after, the Weiner family's comfortable suburban life falls apart when Missy is kidnapped. Although she is returned safely, Missy's ordeal helps to make abundantly clear Dawn's position in the family and her mother's parenting inadequacies.

The children in this film, especially Dawn and Brandon, are beautifully portrayed. The characters seen on screen are very real and very complex individuals. Unfortunately none of the adult portrayals can match them. All of the adults are flat, cardboard characters with no depth, interest or subtlety to them.

MPAA: Rated R. Canadian Home Video rated 14-A. Frequent coarse language and talk about sexual matters.

WHERE THE DAY TAKES YOU ★★★

Credits: VHS/1992/USA/Colour/107 minutes
Director: Marc Rocco
Screenplay: Kurt Voss, Marc Rocco and Michael Hitchcock
Cast: Sean Astin [Greg], Adam Baldwin [Officer Black], Lara Flynn Boyle [Heather], Peter Dobson [Tommy Ray], Balthazar Getty [Little J.], Ricki Lake [Brenda], James Le Gros [Crasher], Kyle MacLachlan [Ted], Dermot Mulroney [King], Laura San Giacomo [the Interviewer], Christian Slater [drug counsellor - uncredited cameo], Will Smith [Manny]
Genre: A gritty, depressing drama about street kids and the grunge beneath the glitter of Hollywood.
Plot: The story follows a few days in the lives of a group

of runaway and abandoned teens trying to survive on the streets of Hollywood. Earning money by panhandling and prostitution, this group lives under a freeway overpass under the general leadership of King (Mulroney), a parolee from the county lock-up.

King's family of young people are all on the run from dysfunctional families. Little J. (Getty) is a violent, volatile youth with a penchant for firearms who at age ten was molested by an uncle. Although even a touch on the face by a gay man repulses him, Little J. now supports himself by prostitution. Greg (Astin), a local kid from a wealthy family, has a severe hard drug problem which he supports by holding up convenience stores and pawning his mother's jewelry. Heather (Boyle), a runaway from Chicago, was raped by her brother. King, at twenty, is the oldest in the group, and the acknowledged head of the family.

Himself the son of a drug addict, King tries especially to keep his family out of the clutches of Tommy Ray (Dobson), a pimp with a stable of teenage hookers. After Little J. kills Tommy Ray in an altercation, King arranges for Heather, Little J. and Greg to leave town with him. Greg, however, OD's on heroin the night before, his body abandoned in a dumpster by Ted (MacLachlan), his supplier. King is then accidentally shot while trying to disarm Little J. in an armed standoff with police officers at the bus terminal, leaving Heather and Little J. to carry on as best they can alone.

MPAA: Rated R. The film contains a great deal of coarse language and several graphic scenes of drug use by teenagers as well as some violent scenes.

The sexual situations are for the most part only implied. Though it is obvious what is occurring, all of the sexual activity takes place off-screen, whether it be Little J. with a middle-aged trick or King and Heather in a motel room.

WHERE THE RIVER RUNS BLACK ★★★

Credits: VHS/1986/USA/ Colour/96 minutes
Director: Christopher Cain
Screenplay: Peter Silverman and Neal Jimenez
Based on the novel *Lazaro* by David Kendall.
Cast: Divana Brandao [the Eagle Woman], Dana Delany [Sister Anna], Charles Durning [Father O'Reilly], Conchata Ferrell [Mother Marta], Castulo Guerra [Orlando Santos], Peter Horton [Father Mahoney], Ajay Naidu [Secundo], Alessandro Rabelo [Lazaro], Marcelo Rabelo [Lazaro, age 4]
Genre: Another variation on the theme of the orphan boy who, raised in the wilds by animals, must learn to cope with the stresses of city life when a well-meaning adult takes him out of his home and attempts to "civilize" him.

White Squall (1996)

In this incarnation of the tale, the jungles are Brazil's Amazonia and the animals are river dolphins.

Plot: Having been turned down by his superiors in his quest to build a hospital and a school at his mission by the Rio Negro, young Father Mahoney (Horton) paddles upstream into the jungle. At the point where the river turns black, he meets a beautiful, mysterious native woman (Brandao) swimming with the dolphins. After making love to her, he is killed by a huge snake while returning down the river. The son (played first by M. Rabelo) born of this liaison lives an idyllic life by the river, protected by the dolphins until his mother is murdered by gold prospectors who also try to kill the boy by tossing him into the river.

Five years later, the young boy (A. Rabelo) is captured by prospectors who take him to the city to display in the marketplace. Father O'Reilly (Durning), recognizing the cross the boy wears, realizes he is Father Mahoney's son. Placed into an orphanage and baptized Lazaro, the boy is forced to adapt to the ways of urban man: bathing, having his hair cut, wearing shoes and clothing. Although rocky at first, the transition appears to be fairly successful until Lazaro recognizes a visitor to the orphanage as the man who killed his mother. Vowing to kill Orlando Santos (Guerra), who is now a candidate in the gubernatorial election, Lazaro and an older boy, Secundo (Naidu), run away from the orphanage.

Secundo is captured and sent to work in one of Santos' gold mines after Lazaro attempts to kill the man. Lazaro follows him into the back country. Escaping from the gold mines, the two boys make their way through the jungle to Lazaro's old home on the Rio Negro where Santos again catches up with them. After a final, fatal encounter with Santos, the two boys, though bound forever by the bonds of friendship, part company. Secundo returns to the city with Father O'Reilly. Lazaro remains in his home by the river where he becomes the stuff of legend.

Although the river water is frequently murky, the scenes of Lazaro swimming with the dolphins, some of which may remind you of the more recent *Free Willy*, are quite memorable, as are the shots of Lazaro's baptism.

One might want to compare this film with others of a similar theme such as the various *Tarzan* films (especially the 1917 and 1932 versions as well as 1984's *Greystoke*), the various renditions of Kipling's *The Jungle Book* and Truffaut's fact based *Wild Child*.

MPAA: Rated PG. Brandao appears nude in the scenes where Father Mahoney first encounters the dolphin woman. Both boys who play Lazaro at various stages in his life wear nothing but brief loin cloths in the jungle scenes. As the older Lazaro at the orphanage, Alessandro Rabelo frequently strips down to his underwear.

WHITE SQUALL ★★★

Credits: VHS/1996/USA/Colour/128 minutes
Director: Ridley Scott
Screenplay: Todd Robinson
Based on an actual 1960 event.
Cast: Jeff Bridges [Sheldon "Skipper"], Eric Michael Cole [Dean Preston], Ethan Embry [Tracy Lapchick], Balthazar Getty [Tod Johnstone], Caroline Goodall [Dr. Alice Sheldon], Zeljko Ivanek [Sanders], David Lascher [Robert March], Jason Marsden [Shay Jennings], Julio Mechuso [Gerard Pascal], Ryan Phillippe [Gil Martin], John Savage [McRae], David Selby [Francis Beaumont], Jeremy Sisto [Frank Beaumont], Scott Wolf [Chuck Gieg]
Genre: An action-adventure drama about a group of teenage boys facing their psyches and the elements aboard a school ship.
Plot: Against the backdrop of the Cuban missile crisis and the first U.S.-manned space flight, a group of teenage boys set sail aboard the Brigantine School Ship Albatross for a year long voyage of self discovery. The trip is under the direction of captain Sheldon (Bridges), a no-nonsense autocrat who manages by sheer force of will to meld the disparate characters into a cohesive unit.

Along the way the individual boys must come to terms with their personal demons. Gil Martin (Phillippe) must deal with his acrophobia and the death of his older brother. Dean Preston (Cole), must overcome his feelings of intellectual inferiority which lead him to cheat on exams and engage in conspicuous acting out behaviour. Frank Beaumont (Sisto) must deal with his feelings about his overbearing father (Selby). Chuck Gieg (Wolf), through whose eyes much of the film is seen, must overcome his feeling that he is a failure in the eyes of his parents. During their voyage, the crew must also encounter various external threats, including venereal disease, prostitutes, and Cuban patrol boats.

It is, however, the gut wrenching disaster which ensues when the ship, by now on the return voyage, encounters a sudden violent storm, a so-called white squall, which is the cinematic and emotional centerpiece of this film. During this freak meteorological phenomenon, the ship capsizes and sinks, with the loss of four lives.

For this maritime disaster, the Coast Guard puts Sheldon on trial, questioning his competence and threatening him with the loss of his Master Mariner ticket. At the hearings, however, the surviving boys rally behind him, testifying on his behalf.

Although there can be no doubt that the storm scenes are the highlight of the film, the cinematic journey to reach this point is definitely leisurely. The film would have benefitted from some tighter editing and fewer stops along the road. I also have some serious questions about the emotional impact of the film. In fact, some aspects of the film left me seething with anger. Was it really necessary for the camera to dwell so long on the faces of those trapped on board the sinking ship? I felt emotionally used and manipulated by these shots. Mawkish and maudlin are the words which come to mind. This anger had me questioning other aspect of the film and the characters portrayed.

Sheldon is seen by the boys as strong and tough but still somebody who makes you want to please him. I see him as a self-appointed charismatic autocrat who demand unquestioning obedience. In truth not too different from the fathers many of the young sailors are rebelling against. Is this a role model best suited to troubled youth in a so-called free society? Or is this the raw material of cults and dictatorships? Compare this aspect of the film with the Austrian film *The Inheritors*.
MPAA: Rated PG-13. Canadian Home Video rated PG. There are a couple of scenes of partial nudity. One occurs when Chuck is interrupted during a shore leave sexual encounter. One has Tod (Getty) pulling his pants down to get a shot of penicillin after contracting V. D. under similar circumstances. There are some instances of violence including one involving the killing of a dolphin as well as those onboard the sinking ship.

WHO SHOT PAT? ★★★★

(Also known as *Who Shot Patakango?*)

Credits: VHS/1991/USA/Colour/102 minutes
Director: Robert Brooks
Screenplay: Robert and Halle Brooks
Cast: Sandra Bullock [Devlin], Aaron Ingram [Cougar], David Knight [Bic], Brad Randall [Patakango], Kevin Otto [Mark]
Genre: A nostalgic comedy about growing up in Brooklyn in the 1950s.
Plot: When Patakango (Otto) shows up at Brooklyn's Alexander Hamilton Vocational High School with a gunshot wound in one arm, everybody, especially the gang-obsessed police, want to know what happened.

When a linguistic misunderstanding leads to a standoff the police think is gang oriented, Bic (Knight) and Cougar (Ingram) are hauled down to headquarters for questioning and a vicious beating. Unfortunately, a false confession leads to trouble with the real gangs from elsewhere in the city.

Meanwhile Bic has started to see Devlin (Bullock), the rich kid from uptown. However, a fist fight in a Greenwich Village coffee house leads them to part company. Despite all these violent undertones, however, the students at Alexander Hamilton have more serious problems to deal with. How to pick up girls? How to top the latest prank? What to do about the school's upcoming talent show.

Although the film has its serious side and tries to deal with issues of teen violence, rich and poor, race relations and abuse, this is primarily a comedy that looks at life through some fairly rosy lenses and should not be taken too seriously. Enjoy it for the laughs, for the '50s music and the occasionally interesting visuals. The scenes where a group of high school boys practice their pick-up skills in a restaurant and then try them out on some unsuspecting girls in the park are particularly memorable.

MPAA: Rated R. Devlin and Bic are seen making love though the sequence is shot quite discreetly. The R rating is primarily a result of the violence that occurs through much of the film.

THE WILD CHILD ★★★★★

(Also known as *L'Enfant Sauvage*)

Credits: VHS/1970/France/B&W/86 minutes
In French with English subtitles.
Director: Francois Truffaut
Screenplay: Francois Truffaut and Jean Grualt
Factual story based on the writings of Jean Itard.
Cast: Jean-Pierre Cargol [Victor], Jean Daste [Philippe Pinel], Francois Truffaut [Jean Itard], Paul Villie [old Remy], Francoise Seigner [Madame Guerin], Pierre Fabre [the orderly]
Awards: Melies Awards (France) 1970: Best Film. National Board of Review Awards 1970: Best Director (Truffaut); Five Best Foreign films. National Society of Film Critics Awards 1970: Best Cinematography.
Genre: A dramatization of the writings of Jean Itard concerning a mute pre-adolescent boy found living wild in the woods of southern France in the late 18th century.
Plot: It is the summer of 1798. In the south of France a boy of about eleven or twelve is found dirty, naked and alone running wild in the woods in the township of St. Sernin. He is covered in scars and scratches, including one scar which suggests that whoever abandoned him some years earlier had intended to kill him.

Lacking even the most rudimentary speech, the boy (Cargol, in an exceptional performance) is brought to Paris and placed in the National Institute For The Deaf And Dumb, where he is exhibited to the paying public as the latest seven day wonder. While at the Institute he comes to the attention of Itard (Truffaut) who objects to the boy's treatment.

Taking the boy into his own home and naming him Victor, Itard and his housekeeper Madame Guerin

(Seigner) begin the long, slow and often frustrating task of trying to educate the boy. Working Victor sometimes to the point of exhaustion, Itard must teach him even such basic skills as walking upright, to say nothing of speaking, reading and writing.

This is a long and difficult task with many setbacks and false leads along the way. Itard must cope also with his own doubts. Often he questions whether he is doing the right thing for the boy. He has taken Victor from the woodland environment which was his home and to which he can never now return. But can he truly hope to integrate the boy into society? Can he help Victor deal with the conflicts which trouble the boy? The conflict between his desire to return to the woods and his new found feelings of affection for Itard and Guerin.

MPAA: Rated PG. For the first seven or eight minutes of the film, Cargol is nude as the young wild boy is chased through the woods by hunters and tracking dogs. Many of the shots are partially blocked by foliage as the boy, frequently running on all fours, tries to hide from his pursuers. There are, nevertheless several brief shots of full-frontal nudity as well as the numerous rear and side shots.

THE WILD LITTLE BUNCH ★★★

(Also known as *The Fourteen*)

Credits: VHS/1972/Great Britain/Colour/95 minutes
Director: David Hemming
Screenplay: Roland Stark
Based on a true story.
Cast: John Bailey [Mr. Sanders], Wayne Brooks [David], June Brown [mother], Liz Edmiston [Sylvia], Frank Gentry [Terry], Cheryl Hall [Reena], Jack Wild [Reg]
Genre: A dramatization of what is said to be the true story of a large family of children trying to stay together as a unit after their mother dies.
Plot: Reg (Wild) and his brothers and sisters live with their single mom [Brown] in a dirty, chaotic, derelict house in a rundown neighbourhood in London. Unkempt, uncouth and unruly, though they are living in poverty this large family is nonetheless very loving and very close. When illness and overwork claim mom's life the children are thrown into crisis and into the arms of the local child welfare authorities. A well-meaning but ineffectual and inflexible homemaker from welfare is soon run out of the house.

Sylvia (Edmiston), the only girl in the family, is able to find a place to stay with an uncle but the boys prove harder to accommodate. Placed at first in a church run orphanage, they last there only briefly. The chaos the boys

Stephane Rideau, *Wild Reeds* (1994)

bring to the previously quiet home proves too much for the poor harassed nuns. Despite pleas from all the boys that they be allowed to stay together as a family, the five oldest, including Reg, who is just shy of his eighteenth birthday, are placed in St. George's Home, an institution which is more borstal than orphanage.

Reg leaves the Home the day he turns eighteen but continues his efforts to reunite the family. Despite his best efforts, however, they only manage to get together briefly at Christmas. Even this is accomplished only by taking matters into their own hands. The realities of a lack of money and a high fever for David (Brooks) soon forces the younger boys back to the Home. The older boys, however, go AWOL from St. George's and quickly become a media cause celebre.

The press and television coverage that centres on the refusal by Terry (Gentry) to give himself up does bring some results. A farm family is found who can give a home to the younger boys. The family must come to a decision. Do the younger children stay on the farm? Or do they continue to hold out for a place where they can stay together?

MPAA: Not rated. Frequent coarse language. There are several nude scenes showing young boys bathing and showering. These include casual full-frontal shots of several of them most notably of Wayne Brooks as David.

WILD REEDS
★★★★

(Also known as *Les Roseaux Sauvages*)

Credits: VHS/1994/France/Colour/ 113 minutes
In French with English subtitles
Director: Andre Techine
Screenplay: Gilles Taurand, Olivier Massart and Andre Techine
Cast: Elodie Bouchez [Maite], Frederic Gorny [Henri], Gael Morel [Francois], Michele Moretti [Alvarez], Stephane Rideau [Serge]
Awards: Cesar Awards (France) 1995: Best Director (Techine); Best Film; Best Screenplay. Los Angeles Film Critics Association Awards 1995: Best Foreign Film. National Society Of Film Critics Awards 1995: Best Foreign Film.
Genre: A drama about a French high school student coming to terms with his homosexuality.
Plot: Played out against the political and social backdrop of the Algerian War for Independence in the 1960s, *Wild Reeds* follows the lives of four French students from widely varying backgrounds.

Serge (Rideau) is the son of immigrant Italian farm workers. Francois (Morel) is the son of a wealthy farmer. Henri (Gorny), a few years older than the other boys, is from a wealthy French Algerian family now in exile, refugees from the violence. Maite (Bouchez) is the daughter of Alvarez (Moretti), a teacher at the school and a high-ranking member of the local Communist Party organization. The three boys are also roommates in the dormitories of the school.

Although a constant companion of Maite, Francois is struggling with his growing realization that he is gay. As he gradually comes out to his companions, he finds himself receiving varying degrees of support from them. He and Serge, who is straight, have a one-time sexual encounter in the dorms, as well as several other tender, though non-sexual, moments.

Henri challenges Francois to "go for it," an attitude which puts the youth off. Maite welcomes him as a friend who puts no sexual pressures on her.

The least sympathetic reaction Francois receives is from the owner of a local shoe store. Although he is a gay man in a long-term relationship with his partner, he is unwilling, out of fear, even to talk to Francois, let alone offer advice or counsel, leaving the teenager to find his own way through his problems.

MPAA: Not rated. Serge and Francois are seen making love once in the school dorms. There is also a lot of sexual talk among the four principles. There is no actual nudity on-screen, however Serge and Francois have several scenes, some quite lengthy, swimming in their underwear.

WISH YOU WERE HERE ★★★★

Credits: VHS/1987/Great Britain/Colour/ 92 minutes
Writer/Director: David Leland
Based on the memoirs of Cynthia Payne, the famous British madame.
Cast: Tom Bell [Eric], Jesse Birdsall [Dave], Geoffrey Durham [Harry Figgis], Pat Heywood [Aunt Millie], Geoffrey Hutchings [Hubert], Emily Lloyd [Lynda], Chloe Leland [Margaret]
Awards: British Academy Awards 1987: Best Original Screenplay. National Society of Film Critics Awards 1987: Best Actress (Lloyd).
Genre: A comic drama about a rebellious early 1950s British teenager who is sometimes too clever and too precocious for her own good.
Plot: Lynda (Lloyd), the fifteen-year-old daughter of a Brighton barber, is constantly at odds with her straight-laced father (Hutchings). Her racy language and sexual forwardness don't fit with his view of the world. Her impetuous tongue and questionable antics, he says, reflect upon his own good name and honour in the town. In fact, he views them sufficiently serious enough that he schedules a session with a psychiatrist for her. They also prevent her from keeping any job she manages to land. A week seems to be long term employment for Lynda.

Her delight in her own sexuality leads Lynda to several affairs, some with boys her own age, some with men her father's age. When she becomes pregnant by Eric (Bell), a much older man, she is faced with several crises, a complete break with her father and abandonment by Eric. The only person willing to stand by her is Aunt Millie (Heywood), the closest thing to a sympathetic adult in her life. The pregnancy forces a decision on Lynda: abortion, adoption, or single motherhood. Not an easy decision for any woman in her position, especially in the 1950s.

Although set in the early 1950s the film touches on many topics which are still relevant, still current more than 40 years later. Teenage pregnancy, abortion, single motherhood, psychiatric treatment for unconventional sexuality, parents more concerned about their own standing in society than their children's best interests:

none of these issues has disappeared from the scene.

One could profitably compare this film with the 1972 Canadian film *Wedding In White* for its treatment of the subject of teenage pregnancy and resulting father and daughter relationships.
MPAA: Not rated. There are several sexual situations involving Lynda with several different partners. There is also some brief nudity. Lynda bares her buns at one point while mooning a neighbour who complains about her singing in the back yard. Eric is caught in the garden shed with his pants partway down when a policeman stops to investigate an unlocked gate. There is also a great deal of language that would have been considered shocking in 1950, but would hardly raise an eyebrow today.

Stephane Rideau, *Wild Reeds* (1994)

WONDERLAND ★★★★

(Also known as *The Fruit Machine*)

Credits: VHS/1989/Great Britain/Colour/103 minutes
Director: Philip Saville
Screenplay: Frank Clarke
Cast: Emile Charles [Eddie], Robbie Coltrane [Annabelle], Tony Forsyth [Michael], Claire Higgens [Eve], Bruce Payne [Echo], Robert Stevens [Vincent]
Genre: A thriller about two gay youths on the run from

thugs who have killed the cross-dressing owner of a Liverpool gay bar.

Plot: When Eddie (Charles) and Michael (Forsyth), two gay sixteen-year-old boys, witness the brutal murder of Annabelle (Coltrane), the cross-dressing owner of The Fruit Machine, a Liverpool gay bar, they hit the road. Pursued by both the killers who are trying to silence the boys and the police who believe the boys are the killers, Eddie and Michael are taken in tow by Vincent (Stevens), an aging opera singer. Together the three head for Brighton.

While Vincent is busy seducing Michael, Eddie, who has frequent hallucinations about dolphins, is making friends with the captive animals in the Wonderland, a dolphinarium on the waterfront. After he has been evicted from the Wonderland for making animal-rights speeches during a performance, Eddie sneaks back in after hours to swim with the dolphins in a beautiful underwater sequence.

Unfortunately the killer on the boys' trail has followed Eddie into the building. Although the killer is drowned in the ensuing fight, Eddie too is wounded, succumbing to his injuries as Michael and an animal-rights activist kidnap the dolphins and release them into the ocean. Emile Charles is the younger brother of actor Craig Charles who plays Lister on the cult TV series *Red Dwarf*.

MPAA: Rated R. The film is filled with gay situations, characters and themes. There are a number of sexual encounters in the film.

Michael shares Vincent's bed in the hotel in Brighton and also has a sexual encounter with a woman.

Charles is seen nude, including full-frontal shots, while Eddie is swimming with the dolphins in the Wonderland.

THE YEAR MY VOICE BROKE

★★★★★

Credits: VHS/1987/Australia/ Colour/103 minutes
Writer/Director: John Duigan
Cast: Graeme Blundell [Nils Olson], Loene Carmen [Freya], Lynette Curran [Anne Olson], Judi Farr [Sheila Embling], Ben Mendelsohn [Trevor], Malcolm Robertson [Bruce Embling], Tim Robertson [Bob Leishman], Bruce Spence [Jonah], Noah Taylor [Danny Embling]
Awards: Australian Film Institute Awards: Best Film; Best Director (Duigan); Best Screenplay (Duigan); Best Supporting Actor (Mendelsohn); Members Award for Excellence in Feature Films. Australian Film Critics Circle Awards: Best Film; Best Director (Duigan); Best Actor (Taylor).
Genre: A gently poignant romantic drama, the first of several nostalgic coming of age films from Duigan featuring Noah Taylor, looking back at life in a small town in the Australian Outback.

Plot: Sixteen-year-old Freya (Carmen) and Danny (Taylor) are pals, mates. Freya is an adopted child who has the reputation of being the town tramp. Danny is a cute but gentle, weedy kid with a winning smile. Nicknamed Bandicoot, he is the boy who doesn't quite fit in the small town where they live, the boy who is the butt of everybody's jokes and hazing. Danny is also obviously in love with Freya, almost to the point of obsession. He steals around at night to watch her through her bedroom windows. He steals panties from her clothes line. He even tries hypnosis. Freya, however, is more interested in Trevor (Mendelsohn), the local wild kid, a football player who is prone to joy

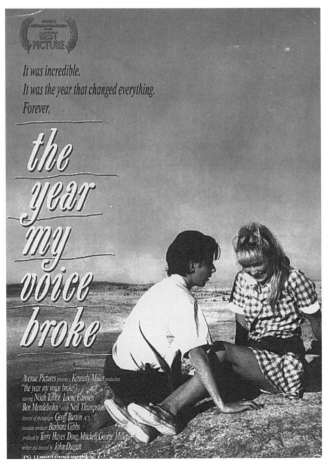

Noah Taylor and Loene Carmen, *The Year My Voice Broke* (1987)

riding in other people's cars, especially Mrs. Ellsman's Mercedes.

When the police finally come for Trevor, he, Freya and Danny spend the night in an abandoned house, known locally as the Ghost House. While Danny watches, Freya and Trevor make love. After Trevor escapes from detention, he is killed in a car accident, devastating the pregnant Freya.

Having by now learned some unsavory truths about her birth mother, Freya decides to leave town and head for the city to have her baby, leaving the distraught Danny behind.

MPAA: Rated PG-13. Freya and Trevor are seen in a number of sexual situations: groping together in the movie theatre, and making love in the Ghost House. In the latter scene, we get a brief flash of Mendelsohn's bare buns when Trevor jumps out of bed and runs out of the house.

YOU ARE NOT ALONE ★★★★

(Aka *Du Er Ikke Alene*)

Credits: VHS/1978/ Denmark/Colour/90 minutes
In Danish with English subtitles.
Director: Lasse Nielson and Ernst Johansen
Screenplay: Lasse Nielson and Bent Petersen
Cast: Anders Agenso [Bo], Peter Bjerg [Kim], John Hahn-Petersen [Justesen], Jan Jorgunsen [Carstensen], Elin Reimer [Headmaster's wife], Ove Sprogoe [Headmaster]
Genre: A lyrical, sunny comic drama which looks at life in a Danish boarding school for boys.
Plot: *You Are Not Alone* interweaves three stories: the relationship between the boys of the school and the youths of the town, the coming to-

gether of the boys when one of their number is expelled and the love affair between one of the students and the headmaster's son.

Ole is the troubled youth who is always pushing against authority. Fed up with the rules around the school, and having already been warned about pin-ups in his bedroom, he plasters the washrooms with centerfolds one night. For this, the school expels the boy. Despite the fact that Ole has an abrasive personality and seems not to be well liked by his classmates, his expulsion provokes a boycott of classes by a majority of the other students.

Against this backdrop of student unrest, fifteen-year-old Bo (Agenso) and twelve-year-old Kim (Bjerg) engage in a romantic love affair, a liaison which is complicated by the fact that Kim's father (Sprogoe) is the school's headmaster. Initially their relationship is little more than eye contact and smiles across the school dining hall, but it progresses quickly. Secretive at first—in one early scene Bo discourages Kim when the younger boy tries to initiate physical contact in public—eventually they are accepted by the other boys as a couple.

In fact, it is their love which the other students use to illustrate the Biblical commandment "Love thy neighbour as thyself" at the school's end of term assembly.

A beautiful scenario. Too bad that in the real world so open an affair between two school boys would be more likely to result in harassment, intimidation and acts of violence. Oh well, one can always dream of a better world. **MPAA:** Not rated. Kim is seen masturbating under the bedcovers one night. In another scene he climbs out his bedroom window in order to spend the night in Bo's bed. The two also share a long embrace and kiss in the closing minutes of the film.

As well, two other boys are found by Bo locked in a romantic embrace in the school showers. One also finds a young woman on the kitchen staff to teach him some of the secrets of kissing and sex.

In addition to the two unidentified boys embracing in the showers, there are several other nude scenes, the most noteworthy being Kim and Bo sharing a shower. This involves extensive full-frontal nudity of both Bjerg and Agenso as well as a lot of sex talk and a loving embrace. Many of the boys engage in sex talk and there is some female nudity seen in Ole's pin-ups.

Ben Mendelsohn, Loene Carmen and Noah Taylor, The Year My Voice Broke (1987)

ZERO DE CONDUITE
★★★★★

(Also known as *Zero For Conduct*)

Credits: VHS/1933/ France/B&W/50 minutes In French with English subtitles.

Writer/Director: Jean Vigo

Cast: Jean Daste [Huguet], Gerard de Bedarieux [Tabart], Delphin [the Headmaster], Du Veron [Bec-De-Gaz], Coco Golstein [Druet], Robert Le Flon [Pete-Sec - Sourpuss], Louis Lefebvre [Caussat], Gilbert Pruchon [Colin]

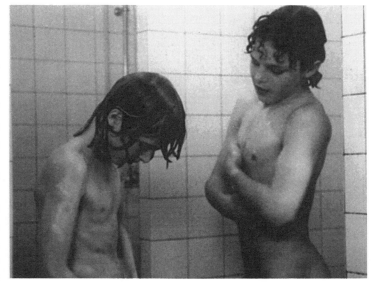

Peter Bjerg and Anders Agenso, *You Are Not Alone* (1978)

Genre: An early comedy about life in a French boarding school for boys centering on four friends who revolt against constant punishment and the implied sexual overtures from teachers.

Plot: A classic film in every sense, *Zero de Conduite* was one of the inspirations for Lindsay Anderson's 1969 film *If...* . The story takes place in a boarding school peopled with eccentrics. One of the teachers does Charlie Chaplin imitations. One steals candy from the boys' desks. One does handstands in class. One openly fondles the boys in class. The headmaster (Delphin) is a midget. The cook serves nothing but beans.

Eventually, Caussat (Lefebvre), Colin (Pruchon), Druet (Golstein) and Tabart (de Bedarieux), revolt against the frequent punishments meted out. The specific impetus for the revolt is a demand from the headmaster that Tabart publicly apologize to one of the teachers. The boy had told the man to go to hell when he openly fondled Tabart in class. Tabart refuses to apologize, and that night reads a stirring call to arms in the dormitory, giving birth to a

rousing pillow fight. The next day at the Alumni Day gathering, the four friends climb onto the roof and shower staff and guest with old books and boots they have found in the attic.

It is implied that Druet and Tabart have a "special" relationship. Tabart is warned about his friendship with Druet by the headmaster. Tabart is portrayed as a somewhat sensitive, effeminate boy, the implication being that he is gay. Remember, this film is more than sixty-five years old. Even today, how many U.S. films have given a sympathetic portrayal of a gay teenager?

Although it may be hard to believe on seeing this film today, it was banned in many places in Europe on first release. This probably had more to do with the director's radical politics (he was an avowed anarchist) than the content of the film. However, there is no denying a political sensibility to the story of four school boys rising up against unreasonable, overbearing authority.

In addition to the direct debt owed to this film by Lindsay Anderson's *If ...* , the imagery of *Zero De Conduite* seems to have been borrowed many times by later French directors. Visual echoes of this film can be found in several of the films of Louis Malle, Francois Truffaut, Techine and others.

MPAA: Not rated. The film includes several shots of nude youngsters, most of them occurring in the boys' dormitories. Many of the boys sleep in short nightshirts and when things get rambunctious these garments have a tendency to fly up, revealing bare bums beneath. In one shot there is a brief frontal exposure of a young teenager as well.

A C T O R   I N D E X

As all the film reviews are in alphabetical order, page numbers are not included.

Brody, Adrien: *King Of The Hill*
Brooks, Wayne: *The Wild Little Bunch*
Broughton, Marcus: *Among The Cinders*
Brown, D. W.: *Mischief*
Brown, Eric: *Private Lessons*
Brown, June: *The Wild Little Bunch*
Bruel, Brigit: *Pretty Boy*
Bruno, Giovanni: *Vito And The Others*
Brush, Peter: *A Separate Peace*
Brynolfsson, Reine: *The Slingshot*
Budin, Gilles: *Blue Jeans*
Budraitis, Yuosa: *The Orphans*
Buell, Bill: *Welcome To The Dollhouse*
Bullock, Sandra: *Who Shot Pat?*
Burayev, Alexander: *Freedom Is Paradise*
Burke, Michelle: *Dazed And Confused*
Burke, Robert: *Rambling Rose*
Burke, Simon: *The Devil's Playground*
Burkov, Georgyi: *The Orphans*
Burlyayev, Kolya: *My Name Is Ivan*
Burr, Butch: *The Genesis Children*
Burruano, Luigi Maria: *Acla*
Burrus, Slade: *The Boys Of Cellblock Q*
Burstyn, Ellen: *The Last Picture Show*
Bury, Sean: *Friends; If....*
Buscemi, Steve: *Criss-Cross*
Bush, Owen: *Soup And Me*
Butt, Paul: *War Of The Buttons* (1995)
Byrne, Cillian: *The Secret Of Roan Inish*

C

Cadieux, Jason: *Lilies*
Cady, Frank: *Soup And Me*
Calderon, Paul: *Criss-Cross*
Calloway, Vanesa Bell: *The Inkwell*
Campbell, Colin: *The Leather Boys*
Capelja, Jad: *Puberty Blues*
Carel, Roger: *The Two Of Us*
Cargol, Jean-Pierre: *The Wild Child*
Carlsson, Ingmar: *My Life As A Dog*
Carmen, Loene: *The Year My Voice Broke*
Carradine, Keith: *Criss-Cross; Pretty Baby*
Carrier, Corey: *Bump In The Night*
Carriere, Mathieu: *The Bay Boy; Beethoven's Nephew; Bilitis*
Carver, Brent: *Lilies*
Case, Bonnie Carol: *Wedding In White*
Caselli, Chiara: *My Own Private Idaho*
Catalla, Charlie: *Macho Dancer*
Cates, Phoebe: *Paradise; Shag: The Movie*
Cattand, Gabriel: *Blue Jeans*
Cattrall, Kim: *Porky's*
Caubere, Philippe: *My Father's Glory; My Mother's Castle*
Cellier, Caroline: *Petit Con*
Cervier, Elisa: *Tendres Cousines*
Cervino, Jose Manuel: *Colegas*
Cervo, Pascal: *Full Speed*
Chabrol, Thomas: *The Rascals*
Chaliapin, Feodor Jr.: *The Name Of The Rose*
Champagne, Lynn: *Mon Oncle Antoine*
Chan, Thang: *The Delta*
Chantepie, Pierre: *Tendres Cousines*
Chapin, Miles: *Bless The Beasts & Children*

Chapin, Tom: *Lord Of The Flies* (1963)
Chapman, Alexander: *Lilies*
Charles, Emile: *Wonderland*
Charles, Josh: *Dead Poets Society*
Charno, Stuart: *Just One Of The Guys*
Chatelais, Jean-Yves: *Tendres Cousines*
Chater, Geoffrey: *If....*
Chauveau, Jacqueline: *Murmur Of The Heart*
Chaykin, Maury: *Josh and S.A.M.*
Checker, Chubby: *Calendar Girl*
Cherstvov, Aliosha: *The Orphans*
Chestnut, Morris: *The Inkwell*
Chicot, Etienne: *36 Fillette*
Child, Vincent: *The Genesis Children*
Chrest, Joseph: *King Of The Hill*
Christensen, Morten Stig: *Friends Forever*
Ciamaca, Julien: *My Father's Glory; My Mother's Castle*
Citti, Franco: *Luna*
Clark, Candy: *American Graffiti*
Clark, Devin: *Prayer of the Rollerboys*
Clark, Ian D.: *Lilies*
Clark, Mickey: *Abuse*
Clark, Susan: *Porky's*
Clayburgh, Jill: *Luna*
Cluzet, Francois: *Olivier Olivier*
Cobos, German: *Hidden Pleasures*
Coburn, Nana: *Return To The Blue Lagoon*
Cochrane, Rory: *Dazed And Confused*
Coffey, John: *War Of The Buttons* (1995)
Coffey, Scott: *Shag: The Movie*
Cohen, Alain: *The Two Of Us*
Colao, Manuel: *Flight of the Innocent*
Cole, Eric Michael: *White Squall*
Colgan, Eileen: *The Secret Of Roan Inish*
Colin, Gregoire: *Olivier Olivier*
Collet, Christopher: *Prayer of the Rollerboys*
Collin, Maxime: *Leolo*
Collins, Bubba: *The Genesis Children*
Colomby, Scott: *Porky's*
Coltrane, Robbie: *The Adventures Of Huck Finn; Wonderland*
Conant, Oliver: *Summer of '42*
Connery, Sean: *The Name Of The Rose*
Conway, Kevin: *Rambling Rose*
Cooper, Chris: *Boys; This Boy's Life*
Cooper, Garry: *Kipperbang*
Cooper, Jeremy: *The Reflecting Skin*
Cooper, Roy: *The Basketball Diaries*
Copans, Sylvain: *Cross My Heart*
Corencia, Antonio: *Hidden Pleasures*
Coryell, Bradley: *Now And Then*
Coulthard, Alice: *The Cement Garden*
Courtney, Jeni: *The Secret Of Roan Inish*
Cox, Peter: *The Devil's Playground*
Crauchet, Paul: *My Father's Glory; My Mother's Castle*
Crawford, Broderick: *A Little Romance*
Crawtem Conrad: *My First Suit*
Croce, Gerard: *Blue Jeans*
Crudup, Billy: *Sleepers*
Cruise, Tom: *The Outsiders; Risky Business*

Cruttenden, Abigail: *Kipperbang*
Cumming, Alan: *Second Best*
Cunningham, Liam: *War Of The Buttons* (1995)
Curnock, Richard: *Paradise*
Curran, Lynette: *The Year My Voice Broke*
Cusak, John: *Stand By Me*
Cusak, Roscoe: *Class*
Cusak, Sinead: *The Cement Garden*
Cusimano, Francesco: *Acla*
Cusimano, Giuseppe: *Acla*
Czerny, Henry: *The Boys of St. Vincent*

D

D'Arbanville, Patricia: *Bilitis*
Da Silva, Erick: *Son Of The Shark*
da Silva, Fernando Ramos: *Pixote*
Dale, Badgett: *Lord of the Flies* (1990)
Damon, Matt: *School Ties*
Danare, Malcolm: *Heaven Help Us*
Daniels, William: *The Blue Lagoon*
Darel, Florence: *A La Mode; Stolen Children*
Darmon, Gerard: *La Teta Y La Luna*
Daste, Jean: *The Wild Child; Zero De Conduite*
Dauphin, Claude: *Madame Rosa*
Davis, Sammi: *Hope And Glory*
Davism Colonious: *The Delta*
Davison, Bruce: *The Cure*
De Bedarieux, Gerard: *Zero De Conduite*
de Falco, Rubens: *Pixote*
de Malberg, Stanislas Carre: *Au Revoir Les Enfants*
De Niro, Robert: *Sleepers; This Boy's Life*
de Torrebruna, Riccardo: *Devil In The Flesh*
Dean, James: *Rebel Without A Cause*
Debell, Kristine: *Meatballs*
Decomble, Guy: *The 400 Blows*
Dee, Maurice: *Kipperbang*
Del Vecchio, Giuditta: *Leolo*
Delamare, Victorien: *My Father's Glory; My Mother's Castle*
Delany, Dana: *Where The River Runs Black*
Delphin: *Zero De Conduite*
Delpy, Julie: *Europa, Europa*
Demers, Kristine: *The Boys of St. Vincent*
Demerus, Ellen: *The Children Of Noisy Village*
DeMornay, Rebecca: *Risky Business*
Dempsey, Patrick: *Heaven Help Us*
Demy, Jacques: *The 400 Blows*
Demy, Mathieu: *Le Petit Amour*
Dengel, Jake: *Prayer of the Rollerboys*
Denise, Shara: *Risky Business*
Denner, Charles: *The Two Of Us*
Denny, Aaron: *Clayfarmers*
Dern, Laura: *Rambling Rose*
Detmers, Maruschka: *Devil In The Flesh*
DeVito, Danny: *Jack The Bear*
Dewaere, Patrick: *Beau Pere*
Di Sanzo, Alessandro: *Forever Mary*
DiCaprio, Leonardo: *The Basketball*

Diaries; This Boy's Life; Total Eclipse
Dickey, Dale: *The Incredibly True Adventure Of Two Girls In Love*
Diedrich, John: *The Devil's Playground*
Dignam, Arthur: *The Devil's Playground; The Everlasting Secret Family*
Dillon, Kevin: *Heaven Help Us*
Dillon, Matt: *My Bodyguard; The Outsiders; Over The Edge*
Dinn, Phillip: *The Boys of St. Vincent*
Dobson, Peter: *Where The Day Takes You*
Dodd, Brian: *The Boys of St. Vincent*
Doillon, Lou: *Le Petit Amour*
Dolan, Michael: *Biloxi Blues*
Donat, Peter: *The Bay Boy; School Ties*
Donat, Richard: *My American Cousin*
Dooley, Brian: *The Boys of St. Vincent*
Dooley, Paul: *Rich Kids*
Doran, Ann: *Rebel Without A Cause*
Dorando, Nils: *The Baby Of Macon*
Dos Santos, Jose Nilson: *Pixote*
Douglas, Suzzanne: *The Inkwell*
Drai-Dietrich, Sebastien: *The Rascals*
Dreyfuss, Richard: *American Graffiti; Stand By Me*
Driver, Minnie: *Sleepers*
Du Veron: *Zero De Conduite*
Duceppe, Jean: *Mon Oncle Antoine*
Duff, Ricky: *Among The Cinders*
Dufilho, Jacques: *War Of The Buttons (1962)*
Duggan, Gerry: *The Devil's Playground*
Dumas, Valerie: *Tendres Cousines*
Dunaway, Faye: *Burning Secret*
Duncan, Lindsay: *The Reflecting Skin*
Dupuy, Philip: *Another Country*
Duran, Biel: *La Teta Y La Luna*
Durham, Geoffrey: *Wish You Were Here*
Durning, Charles: *Where The River Runs Black*
Dushku, Eliza: *This Boy's Life*
Dutton, Charles: *Foreign Student*
Duvall, Robert: *Rambling Rose*

E
East, Jeff: *Tom Sawyer*
Eberts, David: *Burning Secret*
Eccles, Teddy: *My Side Of The Mountain*
Echevarria, Gisela: *In A Glass Cage*
Edwards, Hugh: *Lord Of The Flies (1963)*
Edwards, Sebastian Rice: *Hope And Glory*
Eichorn, Lisa: *King Of The Hill*
Elan, John: *The Incredibly True Adventure Of Two Girls In Love*
Elbsloh, Christoph: *Street Kid*
Elcar, Dana: *The Fool Killer*
Eldard, Ron: *Sleepers*
Elholm, Thomas: *Friends Forever*
Elwes, Cary: *Another Country*
Elwin, Roger: *Lord Of The Flies (1963)*
Embry, Ethen: *White Squall*
Emile, Madame: *Zero De Conduite*
Endre, Lena: *Sunday's Children*
Englund, Robert: *Buster & Billie*
Equia, Jose Luis Fernandez: *Colegas*
Espindola, Oscar: *Chronicle Of A Boy Alone*
Esposito, Giancarlo: *Fresh*
Estevez, Emilio: *The Breakfast Club; The Outsiders*
Etievant, Yvette: *War Of The Buttons (1962)*
Everett, Rupert: *Another Country*

F
Faber, Matthew: *Welcome To The Dollhouse*
Fabiole, Luce: *The Two Of Us*
Fabre, Pierre: *The Wild Child*
Farak, Antonio: *Vito And The Others*
Fargas, Antonio: *Pretty Baby*
Farr, Judi: *The Year My Voice Broke*
Favio, Leonardo: *Chronicle Of A Boy Alone*
Faye, Frances: *Pretty Baby*
Fejto, Raphael: *Au Revoir Les Enfants*
Feklistov, Alexandr: *Lessons At The End Of Spring*
Feldman, Corey: *The Lost Boys; Stand By Me*
Fenn, Sherilyn: *Just One Of The Guys*
Fergus, Tom: *Over The Edge*
Ferguson, Matthew: *Lilies*
Fernando, Daniel: *Macho Dancer*
Ferrell, Conchata: *Where The River Runs Black*
Ferreux, Benoit: *Murmur Of The Heart*
Ferreux, Fabien: *Murmur Of The Heart*
Fiennes, Ralph: *The Baby Of Macon*
Figueroa, Ruben: *Popi*
Filho, Jardel: *Pixote*
Firth, Colin: *Another Country*
Fitzgerald, Gregg: *War Of The Buttons (1995)*
Fitzpatrick, Leo: *Kids*
Flament, Georges: *The 400 Blows*
Flanagan, Markus: *The Beat; Biloxi Blues*
Fleiss, Noah: *Josh and S.A.M.*
Fletcher, Fredde: *Kes*
Fletcher-Cook, Graham: *A Little Romance*
Flores, Antonio Gonzales: *Colegas*
Flores, Rosario Gonzales: *Colegas*
Folk, Abel: *La Teta Y La Luna*
Fonda, Bridget: *Shag: The Movie*
Ford Harrison: *American Graffiti*
Forest, Delphine: *Europa, Europa*
Forsyth, Tony: *Wonderland*
Foster, Jodie: *The Little Girl Who Lives Down The Lane; Tom Sawyer*
Fox, David: *Ordinary Magic*
Fraser, Brendan: *School Ties*
Fraser, Todd: *Clayfarmers*
Frawley, John: *The Devil's Playground*
Frazer, Duncan: *The Reflecting Skin*
Freeman, Cheryl: *Fresh*
Freeman, Kathleen: *Soup And Me*
Fresy, Sami: *Nea*
Fritz, Peter: *Au Revoir Les Enfants*
Frydman, Basia: *The Slingshot*
Fuentes, Tony: *Hidden Pleasures*
Fuller, Kurt: *Calendar Girl*
Furlong, Edward: *American Heart*
Furrh, Chris: *Lord of the Flies (1990)*
Fusco, Giuseppina: *Vito And The Others*

G
Gagnon, Jacques: *Mon Oncle Antoine*
Gainsbourg, Charlotte: *The Cement Garden; Le Petit Amour*
Gaitan, Svetlana: *Freedom Is Paradise*
Galabru, Michel: *War Of The Buttons (1962)*
Gaman, Tom: *Lord Of The Flies (1963)*
Gammon, James: *Criss-Cross*
Ganios, Tony: *Porky's*
Garcia, Nicole: *Beau Pere*
Garrett, Leif: *The Outsiders*
Gassman, Vittorio: *Sleepers*
Gatteau, Faye: *Olivier Olivier*
Gautier, Benoit: *Cross My Heart*
Geer, Ellen: *Over The Edge*
Gelin, Daniel: *Murmur Of The Heart*
Gentry, Frank: *The Wild Little Bunch*
Geoffreys, Stephen: *Heaven Help Us*
Georgouli, Alika: *Landscape In The Mist*
Gerber, Kathy: *Abuse*
Gerrard, Lisa: *Moon Child*
Gerritsma, Tjebbo: *To Play Or To Die*
Gertz, Jami: *The Lost Boys; Mischief*
Getty, Balthazar: *Lord of the Flies (1990); Where The Day Takes You; White Squall*
Gianolo, Beto: *Chronicle Of A Boy Alone*
Gibet, Michel: *Blue Jeans*
Gibney, Rebecca: *Among The Cinders; I Live With Me Dad*
Gibson, Mel: *The Man Without A Face*
Gilmore, Danny: *Lilies*
Giraudeau, Bernard: *Bilitis*
Gish, Annabeth: *Shag: The Movie*
Givens, Robin: *Foreign Student*
Glanzelius, Anton: *My Life As A Dog*
Glaser, Darel: *Bless The Beasts & Children*
Glatzeder, Winfred: *Street Kid*
Glawson, Peter: *The Genesis Children*
Gleason, Paul: *The Breakfast Club*
Gleason, Russell: *All Quiet On The Western Front*
Gleizer, Michele: *Europa, Europa*
Glover, Brian: *Kes*
Glover, Kara: *The Beat*
Goddard, Paul: *The Everlasting Secret Family*
Goetz, Kit: *Pretty Baby*
Goldberg, Adam: *Dazed And Confused*
Golovine, Marina: *Olivier Olivier; Stolen Children*
Golstein, Coco: *Zero De Conduite*
Good, Jack: *The Genesis Children*
Good, Mike: *The Genesis Children*
Goodall, Caroline: *White Squall*
Goodfellow, Joan: *Buster & Billie*
Goodman, Terence: *The Ode To Billy Joe*
Gordon, Ruth: *My Bodyguard*
Gorny, Frederic: *Wild Reeds*
Goulem, Alain: *The Boys of St. Vincent*
Gray, Shane: *The Delta*
Gray, Spalding: *King Of The Hill*

Kidman, Nicole: *Flirting*
Kier, Udo: *Josh and S.A.M.; My Own Private Idaho*
Kinnaman, Melinda: *My Life As A Dog*
Kinney, Terry: *Sleepers*
Kirby, Bruno: *The Basketball Diaries; Sleepers*
Kiser, Terry: *Rich Kids*
Kliner, Kim: *Over The Edge*
Knight, David: *Who Shot Pat?*
Knight, Wyatt: *Porky's*
Knudsen, Ditte: *The Hideaway*
Kohan, Glenn: *The Blue Lagoon*
Kohler, Gilles: *Bilitis*
Koons, Robert: *The Reflecting Skin*
Kotamanidou, Eva: *Landscape In The Mist*
Kozyrev, Voldya: *Freedom Is Paradise*
Krabbe, Jeroen: *For A Lost Soldier; King Of The Hill*
Kramer, Bob: *Bless The Beasts & Children*
Kramer, Michael: *Over The Edge*
Krause, Brian: *Return To The Blue Lagoon*
Kristel, Sylvia: *Private Lessons*
Kristensen, Mona: *Bilitis*
Kroon, Derk-Jan: *For A Lost Soldier*
Krylov, S.: *My Name Is Ivan*
Kussman, Dylan: *Dead Poets Society*

L

Lacombrade, Francis: *This Special Friendship*
Lacy, Jonathon: *The Baby Of Macon*
Ladd, Diane: *Rambling Rose*
Lake, Ricki: *Where The Day Takes You*
Lally, Mick: *The Secret Of Roan Inish*
Laloux, Daniel: *La Revolte Des Enfants*
Lamarre, Jean: *Fresh*
Lamberts, Heath: *Ordinary Magic*
Lane, Diane: *A Little Romance; The Outsiders*
Langrick, Margaret: *My American Cousin*
Lantigua, Luis: *Fresh*
Larive: *Zero De Conduite*
Larson, Henrik: *The Children Of Noisy Village*
Lartique, Martin: *War Of The Buttons (1962)*
Lascher, David: *White Squall*
Laurenzi, Anita: *Devil In The Flesh*
Lawley, Yvonne: *Among The Cinders*
Le Flon, Robert: *Zero De Conduite*
Le Gros, James: *Where The Day Takes You*
Le Mat, Paul: *American Graffiti*
Le Roux, Maxime: *Son Of The Shark*
Leachman, Cloris: *The Last Picture Show; Now And Then*
Leaud, Jean-Pierre: *36 Fillette; The 400 Blows*
Leccia, Francois: *This Special Friendship*
Lee Tai Ling: *Outcasts*
Lee, Cosette: *My Side Of The Mountain*
Lee, Mark: *The Everlasting Secret Family*
Lefebvre, Louis: *Zero De Conduite*
LeGros, James: *Boys*

Leland, Chloe: *Wish You Were Here*
Lena, Lorenzo: *The Flavor Of Corn*
Lenti, Mario: *Vito And The Others*
Leonard, Robert Sean: *Dead Poets Society*
Leone, Pina: *Vito And The Others*
Letts, Dennis: *The Last Prostitue*
Levy, Jeremy: *Rich Kids*
Lewis, Geoffrey: *The Man Without A Face*
Lewis, Juliette: *The Basketball Diaries*
Lewis, Ronald: *Friends*
Leygraf, Jakob: *The Slingshot; Sunday's Children*
Li Bassi, Alfredo: *Forever Mary*
Liden, Anki: *My Life As A Dog*
Lidfors, Lill: *Friends Forever*
Lindsay, Heather: *My First Suit*
Linnros, Henrik: *Sunday's Children*
Lino, Edilson: *Pixote*
Liotard, Therese: *My Father's Glory; My Mother's Castle*
Lisi, Virna: *Ernesto*
Lithgow, John: *Rich Kids*
Lively, Ernie: *The Man In The Moon*
Lloyd, Emily: *Wish You Were Here*
Lloyd, Norman: *Dead Poets Society*
Lo Verso, Enrico: *Stolen Children*
Locane, Amy: *School Ties*
Lockwood, Evan: *Rambling Rose*
Logan, Phyllis: *The Kitchen Toto*
Loiselle, Helene: *Mon Oncle Antoine*
London, Jason: *Dazed And Confused; The Man In The Moon*
Longworth, David: *The Reflecting Skin*
Lonnbro, Harald: *The Children Of Noisy Village*
Lonsdale, Michael: *Murmur Of The Heart; The Name Of The Rose*
Lopez, Charo: *Hidden Pleasures*
Lorenzo, William: *Macho Dancer*
Low, Maggie: *Postcards From America*
Lowe, Arthur: *If....*
Lowe, Rob: *Class; The Outsiders*
Lowery, Andrew: *School Ties*
Ludwig, Pamela: *Over The Edge*
Lynch, John: *The Secret Of Roan Inish*
Lynch, Kate: *Meatballs*
Lynch, Susan: *The Secret Of Roan Inish*
Lyons, James: *Postcards From America*

M

Mabius, Eric: *Welcome To The Dollhouse*
Macchio, Ralph: *The Outsiders*
Machoso, Julio: *White Squall*
MacPherson, Joe: *The Bay Boy*
Madden, John: *Little Giants*
Madio, James: *The Basketball Diaries*
Madsen, Benedicte W.: *Pretty Boy*
Maggio, Pupella: *Amarcord*
Mahinda, Edwin: *The Kitchen Toto*
Makepeace, Chris: *Meatballs; My Bodyguard*
Mana, Laura: *La Teta Y La Luna*
Manesse, Gaspard: *Au Revoir Les Enfants*
Manzano, Jose Luis: *Colegas*
Maraviglia, Larry: *The Boys Of Cellblock Q*

Marchand, Guy: *Petit Con*
Marcovicci, Andrea: *Jack The Bear*
Margolin, Stuart: *Class*
Mariano, Roberto: *Forever Mary*
Marks, Aviva: *Paradise*
Marsden, Jason: *White Squall*
Martens, Rica: *Welcome To The Dollhouse*
Martin, Christy: *Criss-Cross*
Martin, Deena: *Dazed And Confused*
Martin, Duane: *The Inkwell*
Martin, Helen: *A Hero Ain't Nothin' But A Sandwich*
Martin, Maribel: *Moon Child*
Martin, Pamela Sue: *Buster & Billie*
Massari, Lea: *Murmur Of The Heart*
Massaro, Maurice: *Abuse*
Mastalerz, Andrzej: *Europa, Europa*
Masterson, Fay: *The Man Without A Face*
Masterson, Mary Stuart: *Heaven Help Us*
Masur, Richard: *The Man Without A Face; Risky Business*
Matarazzo, Heather: *Welcome To The Dollhouse*
Matheron, Marie: *Le Grand Chemin*
Maunder, Wayne: *Porky's*
Maurin, Dominique: *This Special Friendship*
Mauruer, Claire: *The 400 Blows*
Maxwell, Roberta: *Rich Kids*
May, Mathilda: *La Teta Y La Luna*
Mazhuga, Yuri: *Lessons At The End Of Spring*
Mazzello, Joseph: *The Cure*
Mazzola, Frank: *Rebel Without A Cause*
McCallum, Charles: *The Devil's Playground*
McCarthy, Andrew: *Class; Heaven Help Us*
McCloskey, Leigh: *Just One Of The Guys*
McConaughey, Matthew: *Dazed And Confused*
McCormack, Leigh: *The Long Day Closes*
McDowell, Malcolm: *If....*
McElherron, Fergal: *The Secret Of Roan Inish*
McElhinney, Ian: *Lamb*
McEnery, John: *Romeo and Juliet*
McGaw, Patrick: *The Basketball Diaries*
McGovern, Elizabeth: *King Of The Hill*
McGrath, Doug: *Wedding In White*
McGrath, Liam: *Clayfarmers*
McKern, Leo: *The Blue Lagoon*
McKinnon, Jane: *The Bay Boy*
McLoed, Mary: *If....*
McNamara, William: *The Beat*
McPeak, Sandy: *The Ode To Billy Joe*
Meaney, Colm: *War Of The Buttons (1995)*
Meillon, John: *The Everlasting Secret Family*
Meisner, Gunter: *In A Glass Cage*
Mejias, Isabelle: *The Bay Boy*
Mendelsohn, Ben: *The Year My Voice Broke*
Mercer, Beryl: *All Quiet On The Western Front*

Merckx, Ken: *The Boys Of Cellblock Q*
Mestriner, Marco: *The Flavor Of Corn*
Methe, Francois: *Les Portes Tournantes*
Miles, Chris Cleary: *Second Best*
Miles, Sarah: *Hope And Glory*
Milian, Tomas: *Luna*
Miller, Dennis: *The Everlasting Secret Family*
Miller, Penelope Ann: *Biloxi Blues*
Mineo, Sal: *Rebel Without A Cause*
Miou Miou: *Les Portes Tournantes*
Mitchell, Chuck: *Porky's*
Mitchell, Heather: *The Everlasting Secret Family*
Mitchum, Bentley: *The Man In The Moon*
Molinas, Joris: *My Father's Glory; My Mother's Castle*
Monahan, Dan: *Porky's*
Montiege, Olivier: *Cross My Heart*
Montmarquette, Yves: *Leolo*
Moore, Ashley Ashton: *Now And Then*
Moore, Demi: *Now And Then*
Moore, Maggie: *The Incredibly True Adventure Of Two Girls In Love*
Moore, Sheila: *The Reflecting Skin*
Moquet, Stephane: *36 Fillette*
Moranis, Rick: *Little Giants*
Morel, Gael: *Wild Reeds*
Moreno, Rita: *Popi*
Moretti, Michele: *Wild Reeds*
Morier-Genoud, Phillipe: *Au Revoir Les Enfants*
Morina, Johnny: *The Boys of St. Vincent*
Morozof, Emmanuel: *Olivier Olivier*
Mortensen, Claus Bender: *Friends Forever*
Mortensen, Viggo: *The Reflecting Skin*
Mortifee, Jane: *My American Cousin*
Morton, Joe: *The Inkwell*
Moruea, Jeanne: *The 400 Blows*
Moss, Arnold: *The Fool Killer*
Mottura, Alba: *The Flavor Of Corn*
Moura, Gilberto: *Pixote*
Mouser, Dru: *The Last Prostitue*
Muir, Geraldine: *Hope And Glory*
Mulcahey, Jack: *Porky's*
Mulhern, Matt: *Biloxi Blues*
Mull, Martin: *My Bodyguard*
Mulroney, Dermot: *Where The Day Takes You*
Mumy, Bill: *Bless The Beasts & Children*
Murrey, Bill: *Meatballs*

N

Nadeau, Alex: *Leolo*
Naidu, Ajay: *Where The River Runs Black*
Nat, Lucien: *This Special Friendship*
Nazarov, Yuri: *Lessons At The End Of Spring*
Neeson, Liam: *Lamb*
Negret, Francois: *Au Revoir Les Enfants*
Neil, Christopher: *Train Of Dreams*
Nelson, Craig Richard: *My Bodyguard*
Nelson, Judd: *The Breakfast Club*
Nelson, Sean: *Fresh*
Neri, Francesca: *Flight of the Innocent*

Newton, Thandie: *Flirting*
Nobis, Felix: *Flirting*
Noel, Magali': *Amarcord*
Noonan, Christine: *If....*
Norris, Christopher: *Summer of '42*
North, Jay: *Maya*
Northup, Harry: *Over The Edge*
Novak, Klaus: *The Inheritors*
Noy, Zachi: *Lemon Popsicle*

O

O'Connell, Jerry: *Calendar Girl; Stand By Me*
O'Conner, Derrick: *Hope And Glory*
O'Conner, Glynnis: *The Ode To Billy Joe*
O'Connor, Hugh: *Lamb*
O'Donnel, Rosie: *Now And Then*
O'Donnell, Chris: *School Ties*
O'Neill, Ed: *Little Giants*
O'Neill, Jennifer: *Summer of '42*
O'Quinn, Terry: *Mischief*
O'Reilly, Cyril: *Porky's*
O'Shea, Milo: *Romeo and Juliet*
O'Shea, Paul: *Among The Cinders*
Oates, Warren: *Tom Sawyer*
Ohlers, Henrik: *Friends Forever*
Olds, Gabriel: *Calendar Girl*
Oliver, Tristan: *Another Country*
Olivier, Laurence: *A Little Romance*
Olund, Niclas: *The Slingshot*
Ormond, Julia: *The Baby Of Macon*
Otto, Kevin: *Who Shot Pat?*
Overall, Park: *Biloxi Blues*
Owens, Ayse: *The Long Day Closes*

P

Paaske, Gabriel: *Lakki, The Boy Who Grew Wings*
Pacifici, Frederico: *Flight of the Innocent*
Pain, Didier: *My Father's Glory; My Mother's Castle*
Palaiologou, Tania: *Landscape In The Mist*
Palladino, Aleksa: *Manny & Lo*
Pallascio, Aubert: *Lilies*
Pantoliano, Joe: *Calendar Girl; Risky Business*
Paole, Allan: *Macho Dancer*
Paramore, Kiri: *Flirting*
Pardo, Angel: *Hidden Pleasures*
Paredes, Marisa: *In A Glass Cage*
Parker, Corey: *Biloxi Blues*
Parker, Nicole: *The Incredibly True Adventure Of Two Girls In Love*
Parniere, Oliver: *36 Fillette*
Parodi, Nicholas: *Cross My Heart*
Parry, Natasha: *Romeo and Juliet*
Parsons, Nancy: *Porky's*
Pascal, Christine: *Le Grand Chemin*
Pascali, Tino: *Chronicle Of A Boy Alone*
Patekar, Nana: *Salaam Bombay!*
Patric, Jason: *The Lost Boys; Sleepers*
Patterson, Jay: *Heaven Help Us*
Patts, Mary Margaret: *Soup And Me*
Paul, Sandy: *Puberty Blues*
Payne, Bruce: *Wonderland*

Peacocke, Thomas: *The Bay Boy*
Peck, Bob: *The Kitchen Toto*
Pelikan, Lisa: *Return To The Blue Lagoon*
Pellegrino, Mark: *Prayer of the Rollerboys*
Penn, Chris: *Josh and S.A.M.*
Penot, Jacques: *Les Portes Tournantes*
Pera, Merilia: *Pixote*
Perel, Solomon: *Europa, Europa*
Perkins, Anthony: *The Fool Killer*
Perlman, Ron: *The Adventures Of Huck Finn; The Name Of The Rose*
Perrie, Lynne: *Kes*
Perrin, Jacques: *Flight of the Innocent*
Perrino, Joe: *Sleepers*
Perry-Robinson, Ralph: *Another Country*
Petrie, Doris: *Wedding In White*
Phillippe, Ryan: *White Squall*
Phillips, Courtney: *Return To The Blue Lagoon*
Phillips, Leo: *Wedding In White*
Phillips, MacKenzie: *American Graffiti*
Phoenix, River: *My Own Private Idaho; Stand By Me*
Piccininni, Patrick: *Private Lessons*
Picker, Josh: *Flirting*
Pierce, Justin: *Kids*
Pietropinto, Angela: *Welcome To The Dollhouse*
Pinkett, Jada: *The Inkwell*
Pinoli, Mattia: *The Flavor Of Corn*
Pinsent, Leah: *The Bay Boy*
Pipoly, Danuel: *Lord of the Flies* (1990)
Pirie, Ronald: *The Kitchen Toto*
Pitt, Brad: *Sleepers*
Pitt, Heather: *My First Suit*
Pitzalis, Frederico: *Devil In The Flesh*
Place, Mary Kay: *Manny & Lo*
Placido, Michele: *Ernesto; Forever Mary*
Platt, Edward: *Rebel Without A Cause*
Pleasence, Donald: *Wedding In White*
Plimpton, Martha: *Josh and S.A.M.*
Pomeroy, Julia: *Over The Edge*
Poppiti, Ciro: *Lucas*
Poser, Toby: *The Incredibly True Adventure Of Two Girls In Love*
Posey, Parker: *Dazed And Confused*
Poveda, Miguel: *La Teta Y La Luna*
Powell, Esteban: *Dazed And Confused*
Power, Tyrone, Jr.: *Shag: The Movie*
Powers, Alexandra: *Dead Poets Society*
Preboist, Paul: *The Two Of Us*
Presle, Micheline: *Nea*
Preston, Kelly: *Mischief*
Priestly, Jason: *Calendar Girl*
Prinz, Dietmar: *Beethoven's Nephew*
Prollo, Maurizio: *Forever Mary*
Pruchon, Gilbert: *Zero De Conduite*
Puente, Diego: *Chronicle Of A Boy Alone*
Punzalan, Princess: *Macho Dancer*

Q

Quaid, Randy: *The Last Picture Show*
Quinn, J. C.: *Criss-Cross; Prayer of the Rollerboys*
Quiring, Frederic: *Olivier Olivier*

R

Rabelo, Alessandro: *Where The River Runs Black*
Rabelo, Marcelo: *Where The River Runs Black*
Racette, Francine: *Au Revoir Les Enfants*
Radakovic, Goran: *Hey Babu Riba*
Railsback, Steve: *Calendar Girl*
Randall, Brad: *Who Shot Pat?*
Rapp, Anthony: *Dazed And Confused; School Ties*
Ratliff, Garette: *Return To The Blue Lagoon*
Rebbot, Sady: *Friends*
Reeve, Christopher: *Bump In The Night*
Reeves, Keanu: *My Own Private Idaho*
Reichman, Wolfgang: *Beethoven's Nephew*
Reid, Kate: *Heaven Help Us*
Reilly, John C.: *Boys*
Reimer, Elin: *You Are Not Alone*
Rempel, Nicholas: *Clayfarmers*
Remy, Albert: *The 400 Blows*
Renfro, Brad: *The Cure; Sleepers*
Reno, Ginette: *Leolo*
Reymond, Dominique: *La Revolte Des Enfants*
Reynolds, Ryan: *Ordinary Magic*
Rhoe, Geoff: *Puberty Blues*
Rialet, Baniel: *Le Grand Chemin*
Ribissi, Marissa: *Dazed And Confused*
Ricci, Christina: *Now And Then*
Richard, Jean: *War Of The Buttons* (1962)
Richards, Sindee Ann: *The Fool Killer*
Richardson, Ian: *Burning Secret*
Richert, William: *My Own Private Idaho*
Rideau, Stephane: *Full Speed; Wild Reeds*
Ringer, Michael: *Postcards From America*
Ringwald, Molly: *The Breakfast Club*
Robards, Jason: *The Adventures Of Huck Finn*
Roberts, Pascale: *Friends; Le Grand Chemin*
Robertson, Andrew: *The Cement Garden*
Robertson, Cliff: *Class*
Robertson, Malcolm: *The Year My Voice Broke*
Robertson, Tim: *The Year My Voice Broke*
Robertson, Travis: *Now And Then*
Robins, Barry: *Bless The Beasts & Children*
Robins, Toby: *Friends*
Robinson, Bruce: *Romeo and Juliet*
Robinson, Tina: *Puberty Blues*
Rocard, Pascale: *The Rascals*
Rochefort, Jean: *My Mother's Castle*
Rodriguez, Nelson: *The Incredibly True Adventure Of Two Girls In Love*
Roerick, William: *A Separate Peace*
Rohner, Clayton: *Just One Of The Guys*
Romano, Andy: *Over The Edge*
Ronet, Maurice: *Beau Pere*
Rooney, Gerard: *The Secret Of Roan Inish*
Rose, Bartholomew: *Flirting*
Ross, Charlotte: *Foreign Student*
Ross-Magenty, Adrian: *Another Country*

Rossat, Beatriz: *Hidden Pleasures*
Rouan, Brigitte: *Olivier Olivier*
Rouaud, Cecilia: *Cross My Heart*
Roussel, Nathalie: *My Father's Glory; My Mother's Castle*
Rouvel, Catherine: *Tendres Cousines*
Roy, Lise: *The Boys of St. Vincent*
Ruffelle, Frances: *Kipperbang*
Ruggiero, Allelon: *Dead Poets Society*
Rundgren, Kicki: *My Life As A Dog*
Rusler, Robert: *Shag: The Movie*
Russo, James: *My Own Private Idaho*
Ryder, Richard: *Abuse*
Ryder, Winona: *Boys; Lucas*

S

Sabourin, Marcel: *Lilies*
Sage, Bill: *Boys*
Sahlin, Anna: *The Children Of Noisy Village*
Sahni, Sonia: *Maya*
Salas, Hank: *My Bodyguard*
Saldana, Enrique: *Moon Child*
Salen, Jesper: *The Slingshot*
Sam Chi-Vy: *China, My Sorrow*
Samson, Genevieve: *Leolo*
Samuels, Haydon: *I Live With Me Dad*
San Giacomo, Laura: *Where The Day Takes You*
Sanchez, Genis: *La Teta Y La Luna*
Sanderson, Martin: *My First Suit*
Sano, Bobby: *Macho Dancer*
Santa Maria, Marcella: *Train Of Dreams*
Santos, Zenildo Oliveira: *Pixote*
Sarandon, Susan: *Pretty Baby*
Sardo, Lucia: *Acla*
Savage, John: *The Beat; White Squall*
Sawa, Devon: *Little Giants; Now And Then*
Sbarge, Raphael: *Abuse; Risky Business*
Scales, Prunella: *Second Best*
Scalici, Valentina: *Stolen Children*
Scarfe, Alan: *The Bay Boy*
Scarwid, Diana: *The Cure; Pretty Baby*
Schauer, Roger: *The Inheritors*
Schmidt, Nathalie: *Europa, Europa*
Schneider, Susan: *Abuse*
Schofield, Nell: *Puberty Blues*
Sciorra, Anabella: *The Cure*
Scott, Larry B.: *A Hero Ain't Nothin' But A Sandwich*
Scott, T. J.: *My American Cousin*
Segal, Jonathon: *Lemon Popsicle*
Seigner, Francoise: *The Wild Child*
Seigner, Louis: *This Special Friendship*
Selby, David: *Rich Kids; White Squall*
Semple, Ashby: *A Little Romance*
Serner, Manfred: *My Life As A Dog*
Sevigny, Chloe: *Kids*
Sexton, Brendan, Jr.: *Welcome To The Dollhouse*
Shadbolt, Maurice: *Among The Cinders*
Shao Hsin: *Outcasts*
Sharma, Chanda: *Salaam Bombay!*
Shawn, Wallace: *Heaven Help Us*
Sheedy, Ally: *The Breakfast Club*

Sheen, Charlie: *Lucas*
Sheen, Martin: *The Little Girl Who Lives Down The Lane*
Shepherd, Cybill: *The Last Picture Show*
Sheridan, Richard: *The Secret Of Roan Inish*
Shields, Brooke: *The Blue Lagoon; Pretty Baby*
Shiloach, Yossi: *Paradise*
Shtrel, Ophella: *Lemon Popsicle*
Shuman, Mort: *The Little Girl Who Lives Down The Lane*
Shute, Anna: *Tendres Cousines*
Siemaszko, Casey: *Biloxi Blues; Class; Stand By Me*
Signoret, Simone: *Madame Rosa*
Sigsgaard, Thomas: *Friends Forever*
Simon, Michel: *The Two Of Us*
Sinise, Gary: *Jack The Bear*
Sinutko, Shane: *Soup And Me*
Sisto, Jeremy: *White Squall*
Skagestad, Bjorn: *Lakki, The Boy Who Grew Wings*
Skarsgard, Stellan: *The Slingshot*
Skou, Christine: *Friends Forever*
Slater, Christian: *The Name Of The Rose; Where The Day Takes You*
Smink, Freark: *For A Lost Soldier*
Smit, Maarten: *For A Lost Soldier*
Smit, Rulle: *The Littlest Viking*
Smith, Alexis: *The Little Girl Who Lives Down The Lane*
Smith, Charlie Martin: *American Graffiti*
Smith, Cotter: *The Last Prostitue*
Smith, Kurtwood: *Dead Poets Society*
Smith, Will: *Where The Day Takes You*
Sochet, David: *The Boys Of Cellblock Q*
Somers, Suzanne: *American Graffiti*
Spano, Vincent: *Over The Edge*
Sparrow, Walter: *Now And Then*
Spaziani, Monique: *Les Portes Tournantes*
Spence, Bruce: *The Year My Voice Broke*
Spence, Sebastian: *The Boys of St. Vincent*
Sperandeo, Tony: *Acla; Forever Mary*
Sprogoe, Ove: *You Are Not Alone*
St. Amour, Jason: *Train Of Dreams*
Stafford, Kate: *The Incredibly True Adventure Of Two Girls In Love*
Stahl, Nick: *The Man Without A Face*
Steadman, Alison: *Kipperbang*
Steinmiller, Robert J. Jr.: *Jack The Bear*
Stephens, Robert: *Romeo and Juliet; Wonderland*
Stevenin, Jean-Francois: *Olivier Olivier*
Stevenin, Robinson: *La Revolte Des Enfants*
Stevenson, Parker: *A Separate Peace*
Stewart, Catherine Mary: *Mischief*
Stickney, Phyllis Yvonne: *The Inkwell*
Stone, Philip: *The Baby Of Macon*
Strancar, Nadia: *La Revolte Des Enfants*
Strickland, Gail: *The Man In The Moon*
Stromdahl, Terje: *The Littlest Viking*
Su Ming-Ming: *Outcasts*
Summerville, Slim: *All Quiet On The Western Front*

Sun Yueh: *Outcasts*
Sust, David: *In A Glass Cage; Moon Child*
Sutherland, Donald: *Heaven Help Us*
Sutherland, Kiefer: *The Bay Boy; The Lost Boys; Stand By Me*
Sutton, Dudley: *Lamb; The Leather Boys*
Sverdlin, Rami Nathan: *Pretty Boy*
Swann, Robert: *If....*
Swayze, Patrick: *The Outsiders*
Swoffard, Ken: *Bless The Beasts & Children*
Syed, Shafiq: *Salaam Bombay!*

T

Taft, Andrew: *Lord Of The Flies* (1990)
Taft, Edward: *Lord Of The Flies* (1990)
Taggart, Sharon: *The Last Picture Show*
Tanzilli, Josiane: *Amarcord*
Tapdrup, Christian: *Pretty Boy*
Tate, Larenz: *The Inkwell*
Tate, Nick: *The Devil's Playground*
Tavi, Tuviva: *Paradise*
Taylor, Noah: *Flirting; The Year My Voice Broke*
Termine, Egidio: *The Flavor Of Corn*
Termini, Salvatore: *Forever Mary*
Tevini, Thierry: *Tendres Cousines*
Thewlis, David: *Total Eclipse*
Thibault, Olivette: *Mon Oncle Antoine*
Thomas, Christine: *Wedding In White*
Thomas, Hugh: *If....*
Thomey, Greg: *The Boys of St. Vincent*
Thompson, Susanna: *Little Giants*
Thompson, Tiger: *Over The Edge*
Thorne-Smith, Courtney: *Lucas*
Tierney, Jacob: *Josh and S.A.M.*
Tieu Quan Nghieu: *China, My Sorrow*
Tighe, Kevin: *School Ties*
Tighe, Michael: *Postcards From America*
Tighe, Olmo: *Postcards From America*
Timmerman, Julie: *My Mother's Castle*
Tobolowsky, Stephen: *Calendar Girl; Josh and S.A.M.*
Todorovic, Marko: *Hey Babu Riba*
Tolkachev, Danya: *Lessons At The End Of Spring*
Tomeck, Johanna: *The Inheritors*
Tomelty, Frances: *Lamb*
Tomkus, Vitaulus: *Freedom Is Paradise*
Tonby, Kristian: *The Littlest Viking*
Topping, John: *The Boys Of Cellblock Q*
Torgov, Sarah: *Meatballs*
Tornad, Tony: *Pixote*
Trabaud, Pierre: *War Of The Buttons* (1962)
Trainor, Mary Ellen: *Little Giants*
Treton, Andre: *War Of The Buttons* (1962)
Triola, Nando: *Vito And The Others*
Truffaut, Francois: *The 400 Blows; The Wild Child*
Tucker, Jonathon: *Sleepers*
Turman, Glynn: *A Hero Ain't Nothin' But A Sandwich; The Inkwell*
Tushingham, Rita: *The Leather Boys*

Tyson, Cicely: *A Hero Ain't Nothin' But A Sandwich*
Tzortzoglou, Stratos: *Landscape In The Mist*

U

Uchan, Philippe: *My Mother's Castle*
Ullman, Liv: *The Bay Boy*
Ulrich, Skeet: *Boys*
Urguhart, Robert: *Kipperbang*

V

Vahanian, Marc: *Bless The Beasts & Children*
Valdes, Michael: *The Boys Of Cellblock Q*
van der Wingen, Philip: *Street Kid*
Vance, Courtney B.: *The Adventures Of Huck Finn*
Vandendaele, Ludovic: *Son Of The Shark*
Vantriglia, Damian: *Criss-Cross*
Vargas, Valentina: *The Name Of The Rose*
Videnovic, Gala: *Hey Babu Riba*
Ville, Paul: *The Wild Child*
Villeneuve, Lionel: *Mon Oncle Antoine*
Vincent, Jan-Michael: *Buster & Billie*
Vipond, Neil: *Paradise*
Vithal, Hansa: *Salaam Bombay!*
Vogel, Nikolas: *The Inheritors*
von Bromssen, Tomas: *My Life As A Dog*
von Sydow, Max: *Pelle The Conqueror*
Vrooman, Spencer: *Boys*

W

Wade, Michael: *The Boys of St. Vincent*
Wahlberg, Mark: *The Basketball Diaries*
Wainwright, Rupert: *Another Country*
Waldron, Shawna: *Little Giants*
Walken, Christopher: *Biloxi Blues*
Walker, Clint: *Maya*
Walker, Kathryn: *Rich Kids*
Wanninger, Ashley: *Europa, Europa*
Ward, Asbury: *Clayfarmers*
Ward, Fred: *Train Of Dreams*
Warfield, Emily: *Calendar Girl; The Man In The Moon*
Warwick, Richard: *If....*
Washbourne, Mona: *If....*
Waterson, James: *Dead Poets Society*
Waterston, Sam: *The Man In The Moon*
Watson, Anthony: *The Long Day Closes*
Watson, Woody: *The Last Prostitue*
Webber, Timothy: *The Boys of St. Vincent*
Weber, Nicole: *Street Kid*
Webster, Rupert: *If....*
Weisser, Morgan: *Prayer of the Rollerboys*
Welland, Colin: *Kes*
Welsh, Margaret: *American Heart*
Wendel, Lara: *Ernesto*
Wendenius, Crispin Dickson: *The Children Of Noisy Village*
Wendt, George: *My Bodyguard*

Wheaton, Wil: *The Last Prostitue; Stand By Me*
Whitaker, Johnny: *Tom Sawyer*
Whiting, Leonard: *Romeo and Juliet*
Whitton, Margaret: *The Man Without A Face*
Wiest, Dianne: *The Lost Boys*
Wigdor, Geoffrey: *Sleepers*
Wiggens, Tudi: *My Side Of The Mountain*
Wiggins, Chris: *The Bay Boy*
Wiggins, Wiley: *Boys; Dazed And Confused*
Wilbee, Codie Lucas: *The Reflecting Skin*
Wild, Jack: *The Wild Little Bunch*
Wildman, John: *My American Cousin*
Williams, Cindy: *American Graffiti*
Williams, Robin: *Dead Poets Society*
Wilms, Andre: *Europa, Europa; La Revolte Des Enfants*
Wilson, Georges: *My Mother's Castle*
Wilson, Rita: *Now And Then*
Wilson, Roger: *Porky's*
Wincourt, Marc: *Murmur Of The Heart*
Winfield, Paul: *A Hero Ain't Nothin' But A Sandwich*
Winther, Allan: *The Hideaway*
Witherspoon, Reese: *Jack The Bear; The Man In The Moon*
Wolf, Scott: *White Squall*
Wolfman Jack: *American Graffiti*
Wolheim, Louis: *All Quiet On The Western Front*
Wood, David: *If....*
Wood, Elijah: *The Adventures Of Huck Finn*
Wood, Natalie: *Rebel Without A Cause*
Worth, Irene: *Rich Kids*
Wray, John: *All Quiet On The Western Front*
Wright, N'Bushe: *Fresh*

Y

Yadav, Raghuvir: *Salaam Bombay!*
Yagher, Jeff: *Shag: The Movie*
Yanne, Jean: *A La Mode*
Yates, Marjorie: *The Long Day Closes*
York, Michael: *Romeo and Juliet*
Young, Bruce A.: *Risky Business*
Young, Russell: *Boys*

Z

Zabka, William: *Just One Of The Guys*
Zacharias, Ann: *Nea*
Zanin, Bruno: *Amarcord*
Zeke, Michalis: *Landscape In The Mist*
Zentout, Delphine: *36 Fillette*
Zharikov, Y.: *My Name Is Ivan*
Zinet, Mahamed: *Madame Rosa*
Zischler, Hanns: *The Cement Garden; Europa, Europa*
Zubkov, Valentin: *My Name Is Ivan*
Zutic, Milos: *Hey Babu Riba*

DIRECTOR INDEX

A

Acin, Jovan: *Hey Babu Riba*
Aikman, Anthony: *The Genesis Children*
Amelio, Gianni: *Stolen Children*
Anderson, Lindsay: *If....*
Angelopoulos, Theo: *Landscape In The Mist*
Annaud, Jean Jacques: *The Name Of The Rose*
Antonio, Lou: *The Last Prostitue*
Apted, Michael: *Kipperbang*
Arthur, Karen: *Bump In The Night*
August, Billy: *Pelle The Conqueror*

B

Babenco, Hector: *Pixote*
Baer, Max: *The Ode To Billy Joe*
Bale, Paul Trevor: *The Littlest Viking*
Bannert, Walter: *The Inheritors*
Barron, Zelda: Shag: *The Movie*
Bell, Martin: *American Heart; Streetwise*
Bellocchio, Marco: *Devil In The Flesh*
Beresford, Bruce: *Puberty Blues*
Bergman, Daniel: *Sunday's Children*
Berri, Claude: *The Two Of Us*
Berry, John: *Maya*
Bertolucci, Bernardo: *Luna*
Bill, Tony: *My Bodyguard*
Birkin, Andrew: B*urning Secret; The Cement Garden*
Blier, Bertrand: *Beau Pere*
Bodrov, Sergei: *Freedom Is Paradise*
Bogdanovich, Peter: *The Last Picture Show*
Boorman, John: *Hope And Glory*
Breillat, Catherine: *36 Fillette*
Bresson, Arthur J., Jr.: *Abuse*
Brickman, Paul: *Risky Business*
Brocka, Lino: *Macho Dancer*
Brook, Peter: *Lord Of The Flies* (1963)
Brooks, Robert: *Who Shot Pat?*

C

Cain, Christopher: *Where The River Runs Black*
Capuano, Antonio: *Vito And The Others*
Carlei, Carlo: *Flight of the Innocent*
Carlino, Lewis John: *Class*
Caton-Jones, Michael: *This Boy's Life*
Clark, Bob: *Porky's*
Clark, James B.: *My Side Of The Mountain*
Clark, Larry: *Kids*
Cochran, Stacy: *Boys*
Coolidge, Martha: *Rambling Rose*
Coppola, Francis Ford: *The Outsiders*

D

Da Campo, Gianni: *The Flavor Of Corn*
Dai Sijie: *China, My Sorrow*

Damski, Mel: *Mischief*
Daniels, Alan: *The Boys Of Cellblock Q*
Davidson, Boaz: *Lemon Popsicle*
Davies, Terrence: *The Long Day Closes*
de la Iglesia, Eloy: *Colegas; Hidden Pleasures*
Dellanoy, Jean: *This Special Friendship*
des Roziers, Hugues Burin: *Blue Jeans*
Dinner, Michael: *Heaven Help Us*
Donelly, Dennis: *Soup And Me*
Duchemin, Remy: *A La Mode*
Duigan, John: *Flirting; The Year My Voice Broke*
Dunham, Duwayne: *Little Giants*

E

Escamilla, Teo: *Tu Solo*

F

Fansten, Jacques: *Cross My Heart*
Favio, Leonardo: *Chronicle Of A Boy Alone*
Fellini, Federico: *Amarcord*
Fruet, William: *Wedding In White*
Furie, Sidney J.: *The Leather Boys*

G

Gessner, Nicholas: *The Little Girl Who Lives Down The Lane*
Gibson, Mel: *The Man Without A Face*
Gilbert, Lewis: *Friends*
Gillard, Stuart: *Paradise*
Glatter, Lesli Linka: *Now And Then*
Gonzalez, A. P.: *Clayfarmers*
Gonzalez, Servando: *The Fool Killer*
Gottlieb, Lisa: *Just One Of The Guys*
Grabol, Nils: *The Hideaway*
Graham, William A.: *Return To The Blue Lagoon*
Greenaway, Peter: *The Baby Of Macon*
Gregg, Colin: *Lamb*
Greyson, John: *Lilies*
Grimaldi, Aurelio: *Acla*
Grodecki, Wiktor: *Not Angels But Angels*
Gubenko, Nikolai: *The Orphans*

H

Haedrich, Rolf: *Among The Cinders*
Hallstrom, Lasse: *The Children Of Noisy Village; My Life As A Dog*
Hamilton, David: *Bilitis; Tendres Cousines*
Hemming, David: *The Wild Little Bunch*
Henszelmann, Stefan Christian: *Friends Forever*
Herskovitz, Marshall: *Jack The Bear*
Hill, George Roy: *A Little Romance*
Hiller, Arthur: *Popi*
Holland, Agnieszka: *Europa, Europa;*

Olivier Olivier; Total Eclipse
Hook, Harry: *The Kitchen Toto; Lord of the Flies* (1990)
Horton, Peter: *The Cure*
Hubert, Jean-Loup: *Le Grand Chemin*
Hughes, John: *The Breakfast Club*

J

Johansen, Ernst: *You Are Not Alone*
Jorfald, Knut W.: *The Littlest Viking*
Jutra, Claude: *Mon Oncle Antoine*

K

Kalvert, Scott: *The Basketball Diaries*
Kanievska, Marek: *Another Country*
Kaplan, Jonathan: *Over The Edge*
Kaplan, Nelly: *Nea*
Kavan, Oleg: *Lessons At The End Of Spring*
Kerbosch, Roeland: *For A Lost Soldier*
Kern, Peter: *Street Kid*
King, Rick: *Prayer of the Rollerboys*
Kleiser, Randal: *The Blue Lagoon*
Kramer, Stanley: *Bless The Beasts & Children*
Krom, Frank: *To Play Or To Die*
Krueger, Lisa: *Manny & Lo*

L

Lauzier, Georges: *Petit Con*
Lauzon, Jean-Claude: *Leolo*
Leland, David: *Wish You Were Here*
Levinson, Barry: *Sleepers*
Linklater, Richard: *Dazed And Confused*
Loach, Kenneth: *Kes*
Lucas, George: *American Graffiti*
Luna, Bigas: *La Teta Y La Luna*
Maggenti, Maria: *The Incredibly True Adventure Of Two Girls In Love*

M

Main, Stewart: *My First Suit*
Malle, Louis: *Au Revoir Les Enfants; Murmur Of The Heart; Pretty Baby*
Mandel, Robert: *School Ties*
Mankiewicz, Francis: *Les Portes Tournantes*
McLean, Steve: *Postcards From America*
Menges, Chris: *Criss-Cross; Second Best*
Merlet, Agnes: *Son Of The Shark*
Milestone, Lewis: *All Quiet On The Western Front*
Mizrahi, Moshe: *Madame Rosa*
Moloney, Paul: *I Live With Me Dad*
Mones, Paul: *The Beat*
Morel, Gael: *Full Speed*
Morrissey, Paul: *Beethoven's Nephew*
Mulligan, Robert: *The Man In The Moon; Summer of '42*

Myerson, Alan: *Private Lessons*

N
Nair, Mira: *Salaam Bombay!*
Nelson, Ralph: *A Hero Ain't Nothin' But A Sandwich*
Nichols, Mike: *Biloxi Blues*
Nielson, Lasse: *You Are Not Alone*

P
Peerce, Larry: *A Separate Peace*
Petrie, Daniel: *The Bay Boy; Buster & Billie*
Poitou-Weber, Gerard: *La Revolte Des Enfants*

R
Rasmussen, Lars: *The Littlest Viking*
Ray, Nicholas: *Rebel Without A Cause*
Reiner, Rob: *Stand By Me*
Reitman, Ivan: *Meatballs*
Revon, Bernard: *The Rascals*
Rich, Matty: *The Inkwell*
Ridley, Philip: *The Reflecting Skin*
Ridley, Scott: *White Squall*
Risi, Marco: *Forever Mary*
Robert, Yves: *My Father's Glory; My Mother's Castle; War Of The Buttons*

(1962)
Roberts, John: *War Of The Buttons* (1995)
Rocco, Marc: *Where The Day Takes You*
Roeg, Nicolas: *Walkabout*

S
Sachs, Ira: *The Delta*
Sampari, Salvatore: *Ernesto*
Sandgren, Ake: *The Slingshot*
Saville, Philip: *Wonderland*
Sayles, John: *The Secret Of Roan Inish*
Schepisi, Fred: *The Devil's Playground*
Schumacher, Joel: *The Lost Boys*
Seltzer, David: *Lucas*
Sereny, Eva: *Foreign Student*
Smith, John N.: *The Boys of St. Vincent; Train Of Dreams*
Soderbergh, Steven: *King Of The Hill*
Solondz, Todd: *Welcome To The Dollhouse*
Sommers, Stephen: *The Adventures Of Huck Finn*
Sonder, Carsten: *Pretty Boy*

T
Tarkovski, : *My Name Is Ivan*
Taylor, Don: *Tom Sawyer*
Techine, Andre: *Wild Reeds*

Thornhill, Michael: *The Everlasting Secret Family*
Truffaut, Francois: *The 400 Blows; The Wild Child*

V
Van Sant, Gus: *My Own Private Idaho*
Varda, Agnes: *Le Petit Amour*
Vigo, Jean: *Zero De Conduite*
Villaronga, Agustin: *In A Glass Cage; Moon Child*

W
Walker, Giles: *Ordinary Magic*
Wam, Svend: *Lakki, The Boy Who Grew Wings*
Weber, Billy: *Josh and S.A.M.*
Weir, Peter: *Dead Poets Society*
Whitesell, John: *Calendar Girl*
Wilson, Sandy: *My American Cousin*

Y
Yakin, Boaz: *Fresh*
Young, Robert M.: *Rich Kids*
Yu Kan-Ping: *Outcasts*

Z
Zeffirelli, Franco: *Romeo and Juliet*

GENRE INDEX

Biography

Au Revoir Les Enfants
The Basketball Diaries
Beethoven's Nephew
Biloxi Blues
The Children Of Noisy Village
Europa, Europa
For A Lost Soldier
King Of The Hill
The Long Day Closes
My Father's Glory
My Mother's Castle
Postcards From America
Pretty Baby
Sunday's Children
This Boy's Life
Total Eclipse
The Wild Child
Wish You Were Here

Semi-Biographical Films

The 400 Blows
The Bay Boy
Sleepers
The Slingshot

Comedy and Satire

A La Mode
Amarcord
Beau Pere
Biloxi Blues
The Boys Of Cellblock Q
Calendar Girl
Dazed And Confused
Flirting
Le Grand Chemin
Heaven Help Us
If....
Josh and S.A.M.
King Of The Hill
Kipperbang
Leolo
Little Giants
A Little Romance
The Lost Boys
Lucas
Meatballs
Murmur Of The Heart
My Bodyguard
My First Suit
My Life As A Dog
My Mother's Castle
Petit Con
The Rascals
Rich Kids
La Teta Y La Luna

The Two Of Us
War Of The Buttons (1962)
War Of The Buttons (1995)
Who Shot Pat?
Zero De Conduite

Teen Sex Comedy
A sub-category of comedy, often badly treated.

Class
Just One Of The Guys
Lemon Popsicle
Mischief
Nea
Porky's
Risky Business
Shag: The Movie
Tendres Cousines

Documentary

Not Angels But Angels
Streetwise

Fact-Based Fiction

Acla
The Boys of St. Vincent
Olivier Olivier
Son Of The Shark
White Squall
The Wild Little Bunch

Girls' Stories

The Children Of Noisy Village
The Incredibly True Adventure Of Two
   Girls In Love
Just One Of The Guys
Kids
The Little Girl Who Lives Down The Lane
The Man In The Moon
Manny & Lo
My American Cousin
Nea
Now And Then
The Ode To Billy Joe
Pretty Baby
Rich Kids
The Secret Of Roan Inish
Shag: The Movie
36 Fillette
Wedding In White
Welcome To The Dollhouse
Wish You Were Here

Pre-Teens
Stories in which one or more of the

principal characters is less than thirteen-years old. The majority deal with children on the verge of adolescence: eleven or twelve-years old.

Acla
The Adventures Of Huck Finn
Au Revoir Les Enfants
The Blue Lagoon
The Boys of St. Vincent
Bump In The Night
The Cement Garden
The Children Of Noisy Village
Chronicle Of A Boy Alone
Criss-Cross
Cross My Heart
The Cure
Flight of the Innocent
The Fool Killer
For A Lost Soldier
The Hideaway
Hope And Glory
I Live With Me Dad
Jack The Bear
Josh and S.A.M.
King Of The Hill
The Kitchen Toto
Lamb
Landscape In The Mist
Leolo
Little Giants
The Long Day Closes
Lord Of The Flies (1963)
Lord Of The Flies (1990)
The Man Without A Face
Manny & Lo
Maya
Meatballs
Moon Child
My American Cousin
My Father's Glory
My Life As A Dog
My Mother's Castle
My Name Is Ivan
My Side Of The Mountain
Now And Then
Olivier Olivier
The Orphans
Pelle The Conqueror
Pixote
Popi
Pretty Baby
The Rascals
The Reflecting Skin
Return To The Blue Lagoon
La Revolte Des Enfants
Rich Kids
Salaam Bombay!
Second Best
The Secret Of Roan Inish

The Slingshot
Soup And Me
Stand By Me
Stolen Children
Sunday's Children
La Teta Y La Luna
This Special Friendship
Tu Solo
The Two Of Us
Vito And The Others
Walkabout
War Of The Buttons (1962)
War Of The Buttons (1995)
Welcome To The Dollhouse
Where The River Runs Black
The Wild Child
The Wild Little Bunch
You Are Not Alone
Zero De Conduite

Historical or Costume Tale

The Adventures Of Huck Finn
The Baby Of Macon
Beethoven's Nephew
The Blue Lagoon
Burning Secret
Ernesto
The Fool Killer
Lilies
The Littlest Viking
The Name Of The Rose
Paradise
Pelle The Conqueror
Pretty Baby
Return To The Blue Lagoon
La Revolte Des Enfants
Romeo and Juliet
Tom Sawyer
Total Eclipse
The Wild Child

Holocaust Stories

Au Revoir Les Enfants
Europa, Europa
In A Glass Cage
The Two Of Us

Period Pieces and Nostalgia

Differing from Historical Tales in that they are a look back at events within the lifetime of the filmmaker, or the central characters. The look back need not be a happy, nostalgic one, but can be to a time of terror, abuse or hardship.

A La Mode
Acla
Amarcord
American Graffiti
Another Country
Au Revoir Les Enfants
The Bay Boy
Biloxi Blues
The Boys of St. Vincent

Buster & Billie
Calendar Girl
The Children Of Noisy Village
Dazed And Confused
Dead Poets Society
Europa, Europa
Flirting
For A Lost Soldier
Foreign Student
Le Grand Chemin
Heaven Help Us
Hey Babu Riba
Hope And Glory
The Inkwell
Jack The Bear
King Of The Hill
Kipperbang
The Last Picture Show
Lemon Popsicle
Leolo
Lessons At The End Of Spring
The Long Day Closes
The Man In The Moon
The Man Without A Face
Mischief
Mon Oncle Antoine
Murmur Of The Heart
My American Cousin
My Father's Glory
My First Suit
My Life As A Dog
My Mother's Castle
Now And Then
The Ode To Billy Joe
The Orphans
The Outsiders
Porky's
Les Portes Tournantes
Postcards From America
Rambling Rose
The Rascals
The Reflecting Skin
School Ties
The Secret Of Roan Inish
A Separate Peace
Shag: The Movie
Sleepers
The Slingshot
Soup And Me
Stand By Me
Summer of '42
Sunday's Children
Tendres Cousines
This Boy's Life
This Special Friendship
The Two Of Us
Wedding In White
White Squall
Who Shot Pat?
Wild Reeds
Wish You Were Here
The Year My Voice Broke

Literary Adaptations

Many of the best films about children and teenagers are adaptations of books or short stories.

The Adventures Of Huck Finn
All Quiet On The Western Front
Among The Cinders
Another Country
The Basketball Diaries
Beau Pere
Beethoven's Nephew
Bilitis
Biloxi Blues
Bless The Beasts & Children
The Blue Lagoon
Boys
The Boys Of Cellblock Q
Bump In The Night
Burning Secret
The Cement Garden
The Children Of Noisy Village
Criss-Cross
The Everlasting Secret Family
The Fool Killer
For A Lost Soldier
Forever Mary
A Hero Ain't Nothin' But A Sandwich
I Live With Me Dad
Jack The Bear
Kes
King Of The Hill
Lakki, The Boy Who Grew Wings
Lamb
The Last Picture Show
The Last Prostitue
Lilies
A Little Romance
The Littlest Viking
Lord Of The Flies (1963)
Lord of the Flies (1990)
Madame Rosa
The Man Without A Face
Maya
My Father's Glory
My Life As A Dog
My Mother's Castle
My Name Is Ivan
My Own Private Idaho
My Side Of The Mountain
The Name Of The Rose
Ordinary Magic
Outcasts
The Outsiders
Pelle The Conqueror
Petit Con
Pixote
Les Portes Tournantes
Postcards From America
Private Lessons
Rambling Rose
Rebel Without A Cause
Return To The Blue Lagoon
Romeo and Juliet
Second Best
The Secret Of Roan Inish
A Separate Peace
Sleepers
The Slingshot

Soup And Me
Stand By Me
This Boy's Life
This Special Friendship
To Play Or To Die
Tom Sawyer
Walkabout
War Of The Buttons (1962)
War Of The Buttons (1995)

Musicals

Tom Sawyer

Mysteries and Thrillers

Boys
The Fool Killer
In A Glass Cage
The Little Girl Who Lives Down The Lane
The Name Of The Rose
The Reflecting Skin
To Play Or To Die

Road Stories

Tales in which a journey away from home, whether long or short, figures prominently.

The Adventures Of Huck Finn
Bless The Beasts & Children
Calendar Girl
The Cure
The Delta
Flight of the Innocent
The Fool Killer
Freedom Is Paradise
Friends
Josh and S.A.M.
Lamb
Landscape In The Mist

The Last Prostitue
The Leather Boys
A Little Romance
Manny & Lo
Maya
Mon Oncle Antoine
Moon Child
My American Cousin
My Own Private Idaho
My Side Of The Mountain
Les Portes Tournantes
Son Of The Shark
Stand By Me
Stolen Children
Total Eclipse
Walkabout
Where The River Runs Black
White Squall
Wonderland
The Year My Voice Broke

Science Fiction and Fantasy

Prayer of the Rollerboys

Shakespearean Tales

Films which are based, directly or indirectly, on the plays of Shakespeare, or in which a study of the plays features prominently.

Dead Poets Society
The Man Without A Face
My Own Private Idaho
Romeo and Juliet

Sports Stories

A fair percentage of the films include some scenes of sports activities. The following have some game or sport as a major theme of the film.

Among The Cinders (hunting)
The Basketball Diaries (basketball)
Bless The Beasts & Children (hunting)
Foreign Student (football)
Fresh (chess)
Hey Babu Riba (rowing)
Kes (falconry)
Little Giants (football)
Lucas (football)
Meatballs (running)
My Father's Glory (hunting)
Ordinary Magic (yoga)
Puberty Blues (surfing)
School Ties (football)
A Separate Peace (sports in general)
To Play Or To Die (gymnastics)
Tu Solo (bull fighting)

War Stories

Stories set during times of war, in which the events of the war loom large. Except as noted, all deal with World War II.

All Quiet On The Western Front
Au Revoir Les Enfants
Biloxi Blues
Europa, Europa
For A Lost Soldier
Hope And Glory
My Name Is Ivan
The Orphans
The Rascals
A Separate Peace
Summer of '42
Tendres Cousines
The Two Of Us
Wedding In White
Wild Reeds

SEXUALITY INDEX

Gay Youth

Films that feature gay characters, characters assumed to be gay, characters who are experiencing gay feelings and characters who are called gay by their agemates.

Abuse
Among The Cinders
Another Country
Biloxi Blues
Bless The Beasts & Children
Blue Jeans
The Boys Of Cellblock Q
Clayfarmers
The Cure
The Delta
The Devil's Playground
Ernesto
The Everlasting Secret Family
The Flavor Of Corn
For A Lost Soldier
Forever Mary
Friends Forever
Full Speed
Heaven Help Us
If....
Josh and S.A.M.
The Leather Boys
Lilies
The Long Day Closes
Macho Dancer
My First Suit
Not Angels But Angels
The Ode To Billy Joe
Outcasts
Petit Con
Pixote
Postcards From America
Rebel Without A Cause
Street Kid
This Boy's Life
This Special Friendship
To Play Or To Die
Total Eclipse
Wild Reeds
Wonderland
You Are Not Alone
Zero De Conduite

Lesbian Youth

Far less common than films about gay youth.

American Heart
The Incredibly True Adventure Of Two
   Girls In Love
Streetwise

Straight Kids, Gay Encounters

Films in which heterosexual teenagers come face to face with gay characters, either agemates or adults, and must examine their feelings about the gay person in light of this.

Acla
The Basketball Diaries
The Bay Boy
Cross My Heart
Europa, Europa
Forever Mary
Friends Forever
Full Speed
Hidden Pleasures
The Leather Boys
Lessons At The End Of Spring
Luna
Macho Dancer
Petit Con
This Boy's Life
To Play Or To Die

Homophobia

Both gay teenagers as victims and teenagers as perpetrators. In a few instances straight youths as victims of homophobia as a result of society's misconceptions.

Another Country
Biloxi Blues
Blue Jeans
Clayfarmers
Cross My Heart
The Cure
Friends Forever
Full Speed
Heaven Help Us
Hidden Pleasures
Josh and S.A.M.
Just One Of The Guys
The Leather Boys
The Man Without A Face
The Ode To Billy Joe
Outcasts
This Boy's Life
To Play Or To Die
Wonderland

Cross-Dressing

Cross-dressing children, teens and adults. Some of these cross-dressing scenes indicate a true sexual orientation, some are comic scenes, some fortuitous, some for disguise.
The Adventures Of Huck Finn
American Heart

The Cement Garden
Class
Ernesto
The Everlasting Secret Family
Forever Mary
Just One Of The Guys
Lilies
Murmur Of The Heart
Pixote
Postcards From America
Pretty Boy
Risky Business
Soup And Me
Tendres Cousines
Wonderland

Man and Boy

Probably the most reviled form of intergenerational sex, seen as "recruitment." Several of these encounters are fully consenting for both partners, others are abusive.

Abuse
Acla
The Basketball Diaries
The Bay Boy
The Boys Of Cellblock Q
The Boys of St. Vincent
Bump In The Night
Burning Secret
Colegas
The Delta
Ernesto
The Everlasting Secret Family
The Flavor Of Corn
For A Lost Soldier
Forever Mary
Friends Forever
Hidden Pleasures
I Live With Me Dad
In A Glass Cage
Lakki, The Boy Who Grew Wings
Macho Dancer
The Man Without A Face
My Own Private Idaho
Not Angels But Angels
The Ode To Billy Joe
Olivier Olivier
Outcasts
Pixote
Postcards From America
Pretty Boy
La Revolte Des Enfants
Sleepers
Street Kid
Tendres Cousines
Total Eclipse
Vito And The Others

Wonderland

Man and Girl

In real life probably the most common form of intergenerational sex, and historically considered normal behaviour in many societies.

36 Fillette
Beau Pere
Hey Babu Riba
Landscape In The Mist
The Little Girl Who Lives Down The Lane
Nea
Pretty Baby
Stolen Children
Streetwise
Tendres Cousines
Wish You Were Here

Woman and Boy

Many a teenage boy dreams of an older woman who will initiate him into the mysteries of sex. These screen characters have lived this dream. These relationships are the most likely to be consenting of any intergenerational sexual relationship. Some of these encounters are with prostitutes.

Amarcord
Among The Cinders
Boys
Class
Devil In The Flesh
Ernesto
Europa, Europa
The Everlasting Secret Family
Freedom Is Paradise
Friends Forever
Hey Babu Riba
Hidden Pleasures
The Inkwell
The Last Picture Show
The Last Prostitue
Lemon Popsicle
Luna
Murmur Of The Heart
The Name Of The Rose
Le Petit Amour
Petit Con
Pixote
Private Lessons
Rambling Rose
Summer of '42
Tendres Cousines
La Teta Y La Luna
Vito And The Others
White Squall
You Are Not Alone

Woman and Girl

The least common form of intergenerational sex in life and on-screen.

Bilitis

The Incredibly True Adventure Of Two Girls In Love

Boy and Boy

Youths who find happiness with each other or abuse each other.

Another Country
The Boys Of Cellblock Q
The Devil's Playground
Forever Mary
Full Speed
Lilies
Macho Dancer
La Revolte Des Enfants
Vito And The Others
Wild Reeds
You Are Not Alone

Boy and Girl

Classic heterosexual teenage experimentation.

A La Mode
The Basketball Diaries
The Bay Boy
Beethoven's Nephew
Biloxi Blues
The Blue Lagoon
Buster & Billie
The Cement Garden
Colegas
The Flavor Of Corn
Flirting
Foreign Student
Friends
Friends Forever
Full Speed
Le Grand Chemin
Hidden Pleasures
Hope And Glory
If....
The Inheritors
Just One Of The Guys
Kids
The Last Picture Show
The Leather Boys
Lemon Popsicle
Leolo
The Little Girl Who Lives Down The Lane
The Lost Boys
Luna
Macho Dancer
The Man In The Moon
Manny & Lo
Meatballs
Mischief
Murmur Of The Heart
My Own Private Idaho
Olivier Olivier
Over The Edge
Paradise
Petit Con
Prayer of the Rollerboys
Pretty Boy
Puberty Blues

The Rascals
Return To The Blue Lagoon
Risky Business
Romeo and Juliet
Shag: The Movie
Street Kid
Summer of '42
36 Fillette
Tendres Cousines
Who Shot Pat?
Wild Reeds
Wish You Were Here
The Year My Voice Broke
You Are Not Alone

Losing Your Virginity

Losing it or giving it away. For many the quintessential coming of age experience.

A La Mode
Among The Cinders
The Bay Boy
Beau Pere
Biloxi Blues
The Blue Lagoon
Class
Ernesto
Europa, Europa
For A Lost Soldier
Friends
Friends Forever
Hey Babu Riba
The Incredibly True Adventure Of Two Girls In Love
The Inkwell
Kids
The Last Picture Show
The Last Prostitue
Luna
Mischief
Murmur Of The Heart
The Name Of The Rose
Nea
Not Angels But Angels
The Ode To Billy Joe
Paradise
Le Petit Amour
Petit Con
Pretty Baby
Private Lessons
Puberty Blues
Rambling Rose
The Rascals
Romeo and Juliet
Shag: The Movie
Summer of '42
Tendres Cousines
36 Fillette
Wedding In White
Wild Reeds
Wish You Were Here
You Are Not Alone

Anal Intercourse

Not always consenting, sometimes just talked about or implied.

Another Country
The Boys of St. Vincent
Ernesto
For A Lost Soldier
Friends Forever
Not Angels But Angels
Outcasts
Pixote
Postcards From America
Sleepers
Street Kid
Total Eclipse
Vito And The Others

Oral Sex
Can be straight or gay, consenting or forced.

The Basketball Diaries
The Boys of St. Vincent
Colegas
The Delta
Devil In The Flesh
Ernesto
The Everlasting Secret Family
In A Glass Cage
The Inheritors
My Own Private Idaho
Not Angels But Angels
Postcards From America
Sleepers
36 Fillette
Vito And The Others

Incest
Several variations on this theme.

Beau Pere (stepfather - stepdaughter)
The Cement Garden (brother - sister)
Luna (mother - son)
Murmur Of The Heart (mother - son)
Olivier Olivier (brother - sister)
Street Kid (stepfather - stepson)

You Show Me Yours, I'll Show You Mine
In which children, usually pre-teens, compare notes, usually with the opposite sex.

Acla
Criss-Cross
Le Grand Chemin
Hope And Glory
My Life As A Dog
The Rascals
The Slingshot

Measuring Up
A variation on the preceding in which the boys, usually teenagers, grab a ruler to answer the age old questions "How big is it?" and "Whose is bigger?"

Lemon Popsicle
Lucas

Murmur Of The Heart
Porky's

Masturbation
Talked about, implied and suggested. Almost a universal practice among teenage boys, and for most, the first encounter with their own sexual urges.

Amarcord
Au Revoir Les Enfants
The Basketball Diaries
Biloxi Blues
Bless The Beasts & Children
The Blue Lagoon
The Cement Garden
Colegas
The Devil's Playground
The Flavor Of Corn
Foreign Student
Forever Mary
Full Speed
Heaven Help Us
In A Glass Cage
Lakki, The Boy Who Grew Wings
Leolo
Luna
Macho Dancer
Murmur Of The Heart
Petit Con
Pixote
Sunday's Children
To Play Or To Die
Wild Reeds
You Are Not Alone

First Love, First Kiss
Not always the sweetest.

The Bay Boy
Beau Pere
Bilitis
Biloxi Blues
Blue Jeans
The Blue Lagoon
Boys
China, My Sorrow
Criss-Cross
Cross My Heart
Dead Poets Society
The Devil's Playground
Europa, Europa
The Fool Killer
For A Lost Soldier
Foreign Student
Fresh
Friends
Hey Babu Riba
The Hideaway
The Incredibly True Adventure Of Two Girls In Love
Jack The Bear
King Of The Hill
Kipperbang
Lilies
Little Giants

The Little Girl Who Lives Down The Lane
A Little Romance
The Man In The Moon
Mischief
Murmur Of The Heart
My American Cousin
My Life As A Dog
My Mother's Castle
The Name Of The Rose
Now And Then
The Ode To Billy Joe
Paradise
Le Petit Amour
Prayer of the Rollerboys
Pretty Baby
Private Lessons
Rambling Rose
The Rascals
Return To The Blue Lagoon
Rich Kids
Romeo and Juliet
Son Of The Shark
Summer of '42
Tendres Cousines
This Special Friendship
Tom Sawyer
Welcome To The Dollhouse
Wild Reeds
The Year My Voice Broke
You Are Not Alone

Nudity
Many of the films included in this book have scenes of full or partial nudity. Although not strictly speaking scenes of sexuality, I have included them here as well. In the lists which follow I have not differentiated the scenes by age: the performer seen nude may be anything from a young child to an adult, though if the only nudity involves toddlers or infants, it hasn't been listed.

Bare Breasts
Female nudity which involves only upper torso shots. There may be instances of bare buns and male nudity in these films as well.

A La Mode
Amarcord
American Heart
The Bay Boy
Beau Pere
Beethoven's Nephew
Calendar Girl
The Cement Garden
Class
Criss-Cross
The Delta
The Everlasting Secret Family
Flirting
Foreign Student
Friends
Friends Forever
Full Speed

Le Grand Chemin
Hey Babu Riba
The Hideaway
If....
The Incredibly True Adventure Of Two
  Girls In Love
The Inheritors
Just One Of The Guys
Kids
Leolo
Luna
Mon Oncle Antoine
Murmur Of The Heart
My Life As A Dog
My Own Private Idaho
The Name Of The Rose
Nea
The Ode To Billy Joe
Olivier Olivier
The Orphans
Petit Con
Prayer of the Rollerboys
Pretty Baby
Pretty Boy
Private Lessons
Puberty Blues
Rambling Rose
Return To The Blue Lagoon
Risky Business
Romeo and Juliet
Son Of The Shark
36 Fillette
La Teta Y La Luna
Total Eclipse
Walkabout
Where The River Runs Black
Wild Reeds

Bare Buns

These films aren't differentiated by age or gender. The bare buns may be those of a child, a teenager or an adult. They may be those of a boy, a girl, a man or a woman. Films which also include full-frontal shots, either male or female, are not included in this list as all the films having full-frontal nudity also have shots of bare backsides.

A La Mode
The 400 Blows
All Quiet On The Western Front
American Graffiti
Another Country
The Basketball Diaries
Calendar Girl
The Children Of Noisy Village
The Delta
Ernesto
The Everlasting Secret Family
The Fool Killer
Foreign Student
Fresh
Friends
Full Speed
Le Grand Chemin
The Incredibly True Adventure Of Two

Girls In Love
Just One Of The Guys
Kids
Lemon Popsicle
The Littlest Viking
Lord of the Flies (1990)
Lucas
Maya
Mon Oncle Antoine
My Bodyguard
My First Suit
My Life As A Dog
My Own Private Idaho
My Side Of The Mountain
Now And Then
Olivier Olivier
Postcards From America
Pretty Baby
Private Lessons
Puberty Blues
The Reflecting Skin
Rich Kids
Risky Business
Romeo and Juliet
School Ties
Son Of The Shark
Soup And Me
Streetwise
36 Fillette
Tom Sawyer
War Of The Buttons (1962)
Where The River Runs Black
White Squall
Wish You Were Here
The Year My Voice Broke

Full-Frontal Female Nudity

All these films also include shots of bare buns, and may include male nudity as well.

Acla
Among The Cinders
The Baby Of Macon
Bilitis
The Blue Lagoon
Buster & Billie
Colegas
Devil In The Flesh
The Devil's Playground
The Flavor Of Corn
For A Lost Soldier
Freedom Is Paradise
Hidden Pleasures
The Last Picture Show
Mischief
Moon Child
Paradise
Porky's
The Rascals
Sunday's Children
Tendres Cousines
Walkabout

Full-Frontal Male Nudity

All these films also include shots of bare buns and may include female nudity as

well. Any shot of a penis, however brief, has warranted inclusion in this list. No indication of the age of the nude male is implied. Some are children, some teenagers, some adults.

Acla
Amarcord
Among The Cinders
The Baby Of Macon
Beethoven's Nephew
The Blue Lagoon
The Boys Of Cellblock Q
The Boys of St. Vincent
Buster & Billie
The Cement Garden
Chronicle Of A Boy Alone
Clayfarmers
Colegas
Devil In The Flesh
The Devil's Playground
Europa, Europa
Flirting
For A Lost Soldier
Freedom Is Paradise
Friends Forever
The Genesis Children
Heaven Help Us
A Hero Ain't Nothin' But A Sandwich
The Hideaway
If.... (Some prints only)
In A Glass Cage
The Inheritors
Kes
The Kitchen Toto
Lakki, The Boy Who Grew Wings
The Last Picture Show
Leolo
Lessons At The End Of Spring
Lilies
Lord Of The Flies (1963)
Luna
Macho Dancer
The Man In The Moon
Murmur Of The Heart
My Father's Glory
The Name Of The Rose
Nea
The Orphans
Paradise
Pelle The Conqueror
Pixote
Popi
Porky's
Pretty Boy
The Rascals
La Revolte Des Enfants
The Secret Of Roan Inish
The Slingshot
Street Kid
Sunday's Children
To Play Or To Die
Total Eclipse
Train Of Dreams
Tu Solo
The Two Of Us
Walkabout

War Of The Buttons (1995)
The Wild Child
The Wild Little Bunch
Wonderland
You Are Not Alone
Zero De Conduite

Skinny-Dipping and Nude Beaches

Where better to be nude than while swimming?

All Quiet On The Western Front
Among The Cinders
The Blue Lagoon
Buster & Billie
Calendar Girl
The Children Of Noisy Village
Chronicle Of A Boy Alone
Clayfarmers
The Fool Killer
The Genesis Children
Heaven Help Us
The Inkwell
The Last Picture Show
Lord Of The Flies (1963)
The Man In The Moon
My Side Of The Mountain
Now And Then
The Orphans
Paradise
Popi
The Slingshot
Soup And Me
Sunday's Children
Tendres Cousines
Tom Sawyer
Walkabout
Wonderland

Child Pornography

Not examples of it! Stories in which young children become the subjects of it, or are rescued just before they become subjects. With the exception of *Bump In The Night* the subject of child pornography is only very briefly touched on.

Bump In The Night
I Live With Me Dad
Vito And The Others

Heterosexual Rape

Not differentiated by the age of the victim or the perpetrator. Some are children, some are adults. Variations abound.

36 Fillette
The Baby Of Macon
Buster & Billie
Forever Mary
Le Grand Chemin
Kids
Landscape In The Mist
Return To The Blue Lagoon
La Revolte Des Enfants

Total Eclipse
Wedding In White

Homosexual Rape

Almost always boys raped by adults or older boys.

The Boys of St. Vincent
Forever Mary
Pixote
Postcards From America
Sleepers
Street Kid
Vito And The Others

Sexual Abuse of Children

Particularly depressing situations to watch, though in most cases the abuse is implied or spoken of rather than shown on-screen. Films which feature young people in consenting sexual relationships with adults have not been included here. In some cases the abuse is alleged by outsiders rather than actually perpetrated.

Abuse
Acla
The Basketball Diaries
The Boys of St. Vincent
Clayfarmers
The Everlasting Secret Family
I Live With Me Dad
In A Glass Cage
Lakki, The Boy Who Grew Wings
Landscape In The Mist
The Last Picture Show
The Little Girl Who Lives Down The Lane
Macho Dancer
The Man Without A Face
Not Angels But Angels
Olivier Olivier
Pixote
Postcards From America
Pretty Baby
Salaam Bombay!
Sleepers
Stolen Children
Streetwise
Vito And The Others
Where The Day Takes You
Wish You Were Here

Abortion

Five films which touch on this contentious issue.

Colegas
Lemon Popsicle
Manny & Lo
Pixote
Wish You Were Here

Juvenile Prostitution

In all of these films a teenager, or some-times even children, turn to prostitution, even if only for a single night. I haven't

differentiated between male and female prostitution.

American Heart
The Basketball Diaries
Colegas
The Delta
The Everlasting Secret Family
Forever Mary
Hidden Pleasures
Macho Dancer
Madame Rosa
My Own Private Idaho
Not Angels But Angels
Outcasts
Pixote
Postcards From America
Pretty Baby
Pretty Boy
Salaam Bombay!
Stolen Children
Street Kid
Streetwise
Vito And The Others
Where The Day Takes You

Kids with Prostitutes

The flip side of the juvenile prostitution problem is, of course, that teenagers, in almost every case boys, become clients, sometimes seeing this as a way to accomplish that vital goal of losing one's virginity. In some cases these films deal with young people who encounter prostitutes on the street, or elsewhere (for example Antoine in the jail in *The 400 Blows*). They aren't customers, but they come face to face with the working women.

Amarcord
Beethoven's Nephew
Biloxi Blues
Blue Jeans
Colegas
Ernesto
Forever Mary
The 400 Blows
Hidden Pleasures
The Last Picture Show
The Last Prostitue
Lemon Popsicle
Murmur Of The Heart
The Ode To Billy Joe
Pixote
Porky's
Risky Business
White Squall

Teen Pregnancy

As a theme in these films it varies from a very minor issue to the prime focus of the film.

A La Mode
The Blue Lagoon

Colegas
Europa, Europa
Forever Mary
Friends
Hey Babu Riba
Hope And Glory
Lemon Popsicle
Manny & Lo
Paradise
Puberty Blues

Return To The Blue Lagoon
Wedding In White
Wish You Were Here
The Year My Voice Broke

Teenage Couples
In which teenagers set up households. Some are joined in marriage, others are not.

The Blue Lagoon
Forever Mary
Friends
The Leather Boys
Paradise
Return To The Blue Lagoon

ADDITIONAL FILMS

The following list consists of 300 additional film titles which could be considered coming of age stories for in some way or another they illustrate the learning experience or turning point aspects of growing up. Unlike the films given fuller coverage in the main body of the book, the titles in this list generally do not deal with questions of sexuality beyond romantic attachment. This has enabled me to include older films produced when it would have been impossible to even suggest on-screen that teenagers might have sexual urges.

These films range from the early 1920s to 1997 release dates. They represent a number of different genres: comedy, drama, action films, family films, horror films, science-fiction, fantasy, and so on. Some are unforgettable classics. Some are barely remembered. What these films do have in common is that they illustrate, in some fashion, some aspect of the juvenile experience.

In a few instances I have listed remakes and sequels, but this is not an exhaustive list. I have, for example, only listed three of the seemingly interminable list of Andy Hardy stories Mickey Rooney appeared in during the late 1930s and early 1940s. I also have included only a sampling of the multitude of Huckleberry Finn, Tom Sawyer and Oliver Twist films which have appeared over the years.

For each of the films on this list I have included only the barest of information needed to identify it: title, country of origin, and year of release. For a few of the films I have also included one or more alternate titles in brackets following the main title. Those titles marked with an asterisk are, or have been, available on video tape, though they may not all be easy to locate.

A

Above The Rim: USA, 1994 *
Across The Great Divide: USA, 1976 *
Adventures Of Huckleberry Finn: USA, 1939 *
Adventures Of Tom Sawyer: USA, 1938 *
African Journey: USA, 1989 * (Wonderworks series)
Alan & Naomi: USA, 1992 *
Alaska: USA, 1996 *
Alex: Australia, 1992 *
Alms' A Man: USA, 1977 *
And You Thought Your Parents Were Weird: USA, 1991 *
Andy Hardy Gets Spring Fever: USA, 1939 *
Andy Hardy's Private Secretary: USA, 1941 *
Angela: USA, 1994 *
Angels With Dirty Faces: USA, 1938 *
Anne Of Avonlea (Anne Of Green Gables: The Sequel): Canada, 1987 *
Anne Of Green Gables: USA, 1934 *
Anne Of Green Gables: Canada, 1985 *
Aparajito: India, 1957 * (The Apu Trilogy)
Ava's Magical Adventure: USA, 1994 *

B

Bach And Broccoli: Canada, 1986 *
The Bad News Bears: USA, 1976 *
The Bad News Bears In Breaking Training: USA, 1977 *
The Bad News Bears Go To Japan: USA, 1978 *

La Bamba: USA, 1987 *
Bananas From Sunny Quebec: Canada, 1993
The Barefoot Boy: USA, 1938 *
Bashu, The Little Stranger (Bashe, Gharibeh Kuchak): Iran, 1990
Bayo: Canada, 1985
The Beniker Gang: USA, 1984 *
Better Off Dead: USA, 1985 *
The Bicycle Thief (Ladri Di Biciclette): Italy, 1949 *
Big Red: USA, 1962 *
Big Shots: USA, 1987 *
Billyboy: USA, 1979 *
Black Beauty: USA, 1933 *
Black Beauty: USA, 1946 *
Black Beauty: Great Britain, Germany, Spain, 1971 *
Black Beauty: USA, 1994 *
Blood: USA, 1975 *
Blue Fin: USA, 1978 *
The Blue Kite: China, 1993 *
Les Bons Debarras: Canada, 1981 *
The Boy (Shonen): Japan, 1969
Boy Of The Streets: USA, 1937 *
Boy Of Two Worlds: USA, 1970 *
Boy Who Loved Horses: Denmark, 1960 *
The Boy With Green Hair: USA, 1948 *
Boys Town: USA, 1936 *
Brainscan: USA, 1994 *
The Brave One: USA, 1956 *
Bridge To Terebithia: USA, 1985 * (Wonderworks series)
Brother Future: USA, 1991 * (Wonderworks series)

Bushwhacked (Tenderfoots, or The Tenderfoot): USA, 1995 *

C

Caddie Woodlawn: USA * (Wonderworks series)
Captains Courageous: USA, 1937 *
Captains Courageous: USA, 1995 *
Carrie: USA, 1976 *
The Champ: USA, 1931 *
The Champ: USA, 1979 *
Cheetah: USA, 1989 *
Children In The Crossfire: USA, 1984 *
A Christmas Story: USA, 1983 *
Christy: USA, 1994 *
Cinema Paradiso: Italy, 1989 *
City Boy: Great Britain, Canada, 1993 * (Wonderworks series)
Clarence And Angel: USA, 1980 *
The Client: USA, 1994 *
Clowning Around: Australia, 1992 * (Wonderworks series)
Clowning Around 2: Australia, 1993 * (Wonderworks series)
Come And See: USSR, 1986 *
The Commitments: Great Britain, 1991 *
Convicts: USA, 1991 *
Cooley High: USA, 1975 *
Curse Of The Viking Grave: Canada, 1991*

D

D. P.: USA, 1980 *
D.A.R.Y.L.: USA, 1985 *
D2: The Mighty Ducks (The Mighty Ducks 2): USA, 1994 *

David: Germany, 1979 *
David: USA, 1988
The Day My Parents Ran Away: USA, 1994 *
Devi: India, 1962 *
Dita Saxova: Czechoslovakia, 1967 *
A Dog Of Flanders: USA, 1959 *
The Dog Who Stopped The War: Canada, 1984 *
Don't Be A Menace To South Central While Drinking Your Juice In The Hood: USA, 1996 *
The Dove: USA, 1974 *

E

East Side Kids: USA, 1940 *
Elephant Boy: Great Britain, 1937 *
Eli's Lesson: Canada, 1993 *
End Of The Golden Weather: New Zealand, 1991 *
L'Enfant Lion: France, 1993
Explorers: USA, 1985 *

F

Fame: USA, 1980 *
The Family Game: Japan, 1983 *
Family Prayers: USA, 1991 *
Far From Home, The Adventures Of Yellow Dog: USA, 1994 *
Father And Scout: USA, 1995 *
Field Of Honor (Champ d'Honneur): France, 1978 *
The Five Lost Days: Germany, 1982 *
The Flamingo Kid: USA, 1984 *
Fly Away Home: USA, 1996 *
Forbidden Games: France, 1952 *
The Forgotten Village: USA, 1941 *
Free Willy: USA, 1993 *
Freeze ... Die ... Come To Life: USSR, 1989 *

G

Gangster's Boy: USA, 1938 *
Generals Without Buttons: France, 1938
George's Island: Canada, 1991 *
Getting Even With Dad: USA, 1994 *
A Girl Of The Limberlost: USA, 1990 * (Wonderworks series)
The Good Son: USA, 1993 *
Greta: Poland, 1986 *

H

Harley: USA, 1990 *
Herman: Norway, 1990
Hide And Seek: Israel, 1980 *
High School Caesar: USA, 1956 *
High School Confidential (Young Hellions): USA, 1958 *
High School USA: USA, 1984 *
Home At Last: USA, 1988 * (Wonderworks series)
A Home Of Our Own: USA, 1993 *
Hoop Dreams: USA, 1994 *
Hoosier Schoolboy (Yesterday's Hero): USA, 1937 *
The House On Chelouche Street: Israel, 1973 *
How Green Was My Valley: USA, 1941 *
Huckleberry Finn: USA, 1931
Huckleberry Finn: USA, 1974 * (Musical)
A Hungarian Fairy Tale: Hungary, 1989 *

I

I Am The Cheese: USA, 1983 *
I Know Why The Caged Bird Sings: USA, 1979 *
An Indian In The Cupboard: USA, 1995 *
Into The West: Ireland, 1992 *
The Invisible Boy: USA, 1957 *
Iron Will: USA, 1993 *
Isaac Little Feathers: USA, 1984 *

J

The Journey Of Natty Gan: USA, 1985 *
Jungle Book: USA, 1942 *

K

The Karate Kid: USA, 1984 *
The Karate Kid: Part 2: USA, 1986 *
The Karate Kid: Part 3: USA, 1989 *
The Kid Brother: Canada, 1988 *
Kid Colter: USA, 1985 *
A Kid For Two Farthings: USA, 1955 *
Kid From Not-So-Big: USA, 1978 *
Kid Vengeance: USA, 1975 *
Kidnapped: USA, 1960 *
Kim: USA, 1950 *
Kim: USA, 1984 *
Kindergarten: USSR, 1984 *
Konrad: USA, 1985 *

L

Lantern Hill: Canada, 1990 *
Lassie: USA, 1994 *
Late Summer Blues: Israel, 1987 *
The Lawrenceville Stories: USA, 1988 *
Leave Us Alone (La'os Vaere): Denmark, 1975
Let Him Have It: Great Britain, 1991 *
Let'er Go Gallagher: USA, 1928 *
Let's Do It (Maske Ku' Vi): Denmark, 1976
Lies My Father Told Me: Canada, 1975 *
Little Big League: USA, 1994 *
Little Buddha: Great Britain, 1994 *
The Little Kidnappers: Canada, 1990 *
Little Lord Fauntleroy: USA, 1936 *
Little Lord Fauntleroy: USA, 1980 *
Little Nikita: USA, 1988 *
The Little Thief: France, 1989 *
Little Tough Guys: USA, 1938 *
The Loneliest Runner: USA, 1976 *
Looking For Miracles: Canada, 1990 *
Lost In The Barrens: Canada, 1991 *
Love And Other Sorrows: USA, 1970 *
Love Finds Andy Hardy: USA, 1938 *
Luke Was There (Tough Kids Need Love Too): USA, 1976 *

M

Marked Money: USA, 1928 *
Max Is Missing: USA, 1995 *

Mexican Bus Ride: Mexico, 1946 *
The Mighty Ducks: USA, 1992 *
Miracle In Milan: Italy, 1951 *
The Miracle Of Marcelino: Spain, 1955 *
Mozart: A Childhood Chronicle: Germany, 1976 *
My Apprenticeship: USSR, 1939 *
My Childhood: USSR, 1938 *
My Dog Shep: USA, 1946 *
My Friend Flicka: USA, 1943 *
My Grandpa Is A Vampire: USA, 1992 *
My Pal, The King: USA, 1932 *
My Summer Story (It Runs In The Family): USA, 1994 *

N

National Velvet: USA, 1944 *
The Navigator: New Zealand, 1988 *
The Next Karate Kid: USA, 1994 *
Nobody's Daughter: Hungary, 1976 *
North Shore: USA, 1987 *

O

Old Yeller: USA, 1958 *
Oliver Twist: USA, 1922 *
Oliver Twist: Great Britain, 1948 *
Oliver Twist: Great Britain, 1985 *
Los Olvidados (The Young And The Damned): Mexico, 1950 *
One Crazy Night: Australia, 1991 *
One Crazy Summer: USA, 1986 *
An Orphan Boy Of Vienna: Germany, 1937 *
Orphans: USA, 1987 *

P

The Paper Boy: Canada, 1994 *
Father Panchali: India, 1955 * (The Apu Trilogy)
Pathfinder: Norway, 1987 *
The Peanut Butter Solution: Canada, 1985*
Peck's Bad Boy: USA, 1921 *
Peck's Bad Boy: USA, 1934 *
Peter Lundy And The Medicine Hat Stallion (The Medicine Hat Stallion or Pony Express): USA, 1977 *
Poil De Carotte (The Red Head): France, 1931 *
Pollyanna: USA, 1920 *
Pollyanna: USA, 1960 *
The Power Of One: USA, 1992 *
The Prince And The Pauper: USA, 1937 *
The Prince And The Pauper: USA, 1962 *
The Prince And The Pauper: Great Britain, 1978 *
Prince Brat And The Whipping Boy (The Whipping Boy): USA, 1995 *
The Prince Of Central Park: USA, 1977 *
Prince Of Pennsylvania: USA, 1988 *
Princes In Exile: Canada, 1990 *
Prison For Children: USA, 1993 *
Pump Up The Volume: USA, 1990 *

R

Radio Flyer: USA, 1992 *
Red Hot: USA, 1993 *

Redwood Curtain: USA, 1995 *
Rivals (Deadly Rivals): USA, 1972 *
The Road Home: USA, 1995 *
Rock Bottom: Poland, 1987 *
Rookie Of The Year: USA, 1993 *
Rudy: USA, 1993 *
Runaway: USA, 1989 * (Wonderworks
    series)
Runaway Island: The Bushrangers:
    Australia, 1983 *
*Runaway Island: Treasure Of The
    Conquistadors*: Australia, 1984 *
The Runner (Dawendah, or The Race):
    Iran, 1984

S

Saltwater Moose: Canada, 1996 *
Sam And Me: Canada, 1991 *
The Sandlot: USA, 1993 *
Sarafina!: USA, 1992 *
The Savage Land: USA, 1994 *
Scalawag: USA, Yugoslavia, Italy, 1973
Scarecrow: USSR, 1985 *
The Second Jungle Book: USA, 1997
Secret Places: Great Britain, 1985 *
A Secret Space: USA, 1988 *
Shipwreck Island: USA, 1961 *
Shipwrecked (Haakon Haakonson):
    Norway, 1990 *
Shoeshine: Italy, 1946 *
Sidekicks: USA, 1993 *
The Sky Is Gray: USA, 1979 *
Smoke: USA, 1970 *
Snow Treasure: USA, 1967 *

Solarbabies: USA, 1986 *
Sounder: USA, 1972 *
SpaceCamp: USA, 1986 *
Sparrows: USA, 1926 *
Spirit Rider: Canada, 1993 *
Stand Off: Hungary, 1989 *
The Stone Boy: USA, 1984 *
Storm Boy: Australia, 1976 *
A Summer To Remember: USSR, 1960 *
A Summer To Remember: USA, 1985 *
The Sun's Burial: Japan, 1960 *
Sunday Daughters: Hungary, 1980 *
Swing Kids: USA, 1993 *

T

Take Down: USA, 1979 *
Thursday's Child: USA, 1943 *
Tito And Me: Yugoslavia, 1992 *
To Sir, With Love: USA, 1967 *
Toby McTeague: Canada, 1987 *
Toby Tyler: USA, 1959 *
The Todd Killings: USA, 1971 *
Tom Alone: Canada, 1990
Tom And Huck: USA, 1995 *
Tom Brown's School Days: Great Britain,
    1940 *
Tom Sawyer: USA, 1930 *
Too Young To Die: USA, 1990 *
Treasure Island: USA, 1934 *
Treasure Island: USA, 1950 *
Treasure Island: USA, 1989 *
A Tree Grows In Brooklyn: USA, 1945 *
Turf Boy: USA, 1942 *
Two Soldiers: USA *

V

Les Violons Du Bal: France, 1974 *

W

A Waltz Through The Hills: 1988 *
    (Wonderworks series)
The Wanderers: USA, 1979 *
The War: USA, 1994 *
The War Boy: Canada, 1985 *
Wend Kuni (God's Gift): Burkina Faso,
    1982 *
Where The Red Fern Grows: USA, 1974 *
The White Balloon: Iran, 1995 *
White Fang: USA, 1991 *
*White Fang 2: The Myth Of The White
    Wolf*: USA, 1994 *
Who Has Seen The Wind?: Canada, 1977 *
Who Slew Auntie Roo? (Gingerbread
    House): USA, 1971 *
The Wild Pony: USA, 1983 *
The Wizard: USA, 1989 *
The Wizard Of Oz: USA, 1939 *
Wizards Of The Lost Kingdom: USA, 1985*

Y

The Yearling: USA, 1946 *
The Yearling: USA, 1994 *
Yellow Earth: China, 1984 *

Z

Zebra In The Kitchen: USA, 1965 *

VIDEO RENTERS' & BUYERS' GUIDE

ALLIANCE RELEASING HOME VIDEO
http://www.alliancevideo.com
Major Canadian producer and distributor of films and video tapes. Lists many foreign films on their web site. Direct on-line sales.

CINEVISTA
560 W. 43rd Street,
Suite 8J
New York, NY 10036
800/341-2463 212-947-4373

CRITIC'S CHOICE VIDEO
P. O. Box 549
Elk Grove Village, IL 60009
800-367-7765
800-544-9852

FACETS VIDEO
1517 W. Fullerton Avenue
Chicago, Il 60614
1-800-331-6197
773/281-9075
Fax: 773/929-5437
E-mail orders: sales@facets.org
www.facets.org
Catalogues, bi-monthly new-releases publication, frequent e-mail listings of new releases available.

GAYWEB
P.O. Box 685195
Austin, Texas 78768
www.gayweb.com

INSIDER VIDEO CLUB
PO Box 93399
Hollywood, CA 90093
1-800-634-2242
(213) 661-8330
Catalogue available. U. S. orders only. (Canadians may want to try Videomatica for some of their titles.) Specializes in gay coming of age titles and gay-interest videos.

MC FILM FESTIVAL
54561 Corporation
P. O. Box 20071
Tampa, FL 33622
800-445-7134

LA BOITE NOIR BOUTIQUE VIDEO INC.
Departement des achats
4450, St-Denis Suite 201
Montreal, PQ
H2J 2L1
Fax: 514/287-1597
(A good source for French language films, including American titles dubbed in French, as well as French language titles from France and from Canada, both with and without English subtitles. Be prepared to conduct business in French.)

MOVIES UNLIMITED
6736 Castor Avenue
Philadelphia, PA 19149
1-800-523-0823
215/722-8398
Fax: 215/725-3683
E-mail:
movies@moviesunlimited.com
www.moviesunlimited.com
Huge catalogue lists all but a handful of the films reviewed in this book. Sales only.

STRAND RELEASING
1460 Fourth Street, Suite 302
Santa Monica, CA 90401
310-395-5002
Website: www.strandrel.com

TLA VIDEO
1520 Locust Street, Suite 200
Philadelphia, PA 19102
1-800-333-8521
Fax: 215/790-1501
E-mail: tlaone@ix.netcom.com
Mail order sales.

VBM (Video By Mail)
P.O.Box 1515, Whitney, Texas 76692
1-800-245-4996 or 817/694-4234
Fax: 817/694-4865
Specializes in coming of age videos. They carry many of the videos mentioned in this guide. Rent or purchase by mail.

VIDEO DIRECT
www.directvideo.com

VIDEO SHOPPERS WORLD
2181 Carling Ave.
Ottawa, Ontario K2B 7E8
613/722-6815
Sales only. No rental department.

VIDEOMATICA
1859 West 4th Avenue
Vancouver, B.C., V6J 1M4
1-800-665-1469 or 604/734-5752
Fax:1-800-606-8867 or
604/734-8867
Catalogue available, lists many American imports difficult to find in Canada. No mail order rentals.

WATER BEARER FILMS
205 West End Ave., Suite 24H
New York, NY 10023
212/580-8185 800/551-8304
Fax: 212/787-5455

WOLFE VIDEO
P. O. Box 64
New Almaden, CA 95042
800/438-9653 or 408-268-6782
Specializes in gay-interest videos.

ZEBRAZ
P.O. Box 15710
San Antonio, Texas
210/472-2800
Fax: 210/472-2828
E-mail: zebraz@zebraz.com
www.zebraz.com

ABOUT THE AUTHOR

DON LORT WAS BORN IN KETCHIKAN, ALASKA BUT HAS BEEN A resident of Canada since he was nine months old. He has taught in Canada and Korea. A long-time film buff, he has also been a video store clerk. He has been a Big Brother to three exceptionally fine young men, as well. Though *Coming Of Age* is his book, though he has contributed to several other film and video guides.

When faced with the impossible task of naming his personal top-ten coming of age films, they are, in alphabetical order: *The 400 Blows, The Boys Of St. Vincent, If ..., King Of The Hill, Mon Oncle Antoine, Murmur Of The Heart, Stand By Me, This Boy's Life, Walkabout* and *You Are Not Alone.*

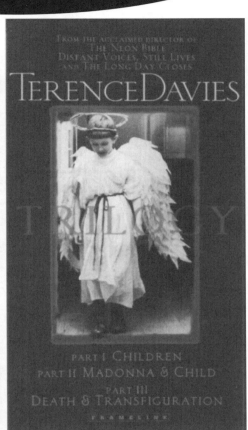

THE DELTA

written and directed by Ira Sachs

BOYS LIFE 2

Latin Boys GO TO HELL

a film by Ela Troyano

FULL SPEED

directed by Gael Morel

STRAND RELEASING www.strandrel.com

© 1997 Strand Releasing

COMPANION PRESS
NAKED CINEMA BOOKS

138002 **The Films of KRISTEN BJORN**
Internationally-acclaimed gay adult video director.
By Jamoo, 152 pages, 8-1/2 x 11, 100-plus nude photos   **$18.95**

527793 **SUPERSTARS—Gay Adult Video Guide**
The Top Porn Stars of The '90s
By Jamoo, 160 pages, 5-1/2x8-1/8, nearly 100 nude photos   **$12.95**

138037 **The X-Rated GAY VIDEO GUIDE**
Over 1,500 Erotic Reviews! By Sabin, 448 pages, 5-1/2x8-1/8   **$12.95**

527777 **FULL-FRONTAL—Male Nudity Video Guide**
By Steve Stewart, 144 pages, 5-1/2x8-1/8, nearly 100 nude photos (BEST SELLER!)   **$12.95**

138045 **The VOYEUR VIDEO GUIDE**
To Special-Interest Male Erotic Videos
By Steve Stewart, 144 pages, 5-1/2x8-1/8, 100 -plus nude photos   **$12.95**

138029 **COMING-OF-AGE Movie & Video Guide** — To Mainstream, Foreign and Independent Movies
By Don Lort, 200-plus pages 8-1/2 x 11, 100 photos   **$18.95**

527726 **GAY HOLLYWOOD Film & Video Guide 2nd Ed.**
75 Years Of Gay & Lesbian Images In The Movies By Steve Stewart, 360 pages, with photos   **$15.95**

138061 **HOLLYWOOD DRAG Video Guide**
Drag Queens & Kings Of The Screen By F. Michael Moore, 200-plus pages, 100-plus photos   **$12.95**

527769 **CAMPY, VAMPY, TRAMPY Movie Quotes**
901 Bitchy Barbs, Wicked Wisecracks & Lusty Lampoons
By Steve Stewart, 216 pages, 4-1/4x6-5/8   **$6.95**

13807X **PENIS PUNS, Jokes & One-Liners—A Movie Quote Book**
By Steve Stewart, 124 pages, 6 x 4-1/4   **$5.95**

For more information about any of these books, or upcoming books,
visit our website coming this Fall 1997:
www.nakedcinema.com

SEE ORDER FORM ON REVERSE SIDE

VISA

COMPANION PRESS
MAIL-ORDER FORM

MasterCard

HOW TO ORDER

Mail Your Order To: Companion Press, PO Box 2575, Laguna Hills, CA 92654
Fax Your Order To: 714/362-9726 (credit card orders only)
E-mail your order To: stewarts@nakedcinema.com (credit card orders only)
Website Orders: www.nakedcinema.com (Order online beginning Fall 1997)

PAYMENT METHODS

U.S. Orders: Visa/MasterCard (Allow 2-4 weeks for delivery)
    Money Orders (Allow 2-4 weeks for delivery)
    Checks (Allow 6-8 weeks for delivery)

Canadian Orders: Visa/MasterCard Only (No Checks/Allow 4-6 weeks for delivery)
Overseas Orders: Visa/MasterCard Only (No Checks/Allow 4-6 weeks for delivery)

SHIPPING RATES

U.S. Orders: 1 book $3.00/2 books $5.00 total/3 books $7.00 total
    4 or more books $8.00 total
Canadian Orders: $10.00 per order (Up to 4 books)
Overseas Orders: $20.00 per order (Up to 4 books)

Quantity	Title	Price (each)	Amount

PRINT
Name _____

Address _____

City _____ State _____ Zip _____

Phone (_____) _____

Subtotal	
Calif. Residents add 7.75% Sales Tax	
Shipping & Handling (See above rates)	
TOTAL	

METHOD OF PAYMENT   ❑ Visa   ❑ MasterCard   ❑ Money Order   ❑ Check (U.S. currency only) Allow 4-6 weeks for delivery when paying by check.

Credit card # _____ Exp. date _____

SIGNATURE REQUIRED for all orders. (I certify by my signature that I am over 21 years old.) _____